Preface

As I descended towards the barbed wire fenc[e]
I saw them before they saw me. Directly opp[osite]
was a group of five men sitting around an ope[n]
were the upturned crates.

Of scruffy appearance, aged between thirty to fifty. They were in possession of two large Rottweiler dogs. As I slithered down the slope towards them, the dogs saw me and began barking ferociously. At the bottom of the slope, I tried to correct myself and stand upright but the bigger of the two dogs made a gigantic leap over the fence and before I could do anything, it was on me. Its sharp teeth snapping at the side of my face. The foul smell of dog breath alone almost knocked me out. The full weight of the dog knocked me backwards and I fell with it on top of me. I was shocked by the sudden attack and for a moment, thought my life was at an end. I struggled to keep hold of my Leki walking stick and was using it to push the dog off when I felt hot, wet saliva being licked across my face. It took a moment for my brain to engage. This dog wasn't biting my face; it was licking me in true Scooby Doo fashion. It was a big heavy dog and the saliva was truly revolting but infinitely preferable to the painful bloody wounds I had expected.

I pushed the dog off and scrambled to my feet noting that the men at the other side of the fence were a mean-looking bunch. To a man, they had greasy matted hair, their eyes were set in deep, sunken sockets, stubble and beards graced their faces, their teeth were rotten and their fingernails were grubby and black. I'd fallen into the camp of a bunch of real desperado's.

Luckily, they were all drunk. As they tried to stand up with their legs crossed, several of them fell back to the ground - fortunately not into the fire. Two of them crawled frantically to the river bank where they tried to hide fishing rods under camouflage netting. They failed miserably, getting tangled up in the net. That left three men and the two dogs. Scooby Doo was now wagging his stump of a tail by my side as if I was a long lost friend. The other quiet, silent-type-of-a-dog, was circling around to one side and I wasn't at all sure about it. Two men were still laid out on the ground, incapable of standing up. A large pile of empty beer cans were strewn around behind them. That left one man, much smaller than me looking directly at me. He said "Och aye, we thought you were the f...ing water bailiff". At least I thought that was what he said in his classic, Rab C. Nesbitt, Glaswegian lingo.

I replied to him, something along the lines of, "Pardon". He clearly didn't understand and continued in a drunken, slurred speech. "See you Jimmy, you f...ing gave us the shits. We thought you were the water bailiff".

He was angry - but not that angry. I decided to confront them head on and climbed over the fence - not very easy to do as I was also trying to keep an eye on the other dog which was now menacingly circling me. On the other side, the lone standing man

3

said something that I took to mean, "Don't be afraid of the dogs, they're harmless". Although he could quite easily have said, "I'd be afraid of the dogs if I were you. That one might be harmless but the other one is a monster". I couldn't understand a word.

The other men were now gathering their senses and getting to their feet and I was soon surrounded by an evil-looking group of men, all swaying unsteadily. They had glazed eyes and foul-smelling breath; they all reeked of stale alcohol, cigarette smoke and foul body odour - truly vile and repugnant. I decided I had been too long in their company, so I told them I was walking along the River Clyde into Glasgow. This caught their attention. I gathered that in all the years they'd been illegally fishing at this spot, they'd never seen anyone come down through the wood from the direction I'd done. I told them about the Clyde Walkway, which I presume will one day be completed to pass this very spot. They had never heard of it. My initial impression of them being evil was, I am glad to say, wrong. They turned out to be very friendly, even offering me a sip of their beer. I was still worried about the silent dog, now right behind me and drooling at the mouth. "Just control that dog, will you?" I asked.

One of the men gave the dog an almighty kick on its side and it went scampering away to the river. Whilst I was relieved the dog was away from me, I wasn't too pleased with the way it was achieved. The soberest man said, "You'll want to see the Roy Memorial". Up to that point, I'd never heard of the Roy Memorial. I had to concentrate really hard as he began giving me directions to it. Apparently, I had to "use the fisherman's' path" which "avoided the big house with walled gardens, the owners being right bastards" and I was warned to "be careful, they'll shoot you if they catch you on their land".

I waved my goodbyes to my new-found friends who quickly resumed drinking, dogs by their sides. I was glad to be breathing fresh air again. After a while, my way was blocked by a large, stone wall which was too big to look over and obviously belonged to a big house. I crept around the wall on a muddy path that led me back into thick undergrowth with rhododendron bushes. Eventually I emerged onto a private lane that did lead to a big house by the river. I turned away from the house and walked up the lane to a gatehouse, escaping onto a tarmac road. A sign on the fence by the gatehouse declared the drive to be private, with no right of way. Thankfully no "right bastard with a gun" was around.

Errata
p.25 mewling should read mewing
p.28 wandered should read wondered
p.44 signets should read cygnets
p.97 Hatton should read Halton
p.112 & p.119
signets should read cygnets

A journey from Bishop Rock to Muckle Flugga

Including a comfortable stroll from Land's End to John O'Groats

By CA Binns

Introduction

One of my favourite books as a boy was 'The Autobiography of a Super Tramp', (1908) by WH Davies. In his preface to that book, George Bernard Shaw wrote 'The Super Tramp was not a slave to convention, but was a free knight of the highway'.

In the 1970's, I read John Hillaby's account of his, 'Journey through Britain', (1968) walking Land's End to John O'Groats (LEJOG), and ever since then, I had thought, one day I'll do that journey.

In 1904 a certain Dr Deighton held the record for walking between Land's End and John O'Groats in 24 days and 4 hours. 'His chief sustenance en-route was a much advertised meat juice'. This spurred Mr George H Allen 'From Land's End to John O'Groats 1905' a vegetarian to set about and break the record which he duly completed later that year averaging over sixty miles a day.

As Yorkshire man, EW Fox wrote in his 1911 book,

'2000 miles on foot - Walks through Great Britain and France'

'I feel in agreement with Robert Louis Stevenson that', 'a walking tour should be gone upon alone, you are free to do exactly as you please, to go or to stay, to walk quickly or slowly, to rest, to make notes or sketches, to talk to yourself to meditate.

Your powers of observation are keener too and more concentrated. If you go in pairs, it is more of a picnic'.

The great A Wainwright in his 1968 book, 'The Pennine Way companion', wrote, 'Walking alone was preferable.... However, on the wilder parts of the Pennine Way it is very desirable to have a companion...'

Wainwright writing in his 1973 book, 'A Coast to Coast walk', declared, 'You don't need an official route, you just need an objective which you are free to walk to, linking footpaths with bridleways and quiet roads. All on foot'.

Hamish Brown had said in his 1981 book, 'Groats End Walk' - 'The Yorkshire Pennine peat roughness will give all the training needed for a walk anywhere else'

I didn't need any more motivation.

In 2007 having retired from West Yorkshire Police; I bought myself a motor home with the intention of using it as a moveable base camp during my walk.

There aren't many people in our hectic world who can find the time, the support and the financial flexibility, to leave home for four or five months, to trek from one end of the country to the other. I was in this enviable position.

I wasn't setting out to break any records. My aim was to wander leisurely through the byways, lanes and footpaths.

My planning was as flexible as the walk was going to be. We (my wife Kay, our Yorkshire terrier dog Ripley), were going to travel from Bishop Rock on the Isles of Scilly to Muckle Flugga on the Shetland Isles including a comfortable stroll from Land's End to John O'Groats; following the spring north.

Mentally I was prepared and motivated. I was to walk alone with the exception of an odd hour here and there when Kay and Ripley would join me. On some days friends and colleagues had expressed a wish to walk a few hours with me, and who was I to deny them their day out?

Physically, I was in poor shape, being somewhat over weight but I had walked all my life and spent many happy hours on the rough Pennine hills around my home in Yorkshire.

The only bookings I made prior to setting off, was the accommodation on the Isle of Scilly.

We set off on Easter Monday afternoon, saying goodbye to Yorkshire as we travelled along the M62 motorway, passing the White Rose emblem.

The next morning, we awoke to a glorious day and drove to Lizard Point, mainland Britain's most southerly point.

At the Polpeor Cove, the land meets the sea with a sheer 250-foot drop over the cliff edge to the rocky shore and sea below. On the plateau above the harbour, an information centre and a café are surrounded by a row of tourist souvenir shops.

We decided to eat in Britain's most southerly café, which had spectacular views across the cliffs and the turquoise sea.

After lunch, we walked down the narrow twisting track to the harbour and the small pebble beach. I was photographed touching the sea and collecting a pebble from the shore, which I intended to carry to Britain's most northerly point.

Back up on the cliff tops we made our way to the RSPB wardens who were encouraging people to look at the choughs through their supply of binoculars. Choughs are the only black birds of the region with a red bill and legs. This distinguishes them at once from black crows and from the smaller jackdaw. They were given their English name because of the 'k-chuff' sound they make, and they feature on Cornwall's Coat of Arms.

The Wardens' explained that the 'Cornwall Chough Project' had bought the fields which bordered the cliffs and were encouraging local farmers to convert the land back into pasture, reversing recent farming trends.

Without the conservation of their traditional habitats, the birds face extinction. The pair we were watching were brooding their eggs, which were on a high, rocky ledge in a cave in the cliff side.

Here on the cliffs we saw the birds in flight. They were much more buoyant in the air than the numerous jackdaws.

Arriving at the heliport, Kay was worried about how Ripley would manage on the flight. She was given a 'sky kennel', a small animal carrying cage.

The flight was brief; just twenty minutes, Ripley adjusted to the noise and vibration and even lay down and rested. The views of the Cornish cliffs, seas and islands were stupendous.

The Isles of Scilly situated twenty-eight miles south-west of Land's End, form a group of five inhabited islands and approximately fifty-one uninhabited smaller islands. The whole of Scilly, much of it still owned by the Duchy of Cornwall, is designated as '*An Area of Outstanding Natural Beauty*', and the coast is a '*Heritage Coast*'.

We landed on St Mary's, the largest of the Scilly Islands, and after alighting from the helicopter, we were greeted by the driver and conductor of the local bus. The conductor even had the leather pouch for his money, just as I remember from forty years ago. They were so polite and friendly loading everyone's luggage onto the bus.

The drive into Hugh Town, along winding lanes that held very little traffic; passing quaint cottages with beautiful gardens was a delight.

The bus dropped us off in Hugh Town square, where the conductor pointed out our lodgings overlooking the pier.

Pier House is a 17th century granite cottage, set next to the sea wall with views over the harbour. It is reputed to have been built in the 1630's as a fish store for soldiers at the Garrison and nearby Star Castle. We were greeted by its owner, a friendly and cheerful man, originally from Keighley, Yorkshire.

The Bed and Breakfast was full of character and our room was adequate if not luxurious. With a bit of neck craning it had a view of the harbour and directly opposite us was the Mermaid Inn.

We stored our bags, and went out to explore. As we wandered around, we noticed that all the gardens still had their iron railings, unlike the rest of Britain, which had them cut down for the War effort during World War 2.

In one shop in the town the proprietor was another Yorkshire man, originally from Horsforth. He had been on St Mary's for twenty-six years but still retained a strong Yorkshire accent. He immediately recognised mine saying, "By heck lad, you're a long way from home".

We continued our walk out of the town and along country lanes. The fields still had a few narcissi and daffodils flowering. These are crops which are grown throughout the winter months in the open fields. We saw corn marigolds and whistling jacks starting to run riot in bulb fields. The hedges were full of white garlic flowers and bluebells. It was April and elegant white lilies were flowering in gardens, and the May tree (hawthorn) was in full blossom.

We reached the Heritage Centre which had internet access. Even though the café was due to shut in ten minutes, the helpful couple who own it welcomed us in and set us up on the computer. They also provided us with large mugs of tea and home-made cake.

Later we followed the footpath down to the coast. We had been told by Matthew, our neighbour back home, that the best beach on the island was Pelistry and that was where we were heading, following the map he had generously supplied. The weather had turned and there was a light mist of rain falling on us which spoiled our visibility. As we walked along the coast path, the sea fret came right onto the land and surrounded us in fog. It was still quite warm and we could see the flowering gorse bushes and the splashes of birdsfoot trefoil that painted the moorland gold as we walked on to Armchair Rock, before returning to Hugh Town.

April · Saturday 14 · Rest day

We had arranged to have our breakfast at 9.30am which would give me plenty of time to get up and have a shower etc. and Kay plenty of time to walk Ripley a mile or so around the old Garrison.

Unfortunately I somehow managed to lock myself out of the bedroom after my shower. What happened next resembled a 'Brian Rix' farce with me stuck on the landing in just my towel, hopping about almost naked waiting for Kay to return. Luckily the guests who were in the other rooms on our floor had breakfasted early and had not returned, which spared my blushes.

I could imagine the headlines *'Naked Cop (retired) confronts lady on hotel corridor'*

Breakfast was a proper English breakfast and cooked the way I like it.

We were off to walk to Old Town along those country lanes. We stopped on the way at a small gallery. It was here we met our first Scilly man, born and bred here. We bought a pot 'Scilly Shrew' from him.

The Scilly Shrew is only found on the island and has no natural enemies, like weasels, stoats etc. It is occasionally seen at the top of beaches, foraging for insects.

Old Town was the main settlement of St Mary's until Hugh Town developed beneath the protective presence of Star Castle. We came into Old Town, past more beautiful gardens, just in time for lunch at a café with seating outside.

Then on to explore Old Town. Old Town developed at Porth Ennor *'the landing place of Ennor'*, was constructed during the Norman period and now greatly enlarged. The centre of authority in the area was a small crenelated keep; Castle Ennor, the remnants of which still survive on the summit of 'Castle Rocks' which rise above the present hamlet.

We walked on to the point at Old Town Bay and then round to the Old Church, where we found thick clusters of dill growing in the hedgerow outside the church.

In *'A Guide to the Old Church of St Mary's (1995)'* we read that it had been built to serve the needs of the Norman overlords and their Celtic serfs in 1130 to 1140 AD

The church was cool and peaceful and smelt lovely as it was full of spring flowers. We sat for a while, enjoying the serenity before moving outside.

The graveyard was in full bloom, bursting with the pale yellow of wild primroses, interspersed with a profusion of white garlic flowers and a riot of blue bells, creating a beautiful and peaceful setting.

We found that the Scillonians, with names such as Mumford, Gibson, Hicks, Tregarthen, and Watts, were lying alongside mariners and passengers washed onto the shores of Scilly from numerous wrecks.

We made a point of visiting the grave of fellow Yorkshireman Lord Harold Wilson, ex-Prime Minister. He was laid to rest in 1995. The grave had a vase of beautiful white lilies and has now become a tourist attraction.

Afterwards we walked back to Hugh Town in time to buy a newspaper. It was only as I flicked through it, that I realised it was Grand National day. Although not big gamblers, we always place a bet on the National.

Today, it was three-thirty pm with a four o'clock start, and I had to use the telephone bookmaker. I selected Silver Birch, at 33/1 and Kay selected Hedge Hunter at 9/1 and with a few minutes to spare we sat down to watch the race. Both our horses managed to complete the course in the lead group and mine actually won.

Celebratory dances over, we decided to have our evening meal at the Mermaid Inn, followed by a pleasant stroll around the Garrison Walk which takes you past the Star Castle, now a hotel, built in 1593. We then walked around the edge of a promontory which is joined to the main body of the island by a narrow strip of land that is Hugh Town, with the quay at one side of the strip and Porth Cressa at the other. The whole area is circled by a walled and fortified enclosure, with cannons still in place in the battlements. On some parts of the walk I noticed an old, hydraulic system made by Adams of York. I'm not really sure what it was used for, but remnants of it were to be found all along the walk.

The area with good paths has been conserved as a wildlife reserve.

April Sunday 15 Rest day

Since arriving on St. Mary's I had been making enquiries about a boat trip to Bishop Rock, the most south-westerly point of the British Isles. The trips are orchestrated by the St. Mary's Boatmen's Association and since our arrival, the weather had not been clear enough to take a boat to the rock. Each time I enquired, I was told, "Not today, but keep trying".

As we were leaving the next day, this was my last chance to get to Bishop Rock, so getting up early, I went to the harbour kiosk to try and book a trip. Unfortunately, it was not to be Although we had sunny weather, there was a sea mist and visibility was not good enough. A couple who stood nearby said, "We have been coming here for five years and have never made it to Bishop Rock".

"You should have been here last week, we took a boat out every day" came a voice from the kiosk.

"Hmmm - I'll have to settle for a view of Bishop Rock with its Lighthouse then", I said.

So, I booked a trip out to St. Agnes; the nearest island to the rock; via Annet.

The harbour was full of boats of all sizes. The quayside was packed with people queuing for boat trips. The Island of Tresco with its gardens, appeared to be a popular destination.

Something else that we missed is gig racing, the most popular sport in Scilly. Throughout summer if the weather is suitable, six-oared gigs are raced by both men and women, with the finish line near to St. Mary's quay.

Today, our boat was The Kingfisher, an open boat, quite large with seating for about thirty people, and a cabin forward. There were only seven of us and the boat was moored up at the bottom of some slippery steps which we had to negotiate.

In the harbour before the boat moved out into the open sea, we were far too hot, but as soon as we pulled away the sea became rougher, with deep swells and a cool breeze became a strong cool wind.

Annet is the most important island for seabirds with almost a thousand pairs of storm petrels, over a hundred pairs of Manx shearwaters, breeding common terns, and fifty puffins. April to July was the best time to see them. We didn't see any, we did, however, see three or four grey seal including one mother and baby. We travelled around the Western rocks and I kept trying to see Bishop Rock, but to no avail. The captain said it was about three miles away and we had only a mile and a half visibility. Our boat went around Annet and out to Melledgan; but still no Bishop Rock, and still no puffins. Eventually our captain gave up and headed off to St. Agnes, the most South Westerly inhabited island, where we were to land and explore for a few hours.

It was lunchtime and just up from the quay was The Turk's Head Pub, Britain's most south-westerly pub. We selected a table outside in the sunshine overlooking the lovely bay of Porth Conger. Here in the shallow waters the sea was a gorgeous turquoise, and the beach in the inlet was lovely golden sand. This led across an isthmus to the island of Gugh.

Later we walked across St. Agnes to Troytown. The sun was blazing and everything inland was very still. The gardens were similar to St. Mary's but a bit more relaxed. The hedgerows rang with birdsong. Song thrushes are abundant with ten times more birds here than are found in similar habitats on the mainland. You can't miss them and they are surprisingly tame which is very uncharacteristic. We also saw lots of blackbirds, linnets and house sparrows which ensured our walks were accompanied by uplifting birdsong.

St. Agnes is only a mile across and at Troytown I was tempted by an advertisement for local ice cream. Whilst we ate the ice creams we walked on to Carnew Point where again we tried to view the horizon for Bishop Rock. We could just make out the islands of Great Crebawethan and Little Crebawethan and even Jacky's Rock, but no Bishop Rock.

We slowly made our way along the indented coastline, past the cushions of flowering sea thrift to the quay where we caught one of the frequent boats back to St. Mary's.

Before supper we walked the Garrison again, and not far from Star Castle, we looked out across the sea and there, behind the island of St. Agnes, standing like a lone sentinel, was Bishop Rock Lighthouse - hooray . Britain's most south-westerly point; built out of Cornish granite although one course is reputed to be Irish granite. It served as the finishing post of the famous Blue Riband Atlantic races between the great liners.

In the middle of the night I woke up and went out to look for Bishop Rock's beam. From Star Castle, it is said that you can see nine lighthouse beams, but I was only interested in one, the Bishop Rock beam, and there it was reassuringly winking as the light circled at regulated intervals.

Three days on the Isles of Scilly is not nearly enough; we had barely scratched the surface. It is so beautiful, and the people are so friendly, generous and polite.

* * * *

The only plan I had was in my head and I intended to walk three days up to our campsite and then three days away before moving on to the next site.

Walking Day 1 *Hot and sunny*

Land's End to Marazion - 15 miles

A very informative taxi driver gave us a running commentary on the countryside we passed on our way to Land's End.

He asked me what I did for a living and when I told him I had just retired after thirty-three and a third years in the police, he told me in an authoritative tone, "It's too late, it's in your blood after so long. You can never retire".

"We will see about that". I replied.

He pointed out the road to the Minack Theatre, informing us that in his opinion, the views from the theatre were the best in Great Britain and he recommended we pay it a visit.

At last we arrived at Land's End, which is surrounded by a tacky theme park.

We set off to find the famous Land's End signpost where we hoped to have our photograph taken before setting off on the walk. After a fruitless search, we went into a shop that housed the Land's End to John O'Groats 'LEJOG' Club and the very helpful assistant informed us that the sign was removed at night otherwise it had a habit of being stolen. She said of the photographer who kept the signpost, "Oh he will be here at 10.00 am, he always is ..." We pointed out it was now quarter past ten and he wasn't.

Whilst we were waiting for the sign to arrive, I completed the forms which would help prove I had completed the walk when we eventually made it to Scotland. I had them duly signed, and the assistant gave me a form to be stamped / signed at various points along the way. The signpost still hadn't arrived so we went to the shop to buy our postcards and a 'LEJOG' baseball cap to get us in the mood.

With our forty or so postcards and stamps we headed back to where the signpost should have been. It eventually arrived around to 11am.

I stood at the end of England and gazed out at the Longships Lighthouse. For a very short period of time I was in a unique position; being at that moment, farther west than anybody else in England.

Land's End, the towering cliffs where the land meets the Atlantic Ocean, is spectacular.

Long before the theme park, people amused themselves here by studying these rocks and cliffs and trying to discern some faint resemblance to some famous person. I stared at the rocks but failed to see Queen Elizabeth the First, Queen Victoria, Dr Johnson and others who are said to be, 'clearly visible'.

Then at last we were off. The scenery in all directions was wild and beautiful. The sea was dark blue and white foam frothed as the waves crashed against the rocks. Wheatear accompanied us over the moor down into Sennen Cove, where the shallower waters became a turquoise blue.

We sat on the front overlooking the beach, eating a bacon sandwich and drinking a cup of tea. After our snack we started the steep, hot climb out, pausing occasionally to admire the view of the bay, before we made it to the top. Where we then branched away from the coastal path into the countryside, crossing several fields of luxuriously thick green grass.

On to Chapel Cairn Brea, a rocky, lofty eminence, set between flowering hedges of gorse which smelt of coconut macaroons just out of the oven.

Chapel Cairn Brea is a Bronze Age summit and is the most Westerly hill in England at 650'. Elihu Burritt writing in his book *'A Walk from London to Land's End and Back'* published 1865, visited Cairn Brea saying, *'It is a capital observatory from which to see the best aspects of Cornwall in all its enterprise'*. Back then his view was dominated by hundreds of tin mine chimneys and wheel houses.

We stopped for a drink at the Cairn which is of a type found only in Scilly and the West of Cornwall. The Cairn is surrounded by smaller burial mounds and apparently, in the medieval period a hermitage and chapel stood here and it is that, that gave the hill its name.

Skylarks were singing overhead as we made our way down off the moor and on to a bridle-way which took us to Carn Euny.

Carn Euny is a heritage site which was excavated both in the 1920's and the 1960's. Apparently it was once a small farming hamlet, established around 500BC and continued to be occupied until about 300AD. The site was rediscovered by miners prospecting for tin and has an underground chamber known in Cornwall as a 'fogou'. The remains of the houses and 'fogou' are very clear. The whole setting is very tranquil and the lack of fanfare made the remains of the little hamlet more beguiling.

Off again, across the fields where we clambered over many Cornish stiles. These appear as a gap in a hedge or wall with a stone threshold then a second stone, a foot or more above which forms a step. A third stone is set at the same level as the first but on the other side of the hedge. There are gaps between all the stones. Some can be quite large which can make negotiating the stiles precarious. The whole thing looks a bit like a hurdle. Christine Roche in her 2004 LEJOG book *'Follow the Spring North'*, describes them excellently, as *'Cattle grid stiles'*.

We came down from the hills passing the Sancreed ancient well, hidden in dense undergrowth. It had many tokens, ribbons and coloured glass, from recent pilgrimages. We followed the footpath from here to the church.

Where we explored its interior with its arched ceiling. After a brief moment of quiet contemplation, we were off again.

Now it was road-walking to Tremethick Cross. The weather remained hot and still and by now Ripley was beginning to flag in the heat. She gently knocked Kay's legs with her nose and did a bit of limping and she knew that she wouldn't be refused a ride. Once up in Kay's arms, she was happy to sit and watch the world go by until she got her second wind.

The roads twisted and turned and became busy with rush-hour traffic; not quite the traffic we are used to in Yorkshire but the narrow bends and high hedges make this sort of walking hard work. After miles of road-walking, we came down by Guval and the heliport near Penzance. From here we had a long walk, sandwiched between the railway and the beach, on a raised walkway, with good views of St. Michael's Mount. It took us all the way to Marazion. Ripley was beat and took herself off to bed, not emerging until morning.

April / Wednesday 18 — Rest day

We decided to wake up naturally the following morning and with no alarm, we didn't wake until 9.30 am and as a result decided to change our plans for the day. After lunch we drove out to the Minack Theatre and found that our taxi driver was not exaggerating the spectacular breath-taking beauty of the place. We walked down to the visitors' centre through gardens planted with sub-tropical plants.

The Minack welcomed dogs, and we sat on the terrace outside, mesmerised by the views over Porthcurno Bay to the Logan Rock. The sun was beating down, and the sea was a sparkling turquoise blue. We were a hundred-and-fifty feet above it. The water was so clear that we could see a shoal of fish swimming in the deep water. 'Minack' in Cornish means, a rocky place. The theatre had been built on one of the crags overlooking a small sandy cove. Before even making it as far as the actual theatre we were entranced.

The theatre is open to the air and looks like it was built by invading Romans, but we quickly came to learn that it was in fact financed and built by hand, in the 1930's, by Rowena Cade and her two gardeners. The theatre is a truly wonderful, spectacular, and awe-inspiring place, even more so when you wander round the visitor centre and hear the story of how it all came to be.

We noticed in the 2007 programme, that the Ilkley Playhouse from Yorkshire, a few miles from where we live, would be performing in July.

On the way back we called in at Morrison's supermarket, Penzance, the most southerly Morrison's in Britain. A notice above the door read, '*Morrison's plc, Gain Lane, Bradford*' an address I know well.

April / Thursday 19 — Walking day 2 *Hot and sunny*

Marazion to Helston - 15 miles - Total walked 30

I set off down to the cliff edge through enclosed snickets of flowering blackthorn and wild flowers, out on to the coastal path looking down the jagged cliff to the sea, then away with the open heath land on my left.

There was a cacophony of birdsong from the hedgerows. Up on the heath you know that the warbling song from high up in the air is that of the sky lark. I was accompanied now by a pair of wheatears with their distinctive white rumps, as they bobbed along, flitting from stone, to rock, to bush, their staccato warble calling me on; and seeming to say, "look at us, look at us".

The land became hilly and I heard the croaking 'pruk, pruk' of the raven, as it soared over the cliffs and crags; sometimes looking as if it was going to tumble out of the sky.

I looked at my map and saw that the little village of Perranuthnoe was nearby. I lengthened my stride and soon found myself walking down the main street.

It is one of about five places in Cornwall named after their National Saint, St. Piran, sometimes spelt Perran. He is also the patron Saint of Tin Miners and it is his cross that adorns the Cornish flag, a white cross on a black background.

Back on the coastal path and on to Prussia Cove, which was named after a local smuggler, John Carter, who used the alias 'The King of Prussia'. I passed a complex of large houses with unusual architecture, having tall chimneys and small windows. Here, I was serenaded by piano, cello and violin, all being expertly played by the residents of the fortress like buildings.

I continued, taking in the fabulous coastal scenery, and enjoying the peace and solitude. Praa Sands was a bit of a shock, having had the coast to myself for miles. The beach had a surf school, and was full of children and grownups, laughing and screaming at each other as they played on the beach.

It was lunchtime, so I went into a beach-side bar and ordered a pint of lemonade with pineapple, my favourite thirst-quenching drink. All the seats outside were taken, so I decided to take advantage of the shade inside, and took my drink to a quiet corner table. I set off again, heading for Porthleven. The land sweeping down to the cliff tops was one minute, fresh soft green grass; then the rough red of dead bracken; and then swaths of yellow gorse that seemed to fall right over the cliff edges and into the sea.

Derelict chimneys and mine buildings dotted the landscape against the beautiful backdrop of the sea. The sun beating down on the sea had the effect of silver flecks on the tips of tiny waves. This was iconic Cornwall.

There were many secluded beaches, with golden sands that looked impossible to reach and were in fact empty. Just before Porthleven, I said goodbye to the sea and cliff tops, and struck a course inland, on picturesque back roads and green lanes, sometimes appearing more like green tunnels as the hedgerows arch high into the sky and trees bend over to meet in the middle. As before, the hedgerows were full of flowers, swaths of soft white common stitchwort intermingled with bluebells and red campion. This was a perfect habitat for the numerous blackbird, wren, thrush, chiffchaff and chaffinch.

Then on to an open and dusty farm track. The dust flew up in swirls and covered my face so that the back of my throat felt parched and dry. I began to think of the 1958 film, *Ice*

Cold in Alex, with John Mills, and the famous scene when, after pushing an ambulance across a desert, he and the others arrived at the bar in Alexandria and downed an ice-cold beer in one. Although now a teetotaller, I could appreciate the sentiment and instead looked forward to downing an ice-cold bottle of water in Helston.

Before I reached Helston I still had to walk a mile or two. I pushed on. There was not a soul in sight when suddenly, a Border collie dog was racing towards me, barking viciously, frothing at the mouth, fangs bared. In shock and not a little fear, I backed up against the hedge, where it pinned me, leaping in the air, snarling and barking. A previous experience on another walk had left me with a border collie hanging from my thigh by its teeth, with a farmer beating it off with a shovel, so I stayed where I was and hoped that the owner would appear and rescue me. Sure enough in the distance, I saw an old man ambling towards me.

I shouted urgently at him to, "Call your dog off". He showed absolutely no response but continued to mooch in my direction. There was no let-up in the dogs angry barking and snarling. You'd think it would become exhausted, expending all that energy and rage, but no. I was beginning to get angry now. I heard the man reply, but couldn't understand a word he said over the barking of the dog. It sounded like, "Oh ee ar ... Oh ee ar".

I shouted again, "Call your dog off". and started edging towards the old man. The dog followed, jumping up, frothing at its mouth, and barking unremittingly. By now I was at, "Call your f---ing dog off". And the unconcerned response was, "Oh ee ar".

By now I felt ready to give the dog a good kick and I was in punching distance of the old man, when I heard him say, "You will have to speak up, I'm a bit deaf". His very strong Cornish dialect made him difficult to understand; that and the dog; but he went on, "Don't worry about the dog, he won't bite you".

"We are not used to seeing people walking down this path", he went on.

I thought - I can tell . I said to the chap, "I'm heading for Helston".

"Go straight down here, not left", he told me.

I replied, "Okay".

"Go straight down, don't turn left", he repeated.

"Right", I shouted.

"No. Go straight down here, don't turn left".

This continued for some time so smiling and nodding I walked straight down, not left, into Helston, with the dog pursuing me out of its territory.

I headed straight into Woolworths on Helston Main Street, and 'Ice-cold in Helston', for a bottle of ice-cold water. Most people who walk into Helston head for the Blue Anchor pub, where they have brewed a beer called Spingo for over 300 years, but I was to give it a miss. I drank my water quickly at the till, downing it in one go. I said to the checkout girl, "same again please", to which she replied "This is Woolworths, not a pub".

Helston is famous for its Flora or Furry Dance, a day-long series of dances and merry-making at an ancient spring festival that occurs each year on the 8th of May.

It is also the final resting place of Henry Trengrove, the inventor of the line rocket apparatus used by sailors to 'fire' a line between ships. Trengrove can be credited with saving thousands of lives as a result of his invention. His grave stone is said to be a simple monument in the graveyard; so simple I couldn't find it.

Helston's origins lie in the tin and copper industry. It was originally tidal so exports were shipped directly out. Many centuries ago the Loe Bar cut off the River Cober and was also responsible for the wrecking of HMS Anson in 1807, whose impressive cannon now rests outside the back of the Guildhall.

April
Friday
20

Rest day

Today, we decamped from Marazion and drove to Truro where we intended to stay in a village called Veryan, not too far from the coast.

The Caravan site was very clean and it seemed that the wardens ran it like a military camp. There were signs everywhere telling us what we couldn't do, but thankfully the couple who greeted us were pleasant and friendly. After setting up camp we set off in our Nissan to Truro, to have a look around and collect our mail from the post office. We were taking advantage of the Royal Mail service, 'Post Restante', and having my father-in-law, Kevin, post our mail on to the nearest large post office, and Truro was our first test of the system. We parked in the town centre, and walked a few hundred yards to the post office where we collected our mail without any problems.

April
Saturday
21

Walking Day 3 *Hot and sunny*

Helston to St Stithians - 9 miles - Total walked 39

Kay drove me back to Helston so that I could continue my footsteps from where I'd left off. The start of my walk was a two-and-a-half-mile uphill slog on a B road. My only entertainment, besides dodging vehicles; was watching a soaring buzzard being mobbed by a flock of rooks as it came too close to their rookery.

Without realising it, I was walking through the World Heritage Site of Cornwall & East Devon. This is unusual as it covers only the Tin Mines with their remaining engine buildings dotted around the countryside, many of which I was getting some good views of. I eventually took a quiet lane leading through Boderwenack, then on to Hendra, and by the time I reached Porkellis it was time for my snap.

I headed for the pub, The Star Inn. The landlord was new, having just moved here and the only food on offer was a packet of crisps. My drink was very welcome in the midday sun. I was his only customer. Later I continued walking along the quiet lanes accompanied some of the way by a beautiful big dog fox. Who wasn't at all put off by my presence. The lanes were now surrounded by rough pasture, framed by gorse and bramble hedges, with the odd flowering blackthorn to add a little height. I was finding it difficult to find footpath signs. I could see them clearly marked on my map but there was no sign of them as I walked. After searching for a sign for some time, I saw a young couple and their baby in the garden of a modern bungalow, very close to where the map said there was a footpath, so I asked them if they could help me.

"Footpath? Not round here - we don't do footpaths", came their united response.

I showed them the map and explained that the footpath led to the reservoir.

"No, not round here. We don't 'do' any walking, so we don't know... Sorry".

I thanked them for their time and walked on and within five yards of their house I located the footpath sign.

Now, for the first time since leaving Helston, I was walking on a proper, green footpath, a delight. The path took me through the heath land to Stithians Reservoir, which a signpost assured me, was home to bog and wetland; the whole area was a conservation zone owned by South West Lakes Trust.

Stithians Reservoir was created in 1965 and is of roughly five miles in circumference, with a concrete dam holding back millions of gallons of water. It supplies a huge area with water, down as far as the Lizard Peninsula and St. Agnes. As I walked around the edge towards the dam, I could see people wind surfing and boating. I also passed some fly fishermen. As I crossed the impressive concrete dam, I reached another milestone; the end of my first map; 'Ordinance Survey Land Ranger 203. Land's End / Isle of Scilly'.

With the aid of my new map, I quickly arrived at Stithians with its very majestic church. With the sun still beating down on me, I decided to call it a day and called on Kay.

April
Sunday
22

Walking Day 4 *Hot and sunny*

St. Stithians to Calerick - 8 miles - Total walked 47

Another lovely day in paradise. We decided to explore our immediate area. The Site Warden advised us that internet access was available at a small Harbour Club in Portscatho. Which turned out to be one of the many fishing villages in the area with an old-world charm appearing to perch on the cliffs, surrounded by lovely views.

Dinner-time saw us at the Plume of Feathers. The pub welcomed Ripley. In the bar area there was an oar hanging from the ceiling, which had been signed by Steve Redgrave.

After dinner I decided to continue walking. I collected my kit and Kay dropped me in Stithians where I had finished the day before, and I headed for the quiet country back-roads into Truro.

The hot sunny Sunday afternoon had encouraged all the 'boy racers', with surf boards attached to their roofs, out onto the quiet lanes. Cars came screaming around blind corners, the occupants seemingly oblivious to the dangers. I witnessed three near collisions; that no one was injured nor a vehicle damaged, I can only describe as a miracle.

It was impossible for me to enjoy the scenery - I was too busy making sure I didn't get run over. A dead badger, which I passed as I neared the end of my journey, had not been fortunate enough to avoid some speeding motorist.

Eventually I found a pleasant, dappled shady spot on a leafy lane to await Kay's rescue; where I could admire a fine specimen of a Lords-and-Lady, which until recently, I only knew by the name 'Preacher in the Pulpit'.

April
Monday 23

Walking Day 5 - St George's Day *Fresh and dry*

Calerick to Idless Wood - 4 miles - Total walked 51

We drove into Truro, to find internet access, and hopefully a computer 'geek' - I use that word with great affection. We found both at a computer shop on the outskirts of Truro. Where we learnt how to use the laptop correctly for our email messages. We then walked down into the town centre where we sat in the square in front of the cathedral, listening to an elderly busker.

The cathedral was just opening again for visitors after being shut for a private funeral for a young man killed in a road accident. Kay and I took it in turns to look around the cathedral interior and Ripley kept the pigeons in order on the square outside.

The cathedral was built in the 1880's and copied the gothic cathedral building of earlier centuries, complete with a magnificent 240' spire. The Victorians certainly knew how to do it. The cathedral incorporates the Parish Church of St. Mary's, parts of which date back to 1259. A minor criticism, however, is that unlike a lot of other cathedrals, this one appears to be hemmed in by the surrounding shops and other buildings. I gazed up at the magnificent windows and arched roof vaults. I particularly liked the terracotta depiction of Christ on the way to Calvary, a masterpiece by George Tinworth, and a joy to look at.

It being St. George's Day, I went looking for something connected to St George, and found him slaying the dragon in a beautiful stained glass window. I sat here for a while in quiet contemplation. In the cathedral shop, I bought a card with the Lord's Prayer in Cornish. The only word I recognised was 'Amen'.

Later in the day I resumed my walk, starting where I had left off at Calerick. As I walked, I counted over thirty specimens of Lords-and Ladies, growing in wild profusion. I made my way through the back lanes until I came to a busy main road which I had to cross. The footpath I had been walking on just disappeared, as if the new roundabout had been dropped on top of it. Unfortunately the roundabout didn't take into account pedestrians and there was nowhere marked for me to cross. Traffic was whizzing by in all directions and all I could do was stand teetering on the kerb, waiting for some kind motorist to allow me to cross. Eventually a knight of the road slowed down and allowed me to get to the other side. I saluted him - a lone example of good manners.

Having crested a hill, I now walked down into Truro Town Centre, on Lemon Street, (which was named after William Lemon, a local mine owner). The houses were all built of stone and looked grand. Now commercial premises; these were once splendid homes.

Lemon Street has its own Nelson-like column. A plaque at the base revealed that the monument was in honour of a local man called Richard Landers, who helped map the River Niger in Africa. Landers was the first man to be awarded a gold medal by the Royal Geographic Society in 1832.

People were swarming up and down the street going about their business, and I wondered how many had actually noticed the monument, even though it was of a considerable size; or if the locals had become inured to its presence.

Truro can also lay claim to be the only town in Britain to have had a newspaper with the word 'Royal' in its title (excepting Royal Leamington Spa Times, which uses its full Sunday name when giving a title to its newspaper). Between 1801 and 1951 Truro was home to the Royal Cornwall Gazette. It merged with the still popular West Briton newspaper that has its offices in Truro whilst today the print is over the border in Plymouth, Devon.

On an official town centre map, Truro is described as being '*a town of elegance and distinction*'. I found it to be very pleasant and might even go as far as saying it was 'modern and vibrant'. I also discovered that Truro had not just one river running through it but three . The River's Allen and Kenwyn make their way through the town to join the bigger Truro River.

With a bit of skilful map reading, I found the footpath leading out of town and out into the countryside under a railway viaduct. I soon found myself walking through fields and woods alongside a river. Wild garlic cut swathes through the thick spring grass and at last trees were starting to take on their leaves. I was surprised how quickly the town had been left behind. It started to rain gently as I walked into the village of Idless where Kay and Ripley were waiting and I decided to call it a day.

 Walking Day 6 *Fresh and dry*

April Tuesday 24

Idless Wood to Lanber Mill - 2 miles - Total walked 53

Tonight we were going to the theatre in Truro; 'The Hall for Cornwall', to see Yorkshire's 'Northern Broadside' perform a production of Shakespeare's *The Tempest*. We follow Barrie Rutter and his Halifax-based group. So we were delighted to see them this far south, and be able to include them in our travels. To accommodate the theatre trip, we could only do a short walk today. So it was back to Idless where I had left off the day before and take a comfortable stroll up through Idless woods and back.

Walking along the narrow road through the village to the woods, we saw several signs telling us that Cornwall County Council were dealing with their problem of Japanese Knotweed. I have never seen any similar signs in Yorkshire, so I wondered if we were dealing with ours.

Walking in April in England is fantastic. Spend a while with me here in Cornwall, looking at the hedgerows.

In the hedgerows, there were lots of lovely purple dog violets and the floor of the wood itself was blue with a carpet of bluebells. Ripley was ecstatic at getting us both for her walk and found the biggest stick she could carry in celebration. The trees at the entrance to the wood were deciduous but these gave way to pine - changing the whole feel of the place. The smell of the wood altered as we walked in amongst the pine trees and the carpets of wild flowers just seemed to stop. The path took us along the side of a stream. Noticeable amongst the brambles and ferns, were the florescent green flowers of the wood spurge, looking very vibrant in the shade from the trees. We did 4 miles today but only 2 miles towards John O'Groats.

The Hall for Cornwall is a splendid theatre, with very comfortable seating. I noticed that the stewards and ushers were all wearing exactly the same uniform as those worn in Bradford's Alhambra theatre. More to the point it was an excellent production of *The Tempest*.

Owing to the amount of travelling backwards and forwards up the A30, we didn't have much time to explore the local area and only had the last evening to drive into Veryan, which is a picturesque little village that has some very unusual round houses with thatched roofs and a cross on the chimney. According to legend they were, *'round so the Devil couldn't find a corner to hide in'*.

Walking Day 7 *Hot and sunny*

April Wednesday 25 — Lanber Mill to Indian Queens - 11 miles - Total walked 64

We were up bright, if not early and we packed up and moved our base from Veryan to Indian Queens ... Kay was to drive me down to Lanber Mill and I was to walk back to Indian Queens.

My walk started along quiet, country lanes, with beautiful and very high hedgerows. However, this part of Cornwall is frequented by a disgusting group of people. There was rubbish dumped everywhere: old fridges, television sets, microwaves, old tyres, and general rubbish. How can they do it? It is just as easy to take rubbish to the tip or recycle centre, as it is to drive into the countryside. It was all the more shocking because Cornwall generally is pretty, clean, and well looked after. The only graffiti we had seen up until arriving at Indian Queens was that written by the group, 'An Gof', who seemed to take pleasure in defacing bridges and main roads around the County.

As I understand it, they are a group of people wanting independence for Cornwall.

The day's walking was not very inspiring with the exception of St Enoder's Church. I bought a book on Cornish Saints, by Peter Ellis, 1992, and it just said, *'Nothing is known of the saint who gave his name to St Enoder'*.

The church is large with an imposing tower. Unfortunately it was locked and the graveyard had not been mown in recent weeks. The grass was knee high. Someone else had been there before me, so I followed the trampled grass and explored the graveyard. Most of the gravestones were made from one-inch-thick slabs of slate. At the gate I found an ancient Cornish Cross.

I walked through Indian Queens which was a bit of a hotchpotch; a few houses mingled with an industrial estate and many large building projects. The town appears to have a well-established brass band, with new rooms for them to play and to practice in.

April	**Rest day**
Thursday	
26	

Today was the day we had booked into Rick Stein's Restaurant at Padstow; something Kay had been looking forward to for weeks. Unfortunately, she bent to help Ripley into the motor home and her back decided to have an 'acute episode'. Through past experience we knew she wouldn't be able to function - stand - for at least three days. It was frightening and excruciatingly painful for Kay to be stuck on her back alone in the motor home, so I didn't do any walking that day. With Kay out of commission, I was on domestic duties.

I rang and cancelled the restaurant and then packed up and headed up the A30 to a site at Bodmin. The manager and his wife were from Yorkshire, Allerton in Bradford. He told me he really enjoyed his life down in Cornwall and it depressed him when he went back home to see what has become of his home city.

We met an 83yr old man, widowed a few years earlier. He had sold up and bought a motor home with a little car towed behind like ours. He invited us into his 'home' and explained to us how he was now travelling around Britain. "Much better than spending the last years of your life in a nursing home" He said. We both agreed with him.

April	**Walking Day 8** *Hot and sunny*
Friday	
27	**Indian Queens to Bodmin - 12 miles - Total walked 76** ⟩

Indian Queens is an unusual name. According to Colin Howard in his 1939 book *'Land's End to John O'Groats'*, its name cannot be traced earlier than the 19th century. A coach house inn displayed a portrait of an Indian Queen with an inscription which tells the story of a Portuguese princess; Queen Caroline? Who landed at Falmouth and slept here on her way to London, her swarthy appearance gave the impression she was an Indian. Howard went on to state that local legend speculates that Pocahontas (1595 - 1617), an American Indian princess passed through, thereby giving the place it's unusual name.

The skyline is scarred by the nearby china clay mines which remain a crucial local employer and one of Cornwall's few surviving industries. China clay, or kaolin, was first used in the making of porcelain but today its main destination is the paper industry. Its excavation produces vast pits and enormous, pale waste mounds of clay and quartzes and although some of it has recently been re-landscaped, the area north of St. Austell was once dubbed the 'Cornish Alps'.

It was another lovely sunny Cornish day when we arrived back at my starting point, the roundabout in Indian Queens. It was almost lunchtime and wafting on the gentle breeze was the tantalising smell of cooking bacon. Parked on my starting point was a catering van. It was obviously meant to be.

The owners of the van, a friendly couple, were discussing the word 'Smeech'. I had never heard the word before and the man in the van thought it was a Cornish word meaning 'smell of cooking fat'. (Intrigued by the word I later bought a Cornish dialect book in which it was recorded as meaning *'the smell of burning'*).

I ordered my usual, a 'well done bacon and tomato', and as soon as the words left my mouth the man said, "You're a Northerner".

"Yorkshire", I replied.

"It must be a Northern thing having tomatoes with bacon".

He said I was the first person to ask for it. Ha . Bacon and tomato; a Yorkshire delicacy.

Just after I'd set off, I was walking along the lane when I saw what I thought was a dull grey-coloured stick in the hedgerow. It surprised me when it moved. I looked closer it glided and slithered a bit deeper into the hedgerow. It was a snake . I couldn't see all of it. My initial reaction was to recoil in repulsion and then I wanted to photograph it; but by the time I had my camera out, it had disappeared deep into the hedgerow.

As I walked away from Indian Queens and out into the countryside, I had the beautiful and by this time clean Cornish lanes to myself. The sun was beating down as I passed a house, romantically and appropriately called, *'Swallows Return'*. The sky was full of their pleasant twittering as they swooped and glided above.

I was now walking towards Castle-an-Dinas, a small hill with links to King Arthur and an important prehistoric settlement. It stands seven-hundred feet above sea level, and has extensive views; south and east over Goss Moor to Hensbarrow Downs, north towards St. Breock Downs, and west to Newquay and the estuary of the Gannel. Today however my views were obscured by a heat haze, the laden atmosphere heavy with the drone of insects.

Around 400 BC Castle-an-Dinas had defences comprising three massive circular stone and earth banks with outer ditches, together with a slighter fourth bank. Today as I walked through them, they were coarse grass mounds forming concentric ripples. As I entered the 'inner circle', a buzzard called, the sound adding a certain lonely mysticism to this quiet, magical place.

The inner circle is about as large as a cricket pitch and very flat. Sheep were keeping it tidy and skylarks were performing their aerial dance while singing their liquid song. The stillness of the air meant that 'Cleggs', better known as May flies, were out in force, hovering then darting out of the way as I walked towards them. I decided this would be a lovely place to picnic, and I chose a spot which looked down on the very busy A30. Thousands of motorists sped past and few would even know that this ancient place existed.

I heard my first cuckoo of the season as I walked down the footpath from the hill, past the remains of a tin and tungsten mine. The rusty remains of an aerial skip and lift could still be seen. The footpath, although clearly sign-posted, was very overgrown with gorse and I wondered if King Arthur had been the last person to use this path, or perhaps more realistically, the miners who last worked up here in the 1950's.

From here, my way to Bodmin lay along more narrow lanes that promised to take me through pleasant villages, the first of which was going to be St. Wenn.

To get to St. Wenn my route lay across a couple of fields, whose stiles were clearly marked and a footpath post pointed out the way. Unfortunately the farmer obviously had a problem and he had put an electric fence across the access just behind the signpost and planted his crop in such a way that it was impossible for a walker to get into the field without damaging it. This blatant law-breaking and obstruction quite upset me; in fact, it made me a tad cross.

I found a stick and pulled up a post in the electric fence, so allowing my access into the field. Normally when confronted with a field growing crops, I would carefully walk around the edge, but here I marched across where the footpath should have been, aiming directly for the stile, clearly in view at the other side. I did have a Jurassic Park moment half way across, waist high in vegetation, I expected to be eaten alive by dinosaurs or some other animal the farmer had lying in wait for me, but I made it to the stile, uneaten.

Then on to the prominent church at the top of the hill; St. Wenn's. Another Cornish saint, she takes her name from Wenna, a daughter of Brychan. The church was open and inside it was plain but well kept. I rested a while and read that there had been a church on this site since 1200 AD.

This, like many other small, rural churches, was struggling to stay open, the parishioners pulling together to keep it going. Within five miles of here, there are four other churches, all trying to keep their doors open.

I continued down the lanes and onto Boscome. Even though the walking here was very pleasant, I was glad to reach the Boscome junction and walk along the old railway line, now called the Camel Trail; a well looked after public footpath and cycle way. The trains on this line used to run to Padstow and North Cornwall but like many useful access lines, these are now long gone.

Entering Bodmin, I walked past the old gaol, the last place in England to carry out a public execution in 1909. Special trains were put on for the occasion, causing a near riot in the town as the assembled crowd realised with despair that they were not going to witness the actual hanging. It was to take place inside the prison walls.

Bodmin or 'Bod Mynachan', the abode of monks, was I found a busy little town with a high street containing a variety of shops amongst which I found a bookshop where I was able to stock up on maps for my journey north. Near the bookshop there is an ancient stone pillar, said to be a remnant from the ancient priory. The priory was originally a Benedictine monastery founded either by, or in honour of St. Petroc, the son of a Welsh chieftain. The nearby Parish church, dedicated to St. Petroc, with its churchyard, lies on a very large traffic island in the centre of town.

The town also possessed a Morrison's Supermarket, which we later used to restock our supplies.

Walking Day 9 *Hot and sunny*

Bodmin to St. Breward - 9 miles - Total walked 85 >

Kay was starting to become more mobile and, exercise being the antidote to her bad back, we set off together from Bodmin on the Camel Trail, with miles of easy walking. It being very popular with the locals. It runs along the side of a small stream on the outskirts of town. We spotted quite a few pale green brimstone butterflies as they took idiosyncratic flight amongst the new, green leaves in the woodland hedgerow.

Ripley was happy because we were all out together, strutting ahead with her tail curled over her back, beaming at anyone who showed any interest in her. All too soon we reached a junction and it was time for them to turn back.

The Camel Trail follows the old mineral railway line from Dunmere to Wenford, which linked with the Bodmin to Wadebridge Railway. Originally constructed to transport china clay and sea sand, the line was also utilised for the movement of granite from De Lank Quarry, St Breward. This is the same granite used to build Bishop Rock Lighthouse. The railway line was completed in September 1834, making it one of the earliest steam operations in the country. John Betjeman; poet 1906 - 1984, described it as, *'The most beautiful train journey I know'*. This didn't stop it being axed.

The Trail took me through Shell Woods, which is designated as a Special Area of Conservation.

It is a mixture of deciduous and coniferous trees and is managed by the Forestry Commission. The place was alive with birdsong and chiff chaff seemed to pursue me through the wood.

Every few miles the trail crossed a road with a cottage or two and I looked longingly for somewhere that sold tea. In the distance, I saw a cottage with a shop sign and I started to drool, only to find when I arrived there that it was a craft shop and didn't sell tea.

I was distracted by a 'mewling' in the sky above me and when I looked up, I saw a pair of buzzards, spiralling upwards in the thermals, soaring and calling to one another. Suddenly, one dived, rocketing towards the earth, the other closely following. The second buzzard dive-bombed the first, connecting with feathers flying. The first plummeted upside down for several feet before righting itself and soaring back into the thermals. What an amazing spectacle . I wondered if this was practice for hunting and catching on the wing.

As I was approaching the end of the trail, I saw a small snake. It was about a foot long and was right in the middle of the path. This time my wits were about me and I managed to photograph it. It seemed to pose for some time before it slithered away into the long grass beside the path. (It was a slow worm...which as we all know is a reptile and technically not a snake).

The Camel Trail ended at Poley Bridge, but a path continued past the massive, derelict works of Poley Bridge China Clay works towards Wenford Bridge. The works in their heyday must have employed hundreds. Today the ruins were being taken over by moss, fern and ivy.

I joined the road again and there, right in front of me, was a café doing Cornish teas; I marched into its shady interior and ordered a pot of tea. Most of the other customers were in the garden, having walked no further than the car park and here enjoying the heat of the day.

Refreshed, up the hill I went, past St. Brewards on the left, with its highest pub in Cornwall, The Old Inn and then up past the quarries and eventually out onto the moor. I was surrounded by grazing wild ponies. I walked to Lady Down Cross Roads where I was met by Kay and Ripley.

Before returning back to base, we took a short drive across the moor, to a place I'd seen on the map, called Bradford, a tiny hamlet by a ford and a small bridge over the River De Lank. There was Upper and Lower Bradford.

We stopped to take a photograph of this Bradford, and one of the residents, who had been gardening, came over smiling at us, as we explained that we were from Bradford in Yorkshire. She told us that we were the first 'Bradfordians' in seven years of them living there, to visit. She was from Blackburn, and her husband was from Burnley and neither had been to Bradford in Yorkshire, despite its close proximity.

When they first arrived, they wanted to change the name of their house which was Bradford, but now they were used to it.

We left the friendly Lancastrians living in idyllic Bradford, and drove into St. Breward, where we found a post office which also had an internet café. The post lady was very enterprising and friendly. As well as the post office and internet café, she also made home-made pizza to take away.

No cooking tonight. The managers of the caravan site persuaded us to join them and other campers in a joint order of fish and chips from the local shop who would be delivering to the site. Apparently they were 'continually excellent'. It's a risky matter, a Yorkshireman purchasing fish and chips out of the County, because we have some pretty good 'chip shops', and these tonight were only just fair, a bit of a disappointment.

Walking Day 10 *Hot and sunny*

St. Breward to Jamaica Inn - 8 miles - Total walked 93 ▷

Kay drove me up onto Bodmin Moor so I could pick up where I left off last night. The moor was teeming with people enjoying the sunshine and the open space; riders and dog walkers along with hikers. Kay and Ripley joined me for the first couple of miles. Ripley remained on her lead as we walked through herds of wild ponies and their foals.

The moor looked a bit brown and dry but if you looked closely you could see tiny yellow and red flowers hidden in the coarse grass. Ripley and Kay eventually turned back. It was one of the disappointments of the walk that they couldn't walk with me. However, it wasn't practical for them to walk more than a couple of miles with me.

I walked on, accompanied by a cuckoo and this time I managed to see it.

I left all the other hikers behind and went on alone. I climbed over the Downs and up to the ancient stone workings of King Arthur's Hall. A rectangular compound flanked by raised banks. It is presumed to have been some sort of meeting place or site of worship. Lonely and enigmatic, it's just right for a spot of Arthurian myth-making, or it could have been a large barn to keep the cows in.

In the distance I could see both Brown Willy, the highest hill in Cornwall, and its more photogenic neighbour, Rough Tor, pronounced 'Row Tor' as in 'ow' 'ouch'. My path continued until Garrow, an old farm, then dropped down to cross two wooden footbridges before skirting the flanks of Butter's Tor and climbing directly up the slopes of Brown Willy.

I was accompanied now by a couple of wheatears and I could hear the mewing high in the sky, of a couple of buzzards, lazily circling. I felt right at home as the moor reminded me of my Yorkshire Moors. Bodmin Moor is big but not as big as many Yorkshire Moors. Here I could see the Moors edge with fields and woods. In winter it could be a harsh place; perhaps even in summer if the weather was bad.

As I climbed Brown Willy's flanks I thought I heard voices behind me but I hadn't seen anyone for miles; I could see the trig point not far ahead of me as I climbed up onto the ridge. From here I could see Rough Tor, Cornwall's second highest peak. It is crowned by more weirdly-shaped rock formations and 'clitter' (rock debris), than Brown Willy and I thought that it looked like a good climb; perhaps another day.

Brown Willy's ridge went up and down, up and down, and every time I thought I was at the top, I had to go down again, the trig point always in the distance. After several these false summits, I eventually got there, at last, on top of the highest point in Cornwall - 1,377 feet... just a hill really.

The summit is covered in bilberry bushes and the scent of them filled the air. Guide books claim that on a clear day you can see Lundy Isle. I couldn't even see the sea, it was lost in a haze on the horizon. I made a few attempts to photograph myself at the summit, until the voices I'd heard earlier materialised in the form of a man and his twenty-year-old daughter and I asked them if they would photograph me, which they did.

The man said he was a Londoner and was now settled in Cornwall. I asked if there were any Londoners left in London as they all seemed to be living in Cornwall and he rather wistfully replied, "Well not in the area of London I was brought up in. It's gone completely, taken over by immigrants".

With all these 'immigrants' now living in Cornwall I wandered if the old rhyme, 'By Tre, Ros, Pol, Lan, Caer and Pen, you may know most Cornish men', meant anything these days? His daughter said, "You did really well. We kept trying to catch up with you but you kept going away from us".

My chest swelled and I tried not to look too pleased with myself.

Her dad said that they were using me as a marker as they were in training for next week's Ten Tor's Walk and continued, "Judging by your accent I'd say you were a Northerner?"

I replied. "I'm from Yorkshire and there is a whole world further north than Yorkshire. I'd describe myself as a Yorkshireman first, never a Northerner".

I had my snap on the top, (I actually was brought up to call it dinner and our evening meal, tea) and while I ate, I drank in the views.

After lunch I headed down the long but easy walk eastwards across the Moor to Jamaica Inn, made famous by the novel of Daphne Du Maurier. The old coaching inn has inevitably been turned into something of a tourist trap with gift shops, a museum and the Dame Daphne Du Maurier Memorial Room.

I had arranged to meet Kay and Ripley for tea at the Inn, now bypassed by the A30, standing on a little hill, with a large car and coach park. My arrival coincided with a coach full leaving which meant I was quickly served at the bar; a pint of lemonade and a glass of pineapple.

Jamaica Inn looked and felt grubby. It had the feel of a tawdry tourist trap. Mark Moxon, in his 2007 LEJOG book, 'When I walk I bounce', described it... 'As tacky as a motorway service station'.

The shop was full of the usual cheap tat - I did buy a copy of Daphne Du Maurier's 'Jamaica Inn', but we decided against eating there. The place reeked of stale tobacco and drink. Perhaps they were aiming at authenticity in this regard, as Mary Yellan, the heroine in the book, gave a similar description of the bar on her arrival at Jamaica Inn.

We decided instead to drive down to Padstow to check out Rick Stein's Fish and Chip shop. It was a bit soon to have fish and chips again really, but because of Kay's back, we'd had to forgo the visit to the restaurant and we thought this might be the next best thing - and we were leaving the area within the next few days.

We had never been to Padstow but because of Rick Stein's TV programmes, we had seen several cameos of it and thought it looked like many of the other small, charming Cornish villages we had visited in the past few weeks. The first thing I noticed as we reached the hill going down into Padstow was the sign that - Welcomed you to Padstow *'sponsored by Foleys Fish and Chip Shop - The Locals' Chippy'*.

Padstow wasn't at all how I'd imagined it, I thought it would be a bit like Whitby in Yorkshire, but as we drove down past Tesco, and modern housing, I was disappointed. Even down in the harbour area, with its narrow streets and older buildings, it didn't live up to expectations. It was full with tourists, even so late in the day, so the place must have something. We parked up and went for a comfortable stroll. Rick Stein seemed to own half of the town.

We went into the fish and chip shop which was staffed with efficient Eastern European workers. I ordered haddock and chips twice. They weren't bad but we have had better in Yorkshire . We only intended to have a flying visit to Padstow and our first impressions didn't encourage us to stay and explore. It is obviously very popular but not for us on this occasion. It was May Day in a few days' time and there were many signs of preparation for the town's famous 'horse dance'. This included signs in the shops saying they would be shut, and more off- putting, provision for parking being prepared a long way out of town. Perhaps a victim of its own success?

April Monday 30 Rest day

A day off from walking, so we drove into Bodmin where I attempted to collect our Post Restante. I joined the very long queue, made up primarily of people collecting their benefits and when I eventually made it to the front of the queue, I asked the woman behind the counter if I could collect my Post Restante. She looked at me and snapped, "Oh, it's you is it; having your post redirected here . Well you can't do that . I've sent it back marked 'NOT KNOWN AT THIS ADDRESS' ".

"What" I said. "Post Restante is a Post Office service advertised on its website".

"Well, we are not a Post Office really, we are just a counter in Cost Cutters", she continued, bossily.

I said, "So you are not the main Post Office in Bodmin? It says you are the Post Office outside and even here above your counter?"

She replied, still very officiously, "Yes, we are ... but we are not part of Royal Mail. They have a sorting office at the end of this street".

So I thanked her nicely for her time.

I went to the Royal Mail sorting office and there spoke to a very nice man, who told me something to the effect that the member of staff at the Post Office didn't know what she was talking about; but put much more succinctly, and on the same lines as my thoughts. Apparently, Cost Cutters had recently taken over the Post Office Counter.

He spoke to the 'viper' at Cost Cutters on the phone and very nicely explained about Post Restante and asked her to check again; pointing out that it was a service that they delivered. He gave us his telephone number and said he would hold it at the Sorting Office if it arrived the next day. I went back to the Cost Cutter Post Office later that afternoon and surprise, surprise; my post was there .

Not a good start to the day and I needed to forget about it, so we decided to visit the much-heralded and excitingly-named, Eden Project; one of the few Millennium projects that have been successful. It is now named as one of the *'Marvels of the Modern* World'.

On the drive down we saw the spoils of industry in the form of hideous slag heaps which created ugly scars on the skyline. I found driving through this area of Cornwall depressing. It is sad that in this day and age, some use cannot be found of the waste from china clay workings.

The car parks for the Eden Project seemed to start at least a couple of miles away from the actual attraction. We were lucky to be visiting mid-week and out of season as the car parks were fairly empty and we managed to park in the *'Dog Zone'*, which is right next to the entrance to the project. These were advertised as shady kennels close to the entrance to make it easy for owners to visit their pets. The *'kennels'* were corrugated canopies which provided shade over the vehicles, to help keep them cool in hot weather. I wasn't sold on the idea that they would provide enough shade to keep a car cool enough on a hot day for a dog to be left very long at all. I felt they were merely a token gesture, a market ploy, rather than a solution for families on holiday with their pets. Certainly on busy days they wouldn't be sufficient.

By the time we had parked up it was raining quite heavily, so it was a perfect day to leave Ripley in the vehicle.

The toilets were at the entrance, just where they ought to be. They were very clean and modern and had the best hand dryer I had ever used, a Dyson prototype; he is a genius. It is the only one of the hot-air kind that I have used that dried my hands completely in a very short space of time.

The entrance fee made me gulp - £14 each, plus the guide; a further £4. To soften the blow, they say it's an annual fee and you can get in free for a full twelve months but how many people take advantage of this? It struck me as another marketing ploy. The project has certainly brought employment to the area and has made excellent use of a large old quarry but I am glad we didn't have to pay for our four children .

You notice the Biomes as soon as you enter...described as *'Transparent interlocking domes that appear to bubble from the ground'*.

The gardens surrounding the Biomes looked like work in progress.

People obviously come here for the large Bio domes; green houses, which, when seen from the outside, are *'stupendous works of architecture and a miracle of engineering science, yet from within they are virtually invisible- like a delicate spiders web'*. So we headed for the largest - the Tropical Hot House. The heat hits you as soon as you enter and people were removing their coats and jumpers and gasping for breath as they were enveloped by the humidity.

The guidebook informed us that you could hide the Tower of London in this Biome, and the humidity was controlled to 60 degrees during visiting hours and 90 degrees at night. The plants, palm trees and foliage were displayed in an interesting manner which kept you informed and educated as it drew you further into the 'jungle'.

We slowly walked uphill from 'Africa' through 'Asia' to 'South America' and at the very top there is a large man-made waterfall; a perfect spot for a photo opportunity. Smile as you feel the spray from the waterfall gently covering your head and face, then read the literature informing you it is recycled toilet water . It's perfectly *'harmless and hygienic',* the sign proudly proclaims.

Moving quickly on, we walked through the jungle, sidestepping the dripping of water from the condensation/rain from the roof and the authentic troops of ants which covered the trees and wooden hand railings, all busily going somewhere. After leaving the tropical Biome, we went into the Mediterranean Biome which had familiar planting and a fresher atmosphere.

As we left the Biomes, we passed a strategically placed ice-cream stall from which I made a purchase. Not far from the stall there was an information desk, so I casually asked the attendant, "Are the ants from England or have they come in with the plants?"

"We don't know". He replied.

"What . So they could be nasty jungle ants with horrific bites".

I exclaimed.

He just smiled and said, "We don't know".

I thought, 'I hope someone does'.

Eden is designed to inspire a sense of wonder but I felt a bit let down by it. I don't want to knock it exactly; I know what they have done is fantastic and they have made huge inroads into an area that needs as much help as it can get.

I came away glad that I had visited but not feeling a 'wow' factor, thinking 'I've been here, done it, won't be rushing back'.

Walking Day 11 *Hot and sunny*

Jamaica Inn to Launceston (pronounced Lanston) - 9 miles - Total walked 102

We said goodbye to the friendly Bodmin site and moved to Lydford in Devon. Arriving back at Jamaica Inn at 3 pm. Kay and Ripley joined me for the first mile or so as we set off across Hendra Downs. It was another hot, sunny day and we passed rough heathland where belted Galloway cows were grazing between the golden-flowering gorse. It wasn't long before Kay and Ripley had to turn back.

At Carne Down, the track descends from moorland into gentler farmland, and from here I followed a succession of lanes, crossing two minor rivers by ancient bridges - the River Penpont Water and the River Inny. Aiming to get to Launceston, before nightfall, I took the direct route which involved walking a half-mile alongside the busy A30 which is not to be recommended.

At Kennards House round-about I left the A30 and walked along a country lane into Launceston passing some very large and magnificent houses. The lane took me down a steep hill right into the heart of Launceston, once the ancient capital of Cornwall and its only walled town.

I could see the old, ruined castle upon its hill, originally a Norman castle founded by William the Conqueror's half-brother. By the 17th century it was used as the County Assize and prison.

I had made it to Launceston and waited for Kay by the steam railway. The railway runs on narrow gauge for two-and-a-half miles through the Kensey Valley. The locomotives used here were built in the 1880's by the Hunslet Engine Company of Leeds, Yorkshire.

Walking Day 12 *Hot and sunny*

Launceston to Lydford, Devon - 17 miles - Total walked 119

Launceston had made an excellent job of the roundabout on the edge of town. It was fabulous with an array of small trees, flowers and shrubs.

It was a busy vibrant place, full of life, with lots of people bustling in and out of a good array of small local shops. The town had managed to keep most of the traditional layout and it still had a town square. We did some important banking first and then we looked around, searching for a pet shop. When we found one we had Ripley's name tag engraved with my mobile phone number. If we lost her down here, our home telephone number would be of no use.

The Norman castle which sits high on a knoll looking down over the town was flying the English heritage flag. Launceston looked and felt to be very 'English' and I felt very much at home.

My walk was to take me out of the Southgate Arch - the only remaining gate from the original town walls - and east to Polson Bridge. Passing the rugby club, I eventually crossed the bridge over the River Tamar and entered Devon at last my second county. I had now walked the full length of Cornwall. I had also, according to many Cornish folk, left Cornwall and entered England.

Glorious Devon; the countryside changed from rough moorland to rolling hills and deep wooded valleys. With the bright lime green of spring, even the brimstone butterflies, which were abundant, were pale green. The trees were becoming flushed with their new leaves, and with the heat beating down you could almost smell the green. On the hillside, the bright yellow of the gorse bushes sparkled in the sunlight. Here in Devon gorse is sometimes called by its old name, 'Furze' and it is said that Devon possesses at least three differing types of 'Furze' so that it is very nearly always seen in bloom.

I walked to the long straggling village of Lifton, a 'linear village' which had once been on the main coaching road from Falmouth to London and still had an Old Coaching Inn. On the wall was a plaque which stated a Lieutenant John Richards Lapenotiere, Captain of HM Schooner Pickle, rode twenty-one horses to get the news of Nelson's victory and death, to London from Falmouth. His route became the Trafalgar Way, now developed into a long-distance walk.

On the edge of Lifton there is a massive factory, most of it cleverly concealed behind trees and shrubs. It looked like it was a major local employer, and signs on the security gate just said 'LIFTON'. I was a little intrigued as to what a factory was doing, seemingly in the middle of the countryside, until I eventually noticed another sign saying, 'Premier Foods', which sounded to me like dog food. Closer inspection revealed that this was where the Devon Cream comes to go into Ambrosia Cream Custards and Rice Puddings. Locally the factory is known as 'Ambrosia'.

At a very quiet spot, miles from anywhere, I came across a line of parked cars - about a dozen of them. In every car, the driver was sitting behind the steering wheel just waiting.

It seemed very strange behaviour. It was just a quiet country road with nothing there; not even a footpath sign ... they were just sitting staring ahead. Then the answer arrived in the shape of a coach full of school kids, who noisily disembarked; (was it that time already.) - And ran to the waiting vehicles. It was the school run.

These were local children who, with the demise of village schools, had to be bussed out to the nearest large town that housed a school.

Further on, I walked into the village of Lewtrenchard, known as the home of the Revd. Sabine Baring-Gould, he is best known for writing the hymn, Onward Christian Soldiers, which he wrote at Horbury near Wakefield, Yorkshire, whilst he was a curate there. The Reverend was a Victorian gentleman, a gifted linguist, a collector and writer of novels and travel books. In and amongst his scholarly pursuits he managed to fit in the rolls of being both the village squire and parson for over forty years.

The Old Rectory is big enough to be a small hotel and the church is fabulous. The guidebook to the church states that it was rebuilt in 1261 and again in 1520. As I walked in through the doors, a feeling of peace and warmth stole around me. After a few moments of quiet reflection, I looked around. The most striking feature in the church is the beautiful Rood Screen. This is a Victorian reproduction of the original sixteenth-century screen, which had been demolished and contains some original bits that the Revd. Baring-Gould had managed to rescue. The Paschal Cross, in painted wood, was also reclaimed by him when it was 'thrown out' from a small Chantry Chapel that sits on the bridge in Wakefield, Yorkshire, when that was renovated in 1840. The church also boasts a beautiful double-barrelled green coloured ceiling.

Exploring the graveyard, the first gravestone to attract my attention had the inscription: 'I was once like you - Alive - Now I am dead - You will be soon like me'. Hmmm.

The Revd. Sabine himself lies in the churchyard beside his wife Grace, a Yorkshire mill-girl. A paragraph in the guide to St. Peter's states *'There is a quiet here, broken only by the song of the birds and the hum of the bees in the great lime trees. Here we can pause for a while and feel about us for a nostalgic moment, something of that older, more peaceful England, whose rhythms were based on the eternal things; on sunrise and sunset; on seed-time and harvest; that rural England that the younger generation has never known and which it becomes harder yearly for us older ones to recall, but which Sabine loved and understood so well'.*

I continued via Lew Mill and a permissive path across Galford Down. This involved a steep uphill climb but it is a lovely place. Here the Saxons, under King Egbert of Wessex, defeated a Celtic uprising in AD 825; the Saxons won the day and went on to anglicize this part of the world.

My crossing of the Down entailed another battle, this time involving a very large herd of young cows. "Mush, Mush" and they eventually condescended to part enough for me to stride on by.

I now had wide views over the surrounding countryside, not least of the huge bulk of Dartmoor, drawing close. From the Downs I joined a quiet lane that led me to Lydford. Horror of horrors! I was developing a blister on the base of my left big toe, the first blister of the walk.

Walking Day 13 *Hot and sunny*

May Thursday 03

Lydford to South Zeal - 12 miles - Total walked 131

Another scorcher of a day. Kay and Ripley joined me for the first hour of the walk, and Ripley insisted on carrying my hat in her mouth. The fact that the hat is almost as big as the dog drew all the usual "aah's", which we think is why she does it.

We headed north, skirting Dartmoor to the east, on a disused railway line that has been transformed into a National Cycle Way. The path is excellent and was bordered on both sides with trees and shrubs, these giving way to rolling pastures deep in the lush green of spring and then opening further to superb views across Fernworthy Down.

Alongside the path, surviving in the shade of the hedges, were small pools of water which were full of tadpoles. Ripley, already very hot, could not resist jumping in and paddling up and down before succumbing to the ecstasy of lying out in the cool water.

At the first road junction, it was time for Kay and Ripley to head back 'home' again. I set off across the road hoping to re-join the 'way' at the other side. I could see the railway line going through gardens. The cycle-route, excellently signposted up to this point, came to a complete stop. With no indication; where the route went, I checked my map and could see that, if I could follow the disused railway line to the next bridge, I would or should be back on the cycle-way. Forging forward I followed a track that skirted the foot of the gardens, which became more and more overgrown, until I eventually managed to scramble back onto the railway line, pushing through shrubs and small trees, which then became a jungle of thorns and nettles, tearing at my trousers and shirt, scratching my arms and drawing blood. I was waist-height in nettles and bramble bushes.

I could see the bridge ahead and decided the distance was less to go forward than to struggle back. I was getting angry. I struggled forward for another twenty minutes and at last made it to the foot of the bridge, which was guarded on one side by a six-foot, solidly-built wooden fence and a steep shingle cutting on the other. I cursed the cycle way planners for their lack of sign-posting, before deciding to attempt the climb up the steep cutting to the bridge parapet. The earth was very loose underfoot; every other foot forward had me sliding back down; and the loose earth was full of sharp stones and broken glass. After a long struggle which left me with bleeding fingers, I managed to reach the top of the earth bank; but this still left me well below the bridge parapet. I was surrounded on three sides by brambles, nettles and thorns. By stretching my arms to their fullest extent, I could just reach the parapet with my fingertips but I couldn't find a foot hold in the stonework, or anywhere to give me the boost I needed, to pull myself up. It was very frustrating, especially as I could hear the traffic racing by over the bridge.

I turned to look back from where I had climbed out ... wow, it was steep; very steep; there was no way I was going back down there! The only choice was the apparently impenetrable jungle of brambles and thorn bushes. Luckily I had my trusty 'Leki' walking stick, and with it I thrashed at the thicket until sweat poured out of me in rivers, and I had cleared a small area large enough for me to stand in with some degree of safety. I continued in this manner until I made it to another fence - six feet tall like the last, but topped with barbed wire! Blood was running down my arms and hands but at the other side of the fence was a lovely, green field. The fence looked as if it should have been guarding a prison camp. I hacked my way to a junction post where I managed to climb onto the top of the post, balancing like an overweight fairy on the top of a Christmas tree. I flung myself into the air, propelling myself upwards and forwards away from the barbed wire and landed on the soft, grassy earth with a heavy thud. I had made it with no broken bones. In just over an hour I had progressed two hundred yards towards my goal … exhausted and bloody.

The empty cycle way continued at the other side of the bridge as if it had not been interrupted. My blister was throbbing; the heat and the tricky terrain hadn't helped; so I decided it was time for a rest and something to eat.

After my snap I set off along the trail and within a short distance I came across a small, oval pool, about a foot deep with a muddy bottom. I was about to wash the blood from my hands and arms when I was pleasantly surprised to spot several newts lying on the bottom. The newts were pale green and only as big as my index finger, and seemed to be basking in the lovely sunshine. It was years since I last saw a newt and I stayed and watched them for a good few minutes.

The walk took me over the 'Lake Viaduct', a large stone structure that handsomely complements the scenery it traverses; it almost looks like it has grown from the granite floor, to bridge the gap between the hills. The railway line that once travelled across the viaduct was another victim of cuts in the early 1960's. Today, this line, if it was still open, could be used as a tourist line, bringing people into this beautiful area by train. Exeter could be within commuting distance by train.

I soon came to another viaduct, this time constructed from steel; the Meldon Viaduct built in 1874, which is a scheduled ancient monument. I leant over the edge and tried taking photographs but they didn't do it justice and I had to content myself with seeing the picture on a notice board. Like most viaducts, they are best appreciated from a distance.

As I crossed the viaduct, cyclists started to join me; first one or two, and then lots of them; these were the first people I had seen since leaving Kay and Ripley.

The Meldon Viaduct is next to the working Meldon Quarry. It is a massive hole, dug into the hillside, where Devon granite is extracted, crushed and used as aggregate on railways and roads.

From here I could hear the constant rumble of the A30, and it wasn't long before I was walking between the still in use railway line, (used to remove the granite aggregate) and the main road. Eventually my path took me under the A30 via a narrow tunnel, which looked like a dark chute as I walked towards it.

On the other side of the tunnel, I entered Okehampton via the relative peace of its golf course. I walked along the edge of the course and over to my left, were the ruins of the Normans' motte and bailey of Okehampton Castle. A sign declared *'Town Centre via Park'*, so I descended through beautiful parkland to a large curve in the river which was surrounded by green fields and flower beds. In the distance, I could see a college building set in these idyllic surroundings. I pinched myself and wondered if the people living here realise how lucky they are.

Okehampton is a pleasant place. It has a main shopping street with plenty of shops.

I took a photograph of an interesting mural on the side of a house, which showed a walker resting on his stick as he stared out across Dartmoor. A stone set in the pavement declared, *'For centuries, Okehampton has directed the spirited hiker to enjoy the freedom of the wild, natural beauty of North Dartmoor'.*

Having descended through the park into the town, I had a good idea I would have to climb back out of it and so, bolstered by a cup of tea, I began the long, uphill climb out of town on the Exeter Road. I walked through several construction sites which give the impression that Okehampton - or 'Okey' as the locals call it - was booming. Halfway up I started being overtaken by mothers laden down with shopping bags, pushing prams. I consoled myself as I plodded upwards in their wake, with the thought that this was the school run, and that these young mothers climb this hill twice a day, five days a week. I was into a rhythm and happy just to keep my pace.

Not far outside Okehampton, I came to the Dartmoor National Park signpost and from here a lovely bridleway brought me to the village of Sticklepath. As I walked along the Main Street I was charmed by an array of thatched cottages. In the middle of this historic village, tucked away in a peaceful setting behind Finch's Foundry, (an old forge and shovel maker), on the banks of the tumbling River Taw, is Sticklepath Quaker Burial Ground. In the early 1700's up to two hundred Quakers lived here. The National Trust now owns the property.

I walked up and out of Sticklepath and on for another mile-and-a-half to South Zeal, another lovely village with thatched houses and an ancient church and market cross in the middle of the main street. Kay collected me and we headed back to Sticklepath, where we had a stroll which took in the reproduction of the ancient pillory, having our evening meal in the enclosed garden of the Taw River Public House.

May Friday 04 **Walking Day 14** *Hot and sunny*

South Zeal to Crediton - 14½ miles - Total walked 145½

A beautiful spring day to find myself back at South Zeal and from here a short stroll to unspoilt South Tawton along peaceful country roads; another thatched village with a lovely large church - how do they keep them maintained?

I came to the Dartmoor National Park sign on a large boulder but I was leaving the Park, not entering it. There was a female chaffinch sitting on the boulder flashing her 'derriere' at a male who was in a bush just above her. He quickly seized his chance, swooped down and copulated with her and seconds later resumed his position in the tree. Fancy. And so early in the day.

I continued my walk along deep winding lanes lined with oak trees which are my favourite trees. They are so English and to me, they look like 'curmudgeons' squatting in the hedgerow, strong and knobbly, full of character.

The hedgerows were bursting with birdsong and spring flowers, many of which I couldn't name so, armed with digital camera, I 'clicked' away, recording the different species for Kay's later examination.

We were riding on the crest of the spring wave with flowers bursting into bloom as I walked from one place to the next, nature seemingly suspended at the same moment as when we were on the Scilly's.

Everything seemed benevolent and peaceful as I listened to the subtle nuances of sound. I felt I was developing new listening skills and thought of how American Red Indians in Western films knelt, putting their ear to the ground and declaring, "Big train coming here in three days". For me it was more like, "Ey up ... bloody hell a tractor is upon me", as I scrambled into the nettles and brambles. The idyllic, deep, winding lane, not now quite so benevolent and peaceful.

I passed farms with dusty lanes which sparrows seem to delight in; dust baths seemed to be the order of the day. I could see on my map I was heading for Dragdown Hill. On a hot day like today I knew I would prefer to be going downhill but as I reached its foot it became clear I would be walking up hill. Here is a pretty little bridge over a stream with a large modern house surrounded by beautiful gardens. The heat was beating down and it was so hot that the tarmacadam on the road was melting, I couldn't put it off any longer so, with my handkerchief in hand to mop my sweaty brow, I climbed the hill.

Dragdown Hill led me to another pretty Devonshire village, Spreytown. First stop was the large church which was hidden within trees. This gave lovely dappled shade to the church bench that provided a perfect spot to eat my snap.

Back on my feet, I walked the few yards and passed the Uncle Tom Cobbly public house. A sign on the wall read: *'In 1802, from this village, the following left for Widdecombe Fair: Bill Brewer, Jan Stewer, Peter Gurney, Peter Davy, Dan Widden, Harry Hawke, and Old Uncle Tom Cobbly and all'.* The pub looked inviting but having just finished my lunch, I decided to keep walking.

I tried to remember the song that the Uncle Tom Cobbly 'ditty' came from but all I came up with was a few lines from Scarborough Fair and then for some reason I was singing, "Hey diddle de dee, a circus life for me ..." Unfortunately, that was as much as I could remember but the refrain drove me mad for the rest of the day: "Hey diddle de dee, a circus life for me" ... I remembered it was from Pinocchio when he meets up with the two 'baddies', having run away from home. To blot the refrain from my mind, I tried singing "Onward Christian Soldiers" but, "Hey diddle de dee, a circus life for me ..."

I saw my first pig sties; a huge pig was out in the muck. It was so big I decided to get my camera out but as I put my hand in my pocket the pig shot into its sty. I have never seen a pig move at such speed.

I stopped to watch a thatcher at work; a skilled craftsman and his mate. I took a couple of photographs of the gable-end and the roof. The two men were at the far end on top of the scaffolding. I walked around to get a good photograph of the thatcher's as they worked and as I looked up at them, both men shouted down, "Hello", and toasted me with their tea cups! A true English craftsman knows the benefit of a good cup of tea. I never did get a photograph of them working, just drinking their tea.

I walked away from Yeoford. The lanes became more undulating and I noticed the earth had changed colour to a startlingly rich red brown. In one field, there was a herd of Devon Red Ruby beef cattle. Their colour mirrored the shade of the soil.

I walked into Crediton and saw that many of the more distinctive, older buildings were made from red sandstone. Crediton was a prosperous, medieval, wool town that was in fact the seat of the first bishopric in Devon, until it moved to Exeter in the 11th century.

I met Kay and Ripley in the Old Market Square, which previously doubled as a car park and market place but had recently been turned into a 'boules' area, and was subsequently deserted. On the edge of the square was the Three Pigs pub and I had a swift drink before we walked to the park where there is a statue of St. Boniface. I hadn't heard of St. Boniface until that day but he was born in Crediton in AD 680 and is the patron saint of Germany with strong links also to The Netherland's (St Windfrith). While we were admiring the statue, a Dutch trio came to do likewise.

As we walked back to the car I saw a sign in a shop window on the main street, 'Use your local shops or lose them'. Exeter with its supermarkets and shops is only seven miles away. We would have liked to use the shops in Crediton but as strangers we couldn't find any suitable parking. The main shopping street is also the main road and was heavy with traffic.

May Saturday 05 | Rest Day

The bank holiday weekend had crept up on us and as a result we couldn't book ahead at any caravan sites as they were all full but we were lucky enough to secure our pitch for a few days longer here at Lydford, which wasn't a bad thing, as it allowed us to explore Lydford Gorge and Exeter.

Before going down to the gorge we had a quick look around the ruins of Lydford castle. Lydford, we discovered had been a Stannary Court town where under a charter of Edward I, the tin had to be officially weighed and stamped. Heavy penalties were imposed on those caught adulterating the tin with inferior metal. In what became known as the 'Lydford law', offenders caught with adulterated tin were made to swallow spoonful's of the molten metal.

The castle was used as a prison and was once described as 'one of the most detestable places in the realm'.

Today with the sun shining it was hard to describe this picturesque ruin as a 'detestable place' (NT leaflet).

Lydford Gorge is the deepest gorge in the South West of England. It was cut by the melt waters from the retreating glaciers at the end of the last Ice Age and continues to be eroded by the River Lyd, whose source is on Dartmoor.

We set off to explore the intriguingly-named Devil's Cauldron. It was another very hot and sunny day and we were looking forward to walking through the shade of the woods. These ancient woods are beautiful; the sunlight streamed through the trees. Oak trees were predominant, with beech, ash, hazel, holly, laurel and sycamore.

There were still large areas covered in bluebells which were dotted with red campion and greater stitchwort. We walked through the Pixie Glen following the path by the river which was clear and barely moving. Brown trout could be seen basking in the centre of the stream, just giving the odd lazy swish of their tails to keep them in place.

At the Devil's Cauldron the river is contorted and squeezed down through a narrow channel in the black slate rock, the pressure causing it to crash down into the potholes below where the water appears to boil. The slate is polished into smooth, black curves, which contrast with the foaming white mass of spray.

To reach the Cauldron we had to walk down some narrow, stone steps, which hugged the sheer side of the Gorge. We wondered how the suspended metal walkway over the Cauldron had been put into place; there were no natural paths near the actual Cauldron and the rocks at that point formed a vertical rock face that bowed out overhead before sweeping in. Ripley was not happy; Kay picked her up. We followed the path out of the Cauldron, on through the wood, where the river soon returned to its peaceful meandering.

We were hoping to spot a red-haired gubbins who according to legend lived in the Gorge and made their living stealing sheep and cattle from the Moor. Instead, at Tuckers Pool we saw three young teenagers skinny-dipping; even in the dappled shade of the trees it was very hot so I was quite envious of them as they bombed each other, jumping from the rocks into the pool.

It was nearly lunchtime so we made our way back to the information centre where there was a picnic area. Later we set off for Exeter, managing to park in a multi-storey car park in the city centre. (The Celts knew it as 'Caerwise', and the Saxons as 'Exonceaster'). We recognised immediately that this city was thriving; the streets were thronged with shoppers, students and sightseers. We did a quick tour of the shops, then it was on to the cathedral.

We were a bit distracted at our first view of the magnificent west front of the cathedral due to the sheer number of people taking advantage of this beautiful setting. The lawns in front of the building were full of young people picnicking, sunbathing, and playing games. The cafés in the surrounding Close had tables and chairs with sun umbrellas set up outside and they all seemed to be full. The whole area had a happy buzz. We took in the outer splendour of the building, which features two massive towers that were part of the original Norman building when it was consecrated in 1133, before entering the peaceful and relaxing interior.

We sat for a while feeling very blessed and soaking up the atmosphere before moving on to admire some of the finest medieval sculptures in England. The building radiated beauty with arched ceilings and the longest uninterrupted stretch of decorated Gothic vaulting in the world.

A quick 'pit stop' at the Cathedral Café to wet our whistles before visiting the historic quayside which embraces its industrial heritage. Again, we were beaten to it; there were ice cream licking crowds of people everywhere.

There has been a quay in Exeter since Roman times but by the 14th century boats could not get up the river because of all the weirs built across it, so in the 1560's, John Trew built a canal to provide access to the quayside.

We spent some time enjoying the sunshine, wandering around the many tourist and antique shops, and watching the boats on the River Exe, before deciding it was time to head back to Lydford. Half a day is not nearly enough time to do justice to a city as big and as beautiful as Exeter.

May Monday 07 Rest Day

We moved from Lydford and travelled up the A30 and M5 to a Caravan Park near Wellington, Tiverton. It rained heavily but the journey ran smoothly and without any problems.

It was a lovely site next to the Grand Western Canal where bulrushes were just beginning to break out amongst mare's tail and flag iris. A garden warbler warbled away above coot and moorhens with their chicks. There were nettles everywhere as well as cow parsley, speed wort, buttercups, daisies and bush vetch that mingled amongst flowering chestnut and cherry trees with green cherries.

May Tuesday 08 Walking Day 15 *Hot and sunny followed by rain*

Crediton to Tiverton - 14½ miles - Total walked 160 >

Crediton was busy. It was post bank holiday Tuesday and it seemed the whole world wanted to drive into Crediton. The post office was packed. A sign asked customers to, *'Bear with us, staff shortages'*. I collected my post, bought some maps from a stationer nearby, used the internet at the library and walked out of Crediton.

I was looking for a footpath across Lords Meadow - a big, well-used footpath that crosses the river by a footbridge. Try as I might, I couldn't find it. I walked around the leisure centre. I walked around a football pitch and changing rooms. I walked into a works entrance. It was here somewhere? I needed a footpath sign - anything! I saw a woman pushing a pram. She went around the back of the football pitch changing rooms. I followed - and found the path - through the children's playground and a nearby housing estate. No footpath signs!

Having crossed the river and walked a mile uphill, I came to the village of Shobrooke where footpath signs were at every corner, all pointing the way to somewhere I didn't want to go.

I saw a bus shelter with four domestic chairs with seat cushions on. It looked like someone had just put them in there whilst they cleaned around their kitchen table.

On the road to the village of Thorverton I passed several spectacularly clean lay-bys. No litter. No contractors' rubble. No tyres. The good people of this part of Devon are very clean and their contractors must be the only ones in the country to pay the landfill tax and dispose of their waste correctly. As I was coming into Thorverton I saw a foxglove flowering, the first that year.

The Bell Inn opposite the church, was open. I had a much-needed drink before having a walk around the church. There were some interesting stone carvings on the ceiling of the porch. The interior was mainly Victorian.

Thorverton does have a shop! It also has a post office. The former is in an old bus and the latter is a portakabin on the main car park. Houses are much sought after here and the former shops, now converted into houses, forced the shopkeeper to acquire their modern and awful appearances

On leaving Thorverton I climbed a big hill and even though it was raining, I still had good views of the Exe valley. Near to an oak tree I photographed a 'new-to-me' wild flower. It turned out to be a yellow archangel.

I walked on getting very wet. I reached Bickleigh Castle. It looked more like a moated manor house than a castle. The north side of the inner courtyard was an impressive facade topped with a tiny and unusual thatched clock tower. Bickleigh Mill was situated nearby, over an old sturdy arched bridge spanning the wide, tree-fringed River Exe - much photographed and said to have inspired Paul Simon to write, *'Bridge over trouble waters'*. I doubted that; the water looked anything but troubled; the whole area looked affluent, and gentle - even in the rain. It was beautiful. I would have liked a cup of tea but everything was shut, even the model railway centre.

I followed the Exe valley way through woods and fields to Tiverton. Highland cattle were in the fields. The woodland path was a pure delight. Alan Plowright, in his 2002 book, *'LEJOG in Fifteen Years'*, described this section of the walk as a *'disappointment, being a muddy confusion of wooded paths'*. He must have been walking through a different wood.

May
Wednesday
09 **Walking Day 16** *Fresh and dry, followed by rain*

Tiverton to Sampford Peverille -7 miles - Total walked 167 >

On driving through Tiverton the other day I wasn't impressed; true it was a Sunday and everywhere was closed but today walking through it, I saw it in a different light. It was a friendly, busy little town and I liked it. There is a big school - 'Blundells'. Its campus is set across two sides of a road, the delightful old school buildings set around a grass courtyard with a date stone, 'Old Blundells, 1604'. Blundells School was founded in that year by a local wealthy wool merchant, Peter Blundell. Through the Wool trade, 16th century Tiverton became the most prosperous of the Devonshire towns.

I saw lots of school pupils in immaculate school uniform, walking between classes. They all looked well-groomed and well-mannered. Blundells must be doing something right; if only all schools were like this one. I smelt bacon cooking. I was immediately tempted by the smell and followed my nose until I came upon a burger-van. The man in the van looked foreign and indeed he was. He told me he was a Kuwaiti. I ordered a well-done bacon and tomato sandwich. "I've never been asked for that before", he said. "I don't have any tomatoes". What is it with the South? Bacon goes with tomato. It's well-established - like beans on toast.

I made do with well-done bacon. As it cooked I got talking to the Kuwaiti, one of the few immigrants I had met in the South-west. He explained how he had lived in Germany for many years before coming to England. He explained that when he first arrived, he went to Birmingham which he hated, stating there were too many immigrants, that it wasn't English enough. He told me his brother was living in the U.S.A, in Los Angeles, California, and that every year he visits him there. He said he hated Los Angeles; it was like Birmingham but hotter. I told him I thought Kuwait was a rich country. He smiled. I told him I was surprised to see him cooking bacon as many Muslims refuse to even touch it. "They are religious fanatics and they have ruined my country", he said.

"Kuwait?" I asked.

"Okay, I'm from Iran really, but everyone around here thinks I'm from Kuwait". I took my sandwich and moved on, thinking: One - he must be legal if he takes a holiday to the U.S.A. every year and Two - he must be making enough money in his burger van to do so. Good on him.

Tiverton has a cinema - the Tivoli. It has been showing films continually since 1932. There was a campaign to save it; I wish them well. Go see a film.

On the outskirts of Tiverton, on an embankment, I saw two beautiful floral displays with the names, 'Tiverton - Mid Devon'. Nearby were a group of six litter pickers busy at work; this is what I like to see, but to be honest, I didn't see much litter that needed picking.

The walk out of Tiverton goes first along a disused railway line and then continues to the Grand Western Canal, which was originally intended to form a major transport link between the Bristol Channel and the English Channel, thereby avoiding the dangerous route around Land's End. It took over forty years to fully open and by then the railways had arrived. The canal had lifts to raise and lower boats to differing levels; boats floated into a 'caisson tub' and as one rose, the other fell. None now remain.

The National Cycle Way follows the canal but the whole time I was by it I didn't see any cyclists. I did see some dog walkers. At a bridge on the canal I saw a barge full of elderly people on a trip. They were all happy, chatting and smiling.

Whilst walking by this peaceful stretch of the canal I came across a horrific scene; a rape. The female, a dull brown duck, was being pursued by four colourful mallards. The strongest and fittest Mallard caught her up and immediately mounted her. She went under the water with plenty of quacking and spluttering and there she remained. The three other males tried to muscle in but the strong duck was having none of that, whereupon a fight ensued between them. The female was still under the water with four male ducks on top of her. 'Come on, get up', I thought.

She came up and quacked for breath and then down again, all four ducks on top of her, the strong duck pushing the others away.

She must surely drown I thought.

Suddenly she was up and the male ducks eased away; she was alive and swimming away.

Just before I reached the village of Halberton I came upon a couple of mute swans with eight signets. I counted six at first and then I realised two were riding on the back of their mother, hidden under her wings.

At Halberton I took refuge from the rain in the church. Dedicated to St. Andrew, it is mostly Victorian in character.

Once the rain eased I moved quickly on along the beautiful canal tow path which was separated from housing by a wonderful beech hedge which had recently been pleached or laid (in some parts of the country they spell it 'layed') ...that means to cut almost through in order to encourage the young shoots to spring from the old stumps. The cut pole is bent and sometimes woven, sometimes pegged back into the hedge. I admired the workmanship.

Between Halberton and Sampford Peverell, the canal was alive with coots and moorhens busy with young chicks. It was siling-it-down with rain, so I headed home.

Devon Badger Watch. I picked up a leaflet at the Information hut at the campsite and we were soon getting instructions on how to get to the Badger Watch, on an old dairy farm near some woods not far from Tiverton, and being advised to, *'Wear dark clothing and don't put on any perfume or aftershave'*.

Later that evening after a short drive, we assembled in an old barn next to the secluded farmhouse; a small group of like-minded people. The path down to the hide, through some fields and woods, was well lit - the lights went out after we had met at 7.30pm and been briefed by 8.00pm. We were in a purposeful hide above the main badger sett. The hide was created in such a way that you observed the badgers at eye level and from only about a foot or two away, through glass. This sett had numerous openings across a large area. The farmer's wife spread peanuts on the ground and we waited - not long; four badgers graced us with their presence and we spent a good hour watching them.

Walking Day 17 *rain*

Sampford Peverell to Taunton, Somerset - 17 miles - Total walked 184

The walk out of Sampford Peverell along the canal bank clothed in Flag Iris was a joy; until it started to rain, and rain. Kay and Ripley, who had set off with me, turned around to go back. I carried on walking between bridges with names such as Whipcott and Fenacre. According to the maps, I was missing ancient chapels and priories but, wet through and dodging puddles, I walked quickly between the bridges and took shelter as best I could.

At Waytown, the Canal goes through a tunnel. In order to get a good photograph of it, I used my stick to whack a few nettles out of the way. In so doing a stray nettle leaf flew up and landed on my hand, stinging me in about six places. I hunted down a good-sized dock leaf and with it rubbed green onto my hand, which brought instant relief to the nettle pain. With the photograph in the camera, I walked on and soon came to the end of the canal - and Devon.

In 1904 George H. Allen completed his Vegetarian record breaking LEJOG walk, sustained throughout Devon by a then well-known local delicacy, Devonian Junket, (sometimes known as Dartmoor Junket), a milk pudding. Today it is hard to find, having been replaced in the 1970's by packets of Blancmange's and Angel Delights. What Allen didn't know was that traditional Junket is made with rennet, an animal by product which today is shunned by Vegetarians. I had crossed Devon and not once had I seen it for sale or even advertised...which is a shame.

The Grand Western Canal does carry on in name. From here to Taunton, the canal is derelict, drained and in parts, overgrown with trees. Devon has turned its part of the canal into a country park and looks after it very well.

The boundary into Somerset was a shock. The canal towpath vanished into a jungle of trees and high grass. There were no footpath signs and stiles, if present, were broken or damaged, enveloped by nettles and impossible to use. I struggled to find the way.

I tried to shelter under the trees but was being eaten alive by midges. Swallows and house martins were having a field day with the flies; I wasn't. The illusive yaffle of a green woodpecker kept me alert as I walked along the line of the old canal, which here was like a mangrove swamp. My Tilley hat kept my head dry. My feet, in my Brasher boots, were dry and my raincoat kept the rain out for a while, although the wet eventually seeped in to my clothes and I carried on, wet, wet and wet.

All the while I could hear gun shots; sometimes near, sometimes far off. I don't know what was being shot at or who was out shooting in such weather. I always cringe when I hear a gun shot. It might be farmers out with their dogs, not expecting walkers, and who would think someone like me would be out walking on overgrown footpaths on a day like today.

I came out onto a quiet tarmac lane and there in the gutter was a dead badger. Surprisingly it hadn't been shot but run over by a vehicle, one of 50,000 badgers to be killed on our roads each year.

I walked on and crossed the main railway line at a road crossing called the *'Bradford Crossing'*. I came to the medieval bridge which crosses the River Tone and walked up into Bradford which looked a nice place with its pub that once also sold petrol from an out sales window, its post office and 14th century church with an impressive perpendicular tower.

Bradford is also the home to Sheppy's traditional farmhouse cider, made here for over 200 years.

Everywhere was closed. Someone ought to open a café here to refresh the lone walker like me in need of a cup of tea.

Back down over the bridge, I followed a footpath alongside the River Tone, all the way to Taunton. At Bishop Hull a funeral was taking place, and people in dark clothing were milling about under umbrellas. I asked a man for directions into Taunton town centre. He gave me them as if I was in a car, sending me miles in the wrong direction; miles which I didn't go, I checked the maps and found a much quicker way on foot.

May Friday 11 Rest Day

We moved camp to Cheddar. It rained. In the afternoon, we drove to Wells, England's smallest city. It boasts one of the oldest medieval streets in Europe, being completed in 1348.

We walked, Kay, Ripley and I, along a busy, narrow, main street, and came out onto Cathedral Close (actually, a large open lawned area) to see the magnificent west end of the cathedral. It has a most-decorative, elaborate facade with many statues, including a representation of the last Judgement, which ranks amongst the finest in Europe.

We walked across the Close in the rain and entered the cathedral and were greeted by a stuffy old man wearing a blue sash. He was not a good 'greeter'. He might be the right man but I believe today he was in the wrong position. Greeters need to be warm and friendly not cold and stuffy like our man today.

However, we enjoyed the cathedral. The guide book stated the average tour takes an hour and that's what we took. We saw the famous 14th Century clock strike at a quarter to the hour and the knights coming around the outside to joust.

The Chapter House with its fluted ceiling-'wow' is one of the most striking and perfectly formed chapter houses in Europe.

The inner meaning of this great room is 'consent' or consensus. The tradition of the Chapter in Wells is that something of a common mind must be reached about the matter being discussed. Debate continues until all are content and a common mind has been reached. In this quickly changing diverse world, common ground is increasingly hard to find but if it can be found, then I believe it could be in a room like this.

Outside, the market square, with its ancient gateways, is a gem. Penniless Porch, which was built circa 1450 and the main street with its stream running in the gutter, is all pleasing to the eye and the school children who now frequented the street in large numbers were all well-behaved and smartly dressed.

May Saturday 12 — Walking Day 18 *Heavy showers all day with dry spells*

Taunton to Burrowbridge - 13 miles - Total walked 197

Taunton on a Saturday morning was busy. My walk led me down into Taunton town centre, past all the crowds and shops. Somehow, I missed the County Cricket ground and the interestingly named, 'Whiligig Lane'.

I was carried along with the crowds of shoppers down the ubiquitous shopping street that could have been anywhere in England.

On the road, out of the town centre, I passed by the ancient alms-houses with their tall chimneys. The town centre gave way to a council estate with boarded-up houses and kids riding on mopeds without helmets. It reminded me too much of work.

The way ahead led under the motorway using an underpass, with its graffiti and smells. Eventually I reached the Taunton and Bridgewater canal, which led out of the town with industrial estates on either side. It was a busy path with cyclists, dog walkers and mums and dad's pushing prams. I was never alone for long. I passed some interesting milestones which marked individual planets, Neptune and Uranus. Presumably the other planets were marked in similar fashion throughout the length of the canal. The milestone was a granite block with a metal orb representing the planet depicted and had a plaque, which gave interesting facts about each planet.

When I was a boy at school, a teacher pinned a map of the solar system on the corridor wall. I learnt some of the planets' names, Saturn being easy to remember because of the rings but I never learnt the order of the planets from the sun outwards. Years later, as an adult, I read how some American school kids were learning the solar system with excellent results. I too learnt it and can remember it to this day.

It goes like this; The sun is in the centre. A small ball of 'Mercury' was being played with by a girl called 'Venus'. She was in her back garden, 'Earth'. An angry man lived next door, 'Mars'. His neighbour was a big jolly chap called 'Jupiter'. He was wearing a sun hat on his head with the word sun thereon. 'Saturn', 'Uranus', 'Neptune'. He had a little dog on his shoulder called 'Pluto'. And that's it, easy.

I came to a golf course, and left the canal crossing a railway line by a bridge to reach the River Tone once again. The flat lands of the Somerset levels were before me. The river was deep inside embankments which flanked either side; embankments that carried footpaths according to the maps. A large dog fox was watching me but I saw it first. Then it was off - as fast as if it was being chased by a pack of hounds.

Gates on the footpath were tied with farmers' bind; orange nylon tape stuff. I had to climb one of them. The path was ridiculously overgrown in some places and I found myself up to my chin in nettles and grass. Royal-blue dragon flies darted about. I'd forgotten to bring my stick and wished I had it with me. It was flat as far as the eye could see and no one, only me was about. It rained heavily. I climbed another gate and slipped on the ground on the other side; ground that had been churned up by the hooves of cattle. The ground was uneven and slippy with wet clay. Cow flaps were everywhere. I slipped and fell on my face, my chest hitting the ground. My arms out-flung took some of the fall. I was winded and shocked. I lay still. I was breathing now and could smell the earth. It rained and rained. Slowly - very slowly - I got up. No broken bones. No broken skin, just mud, everywhere, mud, glorious mud. Miraculously I had missed the cow flaps. I heard a trill and saw with a flash of blue, a kingfisher dart by, raising my spirits. A little further on, a cormorant took flight before me. In a field, over to my left I saw a large flock of mute swans.

On a wet Saturday afternoon, I was alone in Somerset - who said Britain is a crowded place? Over to my right as I walked alongside the River Tone, was Sedgemoor, a huge tract of boggy land. In July 1685, it was the scene of a battle involving on one side, a rebel Protestant army, made up mainly of Devon and Somerset men led by the Duke of Monmouth, pitted against the professional army of Catholic King James II. The rebels lost the battle, which was fought under cover of night, losing over four hundred men in the immediate fight and over one thousand men in the subsequent pursuit.

Later Judge Jeffreys in the Bloody Assizes, sentenced over three hundred men to death. They were hanged and dismembered; their heads and limbs were preserved in boiling pitch and scattered in ghostly warning across the county. Eight hundred and fifty men were transported, sold into slavery in the West Indies. As I walked by, Sedgemoor was peaceful and silent, with no hint of its notorious bloody past.

I crossed over the river on a farm bridge and walked along with acres of land over to my right being used to grow willow trees or witheys. At the village of Athelney I came across a withey yard where men were working making the witheys into fence hurdles. I stood in the rain and watched; watching men work is mesmerising, especially when the work is unusual or rare to the watcher. The Somerset Levels is the heart of the English willow industry which has been carried on more or less unchanged for hundreds of years.

Over to my left the land rose slightly to what was called the Hill of Athelney. It was barely a few feet higher than the land I was walking on. In times, past it was known as the Isles of Athelney. Here in AD 879, King Alfred the Great retired with a few followers, having been severely routed by Danish invaders; and burnt the cakes. So much history; all in one day. I came to a lane and passed fields of orchards; apple trees everywhere.

I walked on towards Burrowbridge with its ancient and ruined chapel of St Michael on top of its 'mump' - Burrows Mump.

I met Kay and Ripley, who joined me in the short but very wet climb to the top.

Walking Day 19 *Heavy rain, becoming fine later in the day*

Burrowbridge to Glastonbury - 13 miles - Total walked 210

It was raining - heavily. I didn't have to go but I was up for it and itching to get off. I'd never been to Glastonbury before and I was looking forward to reaching the place. As I stepped out of the car at Burrowbridge Mump, water flooded my boots and I found myself ankle deep in a lake. It was raining so heavily I was instantly soaked through. "Are you sure you still want to go?" Asked Kay. "Yes - a bit of rain never hurt anyone; we're tough from Yorkshire".

Kay had taken to writing letters home, to a large circle of family and friends. Letters are so much better to receive than the usual bills and junk mail. Her letters were - we were informed - well-received.

This morning's walk from rainy Burrow Mump had her describing it thus:

'I drove Christopher in torrential rain, to Burrow Mump, to the spot he'd finished at the evening before. The rain was so severe, I couldn't see out of the windscreen; it was as if someone had a hosepipe on the car but off he went to walk the wet, very wet, Somerset levels'.

The route away from the Mump first took me along a stretch of the main road which resembled a river in flood. Cars sped along with wipers on full speed and lights on. I could just make out some of the drivers' faces when they suddenly saw me, a lone walker, wet through, walking in this weather.

Cars swerved to avoid me, there was no footpath. I leant into the hedge as a large lorry came by at speed and sprayed me with huge volumes of water. It couldn't get any worse I thought.

The much-needed public footpath sign appeared and I took instant refuge. A few feet along the track, it was closed by a signed gate which read, *'Nature Reserve. No public access. Permits available'.* My map indicated a public footpath and I could see a wet and muddy path going the way I wanted to go, so I climbed over the gate and continued out onto the levels, alone and wet.

The whole area was criss-crossed with ditches and drains, locally called 'rhynes' (pronounced as 'Reens'). The levels are liable to flooding and these rhynes looked perilously full.

Continuing along a straight narrow country lane full of puddles, several nesting mute swans were my only company. Their nests appeared to float on the edge of the only bit of road.

A dry spell allowed me to remove my waterproof leggings but as soon as I had packed them away, the heavens opened and it pelted it down. Or as we say in my part of Yorkshire, it was 'siling it or teeming it down'. So - back on with the leggings. I must have looked a sight, hopping about on one leg, splashing through puddles as I pulled the leggings back on.

I spotted a 4x4-type vehicle ahead, in a narrow passing place. There was water in drains on both sides, lapping up, ready to flood the road. I could see a grey-haired, wizened-looking man sat in the cab of the vehicle smoking a cigarette; I took him to be a local farmer. As I passed he said something that I couldn't quite make out. It sounded like, "Naen". I nodded back to him, and then as I walked away I was puzzled at what he had just said. Was it an insult, or a greeting? I worked out, to my own satisfaction, that what he had said was in fact, "Now then" - as in the Yorkshire, "Na' then".

The vast area of low-lying wetland goes under the name of 'moor' and I was crossing Butleigh Moor but it was not a moor like that I had ever seen before; not like my Yorkshire moors for sure. The skies are big out here; today's sky was all grey and brooding. In the distance, I could see Watton Hill, one of the Polden Hills. I was heading for them and well in my stride. Although I was wet through, it was at least warm.

On top of Watton Hill there is a sail-less windmill which for some time looked like a church. As I got nearer I could make out its round shape and what I took to be crenellations turned out to be chimneys. I took a bridleway which led up through trees, away from the levels and up the hill to the windmill. The track was a slippy, mass of wet clay and mud. At a stile, with a *'Samaritan Way'* marker, I slipped and once again went falling with my face into the earth, my arms taking much of the fall. The wet clay was soft and no damage was done - except me being filthy.

The windmill was now a private house, disappointingly fenced off. I slowly turned away from the windmill and there before me was the most famous and sacred landmark in the West Country - Glastonbury Tor; away across the plain but visible and hopefully achievable. It was the first time I had seen it and as if by some strange magic, the rain stopped and the sun shone out.

I walked downhill to the village of Street, through fields where clover leaves were in competition with giant-sized dock leaves; orange-tipped butterflies were flying ahead of me, urging me on. Street is where Clark's shoes originated from in 1825. It now has a factory outlet shop and a museum to shoe manufacturing. I saw the old Clarks Headquarters, and a hall built by the Clarks' family for the villagers.

Street was busy with coach parties. For such a small village, the main street has an impressive row of shops, banks, cafes, etc., and I could quite easily have ended my day's walk here.

Street and Glastonbury stand alongside each other and are separated by the River Brue. I walked into Glastonbury across the Pomparles Bridge; an interesting name for a monstrous modern concrete construction of a bridge. I planned to walk along a footpath and up Wearyall Hill to the town centre.

Legend has it that the boy Jesus was brought to Wearyall Hill by Joseph of Arimathea so it would have been good to walk in their footsteps but I couldn't find a sign to show me the way onto the hill. At one point, I thought I had found it that is until I saw a sign which stated, '*Alsatians live here*', so instead, I walked up a street called Tor View Avenue. Most of the houses on the Avenue looked like rough estate types with rubbish in their gardens; even the telephone kiosk had its door hanging off. In fact, the whole area looked tired and run down, shattering all the illusions I'd held of the place.

I later read that the Glastonbury Pop Festival in June, isn't even held in Glastonbury, but in a village called Pilton, which is a few miles away. "Hey, let's go to the Pilton Festival", just doesn't sound the same, does it? Yet back in the early 1970's it was in fact called The Pilton Pop Music Festival.

May Monday 14 Rest Day

It was raining again. My very necessary and important back-up team - Kay and Ripley - were going stir-crazy having been cooped up in the van for three days. I didn't fancy walking in the rain again, so we took a day off. We'd been in Cheddar for three days and hadn't visited the Gorge, so we followed the crowds up Britain's largest limestone gorge. A limestone crack, famous for its vertical cliffs and deep caves that leads from the Somerset Levels up onto the Mendip Hills.

Once at the top we parked up by a nature reserve. The rain had stopped and we went for a walk along a limestone plateau - The Mendip Scarp. This area is internationally important, flower-rich, limestone grassland. Rock roses, thyme and spring cinquefoil abound. Feral Soay sheep from the Hebrides have been introduced to help keep the scrub at bay. We had the peaceful Scarp all to ourselves.

After the walk, we drove slowly down the Gorge taking in the views. At the bottom, we looked for somewhere to park around the tacky tourist shops. We found free parking at the back of a pub. We missed Britain's most beautiful cave - Gough's Cave. The garish signs that littered the site were to us, off-putting. A simple, clear and easily-understood sign may have enticed us in. The tatty and tactless signage that abounds in Cheddar - in my opinion - spoils and detracts from the natural beauty. I'd heard about the famous Jacob's ladder - 274 steps that climb up from the bottom of the Gorge to the top - 'close to heaven'. I later learned that it has been re-branded with a view to enticing a younger generation who had not been brought up on bible stories; it is now called, 'The Lookout Tower' with no mention of Jacob at all.

The shops at Cheddar Gorge were truly awful and reminded me of what had been done at Land's End. The American Jesse Gardner wrote of Cheddar in his 1930 book '*From Land's End to John O'Groats*', '*We emerged in the midst of yelling hawkers and vulgar advertising methods which caused us to hurry past the entrances to the caves*'.

Nothing has changed there then.

Down near the ancient market cross, we found a farm shop which sold authentic

West Country farmhouse Cheddar cheese. I had to sample some. I bought a one-inch block; I only wanted enough to make cheese on toast and to drink it down with some Somerset cider.

That evening we went to an Indian restaurant which was excellent, a truly brilliant place and the best curry we had had for a long time. We could park right opposite and keep an eye on Ripley as she waited on the parcel shelf of our car. After the meal, I wrote in the comments book, 'As good as, if not better than, the best curries in Bradford'.

May Tuesday 15 — Walking Day 20 *Rain at first then fine and dry later*
Glastonbury to Cheddar - 13 miles - Total walked 223 ▷

We drove into Glastonbury and parked up near the Tor. As we got out of the car it began to rain. A green woodpecker was 'yaffling' as we climbed up on a modern, much out of place concrete path. The Tor stands 521feet above the town. (The word 'Tor' is of Celtic origin and means 'hill').

The Tor, a sandstone island which at one time was surrounded by the flooded levels.

Its dominant feature is St. Michael's church which was built in the 15th century, replacing an earlier one which was destroyed by an earthquake in 1275.

At the dissolution of the monasteries in 1539, the Tor was the scene of the public hanging of Richard Whiting, the last Abbot of Glastonbury. As we reached the top the rain became heavier so we headed for the church tower. However, no shelter was to be found owing to it being a ruin. Still, we had the place to ourselves and the views from the top are fantastic. Although it was raining, the sun was also shining brightly causing the whole hill to glow a golden magical colour, helped also by the flowering buttercups that were everywhere to be seen.

On the way back down, the green woodpecker flashed its golden green back to us as it flew downhill in front of us. The bottom of the Tor is surrounded by apple orchards, many of them growing traditional Somerset varieties such as Kingston Black and Yarlington Mill.

I left Kay and Ripley at the bench by Tor View Avenue and headed into Glastonbury, to the abbey, where that legendary place, the Isle of Avalon, is supposed to have been. It is that mystical, English place where the sea meets the land: *'The meeting place of the dead, where they passed to another level of existence'*. I didn't meet any dead people in Glastonbury; just a coach-load of German tourists.

I went for a walk around the abbey to take a look at the ruins. It was raining and the Germans crowded into the cafe. I made my way into the main ruin and went downstairs to an underground altar where I sheltered from the rain and ate my snap. The altar is where King Arthur is said to be buried. Whether it was King Arthur that the monks found in 1191 and reburied in 1278, is open to speculation but King Edward 1 was present at the reburial ceremony. Links to King Arthur have brought in the pilgrims and tourists ever since. A group of rain-sodden Germans made their way downstairs into the King Arthur's tomb chamber. They were watching me with folded arms and tutting disapprovingly. I felt like an animal at the zoo. It wasn't until I had finished my snap that I noticed a sign saying, *'Please do not picnic in the ruins'*. Ooops!

Glastonbury town centre with its many book shops, mystic tat shops and so on, was a bit more like I had imagined it to be and worth just a few minutes mooching. As I left Glastonbury on the road to Godney, I came across a group of four local teenage girls, all drunk and weaving across the road and swearing at the top of their voices. Good old English girls, I wondered what the German tourists would think of them. They all deserved to be arrested for being drunk and disorderly; (in my day they would have been) but no police were in sight. Both entrance to and exit from Glastonbury were thus marred.

I was walking back on the Somerset levels, now overflowing with water. It was here that archaeologists found a 'Celtic lake village' on the very edge of Avalon. There was nothing left to see now other than some concrete marker posts.

I was walking towards the village of Godney, a village that can trace its history back to 250 BC, when, like Avalon, it was a lake village or a 'Burtle' (a small clay island). Godney means 'God's Island'. Coming from God's county, Yorkshire, I was surprised by this fact. What was going on? Why should God want an island in Somerset when he has a whole county?

Approaching the village of Godney I saw the remains of a number of World War 2 pill boxes. What were they doing out here? It puzzled me. I later learnt that these WW 2 pillboxes formed part of the 'Stop Line Green', 100 miles of continuous, semi-circular defence lines. These are sometimes known as the Bristol outer defence line, built to defend the port of Bristol, on the *'assumption that the Germans had successfully invaded from the east and had made it across country to this point. The defence line was designed to defend Bristol and keep the port open for evacuation, re-supply and reinforcements'*. (From *'War Walks'*, by Major Green, 1999.)

On the map, I could see a good footpath leading over the first of the Mendip Hills. Any footpath signs that had once been in place were now no longer to be seen, although I did see a sign saying, *'Removal of this footpath sign is an offence'*.

The lower Mendip Hills were covered with golden buttercups and it was through fields full of these flowers that I walked into Westbury-sub-Mendip. From there the only way to Cheddar was along the busy main road which in many places had no footpath. I walked quickly and waved my stick wildly at motorists who were driving at me at speed, forcing them to swerve away from me.

Along this road there are several stalls selling fresh, English strawberries, which are grown in fields around here. I stopped at one stall and bought a punnet I walked on and soon arrived in the outskirts of Cheddar and the finishing line to another day's walk.

Walking Day 21 *Fine then heavy rain, fine and dry again later*

Cheddar to Congresbury - 10 miles - Total walked 233 >

First thing this morning we moved camp to Congresbury, where we found a quiet site on a well-kept working farm. The Farmer being a friendly old man. Having set up our pitch we drove back to Cheddar to my starting point. I left Cheddar passing the ancient market cross and headed out of town. I managed eventually to get onto the footpath around the edge of a large reservoir. The footpath is on the disused strawberry railway line which was built in 1869 - 1870, as a branch line of the Bristol to Exeter railway. It closed in 1965. During its life, it became famous for transporting the early-season Cheddar strawberries, hence its name.

People were sailing dinghies on the reservoir which was a hive of activity. I walked on to the village of Axbridge which has an old 14th-century church - St John the Baptist - just set off from the square. The entrance up to the church by steps is narrow and so the full beauty of the building is not apparent until you are almost near the top. Clearly access for all was not a concern in those days. The church is built of limestone and decorated with Doulting stone. (The local limestone quarry, worked since Roman times). The pierced parapets are an attractive feature. The church was calm and cool inside and I was surprised to see that I was not alone. I quietly moved around under the watchful eye of an elderly woman who was wearing a badge, '*Church Greeter*'. Our eyes met a few times and I smiled at her. She never responded but kept a blank expression on her face. I left my usual mark in the visitors' book and then I said to her, "You have a beautiful church". Not a blink or a twitch. No response at all from the lady. I raised my voice, thinking she might have been deaf. "It's very peaceful here". Still nothing. No sign of life. She looked straight forward and never moved. I sensed she was alive but only just. Perturbed by her behaviour, I finally left the church. Halfway down the steps I heard a voice behind me. "Excuse me". It was the 'Church Greeter'. "You have left your walking stick in the church". She was waving a walking stick above her head and looked very much alive. I smiled at her and said, "No, thank you, I haven't, I've got mine here". I walked away, tapping my walking stick in a Charlie Chaplin manner.

Axbridge also has some interesting old buildings and was an important market and wool town in the middle ages. It even had its own mint with its coins showing the town's symbol - the Lamb and Flag. Some of the buildings are in the medieval black and white style and are pleasantly placed around the square. To say Axbridge has this fabulous medieval square as a feature which should be shown off is true but I'd sack the conservation officer. The square has been ruined. A modern telephone kiosk sits here and looks awful and out of place. Surely a traditional kiosk could have been retained here - I've seen plenty of them around. Secondly the council have 'plonked down' a number of circular, concrete flowerbeds in strategic positions around the square, all of which were devoid of flowers and looked even more out of place -

truly horrible. Lastly, the whole area was surfaced with 1980's style grey herringbone bricks - ghastly and not at all in keeping. Whilst many villages that I passed through in Somerset, including Cheddar, still retained their market cross, the one at Axbridge was demolished in 1830. Today its presence is marked out in the1980's herringbone bricks. I'd prefer it if they built a reconstructed one.

With Axbridge behind me, I re-joined the strawberry line, which I could follow all the way to Congresbury, where the line passes through the Cheddar Valley Nature Reserve. Walking was good. Near Kingswood, I approached the very long Shute Shelve Tunnel. I could just see a pinprick of light at the other end, and asked myself, "Do people really walk, cycle or run through this tunnel? Alone?" Probably not, I thought. However, I had to, so off I went into the dark.

The walls and roof were cut from the rock. The tunnel got darker and darker. I looked behind to check that I hadn't been followed by some hideous ghoul; no I was alone. I walked on into the dark. I could just make out the other end and I walked towards it. Water dripped from the ceiling, slowly at first and then as I got about two-thirds through it was gushing through the ceiling. I walked on through mini waterfalls. The tunnel walls became brick lined with their bolt holes appearing every so often. The exit light was getting stronger ... nearly there ... keep going. At last I came out of the tunnel, alive and well. Phew!

As I approached the village of Winscombe, the strawberry line began to fill with joggers, cyclists, dog walkers and school kids. I asked some joggers if they ever ran through the tunnel. "No, we just run to it and then back", they replied. I didn't really see Winscombe as the line took me around the back of it, so I missed seeing West End Farm, dating from 1278 and said to be 'one of the earliest recorded continuously occupied domestic buildings in all England'. (Winscombe village web site).

At the old station the area had been turned into a village park and it had been done very well indeed. I also passed a cricket pitch where people were practising in the nets and preparing a pitch. I hadn't seen any cricket pitches up to this point and I stopped to think of all the villages I'd passed through; surely, I must have seen one in Cornwall or Devon? No, I couldn't think of any.

At Sandford, the line is blocked by buildings belonging to the Thatcher Cider Company. I had to walk along the roads around the Thatcher complex. The smell of cider was thick in the air. I walked along the lane with apple orchards on both sides. A footpath sign indicated that the Strawberry Line Walk continued this way. I looked down an overgrown snicket and rechecked the sign. I checked my map and then off I went, smashing my way down the overgrown path, at the end of which I climbed a stile into a field full of horses. They saw me and raced towards me, whinnying wildly and just pulling up short right in front of me. They obviously thought I had brought them something to eat. I looked past them to see if I could follow the path. I couldn't - I couldn't even see the path. "Where's the path gone", I shouted at the horses, who turned and ran away.

Dejected at losing the path, I climbed over the nearby fence and walked through a jungle of trees. This led me onto a road where by looking at the map, I could now see where I had gone wrong. I walked back the long way, avoiding the crazy horses and jungle. Someone in authority had placed the Strawberry Line footpath sign in the wrong place. I walked until I found the proper way onto the line which again had been diverted to allow Thatcher's to plant another orchard. Once on the Line I found a good footpath leading straight to Congresbury, I even managed to photograph some wild strawberry plants on the Strawberry Line.

The last mile into Congresbury was made pleasant by a warbling brown bird with a fawn-coloured chest, which accompanied me along my way; I later identified it as a sedge warbler. The Village of Congresbury has links to early Christianity. It is thought that St. Congar, the very first British saint founded a Christian community here in the 5th Century. He is credited with miraculously *'causing his walking stick to grow into a yew tree to provide much needed shade in the church yard'*. My day's walk ended back at the camp site.

Walking Day 22 - a month into the walk *Fine and sunny*

May Thursday 17

Congresbury to Pill - 10 miles - Total walked 243

I found a back lane into the village of Congresbury, then on to the village of Yatton, (an old English name possibly meaning gateway to the hills) and passed the Cadbury Hill with its Iron Age fort. It is a site of archaeology and legends, one example being that the ghost of a Roman legionary walks the site. There are two Cadbury Hills in Somerset. This one is known as Cadbury Congresbury and has no connection with King Arthur that being at the other one. A Spa Hotel looked like the kind of place Kay would have liked so I moved on quickly.

I soon arrived at Claverham, a neat village, originally a farming hamlet that is now very much a commuter town for Bristol. On the outskirts of the village there were big houses with fields full of horses and stables. Several lady riders passed me as I went on my way.

At Westown, a lovely village set in a green valley, yet just six miles from Bristol city centre, I had to re-join the busy A370 to Bristol. Lorries and cars whizzed by but at least the road had a footpath. This road was where in 1967 the first ever Briton was breathalysed, (Flax Bourton village website). At Flax Bourton, I turned off and crossed the railway and emerged at the North Somerset Showground, a large flat field, named as the Bathing Pond Farm. There has been an agricultural show hereabouts for over 150 years. The first shows were started as ploughing matches and continue today. The agricultural theme is alive and well with Terrier racing and bale stacking competitions as well as Livestock entries. The show has been on this present site since 2002 and is an annual event taking place on May Day Bank Holiday, so I had just missed it.

Beyond the show ground, a beautiful hillside covered in deciduous trees looked inviting but the climb was steep. At the top, I saw the name of the hill was Belmont Hill but on the other side of the road, a sign declared it as Ashton Hill; two hills for the price of one.

Another commuter village lay ahead - Failand; a nice-looking village with neat gardens and manicured lawns. The people who lived here did not look like they had 'failed' to me; expensive cars were everywhere. At the end of the village I came across the post office, a gem of a shop. As well as having most things for sale, they also served tea and coffee, so I ordered a cup of tea, which the lady made and brought to me outside. It was perfect and a truly refreshing drink. I missed seeing the 'impressive tapestry depicting the Canterbury tales' which is in the church as there was a funeral taking place. From here I got my first view of the Severn Estuary with its two dominant bridges and distant views of Bristol.

I found a path that led downhill from the limestone edge I had been following, through glorious woodland, accompanied by a stream. This was Gordano Valley, a site of Special Scientific Interest (SSSI).

The Gordano Valley is now also the name of a motorway service area on the nearby M5. Gordano is an unusual name for an English valley; it sounds Italian but it isn't, it's Old English for *a muddy triangular piece of valley*, (1988 *English Place Names* by Kenneth Cameron).

The valley sides are made up of wet reed bed meadows. It was an idyllic way to end the day, leading as it did, to the village of Pill by the busy A369. Just before I left the woods, I coggled over on my ankle on some uneven ground. I went down and lay still, in agony.

After a while I got up and gently put weight back on my foot. 'Ouch!' Nothing to it but to get walking, what else could I do?

May Friday 18 Rest Day

We moved up to Aust, to a farm site on the cliff edge overlooking the Severn Estuary and both Severn bridges, the 1960's Severn Bridge to the right and the modern Severn Bridge to the left. From this spot, we were hoping to be able to see the famous Severn Bore but unfortunately, we missed it.

I'd always wanted to go to Portishead, Bristol. It's where the BBC Wildlife Unit is based; those responsible for Planet Earth and David Attenborough projects.

I'd arranged for my post to be redirected here. At the post office, no one had heard of the 'Poste Restante' service and my post wasn't there either!

This put me in a bad mood and Kay and Ripley took the brunt of it. We drove out of Portishead and headed for Bristol. I wanted to see the Clifton Suspension Bridge. On the road into Bristol I was looking for signs saying 'Clifton Suspension Bridge Viewing Area', or something similar. We drove for some time through Clifton, before seeing a sign which read, *'Clifton Suspension Bridge'*.

Almost immediately the bridge was before us and we found ourselves in the queue to pay the toll, which we didn't want to do, so we doubled back and drove through some back streets, coming by chance upon a lay-by next to Leigh Woods, a National Trust-owned piece of woodland.

Here we decided to take Ripley for a walk in an area of the woods called Nightingale Valley. An information board stated an ancient British camp, 'Stoneleigh Camp', had been excavated here by archaeologists. We listened for nightingales but didn't hear any. We walked on through the wood and came to a viewing point overlooking the gorge and Clifton Suspension Bridge, which is seven hundred feet long and two hundred and forty-five feet above the muddy Avon below.

It was brilliant! Our view point was on top of the gorge and very close to the cliff edge giving an uninterrupted view of the bridge, which was designed by Isambard Kingdom Brunel (1806-1859), who died before the bridge was finished. This view point should be highlighted on the information board at the entrance to the woods.

After our walk, we drove to the massive and modern shopping mall complex called Cribbs Causeway. I hated the place. We went quickly to W.H. Smiths to buy maps and M & S to buy jeans, and then got out fast. Why people like to waste their lives wandering around these places is a mystery to me.

We drove back to Aust and into the village. Here, we found a picturesque pub, The Boar's Head, where we spent the evening. It had been windy all day. Our exposed pitch with a fantastic view of the estuary didn't seem that good when we were being buffeted by gusts of strong winds. We soon realised why we were the only ones pitched up here. The wind shook the motorhome ferociously. Try as we might, we just couldn't get off to sleep. It was like being on a constant roller coaster. About 3.00 am the gusts of wind grew stronger and we decided to move the motorhome back away from the edge. This entailed removing the security bolts on the wheel and driving in reverse in the dark, struggling all the time against the strong wind. At last safely away from the edge we parked up between two caravans in storage and soon nodded off to sleep.

Walking Day 23 *Fine and dry*

May Saturday 19

Pill to Aust - 13 miles - Total walked 256

We went back to Portishead to check if my post had arrived. 'No', it hadn't. I was giving up on Poste Restante. The Royal Mail was letting me down. I needed to get walking.

At Pill it was Christian Aid weekend and the good people here were flocking to the church hall where they were having a plant and cake sale. I walked on and came to the post office where I decided to get my Lejog verification certificate stamped. It was busy and I joined the queue. Two women were behind the counter. The older one of the two was slow and inefficient and looked as if she was sucking on sour lemons.

The younger woman was whizzing through the queue and I soon came to be served by her. I produced my certificate and asked if she could kindly stamp it and so verify my being there. She looked at the certificate and declared in an officious voice, "Oh no we can't possibly stamp this". The 'lemon sucker' interjected, "What's that?" She looked at my certificate and then at me, over the top of her spectacles and then shouted in a screeching voice "Oh no we can't stamp that". At the same time, she dropped the certificate away from herself as though she had just picked up a piece of dog dirt. I looked at both women; the queue of people looked at me; the queue was getting longer. I picked up my certificate and calmly said, "It's been stamped at other post offices without any problems". The 'lemon sucker' took the certificate back and re-checked and then turned hesitantly and said, "I don't think we can stamp it" I quickly said, "You don't think you can do it. All I want is a stamp". She looked up at the queue and looked back at me. People in the queue fidgeted restlessly. Then she relented and stamped the certificate. "Thank you", I said and walked out of the post office and out of Pill.

I found the footpath that runs parallel with the River Avon between Pill and the Avon Bridge (M5). As I approached the massive motorway bridge I came upon a metal sculpture of a huge hammer and spanner. Created by Pat Daw, it was called 'Stronghold' and commemorates the strengthening of the bridge in 2001. It's such a pity that it's tucked away on a footpath underneath the bridge where it cannot be seen by the thousands of people who use the bridge.

I climbed the footpath alongside the M5 motorway and crossed the bridge which stretches a mile across the estuary on gigantic, concrete stilts. As the traffic thundered past me at terrific speed, I felt safe in the path zone with high metal grilled fences on both sides; on one side the motorway, on the other, fantastic views of the River Avon and a boatyard - probably the only one left of many.

I could also see the villages of Pill and Shirehampton, the latter being on the north side of the river. Before the bridge was built, the two villages were linked by ferry and I couldn't help thinking that at that time the two communities were likely to have been in better communication with each other. I imagined that in the past, they may have had pub skittle competitions, very common in all the pubs around here where they have skittle alleys but now the bridge is here, I doubt if they get together any more.

As I paused to take a photograph I could feel the bridge wobble. For some reason, the grilled fencing which made me feel safe and secure before, became lower, the higher I walked.

A sign on the bridge said, 'Pedestrians and cyclists 15mph speed limit'. I wish! I followed the signs off the bridge for the National Cycle Trail No. 41. This took me away from the motorway to a nature reserve which had been the site of a Roman villa. Today there was no sign of it.

The village of Shirehampton was away to my right and up to my left was the town and large industrial area of Avonmouth, known as 'oil basin', with its storage tanks, cold stores, grain silos, factories and smelting works.

It was fine and dry, and I was walking through a lovely reserve. I passed the entrance to the Lawrence Weston Urban Farm where staff looked up, hoping that I was a much-needed visitor. I wasn't but where were all the visitors on such a lovely day?

Near to the farm and over to my right as I walked, was a huge housing estate. I walked past a burnt-out car which was still smoking. It reminded me too much of work. I came to a cycle and skateboard park. I would have expected such a place to be packed. Not here; there wasn't a soul in sight.

The route took me through a nature reserve which cleverly utilised all the surrounding areas and even though large industrial premises were close; the path was a delight to walk. A fox crossed my path, stopped to look at me and then ran off into the grounds of a power station.

I was now walking along the well-signed Severn Way footpath, which has for its symbol, a 'Trow' - a flat-bottomed boat that used to be a common sight on the Severn Estuary. It led me across the railway line and onto a strip of bush land between railway and estuary beach. I climbed a metal stile; the first metal one I'd seen so far on the walk. I walked into the town of Severn Beach along the concrete sea wall.

Severn Beach had the look of a resort. It also looked shut. It was a lovely, sunny afternoon and no one was about. They couldn't all be watching the football - F.A. Cup Final - could they? I came to some parkland behind the sea wall. A large African / Caribbean family were playing on the grass. There were about twenty of them; four grandmother figures, four mother figures and eleven children all under the age of thirteen years. Some of the kids were playing football, some tennis. They were all smiling and happy. Where were the older teenagers and men who were missing out on a good family outing?

I walked on the sea wall. Here it is known as the Binn Wall which I thought was unusual and so close to my own name. I haven't been able to find the origins of the sea wall's curious name. This modern sea defence was completed in 1998, reusing some of the original stone. The original Binn Wall was constructed in 1815 to provide flood protection for the villages of Severn Beach and New Passage.

The land to the side of the wall is now a site of special scientific interest. From here the full majesty of the Severn Estuary can be seen. Thousands of tons of water pass through here twice daily - the famous Severn Bore; one of the highest tides on the planet and I didn't get to see it. The Estuary is important for fish including what they call the Seven of Severn; seven migratory species such as salmon, trout, lamprey and shad. Perhaps most amazing are the tiny elvers of the European eel which travel from the Sargasso Sea in the mid-Atlantic to the Severn, an epic two-thousand-mile journey.

I walked on under the M4 Bridge, a massive concrete structure built in 1996, which takes the English traffic to Newport - over 250 million vehicles a year. The new bridge looked impressive at close quarters and far from being straight, a distinct curve could be detected.

It was noisy above but peaceful underneath. I marvelled at the construction techniques and was glad I was on foot, not realising that below me was the main railway line running from South Wales to London, running in a tunnel built underneath the bridge! Still, I didn't stay underneath for long and escaped into the countryside past an old firing range and into cow fields towards the old Severn Bridge. Its twin-fabricated metal supports thrusting skywards, dominating the skyline.

Kay and Ripley joined me from the Aust side and we walked back together, avoiding cows and horses as we went. A large group of Army cadets straggled past us in a long and unregimented line. Those at the back, including a group of girl cadets were hobbling along in agony, suffering from blisters in large and uncomfortable looking boots.

I left Kay and Ripley at the motorhome and carried on for a short walk past the Aust Gypsy site. They were all out with their horses and trotting carts. Their site was an official one. It looked a mess. Dogs barked, kids screamed, there were piles of tarmac and rubble everywhere. The men and their dogs looked dirty and scruffy, yet none of the dogs bothered me; they had them under control - which is more than can be said for some farmers and their dogs that I'd met so far along my journey.

The gypsies weren't at all interested in me. I guess they were too busy with their ponies and trotting carts, plus this was a national cycle trail and path to the bridge so I think they are used to walkers near their camp.

I came to the Severn Bridge, now part of the M48 into Chepstow, Wales; built in 1966, its white suspension supports changing colour as I walked, flashing from Grey to White when seen from differing angles in ever changing light. I walked up to the bridge and watched a fantastic sunset over the Severn Estuary before calling it a day. The bridge crossing could wait until tomorrow.

May
Sunday
20
Walking Day 24 *Bright and sunny*

Aust to Tintern Abbey - 10 miles - Total walked 266

We moved camp-site up to the Forest of Dean. Once we were settled, Kay and Ripley drove me back to the other side of the Severn Bridge and I began the awesome crossing into Wales.

The views down the Severn Estuary to the new motorway bridge and beyond were spectacular. I know the Severn from here has been described as *'a sulky old grey brute'* (using the words from a Robert Bridge's poem). The tide was in and it reminded me again that I still hadn't seen the famous tidal wave; the Severn bore.

I wasn't the only one crossing the bridge; there were hundreds of motorists zooming past at speed. Cyclists and other walkers were also taking advantage of the good weather to make the walk from England to Wales. The footbridge and cycle path are toll free; motorists from England entering Wales have to pay a toll of £5.20 for a car;

motorists from Wales to England travel toll-free. The towers of the bridge rise four hundred feet above the sea with the road being just one hundred feet above.

Halfway across the bridge I stopped to inspect a plaque commemorating the bridge construction, with the loss of six men's lives. Their names are listed on the plaque. Most motorists never read them.

Shally Hunt in her 1997 book 'The Sea on our left', describes her crossing of the bridge, 'I was suddenly aware of the magnitude of the bridge, its delicate strength. We crept across like tiny terrestrial insects hovering above the vast expanse of air and muddy brown water'.

Chepstow has an English name which means, 'market town'. I walked into Chepstow under the motorway through a tunnel at the end of the bridge. Motorists don't see this tunnel; it's for cyclists and pedestrians. 'Croeso in Cymru' or Welcome to Wales.

I moved into the housing estate called Bulwark. There were three Chinese takeaways within half a mile - the Welsh must like Chinese food. Kids were playing in the gardens and a group of them aged about eight or nine were wearing England football shirts, which I found odd being in Wales.

Two hundred years ago, Chepstow was a busy port plying the Wye Valley and Bristol Channel. Today it's much gentler. The main street looked like any other main street does on a Sunday; everywhere was closed, including the fortified gateway which formed part of the town wall or port wall. It was built between1272 and 1282.

Whilst walking along I came across a man in his seventies who was banging on the window of the closed police station. "I want the police", he said to me, in a Welsh accent. "They don't appear to be in". I told him to pick up the yellow telephone by the door hoping it was linked to a control room somewhere. It was and I left the man happily talking to the police on the telephone.

I made my way through the car park and into the grounds of the magnificent Chepstow Castle. It is a long castle with lots of ramparts topped by Baileys joined end to end, a plan forced upon the builders by the natural ridges they stand upon. Building began in 1069 by the newly-arrived Normans.

After the English Civil war, a Parliamentarian called Sir Henry Marten, who had signed the death warrant of Charles 1st, was held prisoner here for 20 years by Charles II.

The grounds of the castle are more like a park. Lots of families were picnicking in the sunshine.

I made my way downhill to the Wye Valley Tourist Information Centre. There were two information boards: one for the Offa's Dyke path and one for the Wye Valley path. They both led to Tintern Abbey my hoped-for-destination. Offa's Dyke seemed to take a more twisting route, whilst the Wye Valley Way appeared more direct. I chose the Wye Valley Way and climbed back, out through the beautiful castle grounds.

At Chepstow's Leisure Centre the signposts disappeared and I was left wondering which way to go? I chose wrongly and ended up going around a school where people were playing tennis and a whole army of lads were playing football. They all stood and stared at me as though I was some alien from outer space. They all knew I was hopelessly lost or I wouldn't have been there. I marched confidently past them and crashed through the nearest hedge. The path had to be here somewhere. With a bit of difficulty, I found it - a nice wide path through thick woodland.

I hadn't been walking through the woods for long when I was suddenly confronted by a large Alsatian dog. It was loose and staring at me ready to pounce. "Hello boy", I said, "Where are your stupid owners?" It didn't answer. My stick was at the ready. Just then the dog's owners came up. They apologised for letting their dog off the lead but they hadn't expected to meet anyone here. What, on a Sunday afternoon, on a national trail? As it turned out, they were in fact, the last people I saw walking on the entire route to Tintern.

Over to my right I could just make out the River Wye, winding its way through tree-covered, steep-sided hills. Off to my left was Chepstow Racecourse, the home of the Welsh Grand National. The Racecourse opened in 1926. It is set on the Piercefield Park which is the scene of the beginnings of the tourist industry as we know it. Way back in the 18th Century, Valentine Morris, the owner of Piercefield Park, built grottos and began to scratch out the paths through the woods to bring people up from London to see these beautiful sites. This, at a time when very few people travelled, certainly not for leisure.

Today the racecourse was home to a huge car boot sale, packed with people and in the middle of the course, a gymkhana. The voice on the loudspeaker was that of a very snooty English lady, not at all Welsh; "Penelope is doing very well on Prancing Pony. Let's give her a big hand". She said.

My path looped through the woods to take in such delights as 'lovers leap', a near-vertical drop down hundreds of feet to the river and rocks below and to an ancient fort, all covered by bushes. The voice from the gymkhana loud speaker was getting faint and distant as I carried on. The path was getting narrower and narrower. Cobwebs covered the way and I had to slice my way through them.

The gymkhana loudspeaker was now getting louder and louder. What was going on? I was walking towards the racecourse again; I'd thought the course was well behind me! "Tara won this event last year and she is doing really well again today". Declared the snooty-voiced lady. Through the trees, I could now see the gymkhana. It was behind me thankfully. I came to a diversion sign. There had been a landslip and the path was being diverted - backwards. I forged ahead and stumbled through the undergrowth until eventually I came out onto the main road to Tintern.

The road was busy with cyclists all pulling up the incline from the valley floor. They all nodded in a friendly manner as they passed. There were so many cyclists that I couldn't believe there would be any more to follow. Yet on they came, hundreds of them. Were they heading home to Chepstow or even to Bristol, perhaps? I continued down the road until Tintern Abbey came into view. It is set in beautiful surroundings that painters and poets have swooned over for centuries.

My eyes were distracted from the Abbey to the large car park at the side. People, hundreds of people, that's what I focused in on. Coach parties, ice-cream vans, motorcyclists, cyclists, grannies, lovers, families, hundreds of people. It was a beautiful, sunny evening and the people were lingering, making the most of it. I'd been alone in the woods for so long and now felt I was walking into what looked like a scene from hell; not at all what Wordsworth wrote about, or Turner painted.

The Victorians came to Tintern Abbey by train. They came especially in September to see the harvest moon caught in the huge, open, rose window of the Abbey. I reached a plaque on a wall that declared, *'Here near this spot, brass was first made by alloying copper with zinc'*.

I called it a day and joined the queue for an ice-cream.

May **Walking Day 25** *Fair and dry*

Monday 21 | **Tintern Abbey to Monmouth - 10 miles - Total walked 276**

I went back to Tintern Abbey and with the crowds gone, I found the time to have a look around. I couldn't help making comparisons with Bolton Abbey in Yorkshire. I read a sign on a wall declaring that buzzards are usually seen flying above Tintern. I looked up and immediately saw two buzzards flying over the ruins.

Over in the tearooms, the woman serving on was a Scottish widow. I asked her how a Scot managed to find herself here in Wales near the English border. She laughed and didn't answer the question but said she loved it when coaches arrived, full of Americans who squealed at what a lovely Welsh accent she had.

A little further on I came to the small Tintern Parish Church where a notice board declared that the Bishop was coming the following week to induct a new parish priest. I reflected on the monumental majesty of the ruined Abbey and on this tiny little church, tucked away on the edge of the village; Christianity continuing in its many forms.

I came to a modern art piece in the grounds of the old Tintern Railway Station, 'The Circle of Legends' Sculptures', to give them their full title. These were created in Oak by sculptors Neil Gow and John Hobbs. There was King Arthur, King Offa and Eleanor of Provence, all magnificent life sized pieces, expertly carved. They made an impressive picture. Some of the legends I knew, others I did not and I made a note to read up on them. Like 'Sabrina of Hafren': who was she and what did she do? (A Welsh princess, killed by a jealous queen, who had her thrown into the river. The River Severn takes its name from her...the Welsh for that river is Afon Hafren) Or King Tewdrig? (A Sixth Century King of Gwent, who gave his kingdom up to his son and retired to be a Hermit at Tintern. Returning from retirement to help fight for his son, he was wounded and died in battle).

A bit further on the old station buildings were bustling with tourists. There was a shop, tea rooms and some old railway carriages on the lines. I walked along them until I came to one that had been converted into a cinema. I went in and sat down. I watched a brilliant twenty-minute film show about the Wye Valley railway line from Tintern to Monmouth, most of which I was going to walk today. The line closed in 1964. I liked Tintern Station and what they'd done to it. True, it would have been so much better if they had kept the line running. They were still building railway stations or 'halts' as they called them in the 1930's.

The disused line, now the Wye Valley Path, led away from the station complex on an excellent way. After about a half a mile it came to some steps and the sign indicated that the path left the disused railway line, now covered in brambles, and climbed up into the woods. They were beautiful woods; a mixture of deciduous and pine trees. The path forked and was not sign-posted. I chose the right-hand fork and carried on. After six hundred yards the good path came to an abrupt halt in a nest of brambles and nettles.

I couldn't believe it. I slithered down a dangerously steep, wooded embankment until I hit the road near Brockweir Bridge. I followed it until I came to the English village of Whitebrook. It was here that a combined German and Scandinavian enterprise began the very first wire making works in the country. They were a big user of the railway.

Once this valley, now so peaceful and tranquil, had been a very busy hive of industrial activity based on coal, quarrying and iron ore workings. Today, quarrying still exists and coal-mining stopped only quite recently.

The Wye Valley route is one minute in Wales and the next it's in England. So, it was with the railway line which I was now back on and walking on towards Monmouth. The going was good. I came to a sign that read, 'Monmouth 4km'. I checked my map; Monmouth was a good four miles away. The politically correct route-marker sign makers had got it wrong. They'd got it wrong for going metric and they'd also got it wrong by placing this signpost here.

I walked on into a green wonderland. Everywhere was green; many varied shades of green; even the river was green. I was getting an overdose of green. Not that I was complaining. I looked up at the sky and then at my own hands to get a fix on another colour. I was looking at the green verges to see if I could spot other colours and then I did - some small, yellow buttercups. They were like tiny children in a crowd of adults, pushing to the front saying, "Let me see". With more detailed study I saw the purple of red campion and herb robert, and later on I saw flowering foxgloves, both pink and white.

The railway line closely followed the river and here in the river, people were canoeing or fishing. I crossed over the river by a metal bridge, the metal footpath being the only bit of this old, eye-catching railway bridge which spans the river on massive stilts, still in use and into the village of Redbrook. Years ago, home to many in the massive tinsmith industry that lived here; now sadly all gone.

Not much further on, there was a large, flat rock in the middle of the river. In the railway film, I'd seen earlier, a group of boys were filmed swimming in the river and climbing onto this rock and waving at the steam train as it went by. The rock didn't look as if it had been put to such use in years. Health and safety conscious parents had put a stop to that.

The railway line 'disappeared' into a narrow path alongside the river. I was on the final approach to Monmouth when I came across a large oak tree that had fallen over the path. It had obviously been there for some time and its branches were still growing and covered with leaves. There was no path around it and it was too high to climb over. I pulled some branches back and wriggled on my stomach under it. It was a true assault course. I had to push my rucksack ahead of me as I continued through the soil and undergrowth that was swarming with ants. When I eventually came up for air, I was exhausted.

I walked out of the wood and into the large, flat fields of the Monmouth Show Ground. The Monmouth show is described as the biggest one day show in Wales. This year (2007) it was moving to these fields, set in an idyllic location by the banks of the River Wye in an area of outstanding beauty, yet still conveniently close to town. The organisers have done well to secure such a location for the show which takes place on the last Thursday in August every year... Another show missed.

Swans and cormorants were on the river over to my left, as were huge swarms of midges which seemed to zoom in on me. I swallowed a fly, drank some water and then walked into Monmouth singing the song, "There was an old woman who swallowed a fly that wriggled inside her ... etc." I was impressed by the many verses I could remember. It finished with, "She swallowed a horse .... She's dead, of course".

Monmouth used to have four railway stations. Today it has none.

I reached Monmouth by the remains of a railway bridge.

Walking Day 26 *Hot and sunny*

May
Tuesday
22 | **Monmouth to Llangarron - 10 miles - Total walked 286**

We drove into the nearby English town of Coleford. I had a walk around the town centre with Ripley. I liked the feel of Coleford. It was clean and tidy and the people were friendly.

It was a hot sunny day and I'd noticed at least three barber shops displaying their traditional red and white poles.

I decided to get my hair cut. Of the three shops, I was attracted to a rather scruffy-looking shop on the edge of the square; a true barbers shop, not a 'jazzy' hairdresser. The barber was a gaunt, skinny fellow of 65 years. The inside walls of his shop had a display of photographs of historic Coleford. Some that attracted my attention were ones that showed deep snow drifts in the town square and others showing Home

Guard troops but the ones that really caught my eye were photographs showing the demolition of the ancient Market Hall. These photographs were taken in 1968 and showed bulldozers smashing into the lovely and architecturally stunning market hall. They showed crowds of people with no crowd barriers or safety signs at all. In fact, the workmen wore flat caps; not a hard hat to be seen.

The barber was a quiet, shy type who barely spoke at first until I asked him about these photographs. He then opened up and talked passionately about the destruction in the 1960's, of his beloved Coleford. "They ripped the soul out of the town. It's a crime what they did. The Market Hall should have been preserved". He followed on with, "They promised us a state-of-the-art Community Centre on the edge of town as a replacement. It's had three new roofs since it was built and it's now a dilapidated eyesore. It's a mess". I had to agree with him. We'd seen the Community Centre. How anyone could have destroyed the market hall is unbelievable. It cried out, 'ancient building needing tender loving care', not demolition. He gave me a good hair cut for £3.50; he must have thought I was a pensioner. I wonder what will happen to this wonderful barber shop in Coleford when my man retires. It needs preserving just as it is; it was like stepping back in time.

I was dropped off at Monmouth and I took time to look at the ancient and preserved Monnow or Mons Bridge, the only Norman bridge with fortified gateway surviving in Britain. It is here that the River Monnow flows into the River Wye at Monmow, (or Mons mouth).

King Henry V was born in this town in 1387. In Agincourt Square, there is a statue of local man, Charles Henry Rolls, of Rolls-Royce fame. Monmouth was a busy little town and what I saw of it I liked. Teenage school kids and how they look and behave may be a good indication as to how pleasant a town is. The school kids I observed were well-turned-out, clean, respectable and polite.

I walked out of Monmouth on an excellent riverside path surrounded by beautiful, rural countryside. Gentle hills covered with mixed woodland and meadows rich in grass and flowers swept down to the river. At this point the River Wye is wide and lazy. A paddle of canoeists came rowing by.

My route was clearly marked, 'The Wye Valley Way' and was in a good state of repair. Large houses 'peeped ' out from the trees. I came to a junction in the path marked on the map as 'Robin Hood'. Certainly, this terrain was ideal for such a character that I'd always associated with being from Nottingham and Yorkshire, both much further north.

The walk went deep into these woods, following the river which was now 'snaking' slowly around the hills. I was heading for Symonds Yat and I was given two options; one, to follow the river for about three miles around the hills or two, to climb over the hill directly to Symonds Yat. I chose the latter and began climbing the hill on a wide, steep path.

I hadn't seen anyone since the canoeists. The woods were thick with leaves with the sun being shaded out. I heard behind me the panting noise of a human being. I turned just in time to see a man of about fifty, skinny and grey, jogging up the hillside. Sweat poured from him and his clothes were soaked. As he reached me he muttered under his breath. "Don't let them catch me". His face was etched in panic. "Don't let who catch you?" I asked. However, it was too late; the man had jogged on further up the hill and wasn't stopping for a chat. I looked down the hill to see who might be chasing this man; an angry party of trolls or an Orc-like army? I couldn't hear or see anything. Wild boars are said to be roaming these woods but I didn't see any sign of them either. I continued to climb up the path, my hearing sense alert to any noise just in case the man was right and he was being chased.

Just below the crest of the hill I stumbled onto the massive cave system marked on the map as, 'King Arthur's Cave'. Like Robin Hood, King Arthur got around a bit. The entrance to the cave was well trodden. I walked into the cave until I couldn't see where I was going. The cave went deeper but I turned and came out slowly, checking first for the imagined Orc army that had been chasing the jogger. The coast was clear and I moved on over the hill top.

My path merged into another, then another and then another. Suddenly I was confronted by a maze of paths heading in all directions. Which one should I follow? The signs that had been so good up to this point were no longer to be seen. For the first time on this walk I got my compass out. I took a bearing and set off confidently on one of the paths.

I looked down and saw ants, thousands of large wood ants. They were everywhere. I walked on. After ten minutes or so the ants were still being crushed underfoot. I'd never seen as many. The whole wood was moving.

I appeared to be walking around in a big circle on top of this densely-wooded hill. I came at last to a starburst of about seven paths. I looked at my compass. The direction I should be heading in was the narrowest and faintest path of them all. This couldn't be right, but trusting my compass, this was the path I took and after a while, I came to a steep decline in the wooded cliff top. The path went down alright but I think it was made by and for mountain goats. I could hear laughter and human noise below. I felt sure I was now heading in the right direction. I slipped and slithered down the path, eventually coming out through a tiny gap in the bushes onto a narrow lane.

I had reached Symonds Yat West. I turned down the lane past big houses with high fences. The houses had names like, 'Good View' and 'Much Better View'. I didn't have a view. I walked on past 'Private Lovely View' and 'Keep out Beautiful View'. I tried to peer over the fences to get a view

I couldn't. One or two expensive sports cars drove past. I imagined the wife on seeing me, saying to her husband, "Are you sure we put the alarm on?" and he replying, "Yes dear, don't worry and the fence is electrified".

The occupants of these cars were anything but friendly. Steely glares and bitter faces stared at me as if to say, "We know this is a public road but we consider it private really".

I followed the lane down to an overgrown path that eventually led to the river. There was just enough room to stand, either side of me being fenced off with high fences and *'private'* signs. This spot was once a foot ferry crossing - one of over a hundred on the River Wye which is now reduced to having just three.

At least I did get a view of the rapids. Symonds Yat East was back behind me on the other side of the river. I looked at the map and realised, to get anywhere decent I had to climb back up the overgrown path and go back along the narrow lane the way I had just come. The laughter and noise was coming from Symonds Yat East, a much better-looking prospect with pubs, cafes and shops. I couldn't get to Symonds Yat East. There is a 'hailing' foot ferry at the Saracen's Head pub at Symonds Yat East but I couldn't find the path down to it. I walked on the lane and eventually came out at the road junction. There is a garden centre with café from where I bought a much-needed cup of tea. I was still on the Symonds Yat West side of the river. There was a motor boat centre and a motor bus tied up nearby. I decided to walk on and visit Symonds Yat East later with Kay and Ripley.

I crossed the busy A40 by the road bridge and entered the village of Whitworth. From here I walked a few miles on narrow quiet country lanes to the English village of Llangarron which, near to the village entrance, has an interesting 'scrap yard' full of ancient farming implements, chimney tops and cart wheels. The ancient 14th-century church dedicated to Saint Deinst, one of only two churches in England to be dedicated to this saint, is down in the village centre.

The church which I found open, was home to a colony of bats which are protected. Netting had been hung from the ceiling in an attempt to stop bat droppings from spoiling the pews. It didn't work and the pews were in a real mess, not so much from the droppings which just crumble to dust but from the bat's urine which causes a marking and pitting on the woodwork.

The churchyard has won awards for its nature habitat. A piece from an earlier spire now forms part of an unusual sundial. 'Llan' is a Celtic word meaning 'church' or more specifically, the defensive earthen embankment set up around a religious settlement. It is pronounced 'clan'. So, this tiny place in England with a Welsh-sounding name is the place of 'Garron's Church'.

Kay and Ripley picked me up from this peaceful spot and we returned by car to Symonds Yat East, where we had a meal in the attractive and ancient pub, the 'Saracens Head'. The pub is positioned in a spectacular spot right down near to the water's edge. The ceiling of the pub was stuffed with bales of straw. When I asked why, we were informed that the straw 'soaks' up the cigarette smoke. I'd never seen this before and now the smoking ban is in place, presumably I won't ever see it again.

Symonds Yat East needed more exploration and I decided to take a further day off later to revisit it.

Kay, in one of her many letters home, wrote:

'I enjoyed our stay in the Forest of Dean. The site was looked after by the Forestry Commission and we literally walked out of our door and into the forest. We frequently heard the 'yaffle' of a green woodpecker, seeing its flash of brilliant green as it flew up from the field near to our pitch'.

It was a beautiful day. I had devised a route up and down lonely, leafy lanes.

As I walked out of Llangarron, a young man in a car stopped and asked me for directions. I felt smug and satisfied that I could easily help him, being recently armed with this knowledge. After this interruption, the lanes remained quiet as I walked on, listening to the birds of the hedgerows singing. I saw the remains of a bird's egg, cracked open and empty on the floor. At one time in my childhood I would have immediately identified it. It took a bit longer now but I felt sure it was a blackbirds' egg. As a boy in the early 1960's, everyone on my street collected birds' eggs - yes! Some boys collected stamps (as we later did) but we were good at collecting eggs. It's now looked upon as a crime but back then my brother won the top award at school for his 'best presented' egg collection beating a girl who collected tea towels. We always collected a single egg from the nest and we never took the last or a single one. We became experts at finding nests on our patch. All our eggs were expertly 'blown' and presented in boxes which contained saw dust. Although the collection was my brother's, I always felt it was mine because I was the one sent climbing up the tall tree to reach a nest or climb through a thorny hedge to secure a new egg. We had an intimate knowledge of all the birds and their behaviour. The birds bred in the same spots year after year, many having two or three clutches of eggs per year.

After the birds, had fledged - and only after - we gained important 'brownie' points by presenting our teachers with birds' nests for use on their nature tables. Word got around and other teachers in other classes would ask us to fetch nests in for them. The Binns boys would never fail.

I'm not supporting the return of egg-collecting but it is amazing what memories can be brought back by just one broken eggshell on a country lane. They are good memories. Kids in those days knew about nature first-hand and not from a TV or computer screen.

I walked past some orchards and came to the small village of Pencoyd. A village pond was surrounded by ancient red brick houses and a large hall. I arrived at the beautiful little 14th century church of Saint Denys, and found it open. Built in 1330 some of its roof beams are from that date. There are three bells in its tower; the oldest was cast in Gloucester in 1346.

On the outskirts of Pencoyd I saw a planning application notice pinned to a telegraph pole, for a rebuilding of the 'Dhamma Dipa Vipassanna Meditation Centre - a

Buddhist retreat'. I wondered where, down these lonely country lanes, the centre was.

As I walked on, a small blue car slowly approached and stopped short. I saw a small-built Indian man sitting behind the steering wheel. He looked frustrated and annoyed. He peered out of the window and said in a very Indian-accented voice, "Oh please, please can you help me? I'm totally, totally lost".

He was looking for the meditation centre and had been driving around these lanes for ages. By consulting my map and telling him about the planning application notice I had seen earlier, I hope I sent him off in the right direction.

I soon came to the village of Llanwarne with its ruined 13th century church of St John the Baptist down by the Gamber brook, now preserved in a neat well-kept lawned area. An ancient lych-gate led me onto the site which had been abandoned in 1864 due to continual flooding. A new church stood some distance away on a hill. A man was mowing the grass around the grounds of the ruin. He spoke to me in a very strong Hereford accent and I replied in as strong a Yorkshire accent as I could, "Ahm bound for t'ereford". He looked at me quizzically and then said, "It's a bloody long way, a long, long way". I didn't want to hear this having been walking most of the day. I thought I was somewhere near. By my reckoning, I had about seven miles to go which wasn't such a bad thing. The man began telling me to start by heading for the village of Turkey Tump. His route more or less corresponded with mine.

I passed Turkey Tump, a small village which has nothing to do with Turkeys as the name implies. It is named after pigs and means Pig Hill from the Welsh Turkel (pig) and Tump (hill). I made my way to Wormelow Tump; pleasant villages tucked away in the Herefordshire countryside. This was another village with an interesting name. 'Worm' means 'dusky'; 'low' means 'burial mound'.

Here in the late 1890's the Victorians in the name of progress and a road widening scheme, destroyed what has been described by some as a potential *Wonder of Britain*. This was an ancient burial mound, said to be the burial tomb of Amyr (Amr), a son of King Arthur who was murdered nearby. A petrol station and a pub, The Tump Inn now stand on the spot. The pub is said to be one of the most haunted public houses in Britain.

I was passing large fields growing various crops. A sign stated, *'Don't let those Docks, Thistles and Nettles spread, get them mowed off now!'* I climbed up onto Ridge Hill and walked into Hereford along a foot path which gave me good views of the city. The path, well-used by horse riders was heavily churned up. I came out by some pleasant houses in an enviable location on the edge of Hereford.

Some of the houses displayed something that shocked me. The householders had put up wire meshing in an attempt to stop house martins and swallows from nesting under their eaves.

I walked on and came to a gas pipeline construction site that is winding its way across the country. A company called 'Murphy's' was the main contractor and their fleet of green vans, cars and lorries were everywhere to be seen. If the army ever wanted to conscript men quickly, then I suggest they start with Murphy's. They have a ready-made 'army' of fit young men with a fleet of vehicles.

The scenery suddenly changed from affluent edge of town suburbia to inner city housing estate. It was a shock climbing over the assorted junk, broken and abandoned toys and other debris scattered along the road. The way led onto Bishop's meadow, a large flat pleasant park on the edge of the River Wye with people enjoying the sunshine.

I came to the river by the Victoria suspension bridge. It was built to commemorate Queen Victoria's Diamond Jubilee Year in 1897 and replaced an earlier foot ferry at this point. The foot bridge is a beautiful white structure and complements the scene. There are weeping willows by the river's edge pleasantly obstructing the view of the Cathedral over on the other side.

I walked down onto a little beach and began skimming stones. Crouching down I first selected a thin flat pebble from amongst the many others present. Not too light, arm back and then throw along a still piece of water counting up to seven 'skims'. I'd lost none of the skills honed as a boy playing 'ducks and drakes'.

An ice-cream van was stationed at the other side of the bridge and was doing a brisk business. I walked up and onto the bridge intending to join the queue. Suddenly without warning, the van drove off when I was only twenty yards away from it.

The park continued on the other side of the river and I walked into the grounds of Hereford Cathedral which is built of rich red stone. I stopped by the statue of Edward Elgar with his bicycle; Elgar, famous for writing 'Land of Hope and Glory', had been the organist at the cathedral. It was here that I was joined by Kay and Ripley.

In another of her letters home, Kay was to write:

'Ripley particularly liked visiting the park because she had easy access into the river. The hot weather was encouraging her to forget her phobia for cold water. She now flings herself into anything remotely looking like water and wallows in ecstasy'.

Rest Day

May Thursday 24

We took a day off and went back to Symonds Yat - East

We found a parking place in this busy tourist spot and went to have a closer look at the 'hailing' foot ferries. The most popular one is outside the Saracen's Head and it is one of the barmen there who operates it to and fro across the river.

We looked for one of the tourists' boats to take us up river. Tony, our friend from home, had asked us to check up on an old friend of his who was working as a captain on one of the tourist boats. I approached a man who was all kitted out in a captains' outfit. "Are you Gerald?" I asked. To my surprise, he answered in the affirmative and we spent a few minutes talking about our mutual friend from Bingley.

We then got into Gerald's boat - The Kingfisher - and had a very enjoyable and relaxing trip up river with willow fluff everywhere in the air. We sipped coffee and listened to the boatman passionately narrating stories and legends concerning the River Wye.

The record weight of a salmon caught in the Wye is held by a woman, much to the annoyance of all the fishermen, most of whom spend a lifetime fishing the river here.

It was fascinating stuff and hard to take it all in. On the table in front of us were photograph albums of the 2002 floods. Our ears picked up when the boat man gave us his version of how Symond's Yat got its name. According to him, Symond was John Symond, a Yorkshireman who worked at the road toll bar, which he called a 'yat' or gate, hence Symond's Yat. I would have accepted this as fact but later that day at the rock known as Symond's Yat - or Three Counties View - Gloucester, Hereford and Monmouth, I saw a plaque which stated that the earliest record of the name being used was in the 12th century, long before toll roads were in use. Also, long before the 17th Century High Sheriff of Herefordshire, Robert Symonds frequented these parts and is now often quoted as being the person the rock is named after. An old English meaning for 'yat' is 'gap' and it is clear to see the Wye Valley 'Gap' here in the hills.

I prefer my own reasoning for the unusual name which could easily have derived from the Old English dialect term 'simmon gat' meaning a summer pasture; not too hard to imagine once the trees have been cleared.

Back in Symond's Yat East, we had lunch at a little cafe before moving up to the 'Rock' to see the Three Counties View. Legend has it that from here, you can throw a stone into the river at the point where the three counties meet. We were soon busy watching peregrine falcons, aided by RSPB staff and their telescopes. These guys were expert birders and every scope had been set up so we could see the falcon. The male was on a perch by the nest and whilst we were there he was resting, not showing off his great flying skills which was a shame but at least we got some good views of him. The peregrine feeds primarily on birds which it catches in flight. It is one of many of nature's joys to behold.

May
Friday
25 **Walking Day 28** *Dry and sunny*

Hereford to Stoke Prior, Near Leominster - 12 miles - Total walked 310

In the morning, we moved the van up to Stoke Prior, near Leominster (pronounced 'Lemster').

We followed the directions in the book to a site on the outskirts of the village and pulled up near a gate where a stocky man of about seventy years plus was messing about with a few sheep. He had a green bib tied around him with 'farmer's bind'. Just behind him I saw the caravan site sign in the field overgrown in thigh-high grass. At the bottom of the field were a few caravans that were enveloped in tall grass. The farmer was friendly and it seemed that this was to be our 'home' for the next few days. The look of despair on Kay's face was a picture.

The farmer explained that he hadn't had time to cut the grass but now we'd arrived he would see to it, which he did. Everything was there all right: electric hook-ups, chemical disposal, toilet and shower block, and all thigh deep in grass. The farmer wanted us to position our van in between two other vans that were in storage.

As I was driving in I realised that a caravan opposite with a collection of scrap metal, was in fact being lived in by an old man with a large dog. This was not the kind of site we'd been used to. On the plus side, the farmer was a real character and gentleman. He wanted to talk and talk. We ended up talking about tractors. Years ago, he used to own an International Harvester tractor, made in Bradford, which he was full of praise for. He now swears by John Deere tractors, the green and yellow coloured ones that I was seeing all over the place.

Later that day we were glad to leave the site and drive down to Hereford. Kay and Ripley went for a walk in the park and I went to have a look around the cathedral before setting off on my day's walk. As I walked in I was confronted by a vibrant and lively service. Local school children were being educated by an Anti-Slavery travelling exhibition. I stopped to listen and was pleased to hear some facts being read out; the emphasis on slavery today, especially in middle-eastern countries and on how Britain went out on a limb against all the other countries in the world to put a stop to the very lucrative West-African slave trade in the early 19th century.

Hereford Cathedral was bustling but I managed to find a quiet chapel for some prayer and useful relaxation. I was in the little chantry chapel of Bishop John Stanbury who was Chaplain to King Henry VI. The chapel is said to be in the same perpendicular style as the chapels of the King's famous foundations at Eton College and King's College, Cambridge.

My visit to the Cathedral was brief, and I missed the opportunity of seeing the chained library, the home of the Mappa Mundi, the famous map of the world dating from about 1300. I was in no rush and should have taken the time.

I walked through the pleasant shopping streets of Hereford town centre. The sun was shining and the shops were busy. My walk took me up Aylestone Hill just as the College was turning out. Students flocked past me heading down the hill towards town; they were young, happy and bumptious but very well-behaved.

On the outskirts of Hereford, just before the houses gave way to fields, I came upon an enigma. I was standing in front of a very large pair of metal ornamental gates which bore the legend 'RAF HEREFORD'. The gates looked new, and the land behind the gates resembled a nature reserve not an RAF camp - not even a disused camp. The gates couldn't possibly be new. No one today could make such a magnificent structure. On closer inspection, I determined that the gates had been expertly cleaned and renovated. What were they doing here? There was no one around to ask and it was much later that I learnt that the gates had in fact been renovated, having been for many years at the entrance to the now disbanded RAF Hereford. They had, in 2006, been placed here at what was to become Aylestone Hill Park, new parkland for the people of Hereford.

I walked away along a country lane heading north. A mile or so further on I came upon an ancient standing stone, the Wergins Stone. It stands in a meadow some 20 yards from the road to Sutton. The Wergins Stone has a shaft nearly five feet tall, set into an irregular pentagon base just short of four feet wide. In the 1720's Daniel Defoe, in his 'A Tour through the Whole Island of Great Britain', had himself visited this spot and he wrote that during the Civil War the Stone was moved to its present location by 'twelve score places' and that a team of 'nine yoked oxen' were required to draw it.

On this evening, I had the stone to myself. Try as you may not to, you can't help but reach out and touch it. It's the same with all these ancient standing stones; you naturally want to touch them. By touching them you immediately get closer to the stone and the people that made them.

I walked on through the village of Sutton St Michael and on the map I noticed that at the other side of the village there was an ancient iron-age settlement called Sutton Walls. I was eager to see it. It was difficult to get up to it and it's certainly not very photogenic. From every viewpoint that I managed to find, the fort looked nothing more than a high hedge, a continuous hedge and no point of entry. The map showed the hill fort to be 'elongated ovoid shaped'. I never got this view; perhaps an aerial photograph was necessary. In years gone by this hill fort was scandalously used as a gravel pit quarry.

By now it was getting well on into the evening and I still had a good walk to go. I walked into the long straggly village of Marden, which hugs the River Lugg on one side and a slope of a hill called Paradise Green on the other. The ancient St. Mary's parish church sits by the river at the entrance to the village. On the face of it this was another pleasant little village on the outskirts of Hereford with neat houses and well-tended gardens.

Up ahead as I walked, I could see the lights of the village shop open and apparently doing a roaring trade, judging by the crowds of people standing around outside. I was in for a shock. As I got nearer I could see that the crowds of people were in fact East-European agricultural workers. Nearly all were men and very thin, emaciated, with short hair, unshaven chins and dark, deep sunken eyes. They reminded me of the war-time photographs of survivors of concentration camps. None of them looked healthy. They looked poor. More than that they were unfriendly. I smiled and said, "Hello". None of them replied or even smiled back. I felt as though I had walked into the middle of a Zombie B movie. For the first time in months I felt decidedly unsafe. I wanted to get past them quickly but more and more of them kept appearing from side streets, all walking towards me and the shop.

After what seemed like an age, as the evening shadows darkened, I finally left the 'Zombies' behind and made my way up a gentle country lane and out of the village. I had briefly visited Marden without seeing or hearing about any of its three, yes three, Legends.

Theo Lang in his 1948 LEJOG book 'Cross Country' describes all three in detail, Legend no 1 tells, Of the murder at Marden of Christian King Ethelbert in 792AD by King Offa (he of the dyke fame) Legend no. 2 tells, Of the Marden Bell, an ancient Church bell that fell into the River Lugg and was kept under the spell of an evil Mermaid. Legend no. 3 tells, of a Celtic Bangu - a bell that held supernatural powers and used until quite recently to toll the dead. The Marden Bangu is now in Hereford

Museum. There was a definite spooky atmosphere in Marden and it was easy to appreciate that here was a place where a King had been murdered.

At the brow of a hill I came level with a large residential farm complex with well-maintained beautiful gardens. In the corner of the garden and nearest to the road, a large wealthy looking extended family were enjoying a balmy spring evening barbecue. Children ran happily amongst the adults. It was a joyful scene to behold, especially when compared to what I had just walked through. Perhaps it could be said that I was staring. I saw a little girl approach one of the men in the group. He was a fine Errol Flynn-type figure of a man, wearing an open-necked, white shirt with fawn coloured riding trousers and highly-polished dark brown riding boots. The little girl whispered something to him and he immediately looked up and stared directly at me. I imagined the little girl had said to the man, "Daddy, one of our slave workers has escaped and is staring in at us from the road". Initially, the man was tense but on seeing me his body immediately relaxed and again I imagined him saying to the girl, "No, it's alright dear. He's not one of our immigrant workers. I'll get Henry to get the guns and check that they are all back safely in the compound after their visit to our village shop".

Evening was fast approaching and it was getting dark. I still had a good walk to do to get to the campsite. I walked on along a deserted lane. At a junction, I came upon a building with a plaque set high on a wall. It read, *'School house set up 1610 by Jane Shelley, widow of Wm. Shelley, who suffered for plot in favour of Mary Queen of Scots, 1583'*. The building looked well-maintained and was now possibly a dwelling house.

I walked on in the encroaching gloom. I entered the village of Stoke Prior down a steep lane. The village appeared to be made up of detached cottages set well back from the lane in their own gardens. It looked prosperous. I was shocked therefore when I crossed the village centre, a crossroads and saw the village pub which had peeling paint and rotting window frames on the outside. None of the windows, which were dirty, had any curtains. It was a 1960's monstrosity with no warmth or appeal. The clientele didn't look at all like the villagers I imagined lived and owned the delightful-looking cottages I was passing. It might have been the best pub on the entire journey but as it was an awful-looking place, totally out of character with the rest of the village, I kept walking until I reached the campsite.

Walking Day 29 *Dry and sunny*

May Saturday 26

| Stoke Prior to Ludlow - 11 miles - Total walked 321 |

It was a clear and bright day with a slight chilly wind.

Kay and Ripley joined me for the walk to Leominster. We had an audience as we walked away from the site; a young man who worked nights at the nearby chocolate factory and lived in a caravan on our site; he was drinking cans of beer. He assured us that "he was not an alcoholic" but needed the drink to help him get off to sleep. The man, who was a collector of scrap metal who I mentioned before, was up with our night worker together with the owner of the site, our friendly farmer. They all watched us as we took to the lane and walked towards the bridge. The owner of the site had told me that the area was blessed with beautiful walks although "nowadays no one uses them".

We crossed over the busy main road and walked into Leominster through an industrial estate. This route into town gave us the impression that Leominster was scruffy and somewhat neglected. As we passed the railway station we counted numerous teenage girls, all dressed up and leaving their home town by train for the bright lights and shops of some other nearby city, possibly Hereford.

On arriving at the town's main square, we saw a hive of activity with plenty of people shopping. It is a traditional, old English square with many 'black and white olde worlde' timber framed buildings, pubs and shops. Some did need some love and attention but in the main I was pleasantly impressed.

I joined the queue at the post office to get my LEJOG end-to-end certificate stamped. We then left the hustle of the shops and walked down an alleyway into a beautiful park. At the far end of it we could see the historic Grange Court building, built in 1635 and re-located here in 1853 after becoming a traffic hazard. The beautiful black and white timbered building was purchased by the local council in 1938 to prevent it from being bought and moved to the USA.

A friendly cafe tempted us and we sat outside in the sunshine enjoying coffee and bacon sandwiches whilst looking on at a very English scene; a plant sale. The stalls were scattered around the park and people were sauntering between them. The stallholders were a typical bunch of 'eccentric' English men and women. Some of the men, who had names like Rupert, were dressed in whites and had floppy sun hats. The women were elderly, trim and proper. Plants, wrapped carefully in newspapers and cardboard boxes, were exchanging hands at a frantic pace. The whole scene was a joy to watch.

I said goodbye to Kay and Ripley and climbed over a small wall into the mature grounds of the large and imposing Priory Church. I made my way to the church. The vicar was outside the door welcoming a small crowd of well-dressed people. I guessed a wedding was about to take place so I missed going inside which was a shame as I wanted to see the famous ducking stool which is preserved here. It was last used in 1809 to duck Jenny Pipes, the last nagging woman to be ducked in England. Instead I wandered into the grounds of the Priory Abbey gardens, the site of Leominster Priory. Once visited by King John, it had been the home of a monastic community for over 900 years up until the dissolution of the monasteries in 1539.

After a good look around, I left by a snicket and emerged onto a wide street of imposing shops; antique shops. I window-shopped my way slowly along this road, stopping to admire the display in the windows at the 'famous' barometer shop.

I then began my walk out of Leominster along the very busy A49. Cars, Land Rovers and other vehicles, nearly all driven by middle-aged to elderly couples, formed a traffic jam of about a mile heading into town.

I cogitated on the scenario; Leominster obviously supplied the needs of these motorists flocking to the shops this Saturday morning, contrasted against the early scene of teenage girls flocking out of town by train to shop elsewhere.

I walked on a wide pavement along the busy A49 climbing gently away from Leominster. After a mile, I left the busy road and moved up on to a wooded ridge, a footpath marked on the map and named as the 'Stockton Ride'. I was hoping to follow this north for a good few miles. I believe it is an old Roman road. I discovered a good path through mixed woodland well used by local dog walkers. I was striding out, marching through the Hereford Marches, then the footpath began to fade from view; the dog-walkers obviously turn around and go back the way they came. Soon the path became barely visible under a jungle of nettles and bushes. I had to fight my way through, hacking at the nettles with my trusted stick. Eventually the woodland was left behind and the path continued faintly along the tops of some very big fields full of crops. The sky was blue and I could see for miles across the rolling countryside of Herefordshire.

On and on I walked across field after field, each with a stile or gate at the boundary. I felt as though I was the first person to use them in years. As I approached the last field on this route my way forward was barred by a large deposit of sewage slurry. Although the slurry had a crusty top, it wouldn't have been strong enough to hold my weight. The slurry tip was huge and went off in all directions. I had to walk 'miles' around its edges, cursing the farmer for dumping this waste on a public footpath.

I eventually climbed over a fence and came out back on the busy A49 at a place called 'The Hundred'; a tiny hamlet of cottages. I scoured my maps for a way forward. There seemed little else left other than to follow the road, the busy road, which on this stretch had no pavements at all. I made good progress, dodging cars and lorries as I made my way northwards.

At Ashton, I passed by some interesting old barns built of red brick. One had a bell tower in the shape of a cupola. Others had steep roofs with white, fan-like contraptions that reminded me of Kent and their Oast houses. After more dodging of cars, I came to a lay-by with a tea van from which I bought a much-needed cup of tea.

Then a short walk along the road led me into the pretty village of Brimfield, the last village in Herefordshire. Shropshire beckoned.

The church at Brimfield has a striped tower, white wood and red bricks. It is very unusual for an English church. It was locked so I moved on and crossed over the county boundary into Shropshire.

I took a quiet 'B' road into Ludlow. I passed the cattle auction site and walked down to the ancient stone bridge over the River Teme. I stood on the bridge and admired the river scene that was now in front of me. Ludlow is set high on a hill above a bend on the river which is bordered by beautiful woodland. The view of the town is here dominated by the massive 135-foot-high tower of the Church of St. Laurence, one of the largest churches in the county which reflects the prosperity of medieval Ludlow.

Today there are over 500 listed buildings in Ludlow.

I walked up the hill into Ludlow through an old gateway and into the wonderful market square. There has been a market here since at least 1189 when its charter was granted. At the top of Broad Street stands the 16th Century Butter cross building. The market was in full swing, busy with crowds of people. The shops around the square were marked by their individuality and quality. A sprinkling of good-looking cafes and restaurants completed the scene. There was more; the square opened out into a bigger square which marked the entrance to the castle; an 11th century Norman castle set high in its own grounds overlooking the river and woods below. The castle was once the administrative centre for the Council of Wales and the Marches.

The poet, Sir John Betjeman wrote; *'possibly the best little town in England'* and the travel writer A.G. Bradley writing in 1905 wrote; *'the most beautiful and distinguished county town in England'*. I wouldn't quite go along with them but Ludlow certainly has to be up there; if not at the top, then very near it. It's an old town full of charm.

May Sunday 27 — Rest Day

Today we set about moving camp. All the usual suspects came out to watch us, the beer drinking night worker, the scrap metal collector and our friendly farmer. They looked like a scene from 'Last of the summer wine' as they all leant against the fence. Bearing in mind that it had rained heavily during the night and the field sloped upwards towards the road, the three men obviously knew what was about to happen. We innocently hooked up our car to the motor home and waved the three of them good bye. We didn't move an inch; wheels spun round and mud flew everywhere, including all over the sides of the motor home and our Nissan. I tried again, sliding across the field but not progressing an inch forward. I got out and decided to unhook the car. The three men watched and never moved. I got back in the motorhome and tried again. This time I slipped across the field with mud flying in every direction, except at the fence where our audience were safely watching.

Kay got in the rally car (the Nissan) that was hidden under a blanket of mud. The windscreen wipers made little impression to clear a view but she did manage to drive up the by now muddy track towards the gate. We had rescued the car but what about the Motor home? I gave Kay the keys and she had a go. It was like watching a funfair ride as the Motorhome slid all over the place anywhere but uphill towards the gate. After what seemed like an age the Farmer eventually shouted, "This always happens, do you want me to pull you out with my tractor?" Our eager reply, "Yes please" hid my real thoughts of 'Why the bloody hell didn't you say so to begin with'.

His tractor soon had us pulled up the field and to the safety of the metalled road. I thanked him for his help and looked at the mess we had made of his caravan site; it looked more like a battlefield. We moved off and were glad to be away. We vowed never again to park on a sloping grass pitch if possible.

We drove up to Orleton just outside Ludlow. There we found a small site run by an

79

old couple. It was situated in their garden and the toilets were inside a converted shed. We had a grass pitch but at least it was level. I spent some time cleaning both car and Motor home, helped by the rain. It continued to rain heavily.

May Monday 28 | Walking Day 30 *Steel grey skies but mainly dry, just one shower*
Ludlow to Plowden - 11 miles - Total walked 132

Being a Bank Holiday, Ludlow was very busy with crowds of people. I walked away and down the other side of the town by lots of antique shops and passing the famous Feathers pub, built in 1619, with its exuberant timber framing.

Still in the town but at the bottom of the hill I reintroduced myself to the River Teme. Here, overhung by willow trees with swans begging for food from the many passers-by, it completed a perfect English scene. I walked on past the new school buildings and sports centre and then on to the road leading to Ludlow Racecourse.

A good footpath led me alongside the busy Ludlow road. I crossed a railway bridge and was welcomed by a sign that read, *'Ludlow Racecourse next meeting: - October'*. Here today, in May, October seemed a very long time away.

A footpath led into the course itself, on behind the main stands and then behind the stable blocks. I followed it taking in the course sights as I strolled along. My peace and solitude was suddenly shattered by the sound of large dogs barking ferociously. I glanced over to my left and saw, behind the flimsiest of fences, five loose Alsatians. They were going berserk, barking and jumping up at the fence, a fence that looked as if at any moment, it would collapse with the weight of one dog let alone five. I quickly scanned my surroundings for an escape route or place of safety. Being behind the locked main stand building there didn't appear to be one unless perhaps the entrance doors were open. The dogs were by now frantic with excitement; jumping and barking even louder; howling. I might be able to hold one off with my stick but there was no chance with five.

I continued to walk, quickening my pace; trying to look as though I belonged in the place. I couldn't understand why with all this howling, the dogs' master hadn't been alerted. I looked but saw no one. The dogs must surely smash down the fence and be on me. I kept walking and hoping all the time that the dogs would soon be under control. I came to a sign that read, *'Danger, Guard Dogs'*. The sign amused me and I began to laugh. The dogs were now behind me and as if by magic, the danger, whilst not in my direct line of vision, was also behind me. I walked on and away from the dogs.

I left the racecourse behind and walked along a quiet country lane sunk deep between hedgerows. To my left was the railway line and beyond that the River Onny, both of which I followed to the small village of Onibury.

This is still a working-farm-type village with milking sheds that open onto the road. I made my way to the church which was at the centre of the village. It was open.

Here I ate my snap before having a good look around. There has been a church in Onibury since Saxon times. The present building is mainly 13th/14th-century with a semi-circular chancel arch ornamented with zigzags, pellets and beads. It was a joy to explore. An ornate balustrade bearing the coat of arms of Edward 7th adorns a minstrels' gallery at the west end of the church. A 14th-century tower contains a belfry with bells that were rung for the Millennium but normally remain silent due to the 15th-century bell frame being rotten.

I was intrigued by a notice that declared the vestry contained - *'a uniquely designed horse-drawn funeral bier, last used in 1950'*, together with a - *'19th-century hand bier'*. Try as I might, these articles remained out of sight behind the locked vestry door. So, they should. The church silver was stolen in 1783, brass candlesticks were stolen in 1988 and cut-glass replacements were also stolen.

I made a record of my visit in the visitors' book and walked out into the churchyard and sunshine. Between the church and the lych-gate is a magnificent, rare and ancient cedar tree brought over from the Lebanon.

I came to the village notice board where I read and learnt about the Onibury pippin, an apple first cultivated by a Thomas Andrew Knight in 1790. It is said that the apple has a distinctive taste of lemon meringue. I wish I could have tasted one. Unfortunately, Craven Arms, which was the nearest village with a shop, sold only French golden delicious. The Onibury apple trees could be seen in the Onny School playing fields but at this time of year there were no apples of any size on them.

I walked on, crossing the main road and the river bridge over the River Onny, passing as I did the building that once housed the village's railway station. On crossing the railway line, I turned right through a series of farm buildings and up onto a large, recently-ploughed field. I decided to follow one of three way marked routes that merged together heading to the next village of Craven Arms: The Shropshire Way, the Onny Trail, and the Three Woods Walk. All of them were excellently way marked. I made my way slowly up the large field heading to a derelict farmhouse, high up on the horizon. Large parts of the footpath had been ploughed and I soon got clarted-up. Each stride uphill became heavier and heavier as the mud clung to my boots. I climbed over a couple of broken-down stiles and after much effort I reached a good track where I could kick the mud from my boots. The track wound its way down through some beautiful deciduous woodland, high above the river. After the ploughed field this was a delight to walk. The sun even tried to break out and I walked along under a canopy of varied shades of green leaves with dappled sunlight breaking through.

I headed downhill out of the trees towards the valley floor with a view of a magnificent mustard and black-coloured mansion house, the castle of Stokesay, said to be the best fortified mansion house in England. Its English heritage flag flew high from its tower.

The American Jesse Barker Gardner who motor toured from Land's End to John O'Groats wrote about it in his 1930 book of the same name, *'I just stood spellbound before the quaint and beautiful thing, so unique in the combination of military and domestic architecture, dating back to the twelfth and thirteenth centuries and still intact. Its exterior is delightful'.*

As I approached the mansion house I became aware of crowds of bank holiday sightseers. I was soon strolling around the mansion in their company.

I walked on a pavement along the busy road into the village of Craven Arms. I knew that the Craven area of Yorkshire is named after a Celtic word for garlic, 'craf', meaning *'area where wild garlic grows'.* I wondered if there was any connection between the two Cravens. I was given my answer early in the town as an information board informed me that the Earl of Craven (from Combe Abbey, Warwickshire) gave the town its name, developing it as a sheep trading centre. Craven Arms was an early railway town. The sheep were brought in from the local hills and sent away from here by railway. I noted a piece of modern sculpture, of sheep in varying sizes and then made my way into the surprisingly modern town centre.

The cafe was easy to locate being a bank holiday Monday. Swarms of motorcyclists were parked all around it. I stuck out like a sore thumb as I ordered a much-needed refreshing cup of tea. I looked around at the rest of the customers, every one of them, men and women, dressed in black leather motorcycle outfits.

The language being spoken by this group was English with a definite dialect which was strange to my ears. I listened as best I could but couldn't quite make out what was being said. I took it to be a deep Shropshire dialect. I'd like to repeat some of the dialogue but can't. It was a blur of undulating, melodic sounds. The cafe door opened and a man dressed very much like toad of Toad Hall, complete with large goggles, walked in. All eyes swivelled to him and I felt a little more comfortable. The crowds of motorcyclists outside were now crowding around 'Mr Toad's' vehicle, a beautiful old Bentley painted in British racing-green colour.

Craven Arms has its own small supermarket; not Morrison's, Tesco or Asda but 'Harry Tiffins', a small family-run business and long may it last.

I walked out of town along the main road which had a pavement. I wanted to walk the Long Mynd, a famous Shropshire, whale-back hill and I wanted to walk from south to north. To do so I had to deviate west for a few miles to Plowden.

The road to Plowden was very busy, being a main road that eventually led into Wales. There was no pavement and the grass verge was overgrown. It was a dangerous and tortuous route I walked and not to be recommended. Cars and trucks seemed to be aiming for me every few seconds. All I could do was lean into the verge as best I could and walk and trot when the coast became clear. Whilst doing this tedious task I came upon a pheasant sitting on her nest. Even as I bore down on her she resolutely refused to move, except for the flicker of her eyes. The busy traffic didn't seem to bother her as much as it did me. I quickly left her behind. Reaching Plowden which I found to be not so much a village as a hamlet and telephone kiosk on a road junction, Kay arrived to pick me up.

That night we visited an old detective friend of mine and his wife. He had recently retired and moved from Bradford to Stourport on Severn, Worcestershire. We had a really nice evening enjoying a good meal and good company in their lovely home.

It was the first time we had been inside a house in over a month.

It was a long drive back through twisting country lanes which were pitch-black but on our way, we were lucky to see several sightings of badgers, shuffling along the edges of the lanes on their quest for worms. The next morning, we moved camp up to Shrewsbury.

Walking Day 31 *Rain and mist*

Plowden to Leebotwood - 9 miles - Total walked 341

We set off early for a change and relied on our Satnav to guide us back to Plowden. I was a little surprised at first, as I thought the quickest way would have been down the A49, past Church Stretton and back along the A489 to Plowden. The Satnav had other ideas and soon after leaving Shrewsbury, took us on a journey at the back side of the Long Mynd. Rain and mist were on the hills but here, down in the valley bottoms, it was clear and dry. The rural scenery was stunning with beautiful green fields and rolling countryside. The narrow lane we were following had grass growing in its middle. Should we continue to trust the Satnav? We came to a gate which I had to open whilst Kay drove the car through. We came to another gate and then another. We really were exploring the *'back of beyond'* (an Australian term meaning 'the land beyond the mountain range'). In our present situation, it was the land between the Shropshire hills and the Welsh border.

I don't know why but it had a magical feel to it; a land that had been bypassed and forgotten. The lane led us into a stone-built farmyard and we really thought the Satnav had done its worst. However, after opening a gate at the other side of the farmyard we were out and back on the lane with the brooding mist-covered mass of the Long Mynd now accompanying us over to our left. We came to an old quarry turned into a car park. Here Kay took Ripley for a short walk up the hillside. Then with Kay and Ripley back in the car we were off again, soon arriving at the road junction that is Plowden. The rain and mist, far from clearing, had in fact moved down into the valley bottom.

I said goodbye and began the steep climb up the Long Mynd. The mist got thicker and for the second time on my journey I used my compass, setting a north bearing and following it. The path I intended to follow began here in the south and aimed north in a straight line. The problem was that the Long Mynd is criss-crossed with paths from every direction and the mist made path-finding so much more difficult. All the lovely views of the Shropshire hills were lost to me as I climbed up, enveloped in the thick swirling mist. It was cold so I put on an extra layer of clothing and climbed on. I found I was on a well-signed bridleway - the Jack Mynton Way. I climbed up and onto Black Knoll where I saw both heather and bilberries. I was reminded that the Long Mynd is Britain's most southern heather moor where the exclusive British red grouse breeds. I kept my ears open for that exploding alarm call, 'qurrack - rack - rack', or 'go-back, go-back'. Before the day was out I had heard it many times but with the mist swirling in waves like ghosts I never managed to get a good view of one.

Having at last reached the 'northern' heather moors of Britain, could I declare that I had finally moved into Northern England? Maybe, perhaps, but not quite; that elusive line between North and South was here, somewhere about but it is a line much debated and not truly set.

From the first heather bush that I came to, I plucked a sprig of heather for good luck. I later placed it in our Nissan Micra behind the tax disc, and that's where it remained for many a year.

Through the mist, I kept seeing what I thought were people up ahead. As I came closer I realised they were not people but patches of mud. There was no one else up here on a day like this. At last I reached the plateau top and strode ahead on a lovely path of short grass. Not before too long some strange shapes came into view, shrouded in the mist. At first I was puzzled, but very quickly I discovered they were row upon row of glider carriages or towing boxes. One or two gliders were out on the field but it appeared most were locked away in their boxes. There would be no flying or gliding on a day like today. The Glider club was eerily silent as I walked past.

For a while I walked alongside a metalled road which I believe was called The Portway. I thought I might have seen a car on this road but it wasn't to be.

Leaving the road behind I began climbing again, up through the heather to the trig point at Polebank, the highest part of the Long Mynd at 1,693 feet above sea level. Visibility here was atrocious.

As I stood by the trig point I heard from over to my right, what I thought was a baby screaming; a baby in obvious pain. I moved slowly towards where the screaming was coming from and was most relieved to find a sheep mimicking a human baby and not at all in pain from what I could see.

The moor at this point took on a wilder look, enhanced by a darkening, grey sky and the swirling mist and rain... Just what I needed. I could hear the distinct lone cry of a curlew coming from the direction I was heading. Two snipe flew up in front of me and then flew zig- zagging away at speed. A sign declared, *'Ring Ouzel breed in this area'*, but I didn't see any. I walked on and disturbed yet another snipe that flew out from beneath me across the heather.

I came across some Grouse shooting butts named as the Robin Hood butts. (He gets everywhere). I was now walking downhill and after a while I came upon a motor road which was single track and devoid of traffic. I followed it for a good mile or so until I came to the National Trust sign declaring that Long Mynd is owned by that organisation. I was now at the northern-most tip of the Long Mynd and the road began to descend steeply. As I lost height, the sun burst through the mist and I was able, at last, to enjoy some spectacular views of the unfolding Shropshire countryside. Skylarks began singing making the descent even more pleasurable. I followed the road down through the pretty village of Woolstaston which rests at the northern foot of the Long Mynd. I continued further down following a stream of water flowing at the side of the road. I eventually arrived out onto the main road, the A49, at the village of Leebotwood with its distinctive and shapely thatched-roofed pub which goes by the name of the 'Pound'. I walked in and bought my usual thirst-quenching drink; a pint of lemonade and pineapple. I arranged for Kay to pick me up from here and waited for her in the delightful beer garden. I had enjoyed an exhilarating and awesome walk in the mist.

<table>
<tr><td>May</td><td rowspan="2">Walking Day 32 Mixed, heavy showers and sunny</td></tr>
<tr><td>Thursday
31</td></tr>
</table>

May	**Walking Day 32** *Mixed, heavy showers and sunny*
Thursday **31**	**Leebotwood to Shrewsbury - 11 miles - Total walked 352** ▷

I walked away from the Pound Pub and the busy A49 down a quiet country lane with hedgerows in full bloom. The sun was shining and the hills of Shropshire were visible all around. They presented a shapely and more photogenic scene than did the Long Mynd which appeared to be hiding behind rolling countryside. Having studied my maps the night before I knew I was in for a low-level stroll into Shrewsbury. Rich, green hills going by the names of, 'The Lawley', and Welsh sounding, 'Caer Caradoc', loomed around me, looking enticing with ridges that demanded to be walked. Unfortunately, they were in the wrong direction and I reluctantly left them behind.

I found myself walking by substantial working farms with farmers in the yards with dogs, chickens, cows, sheep and horses, all to be seen.

I was walking on a very quiet narrow lane running straight through beautiful countryside. I realised I was on an old Roman road. I thought they would have gone to Shrewsbury but apparently, this was not to be. The road missed Shrewsbury by a good few miles. I discovered that I had been walking along Watling Street West, a Roman road that headed from Wroxeter to Kenchester, (back down to the Welsh border). Watling Street itself headed from Dover to Wroxeter or Virocanium which was much bigger and more important than it is now, being overshadowed today by its near neighbour, Shrewsbury.

The road dipped down and across a beautiful, cobbled ford. The water in the ford barely came up to the soles of my boots. I noticed a stone clapper bridge with a metal railing which crossed the stream for the use of pedestrians. The bridge was overgrown with nettles. I could say with certainty that the Romans hadn't used the bridge but perhaps the Victorians or Edwardians had. Certainly no one recently had used it. Using my 'Leki' walking stick I hacked away at the vegetation until I had cleared a pathway and climbing on to the bridge I said in a loud voice, "I now declare this bridge open for business". A horse in a nearby field nodded its head in an agreeable manner.

A short distance further on I came upon another well-maintained ford with a stone clapper bridge with metal railings all covered in overgrown vegetation. I believed I was experiencing 'de ja vue', until I realised there was no horse nodding in an agreeable manner in a nearby field.

I walked on along this very beautiful country lane. The sun was now beating down and the sky was a bright shade of blue. I walked into the 'sleepy' and pleasant village of Frodesley, where at the crossroads, a wooden bus shelter provided not only shade from the sun but also a seat to rest upon. I ate my snap whilst reading the village notices that had been pinned up on the shelter walls. Frodesley has a busy social life if the notices are anything to go by: bridge clubs, beetle drives, knitting circles, young farmers, gardening clubs, judo and darts evenings. Something for everyone as well as free range eggs for sale with an honesty box for the money. The bus shelter was also home to a lively family of swallows. I sat, mesmerised by their flying antics just a few inches from my head.

Lunch over, I came to a dilemma. A sign at the crossroads pointed to the historic castle and manor house of Acton Burnell, a mere three miles away in the wrong direction. I was heading for Shrewsbury. I had never heard of Acton Burnell so decided to give it a miss. Three miles to reach it would mean three miles to walk back, six miles more than I needed to walk that day.

I have regretted that decision ever since, as Acton Burnell was once the seat of the English Parliament. In 1283, Edward I, that great English King, then fighting the Welsh, had called a Parliament here, in which the merchants were separately represented. It passed the statute of Acton Burnell which made it lawful for a creditor to seize the goods of a man who would not pay his debts and hold them until he did so. Acton Burnell is also home to the Lee family, ancestors of General Robert E. Lee, a Confederate leader in the American Civil war. England is so full of interesting places. I was finding it impossible not to miss some good ones along my route.

I walked on towards my goal for that day, Shrewsbury. On quiet back roads, I passed field after field full of horses; horses everywhere. I walked past the old-World War 2 RAF Condover navigation and cross country training centre. Now the disused airfield complete with old watch tower has been turned into a stud farm and livery centre. A gallop has been laid out around a large flat field and horses were being put through their paces by an army of grooms.

A little further on I came to a sign which read, 'Paddocks for sale' and 'DIY Livery'. Suddenly the quiet road I was walking became very busy with traffic. Women and lots of them in smart little cars containing riding boots and saddle on the passenger seats, all driving fast along the country lane to the stud farm. Their kids obviously at school and husbands at work, they were off riding. What a lovely way to spend an afternoon.

I walked to the pretty village of Condover which has a willow-tree-covered stream running through it. Walking up towards the parish church, passing the rather imposing and impressive grounds of Condover Priory School. This looked like a really good place to be educated if you could afford it.

There has been a church in Condover since Saxon times. The present church of St. Andrew and St Mary dominates the village. It was a Saxon collegiate or minster church with three or four priests attached. The nave is vast and spacious, more so because it lacks pillars. It has a 'hammer beam roof', rebuilt in 1662 and was a delight to see. A notice inside the church tells of a time in the early 19th century when the church plate was stolen from an ancient oak chest which is still there. One Sunday afternoon, a man hid himself in the church and after the service, he broke open the chest and stole the silver plate. The church elders offered a reward for information about the 'evil person' who carried out the theft. Years later a man in prison on another charge, confessed to the crime and led officers to a spot in nearby Bayston Hill where they found the church silver plate buried beside a stream.

Having spent some time inside the church, it was time to move on. I left my usual remark in the visitor's book and went back outside into the glorious sunshine. My way into Shrewsbury was via the Bayston Hill Gap along footpaths and cycle ways. Having been for some considerable time in the quiet countryside, it was something of a shock to find myself crossing a busy outer ring road and stepping into an urban city scene. I walked downhill around the back of the famous Shrewsbury school founded in 1552, an independent boarding school described as *'one of the best schools in England'*.

Then I walked through several housing estates until I came to 'English Bridge' which I used to cross over the River Severn. The same river I had seen down by Chepstow and Aust. Here the River Severn almost encircles the town centre in a gentle embrace.

One of England's finest medieval towns, Shrewsbury City Centre is a fantastic place with lots of quaint alleyways and streets called 'passage ways' and 'shuts', and a bustling shopping centre. Antique shops and book shops jostle alongside dress shops, boutiques and lots of other small independent shops, many housed in quaint 15th century half timbered 'black and white' buildings. I walked past the 'Parade', a specialist shopping centre set in the distinctive surroundings of the Old Georgian Infirmary. I walked by the castle, and library known as Castle Gate Library with its statue of Charles Darwin, erected in 1897 to commemorate Shrewsbury's famous son. Then on to the railway station - 'Wow' - The Victorians certainly knew how to build railway stations and Shrewsbury's is a real gem. It is a fabulous building and looks more like a palace than a railway station. It was designed by T.M. Penson and built in 1848 to service the Shrewsbury to Chester line.

Kay was already there waiting for me. We found a fabulous riverside park, the Quarry, with its show-piece garden, The Dingle, originally laid out as a garden as early as 1719, being remodelled in 1879 and finally being redesigned recently by local man, the late Percy Thrower. It was one of the best we had seen. We finished the day with a Chinese take a way and turned in for the night parked up on our luxury site with all 'mod-cons', secluded bays in a child-free zone, hot and cold water on tap, with waste drain on pitch.

June **Friday** **1**

Walking Day 33 *Hot and sunny*

Shrewsbury to Wem - 11 miles - Total Walked 364 >

I walked into Shrewsbury town centre determined once and for all to resolve one of the 'world's greatest conundrums'; how to pronounce 'Shrewsbury'. I headed for the bank, yes, I'm afraid even when you are on a life changing adventure, you must still do your banking. Standing in the queue I asked a number of locals for the answer to the puzzle, 'Is it Shrowsberry or Shrewsbury?' I received some different replies and nearly caused a riot; on one side Shrowsberry and on the other, Shrewsbury, (supported by the fact that the local football team is known by the nickname, 'The Shrews'). None of this would matter if the place had retained its Welsh name, Pengwern, as it was known before the English arrived in the 7th Century AD.

I headed out of town along the busy Wem Road, being the only person to take advantage of a nature reserve to walk through. I then crossed the busy Outer Ring Road and walked on along a footpath at the side of the quieter Wem Road, now in open agricultural countryside with the hills in the distance. The walking was easy and I soon came to the village of Albrighton.

At the locked church, a fairly modern, red brick building, I looked around the churchyard for the ever-present seat but there wasn't one to be found. So I sat on a wall and had a drink of water and looked out across the fields of crops. Shrewsbury lay below me.

In 1403, the Battle of Shrewsbury took place here and I was viewing the battlefield from the back of the rebel line. The rebels were led by Hotspur, Sir Henry Percy. The King's line was down towards Shrewsbury.

The battle made famous by Shakespeare in his play, Henry IV, Part One. The rebels were defeated by the King's superior numbers. Hotspur was killed and the rebellion put down. I was probably within half a mile of the place where he died, nearer to it than Shakespeare himself had been.

As Hotspur said before his demise, '*Whither I go, thither you shall go too*'. So come on, let's leave the battlefield behind and move on.

From Albrighton I took a back lane through the fields and under a railway line, chuckling to myself at a sign that read, '*Albrighton Hall Farm. No farm traffic*'.

Eventually I arrived at the walled Sansaw Park.

I discovered a gymkhana taking place. I leant on the wall and enjoyed watching the activity. Landrovers were pulling horse boxes. Tents and marquees were already up and bales of straw were stacked up ready for use. In the distance, I could see a show jumping ring with lots of ponies and young girls - nearly all girls - getting ready to compete.

Nearby I found a green metal seat with a plaque that read, '*In commemoration of the Coronation of Queen Elizabeth II 1953*'. Nettles were growing all over and under the seat making it unusable. I soon hacked them down and became the first person to sit on it for some considerable time.

With Sansaw Park behind me, I turned my attention northwards. Rising up from the flat, agricultural land was the modestly high, tree-covered rock face of Grinshill Hill. Stone from Grinshill was used to build the frontage of Number 10 Downing Street.

To one side of this hill was the tall spire of the church at the village of Clive. I set off with a spring in my step eager to explore this new scenery, steadily climbing up a lane that cut deep into the rock, arriving at the top of the hill, near to the Church.

Why do some churches have spires and others have towers? The Naylor brothers in their 1916 'JOG-LE' discussed this topic and came up with this idea; *'In mediaeval times the church tower was often the strongest building in the village. The tower was a good lookout point as well as a strong room where the villagers could shelter safely. Spires were often found in areas where forests and woods abounded. The spires, being visible above the topmost foliage, acting as guideposts'.*

I know churches have towers, usually to hang their bells. All Saints Church at Clive has a magnificent spire at the top of a bell tower.

The church was open and I left the hot sunshine and went inside where it was cool and dark. I found the light switches. I learnt that the beautiful baptistery and magnificent spire had been built between 1892 and 1894 to commemorate a Mrs Bibby, the wife of the squire from nearby Sansaw Hall. Mrs Bibby, was originally from Dewsbury in West Yorkshire and the font here was a copy of the font to be found at All Saints Church, Dewsbury.

After leaving my mark in the visitor's book I made my way out of the village, over the hill and back into agricultural fields. At Shooters Hill, I heard the pee-wit sound of a lapwing and before long I was observing a whole field of lapwings moving about in the stubble. As I walked on, the sound of the lapwings was replaced by the sound of helicopters, lots of helicopters and soon the sky was 'alive' with helicopters. Some were hovering; some were moving up and down. I'd never seen as many helicopters in the sky at the same time. I guessed it was a helicopter school and learnt later it was in fact RAF Shawbury, the home of the RAF Helicopter Training School since 1976.

I walked into the town of Wem. A sign declared that Wem was the home of the Eckford Sweet Pea. Back in 1888 the world-famous hybridist, Mr Henry Eckford, moved to Wem and built up a seeds business which allowed him to continue his work with the sweet pea. Most old-fashioned sweet peas in the world today can be traced back to Mr Eckford. The Sweet Pea Show is held in Wem each year in July.

At the first car park, I came to, Kay and Ripley were waiting for me and we headed for the Co-op to restock.

Walking Day 34 *Hot and sunny*

June
Saturday
2

Wem to Whitchurch - 10 miles - Total Walked 374 >

Wem is a small market town with a population of around five thousand. It can trace its history back to Saxon times when it was called 'Wamm', meaning 'marsh'. I hadn't noticed much marshland walking into the town and on this Saturday morning the market street shops were very busy with shoppers.

I saw the amusingly-named *'Wem treacle mine'* which on closer inspection turned out to be a sweet shop and cafe. I resisted going in as having just set off for the day, it was too early to take a break.

I found a signpost indicating north on the Shropshire Way and followed it out of town. I walked, or rather squelched across fields which had just been muck-spread.

Wem, Drayton and Whitchurch along with this area of North Shropshire, form part of a *'Hundred'* which is a division of the Shire; one of twelve in Shropshire from pre-conquest times, i.e. Saxon. *'A division of the English Shire corresponding to the 'Wapentakes' of Danish areas, e.g. Yorkshire'*. From Brewers Dictionary.

The name of this 'Hundred' is Bradford North and South Bradford as they are more commonly known. It felt strange to be walking in Bradford, a huge area of Shropshire. It contains two boroughs, three market towns, fourteen parishes and seventy-nine villages. It is from this area that the Earl of Bradford takes his title. It has absolutely nothing to do with Bradford in Yorkshire. I have a book called *'Bradford around the world'*, by C. Neville Packett (1997), and I was surprised to find that this Shropshire Bradford is not mentioned in it.

The muck-spread fields gave way to grass land abounding with poppies. I walked by a few impressive large houses with well looked after grounds.

I lost the Shropshire Way footpath signs but found the remnants of the Wem Marsh which was very big. I skirted around the edge of it then my progress was blocked by a number of electric fences. I'd learnt a technique to cross these obstacles, which involved a combination of raising the wire together with one of its poles which I then laid flat, striding immediately over it before re-erecting the pole. Progress was now very slow and laboured.

I was relieved to climb out of this mire and into the village of Whixall, which was mentioned in the Domesday Book.

The first building I came to in Whixall was a Community Centre. I was hoping that being a Saturday, it might be open with a coffee morning or jumble sale or something like that but it was closed and deserted.

I walked along the lane until I came upon the small, Gothic-style St. Mary's Church, built in 1867 of red brick and stone and set upon a raised piece of land. I walked up the path through a pretty graveyard and in a beautiful spot in the sunshine, found the ubiquitous bench I was looking for. I parked myself on it and stretched out my limbs ready for a good rest. I was just getting my flask out of my rucksack when I heard the most awful screeching noise coming from inside the church. I hadn't noticed it was open. The noise startled me. It sounded like a woman in pain. I could hear words being formed within the screeches. I realised a woman was hyperventilating.

I didn't realise until later that I was the cause of all this hysteria. I poured out a cup of tea and was just about to take a sip from it when the sun was blotted out from my view by a tall, gangly young man dressed in morning suit and tails. He had a remarkable resemblance to Peter Crouch, the Liverpool and England footballer. I found out later this young man was called Henry. He had a stutter and like a scene from the film, 'Four Weddings and a Funeral', he said to me, "M m m mother w w w-would like to k k k-know are y y y-ou b b b-bride or g g g-groom". I informed him that I was neither.

He turned sheepishly away and went into the church where I could still hear the hysterical woman sobbing loudly. I began to make out some of her screeched words. "He is ruining the day. That, that tramp has ruined everything".

I still hadn't realised that she was directing all this angst at me. I opened my sandwiches and began to choose one to eat. Henry reappeared and stuttered, "M m m-mother knows y-you are not the b b b-bride's family. Th-th-thats us. C c c-an you c c c-confirm th th th-that you are not the g g grooms side".

I took a bite from my sandwich, chewed it carefully and took a sip of tea   before replying. "Look, I'm not connected to the wedding at all. What time does your wedding start?" Now realising that it was I with whom Henry's mother was upset.

Henry replied that the wedding was due to begin at 3pm but his mother liked to get to the church early, very early and soon her sister and nieces would be arriving and the last thing they wanted to see was a 'tramp' in the church yard. As it was only just turned noon, I reassured Henry that I had no intention of staying until 3pm.

He left me and went back inside the church. I heard his mother screech, "What the hell is he doing here?" Henry replied, "H h h-he's just r r r-resting, mother. Resting. Resting". "Don't you talk to me like that", mother snapped back at Henry.

I continued to eat my snap and just as I finished the last bite a car pulled up containing three women; a mother and two daughters perhaps. They were all dressed-up for a wedding and they began to walk up the path towards the church.

I had taken to treating my inner thighs with Vaseline to prevent chaffing as I walked. To lubricate my legs in such a manner entailed undoing my fly and inserting my Vaseline-covered hand inside twice - one for each side. I thought now would be a good time to perform my daily routine. I imagined the hysterical one fainting inside the church. I left the scene by a side gate and made my way out of Whixall, smiling as I went.

Whixall, like Wem, is surrounded by a bog; a large bog known as Whixall Moss Bog; a site of special scientific interest or SSSI. It is the third largest raised bog in Britain and has been described as a quagmire.

In 1927 a bronze-age axe head was found here. Not wanting to be lost in the bog for such a long time myself, I took some quiet country lanes to Whitchurch, neatly missing the Welsh border at Welsh End and English Frankton. I entered Whitchurch through a pretty looking suburb. Whitchurch prides itself on being Shropshire's oldest, continually inhabited community.

A corner shop with white doves in a dovecote was open and I popped in for an iced lolly, I needed something to settle my nerves after the hysteria of earlier. The shopkeeper turned out to be a South Londoner who was glad to have escaped the 'hell hole London has become' - his words.

On this hot, sunny afternoon, Whitchurch town centre was pleasantly busy with crowds of happy looking shoppers. I strolled through them admiring the good number of varied shops. Some of them were of the old black and white half-timbered style.

There has been a market here since 1284. At the centre of town in the Bull Ring, there is a handsome clock tower dated 1994. Whitchurch is the home of clock towers as local clockmaker J. B. Joyce and Co., established 1690, specialises in them.

I climbed up the street heading north passing antique shops and the like. At the Black Bear Pub, I crossed over the road and went into the grounds of St. Alkmund's Church which towers above everything else here about.

There has been a Church here since Saxon times and this one, built in 1713, is named after a Saxon Prince who was murdered by a rival for the throne of Northumbria. The Church was open and I made my way in.

In the porch, there is a memorial to Lord John Talbot, Earl of Shrewsbury, who was born in Whitchurch and died in France after the Battle of Bordeaux in 1453; the last battle in the 100 years' war. Fifty years after his death his embalmed heart was returned to Whitchurch and buried under the old Church porch. Talbot gets more than a passing mention in Shakespeare's Henry IV, Part one.

Kay and Ripley arrived and we had a leisurely look around the Church.

As well as an interesting modern sculpture entitled Lord of the Dance by John Sutch, there was a striking war memorial in beautiful electric blue, yellow and green coloured tiles depicting St. George and the Dragon, which caught my eye.

Whitchurch is at the northern-most part of Shropshire. It also happens to be the centre of the Cheshire Cheese Industry which is certainly strange as it is in fact in Shropshire. It holds an annual cheese fair and farmers from all over Shropshire and Cheshire attend it.

I was now on my way northwards to Cheshire. The next day we moved the motor home up into Cheshire and for the next few days our base was to be at Delamere Forest Caravan Site.

June
Monday
4

Walking Day 35 *Hot and sunny*

Whitchurch to Bickerton - 12 miles - Total Walked 386

I set off from Whitchurch (known as Medlolanvm in Roman times), by the preserved section of Roman wall, making my way to Jubilee Park - a pleasant urban park commemorating Queen Elizabeth's Golden Jubilee. I found the finishing post of the Sandstone Trail, a 34-mile walk linking Frodsham to Whitchurch, over the Cheshire hills. I was to walk the trail northwards rather than the preferred southerly approach.

I set off, joining the Whitchurch Spur of the Llangollen (pronounced Clangoflen) Canal. The canal runs for forty-six miles, it being a spur of the Shropshire Union Canal but I was to walk just a short distance on it.

I soon came to an unusual swing bridge which, on A frames had a cantilever effect. The canal was extremely busy with narrow boats waiting to go through the staircase locks at Grindley Brook. Which also serves as a major canal user service point with an excellent internet cafe, shop and toilets. I used them all. If you are not careful you can easily get 'sucked in' by watching the canal boats negotiate the locks and I had to pull myself away and move on.

At Willeymoor Lock I left the canal and headed up across gentle hills to St. Chad's chapel which is surrounded by Cedar of Lebanon trees. The chapel, built in 1689, was locked. Services are still held here during the summer including Rogation Sunday, Ascension Day and Rush-bearing Day. It was hard to imagine where the congregation came from as there were no villages hereabouts and farm houses were few and far between.

The fields were full of cows, cow pats and thistles. I negotiated all of them. I passed a large horse-racing training centre and walked for a time along the white-railed gallops, admiring the many fine-looking horses.

My walk led me past some large ponds which were man-made, having been dug originally for sand and 'marl' (composed of clay and lime). The marl was used as a fertilizer to 'sweeten' the heavy soil. Shally Hunt, in her 1997 book, 'The Sea on our left', found a Cornish quote to do with marl; 'A man doth sand for himself, lime for his son and marl for his grandson'.

The walk and scenery changed as I climbed up through the beautiful woods of Larkton Hill and up onto the top of the bilberry-clad hill. I was very surprised to see ripe bilberries so early in the year. Kay makes a delicious bilberry and apple pie from the bilberries that grow on our moor back home in Yorkshire but they never ripen this early. Fluttering amongst the bilberries I noticed a 'new to me' butterfly. It was a 'green hairstreak' and having seen one, it wasn't long before I saw lots more. The name of the butterfly is very descriptive because it is pale green with subtle, dark lines which look like hair.

I was so enthralled by these bilberries and butterflies that it was a while before I straightened up to take in the fantastic view north-west across the Cheshire plain to Liverpool and Lancashire.

At the very top of Larkton Hill there are the remains of the spectacular Maiden Castle; not a stone-built castle but an early Iron Age fort (800 BC to 43 AD), the remnants of which can be clearly seen in the grassy mounds.

I walked on a good path, well-signposted, keeping the views always in sight. I began to climb up Bickerton Hill; like Larkton Hill except it has more tree cover on the top.

Kay and Ripley met me there having parked at nearby Bickerton Church and climbed up through the wood to meet me. I walked back with them to show off the bilberries and the green hairstreak butterflies, not forgetting the fantastic view. It was a lovely, sunny afternoon and we all enjoyed our time up on Bickerton Hill.

Back at the car we drove off to find a country pub next to the Cheshire Polo Ground where we had a pleasant, sunny and relaxing evening in the beer garden.

Walking Day 36 *Hot and sunny*

June Tuesday 5

Bickerton to Delamere Forest - 16 miles - Total Walked 402

On the drive, back to Bickerton I couldn't help but notice that we were passing through a very wealthy area. The houses and gardens were grand and most of them had numerous garages, stables and even helicopter pads. I also happened to notice that we were passing lots of fruit farms; not that these two points could be connected other than that the rich will obviously have plenty of fresh fruit to eat.

It was a beautiful hot and sunny day. Kay and Ripley joined me as we set off from Bickerton, walking uphill through deciduous trees and passing a farm where partridges were scurrying around. We passed spectacular red sandstone cliff-faces, sculpted by the wind and rain.

Each turn in the steep path revealed spectacular new prospects; red cliffs bordered by ancient woodland and dotted with flowering cerise coloured rhododendrons. Eventually we arrived at and touched the trig point, which is the marker at the top of the hill known as Rawhead, 746 feet above sea level, the highest point of the Sandstone Trail. The views were magnificent. Below us were the rich farmlands of Cheshire and over to the north we could see the industrial area of Merseyside and Liverpool.

After posing and taking the requisite 'evidential' photographs I said goodbye to Kay and Ripley who retraced their steps back to the car. I marched forward along the wooded ridge top on a good path.

In 1834, Isabella Bishop, the daughter of the local rector, wrote in her diary of the *'dreadful brigands of Bloody Bones Cave on Rawhead'*, who had been terrorising the neighbourhood and stealing cheeses from the local farms.

Eventually the bandits were captured and eight of them were executed. Other than a passing glimpse of a courting couple yesterday, I hadn't seen another soul so far on this Cheshire Trail and no bandits.

Another climb led me to the top of Bulkeley Hill where, hidden in the woods was an intriguing underground bunker and the remnants of a railway line; all very puzzling, with no immediate answers. It might be nothing more sinister than a covered reservoir.

My attention was then drawn to some amazing ancient oak trees. I have said it before; oaks are my favourite trees. Bulkeley Hill is also home to a fabulous sweet chestnut plantation. Previously coppiced, these magnificent trees were today providing me with much needed shade. The grey squirrel was everywhere and kept me company as I walked on through the woods.

It is always good to look back and as I left the woods behind, I looked back to see, high upon the hill, Peckforton Castle. Built in the 1840's by Admiral Tollemarche and modelled on a Norman castle. It is now a mansion house. My attention was grabbed by a murder of crows mobbing a buzzard. The buzzard eventually escaped their attack - but only just.

Turning to move on, the spectacular view of Beeston Castle was ahead of me. This area is certainly well-endowed with places of interest. I came to the castle's entrance; a well-built gatehouse where English Heritage has its shop and office. I went in, buying cold water and ice-cream which I devoured as I wandered around the ruins.

The castle was built in 1337 by Ranulf Rufus, Earl of Chester, to defend the Welsh border. It is one of the most distinctive landmarks in Cheshire and on this day, I had the place all to myself. With its protecting walls and circular towers, Rufus had it built after the model of those he had seen at Constantinople. It was one of the first to break the mould of the usual English Norman square-shaped castles.

By far the best view of the castle was as I walked away from it and looked back - seeing it perched atop the crags. It seemed to blend in with the cliffs, looking almost natural, as though it belonged there - which it did.

As I was admiring the castle from this angle, a large herd of black and white Friesian cows came plodding up the lane, heavily laden with milk. The farmer at the back of the herd with his dog was a really friendly fellow and we stopped to have a chat. He appeared to be very contented with his lot (which some may say is unusual for a farmer).

I crossed under a busy railway line by a mud-filled tunnel and came out alongside Wharton's Lock on the Shropshire Union Canal. Some boats were going through the lock and again like at Grindley Brook, I had to tear myself away after watching them for a while.

The canal boat people were all friendly, relaxed and healthy-looking. Beautiful neon-blue dragonflies darted about me. They were still with me as I moved away from the canal up along a lane. I learnt later that they were more likely to have been the 'Banded Demoiselle' dragonfly, and it is the male that flutters in small groups. Mark Moxon, in his 2007 LEJOG book, 'When I walk I bounce', describes a similar scene of neon-blue damsel flies darting around his head. He describes it as, 'like I was walking through a Disney film'; a magical scenario I could easily identify with.

I left the lane and crossed fields along excellent paths. I even passed a field full of llamas. The views changed, and over to my right I could see the outskirts of the village of Tarporley, said to be one of the wealthiest places in Britain. I climbed up through fields to the southern edges of Delamere Forest, the paths now steeply climbing up, back into woodland. I crossed over the A54 Manchester to Chester road; the old Roman Road of Watling Street.

Today I was going to end my walk at the Delamere Caravan Site where we were camped but first I had to walk over and through Delamere Forest with its many trails and paths. I tried my best to concentrate and keep on the right track. Ahead of me I could see a large aerial radio transmitter known as 'Old Pale' which could be seen from my motor home on the caravan site, so I knew I was nearly there. The trouble was that this view was with me for a very long time. I kept thinking I was getting nearer then it seemed further away.

Delamere Forest Park, today managed by the Forestry Commission, is just a small remnant of the ancient hunting forest of Mara and Mondrum, used for hunting by the Earls of Chester and later the King; the name sounds like something out of Tolkien's, *'The Lord of the Rings'*.

At last I climbed to the top of 'Old Pale', where I had views across the seven counties: Cheshire, Lancashire, Flintshire, Shropshire, Staffordshire, Derbyshire and Denbighshire. More importantly, I could see my motorhome. I headed downhill towards it passing the Visitor Centre and the natural open arena area where each year, the Forestry Commission put on shows, rock concerts and the like.

June Wednesday 6 — Rest Day

We had a day off from walking and drove into Frodsham where we found a lovely park, frequented by families and well-behaved children. We also found a council-run Internet cafe which was excellent. After visiting the shops, we made our way back to our camp where we put up our sunshade, set the table and chairs outside, and had a lazy time of it in the sunshine, aware that the rest of Britain was being washed away in torrential rain.

It was at this site that we met another Colonel Blimp-type. He marched up to me in a military manner, pipe in hand, pointing at my motor home and declaring, "Ah, yes, a Swift Sundance model 630L. I used to have one, but I traded it in for a Superior model".

I humoured him the best I could for the next half hour or so. You never can shake them off once they attach themselves to you.

In one of her regular letters home, Kay was to write: *'Whilst Christopher was walking, Ripley and I explored Delamere Forest over the next few days. There was a muddy lake not too far from our campsite. The lake was fantastic for wildlife and full of birds. The edges of the lake are smelly bog and mud puddles full of green slime. Ripley managed twice to find her way into the mess - phew. The look of ecstasy on her face as she wallowed made it almost worthwhile. The first time, she was bathed in our fire bucket - which pleased her no end. The second time, she was held under the cold water tap - which pleased her less. I doubt she has learnt her lesson; this hot weather seems to give her an imperative to wallow. Luckily, we managed to find a dog groomers' with a cancellation and with a few snips she is almost naked, quite a bit livelier and much easier to keep clean'.*

I set off from the camp-site on good paths through the forest, and skirted around the edge of the huge lake called Blakemere Moss, which in places is little more than a muddy bog. I left the forest by a back lane which led me through farmland to the edge of Frodsham.

I continued downhill into the historic market town, passing a sign welcoming me and declaring that in 2006 the town had won the *'Best-kept village (large) in England competition'*. It was market day, and busy. As I walked along passing the stalls, I was subjected to friendly jostling from the crowds.

The town has a 'K4-style' public telephone box which is a listed building, it being one of only about twenty left in the country. I stopped to admire it and even went inside. Designed by Sir Giles Gilbert Scott, it is like his more popular 'K6-style', with which we are all familiar, except it is bigger, much bigger and has *'Post Office'* and *'stamps'* named alongside *'Telephone'*. After a full exploration of the telephone kiosk I made my way to the Sandstone Trail marker stone.

The monument, a small obelisk, is prominently placed in the market street and marks the beginning or as in my case, the end of the Trail. I visited the Post Office and had my 'LEJOG' certificate stamped without a problem.

I left Frodsham on the main road heading for Runcorn, passing the ancient fishermen's' cottages, virtually the only evidence left of the fishing industry that was once prominent in this town. On a bridge, I saw a sign advertising a *'Donkey Derby'*. I hadn't seen one of these in years and was pleased to see one being advertised. The health and safety nut brigade would have a field day with a Donkey Derby today I thought.

The main road was busy with traffic but at least I was on a wide pavement. I passed over the River Weaver on an old stone bridge and then across a canal, The Weaver Navigation System on an old, iron swing-bridge which I recognised from years ago. Before the motorway was built this road was part of the route we used to take to get to North Wales for our holidays. The traffic would crawl for miles, and this rusty, old swing-bridge was a landmark back then. Today it is overshadowed by the motorway which passes nearby on gigantic concrete stilts.

I walked into the town of Runcorn. A sign welcomed me and displayed one of those 'PC jazzy strap lines' like a modern-day heraldic motto that read; *'It's all happening in Hatton'*. That's good, I thought but I'm going to Runcorn. Per my map, Hatton was a district of Widnes on the other side of the River Mersey. The truth of the matter is that after the complete organisational 'cock-up' by politicians back in the early 1970's, part of Lancashire i.e. Widnes, was linked with Runcorn, Cheshire and the new district was given the name Hatton so as to offend neither Runcorn nor Widnes. Well it bloody offends me, as do the 'jazzy strap lines' which now seem to spring up everywhere. Lancashire County boundary signs have one that reads: *'Lancashire - the place where everyone matters'*. It is enough to make you sick. I can just imagine a hotel conference room full of self-important people with nothing better to do, wasting taxpayers' money, trying to come up with these 'jazzy' slogans we can all do without.

I walked into town alongside a busy dual-carriageway, on a good footpath and then along Runcorn Heath, parkland that afforded me views over Runcorn, a town of some considerable size with very pleasant suburbs. As I left the park and headed downhill into the town centre a large Grammar School was closing for the day. Hundreds of well-dressed and well-behaved school children were emerging onto the streets. I was caught up with them as they star-burst their different ways home with many heading my way down into town. These are nice kids I thought to myself.

I passed a very large and impressive war memorial. I always stop to read the names and pause to reflect.

I was now heading for the bridge over the River Mersey. I walked through a small area of red brick terrace housing which was obviously the poorer part of town and looked totally alien to anything else I'd seen in Cheshire so far.

I crossed over the Duke of Bridgewater's Canal, built to convey china clay from Cornwall to the potteries in Staffordshire and then to transport the finished products back to the port of Runcorn for onward trading. Here was a direct link all the way back to Cornwall and those 'Cornish Alps' of a few weeks back. I could see 'The Bridge' as it is locally called; a white steel tubular structure that looks like it should be at Blackpool Pleasure Beach or Alton Towers.

The Bridge rattled and shook with the volume of traffic. To my left was an old stone-built railway bridge built from 1864 to 1868, complete with crenellations and machicolations. Why a Victorian bridge should have or need such medieval battlements I'm not sure, but as with all Victorian structures, it looked solid and sturdy. It was very busy with trains heading to Wales from Liverpool.

Halfway across the road bridge a plaque declared the bridge was opened in 1961 and linked Runcorn in Cheshire with Widnes in Lancashire. The River Mersey was down below me, running in a narrow channel in the middle of the estuary of sand and mud. The river looked silted-up and the port of Runcorn down to my right looked isolated and small with some of the quays obviously long-since used. A similar scene awaited me on the Widnes side where some of the old quay walls had been converted into a green park.

I walked into Widnes alongside the busy road until the footpath led me to a subway which I entered. It was a dark, urine reeking subway and in the middle of it, I came across a street artist. She was busy painting a mural on the wall and was squat on a small stool with her paints surrounding her. The mural she was painting was of a Lowry-type street scene and looked impressive. She herself was shy and furtive and wanted to know why I was asking her so many questions. I asked her if the Council was paying her; I got the impression that the mural was unofficial and might be considered by some to be graffiti, which it most certainly was not. It was a good piece of art work that when completed would enhance the subway and I liked it.

I left the artist in peace and re-emerged into the daylight and fresh air. I walked to the end of a quiet road where Kay and Ripley were waiting for me, parked outside a scrap yard with huge mountains of scrap metal. Welcome to Lancashire I thought.

June Friday 8 Rest Day

Today we moved camp up into deepest Lancashire. We found a caravan site at Lathom near Ormskirk. The site was in the grounds of 12th century Burscough Priory. The ruins of which we could see over a wall. Having set up camp we headed into town. Ormskirk turned out to be a friendly place. It had a large Morrison's Supermarket at its centre with plenty of pedestrianized shopping streets leading away from it. I did some banking and found myself talking to a Bradford girl speaking in a familiar accent from behind the cash desk. Apparently, she had married a Lancastrian and moved over to 't'other side ot'Pennines' with no regrets.

We found an abundance of excellent farm shops scattered around the surrounding area, all selling good quality local produce. The delicacy at the time was asparagus; Formby asparagus being noted as the best money could buy. For the next week or so we were to live off asparagus and steaks. Taylor's farm shop at Lathom was particularly excellent; one of the best on our entire journey.

Ripley had developed a limp so we sought out a vet's in Ormskirk. An injection and course of tablets soon had her fit again. Later that evening as we settled into our new caravan site tucked away in a tranquil corner, a lovely tree-lined field in front of us. Our peace was unexpectedly shattered by a large convoy of caravans being pulled onto our quiet patch by several transit vans.

The male drivers were opening cans of lager as they jumped down from their vans. Their next move was to open their back doors and release a horde of kids who noisily swarmed everywhere. A football was produced, a radio was switched on full volume.

To be fair the football only bounced off our van about a dozen times and the kids only swarmed over 'our patch' until midnight. These people appeared to be either related or work colleagues. They were from Liverpool and turned out to be a friendly bunch. Their overt friendliness rubbed off onto us and by the end of the weekend we had enjoyed their company and were truly sorry to see them move off.

June Saturday 9 Rest Day

Another day off from walking. Our friends Tony and Di came over the border from Yorkshire to visit us, bringing with them our post and by now some much-needed memory foam mattresses. They told us we were just over an hour away from home using the excellent motorway network. We were tempted but decided to hold out. Instead we climbed into their large Nissan Patrol and headed for Formby with its National Trust red squirrel reserve.

Formby was just a few miles away. The wooded nature reserve is near a dune filled beach at the end of a very long tree-lined avenue, (Victoria Road). *'The open foreshore, shifting sand dunes, historic asparagus beds and mature pine woods make it a special place for recreation and wildlife'*. (Extract from National Trust leaflet).

With the sun beating down the tree-lined avenue was alive with chattering and laughing people, Liverpudlians, all walking towards the beach. There is a railway station at Formby with a direct line into Liverpool. It appeared the whole of Liverpool was making its way to the beach.

We joined the throng of friendly, good humoured people and walked their way. At the National Trust kiosk after buying a bag of peanuts, we left the crowds and headed into the sand dunes and tree-covered hills. The man in the kiosk shouted to us; "It will be too hot for the squirrels. You might not see any".

After an hour stumbling through the sand dunes searching every branch of the pine trees for red squirrels and failing miserably, we staggered back to the tree-lined avenue with sand stuck between our toes irritating our feet. The tide of humanity was still flowing towards the beach.

Kay, in one of her letters home, described the scene: *'It was like joining a queue outside a nightclub, with groups of glamourous teenage girls with very little clothing on. However, it was their footwear which was most startling; from stilettos sandals to thigh-length boots; I wondered how they would walked on the sand beach? The group of flirty twittering girls were being doggedly pursued by clusters of young men trying their best to be noticed flashing their bare, skinny, and very white chests'.*

Today at Formby, the only red squirrels we saw were ones which had been painted; one on an ice-cream van and the other, the name of a pub. We were desperately disappointed because we'd heard so much about the place. Tony had once been to Southport, further up the coast to, of all places, the crematorium and had seen red squirrels. So, we drove up through Formby's 'Millionaire Row' of fabulous large houses in this 'rich suburb' of Liverpool, to the seaside resort of Southport. I say seaside but you would need a telescope to spot the sea, which seems to be miles out from the promenade. We didn't need a telescope to spot the red squirrels. As soon as we drove into this wooded and shaded grassy area, we saw red squirrels everywhere.

We left Southport and headed back inland. Tony and Di were staying at the Red Lion Pub in the historic and very pretty village of Newburgh. This is also a wealthy village, judging by the quality of the cars parked in the pub's car park. The village has many surviving 18th-century houses along its main street with a village green and ancient cross at its centre. It was once an industrial area with its old coal pits but today it is very refined and is 'the' place to live in Lancashire.

Newburgh's next door neighbour is the village of Lathom, the village where we were camped. The two villages appear to merge seamlessly. The whole area reminded me of the wealthy villages of Cheshire that I had recently left. Not at all like the Lancashire I'd imagined.

During the English Civil War, Lathom, being the seat of the Earls of Derby, was a Royalist stronghold which withstood a massive Parliamentary siege for many months until finally being overrun in December 1645.

The Red Lion Hotel was packed. We squeezed through the crowded bar and headed outside into a courtyard. The rooms of the hotel overlooked this courtyard and the ones upstairs had an open-air balcony corridor which gave the place a continental feel yet it was a typical English scene.

The inn was old and the courtyard would easily have been recognised as such, going back before Shakespeare's time. The Naylor brothers, in their 1916 book, *'JOG to LE'*, give a wonderful description of an old coaching inn, very like this one, where, *'In Shakespeare's time nearly all the acting outside London was done in the courtyards of coaching inns. The actors' covered wagons were drawn into the inn yard while members of their party beat a drum around town to announce their presence. The covers of the wagons were taken off and placed around the sides of the wheels, to act as screens while the actors changed, underneath the wagons. Meanwhile boards, kept at the inns especially for that purpose, were fastened over the tops of the wagons to provide a stage - hence the term - 'to play the boards'. The town's folk came to watch the play and crowded into the inns' stables - more specifically into the 'stalls' - another well-known theatrical term'.*

There was no acting today but the courtyard was crowded with happy and friendly people. It was a young crowd. They didn't look like they'd worked hard all their lives to earn the quality cars parked in the car park. Neither did they look like they'd saved up all the pennies from the years of doing paper-rounds to be able to afford the cars. So, I guessed probably correctly, that mummy and daddy had bought them their cars. Not a cheap banger amongst them.

We managed to find a spare table and spent a very pleasant afternoon in the hot sunshine eating, drinking and trying to do the Daily Telegraph crossword.

 Walking Day 38 *Hot and sunny*

June Sunday 10

Widnes to Windle - 9 miles - Total Walked 421

Tony and Di came around to our site for a stroll and morning coffee before they set off for home. As we waved goodbye we ourselves were leaving the site to make our way back to Widnes. It felt like an age since I had seen the large scrap metal pile welcoming me to Lancashire. Technically the subway artist was the first person I'd seen since crossing the Mersey and technically I was not in Lancashire but Cheshire, seeing as how the 1974 politicians had decreed it to be so. Believe me, Widnes, like it or not, is in Lancashire. It stands out like a wart on the top of Cheshire from which it is separated by the wide and muddy River Mersey.

I made my way on foot to the Victorian promenade. Well-built in granite it looks like it will last forever, which is more than can be said for 'The Bridge', the white steel, tubular structure. A man who looked to be in his late seventies hobbled over to me, "Ah, the bridge", he said. "I worked a good few years of my working life on that bridge. I was a crane driver based on that first stanchion over there", he informed me, pointing to one of about five stanchions.

He went on to tell me that he worked for Fairclough Construction who built the Bridge back in the late 1950's to 1960's.

"It's knackered now; too much traffic using it", he went on. "They're going to build a new one over there", he said pointing up river. I thanked him for his information and said, "Are you a Lancastrian or a man from Cheshire?", "I'm born and bred Lancastrian but the bloody politicians tell me I live in Cheshire now - which I don't". Just as I thought.

The 1961 road bridge replaced an older transporter bridge which had stood on this spot for about one hundred years before it too became 'knackered' by heavy traffic use. The local toy firm, Meccano, made a transporter bridge which they modelled on the Widnes one. I made my way through neat rows of terrace housing, past the huge chemical 'Catalyst' museum, which looked like a good place to visit but it would have to wait for another day.

I took a deep breath and set off through the streets of Widnes town centre. Being from Yorkshire, I have certain prejudices against Lancashire and I wasn't looking forward to this part of my walk. I expected dark, satanic mills and depressing Lowry-type scenes. Many other LEJOG walkers take an inland route up country via Yorkshire and the Pennine Way, but having walked the Pennine Way years ago, and having completed huge sections of it on a number of occasions since then, I'd no desire to walk it again. I'd got this idea to complete my journey without walking in my native county, God's own County, Yorkshire.

Unlike Mark Moxon who, in his 2007 LEJOG book, 'When I walk I bounce', declared many times that he, 'hated the Pennine Way; hated the moor and bogs'. I positively love moors and really enjoyed walking the Pennine Way even in the rain.

So here I was in a 'foreign land'. 'Watch out for the natives', many texts from friends and ex-colleagues were reminding me now that they knew I had crossed over the Mersey. I walked past the town centre pubs with crowds of men standing smoking in their doorways. I expected some 'witty' comments as I walked by in my hiking gear complete with my Leki stick and Tilly hat but to a man, they just stared open mouthed. I judged they were still drunk from the night before.

I left the town centre by a footpath alongside a modern dual carriageway, The Kingsway and walked up hill along it for a good mile or so, passing a huge housing estate on one side and a sixties-style industrial complex on the other.

At Farnworth, remnants of an old stone built village could be made out amongst old red brick terrace housing including, in Pit Lane, an old Bridewell, a stone-built lock-up, now a listed building.

I turned off into quiet country lanes, leaving the town behind and arriving at Clock Face, an old coal-mining village, the Lancashire coalfield having long since closed. The Miners' Social Club was still here in the village along with rows of 'grotty' terraced houses which sadly, had seen better days.

Over a hundred years ago, in 1907, the Lancashire coalfield was at its peak in production; twenty-six million tons of coal per year with over three hundred and twenty pits, employing ninety-four thousand men. The coal was easily obtainable near the surface. The last pit shut in 1993 when economics closed the industry. It is cheaper to buy coal from Poland these days. It is estimated that one hundred million tons of coal is still down there waiting to be dug out. ('NCB and Lancashire Coalfield' website).

I made my way back into the countryside passing large houses, many with a few horses and stables and one with heavy security and large ferocious dogs, thankfully fenced in. The difference between the terrace housing at Clock Face and here was remarkable; two extremes so close together.

I marched on in the sunshine passing not a soul. On the brow of a slight hill I came to the outer suburbs of St. Helen's. Here I could leave the road and walk on footpaths through 'Sutton' nature reserve. With its willow trees, streams and ponds, it made a pleasant escape from suburbia. I had the reserve to myself which eventually led me onto Sherdley Park, a huge heathland adjoining a golf course.

I took advantage of the park to walk downhill into the town centre of St. Helen's. There were quite a few golfers on the course, some dog-walkers and joggers in the park; even a family trying to fly a kite. On leaving the park I came to a huge roundabout with, on the other side of it, a large Macdonald's restaurant. It was packed. I was determined to walk on by but at the last minute decided to go in and buy a cold, vanilla ice-cream milk shake. I was still drinking it when I arrived at another large roundabout, 'Ravenhead', this time with an excellent sculpture of a coal-miner - head and shoulders - and a welcome to St. Helen's, home of Pilkington's glass. The company still manufacture glass here today but mainly window glass.

The roundabout was expertly manicured, clean and as good a welcome as any town could offer to road users. Its name, 'Ravenhead', reminded me of the many beer glasses I used to see with that name and distinctive logo which are, or used to be made here. I was surprised that Ian Marchant, in his famous 2006 LEJOG book, 'The Longest Crawl' hadn't paid a visit here. The traditional British dimpled beer jug with handle, made at the Ravenhead factory in St Helen's by Pilkington's, was discontinued in 2001. Since that time several attempts have been made to restart production but with limited degrees of success; so, we now drink mainly from French-made glasses.

I left the road and joined a canal tow-path to walk past the Pilkington Glass Museum, (I must go back and visit it sometime) and into the very heart of St Helen's.

Rubbish and graffiti were the order of the day. It was truly depressing. A group of about fifteen skinheads with two Alsatian dogs were playing in the canal, jumping in wearing cut-off jeans and not much more. A pipe was pouring what looked like effluent into the canal and these lads were 'showering' under it. I was amazed that none of them had yet cut their feet open on the many broken bottles and empty beer cans that littered both the tow-path and canal.

I walked past them with some trepidation expecting some 'witty' comment. However, like the drunks in Widnes, not a word - not even after I had stopped to photograph their antics. They were a happy bunch - why pay at the local swimming pool when you can come down here for free?

I left the canal and headed into the town centre which looked like it had been completely rebuilt in the 1960's. The only buildings of age were two huge and ugly church buildings. One of them, St Mary's Lowe House Church is a grade II listed building with a Romanesque or Gothic tower and dome. This church has a Carillon of forty-seven bells. From the outside, I'm sorry to say, it looks dark and depressing, not what a church should look like.

Like Widnes, the pubs were busy with people drinking outdoors in the sunshine. Near the modern bus station, one pub was packed with bus drivers, men and women and I couldn't work out if they were just starting, just finishing or half-way through their shift. Two of the options horrified me as they all appeared 'fresh' from their drinking. It reminded me of a scene from the early 1970's classic television TV programme, 'On the Buses'. I looked around to see if a 'Blakey-type' bus Inspector was waiting behind a bus to jump out, catching them all 'at it' and declaring, "Come on you lazy lot, get that bus out". However, there was no bus Inspector and in today's world the bus drivers obviously knew it; they looked so relaxed. Being a Sunday the modern 'Blakey', would be at home having a large Sunday dinner; either that or he'd be on an all-expenses-paid jaunt to Dusseldorf or somewhere like see how the Germans' manage local bus services.

The litter problem was still evident in the town centre and it looked like no one had bothered to clean up after Saturday's market. Just after the town centre I came upon a small but pleasant and clean park, Denton Green Park. It took me away from the centre and out towards the village of Windle. On the outskirts of town, I came to a large crematorium which looked exactly like the one I'd been in earlier in Southport - same architect. The main difference was that here the squirrels were grey and not red.

I waited a short while for Kay to arrive with Ripley and we finished the day by strolling around the crematorium grounds - Oh, I nearly forgot - somewhere between Farnworth and Clock Face, I crossed that modern boundary line between Cheshire and Merseyside! However, as I keep saying, I'm a feet and inches man and it's all Lancashire to me.

June
Monday
11

Walking Day 39 *Hot and sunny*

Windle to Appley Bridge - 9 miles - Total Walked 430

Kay and Ripley dropped me back at Windle Crematorium from where I set off in glorious sunshine. I took a quiet country lane winding through fields. The lane headed down hill, at first towards a bridge over a stream and then rising gently uphill, passing the large Rainford Hall and its park-like grounds, now an independent hospital. As the lane crested the hill I arrived at the small village of Crank. The views behind me towards the coast were glorious, showing an agricultural image of Lancashire that I had not expected. I walked past the unusually-named pub, The Red Cat Inn, which had an ornament of a red cat in its window. It was early in the day and the pub was closed which was a shame as I had heard that the pub, which has become a bit of a 'gastro' pub, adorns its interior walls with snippets of local history, tales of ghosts and the mysterious local Crank caverns, a small network of caves which were frustratingly nearby but well and truly hidden on private land.

I continued for some time along quiet country lanes through similar undulating countryside; very peaceful. I arrived at the village of King Moss, an old coal-mining village, at the same time as a small convoy of cars. I ended up following the cars to their destination, The Collier Pub, which was just opening its doors. The people in the cars were dressed in business suits and were obviously all together, coming here from Liverpool perhaps, to have a business lunch. I nipped into the pub before the crowd had managed to get out of the car park and I ordered my usual thirst-quenching drink. I wasn't surprised to find the glass I was drinking out of was made in France. I moved outside to the beer garden where I studied my maps.

Later, I made my way out of the village, rising gently uphill and passing a large farm shop with cafe and craft shop. I gave the cafe a miss and continued along the lane. At a crossroads, I came upon a taxi driver out of his vehicle and looking over the fields. In a very deep Lancashire accent he asked me, "Do you know where the farm shop and craft centre is please?"

I felt a sense of smugness that here I could give directions to a taxi driver and I sent him on his way with a smile.

At the village of Upholland I crossed into Lancashire leaving Merseyside behind. Upholland, a sleepy dormitory village, has two claims to fame; firstly, in 1323, King Edward II stayed here for a fortnight on his way to Liverpool and secondly, a pig fair was held here every year on Easter Monday.

I passed the railway station and crossed over the very busy M58 motorway and continued along a huge green playing field to the village of Chequer. I passed a nature reserve and fishing lake. An adult fishing day pass cost two pounds. I was heading for another nature reserve I'd spotted on the map called Beacon Hill.

Beacon Hill Country Park is a large hill combining woodlands with meadows, all commanding *'majestic views across the Lancashire plain'*. I was happy with my discovery and I walked on and on. All this walking in hot sunshine was making me thirsty. I kept swigging water from my water bottle but when I saw below me a sign-posted Visitor Centre, I lost height and headed for it, hoping that the Visitor Centre would have a cafe. When I arrived, all I found was an empty field centre classroom and a warden's office, also empty. I reluctantly headed back uphill wondering where all the visitors were. I had the place to myself.

By the time, I reached Ashurst's Beacon, a large stone monolith with spectacular views, I was very dry and thirsty. I took in the stunning views across West Lancashire and headed back to the Prince William Pub I'd just passed. (The ridge I had been walking along was shared with a motor road that I had been ignoring). The instant shade provided by the interior of the pub was very welcome. The only other people in the place were the young barmaid and a female customer. They were both engrossed in conversation and totally ignored me. I stood there listening for a while. It was full of "Get away!" "Never!" "Then what happened?" "I'd never believe it of him!" and "Who was she with?"

Thirsty and irritated by the barmaid's complete ignorance I had to make my presence felt by banging my fist down onto the bar. The barmaid looked up at me, and I took this as my queue to order my usual thirst-quenching drink of lemonade and pineapple juice. Without saying a word to me and still engrossed in her conversation, the barmaid placed a glass of tomato juice in front of me. She immediately returned to her conversation. "Really!" "Go on!" "Then what happened?"

"Oi!" I banged my fist back down on the bar. "What's this?" I said, pointing to the tomato juice. The barmaid looked at me in irritated shock and replied, "It's what you ordered; a tomato juice".

"I didn't order a tomato juice", I retorted.

"Oh, yes you did", she said.

"Oh, yes you did", concurred the female customer.

By now I was ready to explode. I counted to ten and calmly said, "I know what I ordered and it wasn't this".

The 'bitch of a barmaid' eventually gave me what I had ordered and then immediately continued her conversation. I moved away to a corner of the room. I hate poor service of any kind. I could feel my rebellious streak emerging as I decided to leave my by now empty glass on my corner table instead of taking it back to the bar, as is my normal routine. This would teach the barmaid a thing or two I thought, as I slipped out unnoticed by the side door. The incident at the bar irritated me, but the good thing about walking is that you can soon clear your head and that is what I did.

A leafy country lane headed steeply downhill from the pub and I followed it, passing some very large, detached houses in magnificent grounds. This was yet another 'millionaires' row, more akin to those I had seen in Cheshire.

Judging by the unfriendly glares and stares I was getting from the people in their beautiful gardens, I guessed the locals were not used to walkers passing by this way. At a sharp bend in the lane I took a footpath that led through an ancient looking deciduous wood. For a while the footpath followed a stream and it looked and felt as if I was the first person to pass this way for some years. I eventually left the wood and levelled out on the valley bottom, walking alongside the River Douglas, in an area marked on the map as Holland Lees.

The footpath, although visible was incredibly overgrown and my progress was slow. I did manage to get some good views of the river which had a healthy population of mallard ducks with plenty of chicks, a couple of herons and I also saw a kingfisher dart by with a flash of blue.

After beating my way through the vegetation, I eventually arrived back to civilisation in the form of a road bridge. I climbed some steps and found myself at the Village of Appley Bridge. I walked a few yards along the road and came to another bridge, this time crossing the very busy Leeds - Liverpool Canal.

The canal was bustling with longboats and the tow-path was crowded with people, all happy-looking and enjoying themselves. It was a sight I have seen many times near my home in Bingley as this same canal passes through there on its way to Leeds. Just north of Bradford there is a suburb with a similar sounding name called Apperley Bridge, where the Leeds - Liverpool Canal passes through. The canal runs east to west and I was heading north. I left it behind and climbed uphill through the village until I came to a busy crossroads where I called it a day.

June Tuesday 12 — Walking Day 40 *Dull, overcast but dry with slight breeze*
Appley Bridge to Preston - 12 miles - Total Walked 442

In the Village of Appley Bridge there is a small industrial estate. One of the units is home to a business which specialises in deep-sea-diving equipment including mini submarines and at the entrance to the unit, there is an old submarine; it certainly was an unusual sight to see here inland.

The village is also famous for a few other things. I passed the unusually-named Skull House Lane. Legend has it that during the Civil War some of Cromwell's Roundheads chased a monk into the house where he hid in a cubbyhole. The soldiers set a fire and burned the monk out whence he was killed.

His discoloured skull has remained on the mantel piece of the living room ever since. Many residents of the house have tried to get rid of the skull with disastrous consequences. One person threw it in the nearby river only to drown in the same river shortly afterwards. Another man removed the skull leaving it many miles away and later fell down the stairs and killed himself. The list goes on and so the skull remains out on display in the house. Similar skull legends exist in other parts of the country. There is one similar story in the Lake District that I know of but this one here is unique in that a road has been named after it.

As if that isn't enough for a small village there is the story of the meteorite; 33lb of iron rock which in 1914, landed in a field near the village, illuminating the night sky with a spectacular show.

I walked away from the village up a quiet, country lane that led me to Robin Hood Farm. Robin Hood like King Arthur, seems to turn up everywhere. The farm was a busy milk farm with plenty of cows. The country lane wound its way through undulating countryside. I stopped for a while to watch some farmers wrapping silage into big plastic bags using machinery that cleverly wraps plastic sheeting around the cut grass, leaving it to appear as though it is one big, plastic bag. The fields were soon 'littered' with these 'bags'. In some fields the 'bags' were black, in others they were a light blue colour. I don't know what the difference in the colour signifies, if in fact it does?

Some of the farms I passed had farm shops attached and nearly all of them bore signs indicating that *'Asparagus was ready'*. Although the lane was pleasant and easy-walking, I was on the lookout for a footpath. I passed many going east and west but none heading in my direction.

I walked into another wealthy-looking area, the village of Heskin Green. Large detached houses with all the trappings of wealth; swimming pools, sports cars, electric gates and paddocks with stables and horses. The lane took me into the small town of Eccleston. A sign declared it to be the regular winner of the best-kept village in Lancashire.

I walked along its busy main street which had plenty of shops and businesses. Teenage boys with expensive-looking hairdresser hairstyles skated past on skateboards making their way to the sweet shop. A crowd of kids hung around outside. The smell of freshly-baked bread which drifted from a bakers' shop was competing with the smell of fish and chips coming from a small hut-style chippy. I resisted the temptation and headed out of town over the ancient stone bridge that crosses over the River Yarrow.

I could see a beautiful old church across the river to my right but I was in my stride so headed uphill towards a 'thunderingly' noisy and busy main road. After carefully crossing I found a footpath heading north and I escaped the noise and bustle. The footpath turned out to be hopelessly overgrown with thick brambles and no matter how hard I hacked at the vegetation, the denser it seemed to become. I reluctantly gave up and returned, sweating and tired, back to the busy main road.

I headed east along the road for a short while until I reached a quiet road heading north towards Leyland. Amazingly this road possessed a pavement which I followed through pleasant suburbs into the town of Leyland. The town sign declared that Leyland had been making trucks since 1896. I could just make out the massive truck factory with test tracks over to my right.

It was Leyland that gave British Leyland its name, when in the 1960's and 1970's nearly all British motor vehicle manufacturing came under the one name. Truck-making today is still a major employer.

I walked on into the suburb of Earnshaw Bridge with its neat terraced housing and row of shops. I called in to the chemist to restock with Vaseline which I had been using liberally. I was the only customer and I said to the girl assistant, "Is this the lull before the storm?" She didn't understand my meaning and replied, "The weather forecast didn't mention anything about a storm". I left the shop smiling to myself.

At Farrington Moss, I could leave the roads and follow a marked cycle way heading for Preston. I was now in a built-up area but my route was quiet and pleasant. I passed the suburbs of Lostock Hall and Tardy Gate, crossing over railway lines to eventually come out onto the very busy A5083 main road into Preston; at least I had a good pavement to walk on. My entire journey into Preston town centre was accompanied by a constant stream of commuter traffic heading out the other way. The city centre loomed up before me with its many tall buildings of steel and glass, looking like Dallas, from the TV show. Workers making their way home all looked miserable and unhappy, whether on bicycles or on foot; all had a tired gloomy look about them.

At Penwortham, I came upon a beautiful 1930's-style fire station, still being used and complete with a Station Master's house. They don't build them like that these days. I hope it will be preserved.

I walked on into Preston passing row upon row of 'Coronation Street' type housing. I eventually came to an ancient footbridge over the River Ribble, which here is wide and fast. I crossed over the bridge, passing the odd pedestrian. Most people were on the other modern road bridge below that was packed with motorists.

Safe on the other side, I followed the river bank down towards the road bridge through what should have been a pleasant park. Unfortunately, the park appeared unloved; the grass was uncut and litter was everywhere. I found a seat to rest on, surrounded by litter and called up Kay to come and rescue me.

June Wednesday 13 — Rest Day

Today we moved camp up to Cockerham, a lovely quiet camp-site in the woods and fields near Lancaster. Like many of the other sites we had visited, it had a self-service launderette which we took advantage of. On the way, up there we called into a garage where we checked our tyre pressures and gave both our vehicles a good wash.

Through the night, a heavy wind brought thousands of leaves and twigs down onto our recently washed motor home. Well, that's how it goes.

June Thursday 14 — Walking Day 41 *Wet, blustery and showers*

Preston to Garstang - 12 miles - Total Walked 454

Preston has the distinction in English history, of being not just the site of one battle but two. The first was in 1648, when a Royalist force, supported by Scottish troops numbering 24,000, marched south. By the time, they reached Preston the line was spread out over twenty miles from beginning to end. Cromwell, with a force of 9,000 struck in the middle of the line at Preston. Many Royalists were still foraging for food and not at all battle-ready. It was more of a rout than a battle and Cromwell easily won the day.

The second Preston battle took place in 1715 when a Jacobite Scottish army led by Bonnie Prince Charles took over Roman Catholic Preston town and built up its defences. An English Hanoverian force arrived and laid siege to the town. Within days the Jacobites surrendered and their rebellion was all but over. Both battles had strong Scottish connections and this association helped me to realise that I was now nearing Scotland!

I stood in the rain in the Broadgate River Park in Preston which as I have already said, was a complete mess. I was looking at a finely-built row of Victorian terraced houses with 'politically incorrect' staircases leading to their front doors.

The houses have a magnificent view of the wide River Ribble with its ancient stone footbridge. They had once been home to the rich but today they have all been turned into bedsit flats; not very well-maintained ones. Anyone with a bit of money and vision could transform this row of houses back to reflect the grand era that they once belonged to.

I crossed over the road leading to the busy bridge and continued along a lane of industrial warehouses leading to what was once a gigantic engineering works. The works have long since gone and the Manchester regeneration company, 'Urban Splash', have transformed what, on the face of it was a pretty ugly engineering warehouse, into accommodation for the young professional, childless and rich of Preston. The warehouse, as well as containing stylish, modern apartments also had a swimming pool and gymnasium. Looking up from the road I could see into the gym, sorry, fitness lab, through a huge wall of glass.

The compound was secure behind walls and electronic gates. Every now and again someone left the compound in their Porsche or BMW, the gates quickly closing behind them. The apartments in this complex have views across to another ugly warehouse or engineering factory.

At least the old road I was walking along was litter free. On the complex wall, there was a stunning work of art, and I mean stunning. If you are ever near Preston it is worth taking a detour just to see it. It's free and no one else appeared to be walking on foot in this part of town. I doubt you would have to queue to see it. The Sculpture commemorates the previous usage of the Strand Road East Engineering Works, (1863 to 1993). It tells the life story of the metal works starting with early manufacturing of railway engines through to cars, lorries, trams and aeroplanes; all previously manufactured on this spot. This is a piece of public art that deserves more credit. The fact that it depicts an area of manufacturing now all but lost to Britain makes it even more compelling.

I walked on, out of the industrial area and through a huge area of red brick rows of terraced houses. I doubt if many LEJOG walkers ever pass this way, avoiding cities at all cost.

Back in the 1930's Colin Howard in his motor tour described these terraced houses thus: 'The streets abjure individuality in favour of conformity'. He was describing Wigan but his description could easily be valid for Preston except, the streets today contain parked cars which are nearly all different, so conformity is lost.

I avoided the city centre heading out into the suburbs, along road side pavements.

In the Ingol area of town I came upon a newsagent. It had once been a semi-detached house with a garden, the garden having been metalled into a parking lot. A billboard on the wall attracted my eye. It read, 'PNE Mystery'. I stood reading it for some time.

The 'PNE' was a 'mystery' to me and as all good newspaper billboards should, it tempted me to go into the shop and buy the local newspaper. After reading it I kicked myself for not knowing what 'PNE' stood for. I had known but for some reason my brain didn't engage and bring it to the fore. 'PNE' is short for 'Preston North End', the name of the football team hereabouts and the 'mystery' was to do with some financial funding that helped the club over a crisis.

'Wherever I go I always like to buy a local newspaper'. (Notes from A Small Island - Bill Bryson 1995), and so do I preferring to read the local news and letters than those in the politically-slanted morning papers.

The girl assistant in the newsagent's who sold me the paper, whilst filing her fingernails, was slouched over the counter looking bored and fed-up. To make small talk I said to her, "If you are so fed-up you could get a brush and clean up all that litter that is outside the shop". (I'd had to wade through tons of litter just to get in through the door).

Her fed-up look changed to one of hostile anger. "It's not my job to clean up outside", she declared.

"You work here, and it's your shop", I said.

"The shop belongs to Malik and he never bothers to clean up so, why should I?" she replied.

"Okay, but the litter might discourage customers from coming in". I said.

With a sharpness, I wouldn't have given her credit for she quickly replied, "Well it didn't stop you coming in did it?"

True it hadn't but then thirty years of policing, working in the gutter of life, had conditioned me to wade through shit. I left the shop and decided to stop trying to make small talk with the natives.

On the outskirts of Preston, I looked back on a *'Welcome to Preston'* sign. Preston now has a multi-cultural society. The 'politically correct' nut brigade had obviously lost many nights' sleep over what to do with Preston's coat of arms. The traditional sign reflects Preston's Christian history. Preston Means 'Priests' town. Its coat of arms has the symbol of Jesus, as described by John the Baptist as the Lamb of God, (Agnus Dei), usually depicted as a sheep with a cross carried over its shoulder. On the modern coat of arms as seen on many of Preston Council vehicles, the cross has been slimmed down to look more like an arrow and on some signs, I saw a crescent had been placed on top of it taking away the Christian element completely.

The reason for subjecting myself to the city centre walking was so that I could get onto the Preston to Lancaster, Lancaster to Kendal canal, thereby being able to walk right up into deepest Cumbria on traffic-free canal tow paths.

Just before the pleasant village of Woodplumpton, I arrived at the canal but because the canal wanted to keep to its level contour, it took a four-mile loop heading west. On checking the maps, I discovered that by walking a mere mile and a half I could pick up the canal heading north and save myself over four miles of walking. To get there I walked over a small hill and through the village of Woodplumpton. In some places, it's not as grim up north as some people would have it. Here just a few miles out of Preston, I had found a pretty village with houses and cottages, some of which had thatched roofs. In the middle of the village I stopped to admire the well-maintained 14th-century St. Anne's church with its neatly painted windows and beautiful grounds. It was locked and I couldn't get in but from the exterior I could tell it was cherished.

The church occupies a prominent site overlooking the valley of Woodplumpton Brook to the south and west. Amongst the grave stones in the church yard is a large boulder. Legend has it that a witch was buried here and the boulder prevents her from digging her way back out. There was no sign of her digging whilst I was there.

On leaving the village I came to the Moonsbridge Marina and the canal. It was packed with people and boats but once I reached the tow path I left them all behind. I was back in the countryside and apart from the occasional narrow boat, I was accompanied only by huge flocks of sand martins swooping above me with their aerial acrobatics.

The canal is frequently crossed by beautiful stone bridges all of which are numbered, allowing me to count down my progress. Near the bridges were some unusual, three-stone stiles that I hadn't seen before, like those in Cornwall but not quite.

I enjoyed my walk on the canal. As well as sand martins, I saw coots, moorhens and swans with signets. Yellow flag iris was in abundance although mostly weather-blown and battered. On a hillside, I watched a farmer enter a field on his motor trike and begin scattering food in a straight line. The sheep in the field ran to the line like a parade of soldiers on drill parade. A lame lamb at the back responded like Corporal Jones in television's Dads Army by bringing up the rear and being last to get in line.

At one point on the tow path I looked across to my right and saw at the same time the following modes of transport: canal boat on the canal; intercity train on the railway line; cars on the A6 road; lorries and cars thundering north on the M6 motorway. I guessed most of them could be in Scotland by nightfall; except the boat and me of course. For me it would take a few more days to make it to the border. Talking of borders, I was at one point within twelve miles of the Yorkshire border. Over to my right I could see the hills of the Forest of Bowland, that beautiful area of the West Riding of Yorkshire. I was tempted, really tempted but resisted going there.

I crossed over the 'Brock' aqueduct built in 1797 by engineer John Rennie. It is the first major river crossing since leaving Preston. Just prior to entering Garstang I looked over to the ruins of Greenhalgh Castle, which was built in 1490 by the Earl of Derby. In the Civil War the castle was one of the last Royalist strongholds to hold out against the Parliamentarians. I walked into the town of Garstang where I called it a day.

June
Friday
15

Walking Day 42 *Dry and windy*

Garstang to Lancaster - 12 miles - Total Walked 466

Garstang announced itself as, *'The best kept village in Lancashire'*. Another one I thought. I found it to be a small compact village, very well presented with a good selection of shops and a cobbled market square. I called in at the post office to get my LEJOG certificate stamped.

Making my way north out of town Mallard ducks were everywhere. I discovered a new game as I walked along; searching for and reading the many humorous names on canal narrow boats, 'Kingfisher' and 'Mallard' seemed common names but the best were ones like, 'Thursday's child', 'Auntie Rincal', 'No worries', and 'Kids Inheritance'.

I was walking along at a cracking pace playing the game and waving to the ever-friendly boat crews. I was the only walker on the tow-path. I passed a hillside that was full of pig sties and pigs, the greatest number of pigs I had seen so far on the whole journey. I was fast approaching Lancaster and I could see the 1960's built Lancaster University away over to my right on a hillside.

The storm during the night had blown down a huge tree which was now blocking the canal. A traffic jam of canal boats heading into Lancaster was building up on the southern side of the tree. Waterway workers were busy preparing the tree for its removal which I was told would be tomorrow. As a result, the canal and tow-path were closed. The boats could do nothing but pull in and call it a day. I explained to a workman that I needed to get into Lancaster tonight. The tree he explained, was also blocking the tow-path but I could go ahead and try to get over it at my own risk. I marched confidently up to the tree. A large crowd of boaters were examining it on both sides but the way over was high and appeared well and truly blocked.

"You're not going to try and climb over it?" asked interested boaters.

"Yes, I hope so", was my reply. I studied the tree and looked for an easy way over it.

"He'll never do it".

"It's too big".

"He's too big".

The crowd of onlookers was growing.

"Hey, this man's going to try and climb over the tree", someone shouted which drew other boaters rushing to watch. Soon I had a large audience. What had I got myself into?

There I had been, walking alone on the tow-path enjoying myself and suddenly I was in the spotlight, centre of attention to a growing number of onlookers. I studied the tree closer and I thought I could climb over it using some of the stubs from the recently cut branches. I pulled myself up onto its top. A large cheer came from the crowd. Sliding down the other side was easy by comparison. I dusted myself down and continued my solitary way.

I passed the village of Galgate, dominated by its tall railway bridge and embankment. The oldest silk mill in England is to be found here, sadly no longer used as such. At Bridge 91 I entered the Burrow Heights Cutting, built through a glacial deposit to avoid a detour. The cutting is up to ten yards deep and nearly one and a half miles long.

As I rounded a bend in the canal, Lancaster Castle came into view. The bend bears the local name of 'Hangman's corner' for from here, bargees could see the gallows up on the hill.

Lancaster soon crept up on me and I left the canal to walk through the student bedsit area to arrive at the railway station where Kay and Ripley were waiting for me.

Rest Day *Dry and overcast*

Our youngest daughter Charlotte was coming to stay with us and we were up early to go back to Lancaster Railway Station to meet her off the train.

Now I was in the company of two women and outvoted so as a family we went shopping. Being a Saturday morning, Lancaster was busy. Some of Charlotte's friends were at Lancaster University and having visited them her knowledge of Lancaster city centre shops was better than ours so she led us around the pedestrian shopping streets. I thought I might as well take the opportunity to restock with maps and socks. On the high street, we identified two hiking and outdoor pursuits stores which were next door but one to each other. We entered the nearest.

A few people were browsing the selections of clothing and equipment but it was not very busy. A young man stood expectantly behind the till counter. I selected a few pairs of hiking socks and went up to stand in front of him. I was conscious that a woman holding a shirt had come to stand behind me. The young male assistant looked up and somehow, I know not how, looked straight through me and said to the woman behind me. "Yes madam, can I take that from you?"

At this point, the woman should have said something like, "I'm sorry, it's this man in front of me who was first, but she didn't". She stepped to my side and handed the sales assistant her selection of clothes. I had experienced such poor Lancashire service before, in the pub the other day and here I had encountered it again in Lancaster, the capital of Lancashire.

Is it because I'm a Yorkshireman I thought to myself but how would he know that? I hadn't even opened my mouth and I doubt if he'd seen my Yorkshire Rose lapel badge. For a moment, I was stunned by this rude and awful service or should I say lack of service. I placed my selection of socks down directly in front of the young man and said to Kay and Charlotte who were waiting in the store behind me, "Come on we are leaving, I hate poor service" and with that we marched out of the store. Charlotte did manage to mutter something like, "What's up with Dad?" Before I could tell her, we were back out on the street. I doubt if the young man had even recorded the fact that he had missed a sale or been rude.

I went directly into the second of the hiking stores, selected the same quantity of hiking socks and bought them without a problem but by now I had had enough of shopping and managed to persuade the Kay and Charlotte to come for a drive in the car with me.

As a boy, I had been on holiday on many occasions to Sunderland Point which is a wonderful village situated a few miles out of Lancaster. It is as the name suggests, a point on a piece of land sticking out to sea, which at high tide is cut off from the mainland and becomes an island. The merchants of Lancaster in the days of sailing ships built a quay so that the ships could dock here prior to moving up into Lancaster on the tide.

It's a lovely place and I have fond memories of the holidays we had here, especially the ones with my Granddad and Grandma. My Granddad had intended to retire here; he loved the peaceful, island-like atmosphere. He bought a dilapidated cottage and spent a few years renovating it. When it was nearly time to move over to live there permanently my Grandma got cold feet and they stayed at home in Yorkshire.

We drove the few miles to the village of Overton that links Sunderland Point by a coastal road. At the Globe Inn, we saw that the tide was in and the road was submerged, leaving the Point out of our reach for now.

A little disappointed, we drove off and luckily fell upon an old coaching inn, The Stork Pub at Condor Green, which stands in a lovely setting on a grassy bank overlooking the tidal river. Here the River Condor meets the River Lune.

We went into this excellent low-roofed pub with its many quaint and dark rooms and enjoyed a lovely meal. The pub has a large display of eclectic items, the best being a glass-boxed Victorian egg collection. Now definitely illegal to reproduce it looked like a museum piece with tiny eggs in the middle working out in a circle to very large eggs on the outside. All the eggs were from local wild birds.

Dogs were allowed in and so Ripley joined us. After our meal, we took her for a stroll through the nearby woods and fields. We then drove back to Sunderland Point where at Overton we discovered the tide was retreating and revealing the wet and muddy coastal road which I took with care, as it undulated between large, muddy sandbanks and rivulets of retreating sea water.

The sandbanks were alive with birds, curlews and oyster catchers being everywhere together with seagulls and shelducks. One family of shelduck had an amazing thirteen chicks and we stopped for a while to watch their cute antics and voracious eating habits on the mud bank.

The coastal road ends at the pebbly beach at Sunderland Point where non-residents' cars have to be parked up by the toilets and information boards.

Down along the beach towards the village, several brightly-coloured boats were moored. On a couple of the boats farthest away from us I thought I saw a pair of owls; large ones. We reached for our binoculars and soon had the owls in close vision. There was something about them that we couldn't figure out. A man walking his dog noticed that we were observing the owls and told us all about them. They were model eagle owls with moving parts; the heads move slightly. They had real feathers and are supposed to frighten the gulls away from the boats and any fish catches.

We had a good laugh at ourselves and walked on past the first terrace with its 'famous' stone post and onto the second terrace where I identified the house we stayed in during our holidays.

115

Back in the 1960's the tiny village had a post office, a shop which sold bright orange-coloured hand lines with fish hooks and weights. The local boys showed us how to set the lines overnight and we spent many happy days fishing.

Today the shops are gone and so has much of the fishing. Fishing nets hung out to dry between large poles were part of the scene back then but sadly not today.

Features of Sunderland Point are the fishermen's cottages, the walk to the lighthouse on the Point, the view across the wide River Lune estuary to Glasson Docks and beyond to Ploverscar Lighthouse and the views north across many miles of farmers field to the power station at Heysham. For me and probably many others, the highlight has to be Sambo's grave. Sambo was a slave at the height of the slave trade between Africa, England and America. He came here in 1736.

Many Lancaster merchants built their wealth upon the trade and some brought slaves back to work as servants in their fine town houses up in Lancaster. When Sambo died in service, the 'good' people of Lancaster were not quite sure what to do with his body. *'It is recorded that he was a much-loved and respected servant who pleased his masters'*. When he died, they buried him with less respect and love than a dog, in a lonely unconsecrated field at the furthest point away from their mansions. *'Some may say romantically, to be nearer his African homeland'*. *(The story of Sunderland Point*, Hugh Cunliffe, 1984).

Sambo's grave is marked on the ordnance survey maps and many people find their way to it by walking away from the village down a quiet country lane to the far side of the Point. The grave is now marked by a brass plaque and adorned with many flowers, trinkets and baubles left by visitors. It is in my opinion, a very special place and in this year 2007 which records the 200th year of the abolition of slavery in Britain and its colonies, I thought it poignant to revisit the grave and to bring Charlotte to see it.

Whilst still at the grave I used my mobile phone to contact my Mum and Dad. I rang to say "hello" and "guess where I am this week?" Without hesitation, my Dad said, "You are at Sambo's grave on Sunderland Point".

Very spooky. "How did you guess that?" I said. He knew I would make a pilgrimage there if I was near Lancaster.

June **Walking Day 43** *Grey overcast but dry, hot and sunny in the afternoon*

Sunday
17 | **Lancaster to Burton in Kendal - 10 miles - Total Walked 476**

Charlotte was going home today. We enjoyed her company. Her presence brought the familiar comforting feeling of home to us. We said our goodbyes at Lancaster Railway Station. Then I was back at it, walking back into Lancaster town centre, passing its 15th-century priory church and castle with its 12th-century tower and 18th-century prison.

I hadn't been walking long before my progress was impeded by a civic procession making its way from the Town Hall along Market Street, passing the famous Horseshoe Corner. Here, set into the pavement is a horseshoe said to mark the place where John O'Gaunt's horse cast its shoe. The procession made its way up to the church. The Lord Mayor, mace bearers and other officials were all there in their finery. I stood watching them make their way up the hill. A special and fine tradition, I was glad I managed to witness it. It was only after they had gone out of sight that I realised I hadn't taken a single photograph of the event.

It was still early and I put it down to needing a coffee, which I duly found in a bookshop which was open for business. As well as the coffee I bought my much-needed maps and later wished I hadn't, as I had to carry them all day.

On my way out of Lancaster, I walked down Castle Hill and passed by the Lancaster Merchants Cross and the building marked by a blue plaque as the home of Robert Gillow, furniture maker. It was a fine stone-built house of four or more stories.

Robert Gillow (1704-1772), as a ships carpenter, travelled to the West Indies and brought mahogany wood back to England. The rest is history, as they say.

I arrived at St George's Quay by crossing the River Lune, now easily accomplished on the Millennium cycle and footpath bridge, which was opened in 2001. It is an excellent steel structure which complements the historic town behind it.

I came across a modern piece of street sculpture made of sandstone, stainless steel and clear acrylic mosaic. It deserves to be seen by many. It was in the form of a ship. At first glance I couldn't make it out. On closer inspection, and it does need close inspection, I discovered a unique memorial to 'Captured Africans', by a Manchester-based artist, Kevin Dalton Johnson. The memorial utilises copies of original documents and lists the Lancaster Merchants, Captains and their ships that sailed from this port on the slave triangle between here, Africa and America.

The names of the ships are recorded as well as their cargoes, which included tobacco, sugar, rum, cotton and slaves. The slaves are depicted in the deepest holds on each ship and are recorded with no more credit than the ships other cargoes for it is clear to see that that is how the slaves were considered, a common commodity to be bought and sold.

Crossing the River Lune, I found myself in the Skerton district of Morecambe. I walked through the very peaceful Ryelands Park to arrive back on the Lancaster to Kendal Canal. The tow-path was busy with dog-walkers and ever-friendly boat crews.

At Hest Bank I had some magnificent views of the 'purple' mountains and hills of the Lake District away north over the wide Morecambe Bay. I was making good progress on the canal, counting down the bridges and checking for more humorous boat names. At Bolton-Le-Sands, *the very name conjures up images of the huge Morecambe Bay sands that are here visible'* - (W.B. Dawson in his 1934 LEJOG book), I stopped to eat my packed lunch and was surrounded by hungry mallard ducks with chicks. I think the ducks had more to eat than I did.

I walked on and into the busy town of Carnforth. I'd been here before, but never by way of the canal. Carnforth has a railway steam museum and an excellent book shop. The railway station is famous for being used for the station and cafe scenes in the famous 1945 film, Brief Encounter, directed by David Lean and starring Celia Johnson and Trevor Howard.

Whilst I'd been walking along the canal, I had been admiring the British Waterway logo which is in the form of a canal, passing under a stone-arched bridge, with three bulrushes on one side. It is a simple logo which works, which probably means that sometime soon, someone will want to change it. Don't! (Too late! It's changed as it is now called the Canal and Rivers Trust)

As I walked out of Carnforth. The canal passes under the very busy M6 motorway. I came upon an Asian boy aged about twelve years who was fishing. He had a net on a bamboo cane and a jam jar which already had some tiddlers in it. I asked him how he was doing. "Have you caught owt yet?"

He replied excitedly, showing me his jam jar full of tiddlers. Here was a young lad doing what young lads should be doing, fishing on the canal. What was particularly striking to me was his broad Lancastrian accent.

A pair of geese with a huge number of chicks drew my attention to the other side of the canal where they waddled along in the long grass. At Kellet Lane Bridge some distant hills came into view. I recognised them as the hills of Westmorland. Hills I'd seen many times before.

To save another long loop of canal contouring around the level I left the canal and took a quiet country lane over High Keer Bridge to Tewitfield where at a huge marina, I re-joined the canal. The marina was a recent development. Some of it was still being built and it turned out to be the end of the canal for boat users.

From here to Kendal the canal had been abandoned in places, filled in and overgrown but a footpath was still usable. I passed an official looking sign that declared an intention to reopen the canal for boats to Kendal at some time in the future. I then arrived at the M6 motorway which not only blocked the canal but also my footpath, sending me on a circuitous detour to a motorway bridge. The motorway builders lacking vision and believing the canal to be a 'dead duck', built straight over it, blocking it at least twice. The future of the reopened canal seemed very bleak to me.

I walked up the incline still on the old canal that was the Tewitfield Locks; a series of eight locks that raise the canal up seventy-five feet over three quarters of a mile. An old Lock Gate preserved 'land locked' on the tow-path is a sad reminder of what was once there. I stood for a while admiring the skeletal remains which were now overgrown with a jungle of grass and weeds.

At the bottom of each lock there stood a stagnant pool of water.

The sun began to break through the grey clouds and as it did so those stagnant pools began to glisten and as if by magic the 'neon tetra' blue damselflies came out to play.

I stood again, mesmerised by this free show of nature as though I was *'in the middle of a Walt Disney cartoon'*. (Mark Moxon 2007 LEJOG book, *'When I Walk, I Bounce'*)

Stretches of the canal after the motorway still contained water and were being used by fishermen. The footpath was good and I made easy progress to Burton in Kendal where Kay and Ripley had walked out to meet me.

Burton in Kendal is a fascinating village that was once a busy coaching station on the A6. Now by-passed by both A6 and the M6, it is a quiet backwater that retains several impressive inns and buildings that appear too grand for such a quiet village.

That famous Lake District author, Alfred Wainwright, captures the village perfectly in his pencil drawings in his obscure 1974 book on Westmorland villages. Burton in Kendal is worth visiting. Somewhere along this stretch I walked out of Lancashire and into Westmorland (Cumbria).

June Monday 18 — Rest Day *Dry and overcast with rain later*

Today we moved camp to Kendal. The caravan site was packed. It was just outside the town and not far from a large Morrison's supermarket. The warden had reserved us a spot and we were to follow him around the site to it. The spot he had chosen for us was a grass pitch on a very steep sloping hill.

He left us to set up pitch and we set to in a routine now near perfect. To gain any sense of being level required more than our two levelling blocks. I went searching for the warden who came to our assistance carrying a box full of large wooden blocks, obviously well practiced. In next to no time we were balanced four or five blocks up on the front end.

Never had we been so high up on blocks and never since. The warden assured us we would be as 'safe as houses' on the blocks. The situation was made worse for us as tonight we were expecting Kay's Mum and Dad, Kevin and Margaret with their dog Jesse, who were to spend the night with us. So, there would be four of us balancing on rickety stilts on the steep slope. To make matters worse it started to rain and rain with thunder and lightning.

We balanced in the van all night with the rain pouring down and the fear of slithering away at any moment. We played cards, not daring to move around too much. After a fitful night, the morning dawned dry and fine. We had survived the stilts!

June Tuesday 19 — Walking Day 44 *Mild, grey day becoming sunny later on*

Burton in Kendal to Kendal - 12 miles - Total Walked 488

Kay, Ripley, Margaret and Kevin were going to spend the day at the nearby RSPB Leighton Moss Nature Reserve, hoping to see the elusive bittern (which they didn't see). First, they dropped me back on the canal-side at Burton.

I set off followed by large numbers of coots, moorhens and swans, all with their chicks and signets swimming close behind. The views across to Farleton Fell were fabulous and enticing. I walked past the historical coke ovens at Holme, used in the lime-burning industry. The ovens like most things along this stretch, were overgrown with grass but otherwise looked in a solid state. The limestone produced hereabouts was transported south along the canal. Coal was transported north and so the canal got the nickname, The Black and White Canal.

It was a good day for walking and my progress on the easy-going canal tow-path was excellent. Every time the sun managed to peep through the grey sky, butterflies appeared. I was joined by a pair of beautiful Pearl-bordered Fritillary butterflies that flew alongside me for some considerable distance.

Just before I reached the A65 road I came across a man dredging the canal of weeds, using an unusual paddle-wheel-machine-type boat. It looked like something you might see at a fairground. It turned out he was a contractor working for British Waterways travelling the country from his Dorset home to wherever he was needed.

On arriving at the bridge that carried the A65 road over the canal, I had arrived at the spot nearest to my home in Yorkshire. The border with my county was just a few miles to the east. The A65 road links West Yorkshire to the Lake District and it is a road I have travelled many, many times. If ever I was going to pack it in and call it a day, then here would be a good spot but there was no chance of that. I was enjoying myself too much and I hoped Kay was also enjoying our adventure.

The roar of traffic from the nearby M6 motorway shattered the tranquillity and peace, not only that, but the motorway completely blocked the canal, again. Luckily, I could use the nearby 'B' road to go under the motorway and re-join the canal. I came to the old Wakefield Wharf named after the wealthy Wakefield family from nearby Sedgwick. They owned the local gunpowder factories hereabouts and for years brought their goods down to the canal by a horse-drawn tramway, long since gone. The wharf is now home to the little canal cruise boat, the Water Witch. Some of the historical canal buildings have been renovated and the canal is being put to some use again after years of neglect.

I walked on. High up on a sweeping curve of an embankment of the canal, I looked down on the fields that for the previous weekend had been the Westmorland showground. I watched a small army of workmen dismantle the tents and marquees. I was very disappointed to have missed the show. Had I known we were this close to it we would have visited it. After all, here I was walking across the country and a visit to at least one County Show would have been 'the icing on top of the cake' but not this time.

In a field, adjacent to the show tents stood a line of excellent dry-stone walls; obviously, part of the dry-stone wall competition. From my vantage point high up on the embankment it struck me that I would have had a better view of all the dry-stone Wallers than those down in the field on the level. From here I could see straight walls, wavy walls, walls with corners, circular walls and star-shaped walls. Out of context I would have puzzled over this 'weird' construction for ages.

Eventually I came to the end of the canal water. From here to Kendal the line of the canal could still be traced but the canal in places had been filled in or was wildly overgrown with a jungle of vegetation. Forlorn stone bridges still crossed the 'canal' but served no other purpose today than cow shelters. I briefly left this scene and walked into the pretty village of Sedgwick with its rows of neat terraced cottages, once the home of the workforce for the gunpowder factories.

The village is dominated by the Sedgwick Aqueduct; now a listed building. It takes the canal high up above the houses. Today it is used by the villagers as a dog walk. I re-joined the line of the canal up some steep, stone steps. The canal passed from the aqueduct through a small wood and out on through fields on its way to Kendal.

On nearing Kendal I was joined by local people walking their dogs. I knew then I was close to the town and not before long I was walking alongside a high, modern warehouse belonging to 'K' shoes of Kendal.

A large brown rat ran across my path, startling me. I'd not expected to see a rat in broad daylight on such a well-used path but as I am told, rats are never more than ten yards away from us at any time. The route into Kendal passed a few busy school playing fields and row upon row of terraced houses.

What had once been the marina or Kendal wharf was now a sorry sight. Most of it had been turned into a linear car park and except for the excellent and unusual 'change' bridge, renovated in 2002, nothing remains of what was once a busy canal terminal. A few coping stones set in the ground mark the end of the line and for me the end of an excellent canal walk.

I walked to the cemetery where a path around the side took me to the hill atop of which stands Kendal Castle. I had been to Kendal many times but had never been up to the castle and therefore wanted to visit it. Coming at the end of the day it was a steep climb up the hill but it was well worth it.

A couple of other people were exploring the castle which has useful information boards explaining its history in detail. It was a Norman castle, its most famous resident was Katherine Parr, the last wife of Henry VIII, who survived him.

The views alone are magnificent. The town of Kendal below can be viewed from above as if looking at a map.

The River Kent, one of the fastest flowing rivers in England, is spanned by several 18th-century stone bridges and winds its way through the town. It passes many cobbled streets and medieval shambles, each with enclosed yards which were built in stone to afford protection from the raiding Scots.

My eyes focused on the large Gothic parish church, one of the widest in England with five aisles. The busy main street, once sheer hell for motorists now by-passed, is a charming market street with all the shops one could wish for.

After climbing the Castle's towers and walls and looking down wells and cellars, I moved off, heading north towards the edge of town. Before turning in for the night I was joined by Kay and her Mum and Dad and we drove back into Kendal to explore its many quaint features, like Wainwright's Yard off Main Street, recently renamed after Alfred Wainwright of Lakeland fells and mountains guide books fame. He lived most of his adult life in Kendal. Here in the yard is a superb and worthy monument to him, using slate pictures copied from his guide books with 'his' footprints set in the cobbles.

Nearby on the main street there is the ubiquitous 'Burtons' menswear shop. This one had, set in stone high up, *'MONTAGUE BURTON THE TAILOR OF TASTE'* which is something you don't see very often. Or is it?

A bit further down the main street, protruding from the pavement against the wall of the Town Hall, there is a curious, smooth lump of a stone labelled and known locally as the 'Ca' stone (which is short for Call Stone). This stone is believed to be the base of a cross where for centuries proclamations have been announced. Apart from rubbing my hand over the stone I just had to sit on it.

Kendal is known for its many traditional signs displayed high above the shops; a lion above a hotel; a pestle and mortar above a chemist shop. My favourite, tucked away down a side street, is of an Arab smoking a pipe which is above a snuff maker, one of the many small, traditional businesses still found here in Kendal.

Another small but globally-known industry is Kendal Mint Cake, used and carried by every Everest expedition and many Fell walkers all over the world.

For my Lejog walk I always carried Kendal Mint Cake in my rucksack as an emergency food.

June **Walking Day 45** *Dry and cloudy with sunny hot spells*

Wednesday 20

> **Kendal to Haweswater via Longsleddale and Gatescarth Pass - 11 miles - Total Walked 499**

We experienced a little of what the rest of the country had been having; an overnight storm with torrential rain and strong winds.

Another fitful night balancing on the 'stilts' but once again survived. It was enough to send Kevin and Margaret off home with their impression of a rain-soaked Lake District unchanged.

Kay and Ripley joined me for a brisk walk on pavements along the old A6 road walking slightly uphill, out and away from Kendal. After a mile or so the footpath ended. I said goodbye to them both and carried on along the wide grass verge.

The road was blissfully quiet and after a while I came upon the frowsiest tramp I had seen in a long time; a true tramp like the ones in *'An autobiography of a Super Tramp'*. He was walking towards me. His beard was long, straggly and unkempt. It appeared to have a bird's nest in it or was I imagining that?

He looked like a cartoon character with a swarm of flies constantly hovering over his head. As we passed our eyes met and I said, "Hello. Are you all right?"

He replied quietly and sheepishly, "Yes", and carried on his way. At the junction of Longsleddale, I stopped for a rest on a concrete-topped milk churn stand which 'litter' the countryside in these parts. These historic reminders of a bygone age when milk stored in metal churns was placed on stands usually by the farm entrance or as in this case, at the valley entrance to be collected by the dairy wagon.

Today of course milk is stored in a tank on the farm and the dairy wagon collects it directly from source cutting out the need for milk churns. In the 1920's and 1930's milk from this area was collected from the milk churn stands by wagons, taken to the many railway stations, placed on a train and arrived in London, fresh for the capital's citizens in the morning. The old way seems more romantic to me. The new way might be more hygienic but certainly not any faster. Someone somewhere should do a study of these historic little 'buildings' before it's too late. The next generation may not even notice them and will not appreciate what they are and what they were used for.

I left the A6 behind and descended a hill into the Lake District National Park. I crossed the very attractive River Sprint which was to accompany me throughout the valley, over a slate and stone bridge surrounded by white painted cottages. It was an idyllic setting.

The hills of Longsleddale lay ahead of me to my left and right. The valley road headed straight as an arrow to the head of the dale. Throughout my journey up the valley I saw no one else. The hedgerows were in full bloom and birds were all around me, particularly pied wagtails. I passed a wild honeysuckle bush that had been completely smothered by a fog of cobwebs.

Half way up the valley I came to a tiny hamlet with, at its centre, the tiny and very plain St Mary's church, rebuilt in 1863. It was open and I went in through a carved oak door, said to date from 1662. There was a strong musty smell and I believe the church was glad of the fresh air. Having said that, it was a very clean and well-maintained little church.

After making my usual note in the visitors' book I stepped back outside into the glorious sunshine. Directly in front of me, lit by a ray of sunshine, was the smallest war memorial I had so far seen on my walk. It was a small stone cross with a carved wreath. It had just three names upon it, all of whom were lost in the Great War of 1914-1918.

Today the valley was totally devoid of people and I found it hard to imagine how a place without even a village as such could lose one let alone three men. As I stood reading the memorial I was reminded of all the war memorials that I had passed on my journey. Some, like the one at Runcorn, were massive, containing hundreds of names all listed in alphabetical order, not by rank. Others were more modest like this one. As well as being small this one was unusual as it was in the church graveyard.

My fellow LEJOG traveller, Colin Howard wrote, poignantly, the following in 1939 after coming across a war memorial at Kingussie and I make no excuses for quoting it in full. *'Here indeed was a memorial that should last longer than those of a past age, which now commemorate only some quaintness or oddity in their design and attract attention on that count alone.*

Memory is short and when a battle becomes history, it loses the poignancy that should make it serve as a deterrent to warfare.

We of this age (1939) hate war because we lost our husbands, sons, brothers in the Great War, we do not hate it because we lost our ancestors at Sedgemoor or Crecy. will the thousands of war memorials all over Great Britain serve no purpose than to keep us from taking life with the reminder that to take, we must give.

Sorrow cannot last forever. The new skin will grow over our wounds. a new generation shall pick up our arms and learn for itself what war can mean to a land.

I fear that a war memorial, though it be built of the hardest stone, is no less ephemeral than memory'.

Written in 1939, just before the outbreak of WW2, the above deserves a second reading.

I left the churchyard and crossed over to an immaculately clean public toilet block. Next to it was an old-style traditional telephone kiosk. It was full of cobwebs. I decided to use this one and gave Kay a call. I was surprised to see that the minimum call amount was forty pence. At least the kiosk still accepted coins. Most of the ones I'd seen had been converted to credit cards only or pre-paid telephone cards.

From the church the dale scenery got even more mountainous with views of the hilltops and scree-filled slopes. It was Lakeland scenery without the Lakes. I was at home with this kind of territory. At the farm called Sadgill the road carried on up but was no longer metalled. Sadgill has a mountain rescue post and is surely as good an example of misnomer as one could find. The hills 'creep in' to give a cosy feel to the place.

The River Sprint flows down the dale head in a series of beautiful waterfalls. Dippers could be seen flitting about boulders in the stream. Wheatears bobbed along the wall tops. A truly idyllic place (and on a day like today, filled with glorious sunshine), was anything but a 'sad gill'.

I climbed up the boulder-strewn track, pausing now and again to admire the view behind me back down the dale.

As I reached the brow of the pass I stooped to take a handful of fresh mountain water. It was cool, refreshing and thirst-quenching. I rested by an arched, stone bridge that spanned the stream, even though it was narrow enough to stride across. Perhaps the bridge is more of a necessity in winter? Here I ate my daily piece of fruit; an orange. High up here I was joined by cawing ravens. I climbed up the last bit of the brow to reach the Col of Gatescarth Pass which at 1,900ft was the highest I had been on my travels so far. The paths carried on up from the pass in differing directions heading for familiar mountains (all of which I have previously climbed).

My route was the only one now heading down hill. Soon the waters of the Manchester Reservoir, Haweswater, came into view. The blue of the water reflected the blue of the sky; crystal sharp. As I plodded down towards the car park, in places down stone steps, I could see Kay and Ripley out on the fell-side climbing up to join me. A shower of rain came from nowhere and wet me thoroughly, but as quick as it came, it went and the sun came back to dry me.

Kay had parked the car at the car park at the head of Haweswater and we drove back to Kendal via the east side of the lake then via the villages of Shap and Tebay. As we crossed over the M6 motorway, a dazzling display of orchids filled the grass verges and we stopped to admire them.

Walking Day 46 - The longest day *Dry and fine*

Haweswater to Penrith - 13 miles - Total Walked 512 >

For the first time on my walk I was going to be joined by friends; Dick, a retired Crown Prosecution Solicitor and Richard, a still-working CPS Solicitor from Yorkshire who had taken the day off. They joined me in Kendal. Squeezing into our Nissan Micra we set off back to Haweswater where both solicitors witnessed my morning ritual of looping back across yesterday's finishing line.

That done, we said goodbye to Kay and Ripley and set off on a good footpath around the head of Haweswater. The sun was shining and the mountains, high above us, dominated the view and looked magnificent. Our course was going to follow the low-level route along the western bank of Haweswater.

Not long after setting off and just after we'd got into a modest stride we came upon the RSPB hide at Riggindale. We were invited to join the excited little band and dropping our bags, we were soon looking through their binoculars and telescopes at a beautiful golden eagle.

We were reliably informed that this one golden eagle was at this moment the only eagle in England. It was a male whose mate had died about three years ago. He had been holding his nesting site ever since, pining for a new mate but as of that moment none had appeared. It was hoped that a juvenile Scottish golden eagle from Dumfries and Galloway would eventually make the short flight across here to join up with this lonely bird. None of us were in a hurry to leave this spot but eventually we said our goodbyes and moved off.

Nature didn't leave us though and as we walked, Dick spotted some sundew and common butterwort, both insect eating flowers. As we bent down to examine these flowers a beetle of a huge size, (approximately two inches), walked across our path quickly followed by a magnificent yellow and black dragonfly.

We had joined Wainwright's Coast to Coast long distance footpath and it wasn't long before we passed a group of young men walking the route towards St Bee's Head.

Before we left the delights of Haweswater we stopped for a drink on a high promontory with good views. Both Dick and I opened our flasks for a quick slurp. We had almost finished our drink before Richard had even removed his massive rucksack.

I had earlier suggested that he leave his rucksack in our vehicle as I was sure he wouldn't need such a large pack on our low-level walk. However, Richard insisted on carrying it. It had been with him when he trekked through Nepal to the Everest base camp, the Australian outback, the jungles of Borneo and India, the mountains of the Andes in South America and the Rockies of North America. The list went on and on. There didn't seem to be anywhere in the world that he and his trusted rucksack hadn't been to.

I was now putting my flask away and was ready for the off and Richard was down at the water's edge scooping up some water in a billy can. Dick and I watched in incredulous fascination as Richard removed from his rucksack a primus stove, paraffin cans and other tea making paraphernalia. Performing a ritual that he was obviously well used to, he 'pumped' up the stove and soon had it lit with billycan of water boiling away.

Richard then went back into his pack and produced a selection of tea; large cans containing a variety of teas. He had a pint of milk or two in his pack (just in case) but he preferred his tea without milk. He then 'dived' into his pack which was beginning to look like a 'Santa's sack' and produced some cans of Vietnamese fish produce. Richard opened them and offered the foul-smelling 'food' around. I politely refused the offer choosing instead to eat some of Dick's 'Jelly Babies'. Whilst all this was going on, Dick kept us entertained by telling highly amusing 'old war' stories; tales from the days when he prosecuted at Bradford City Courts... all very civilized.

After our 'tea break', we set off crossing the fast and furious Measand Beck by a series of wooden bridges. We saw some of the pretty waterfalls spilling from the fell side and heading for the reservoir. It was here on one of the bridges that the conversation changed onto walking sticks. Dick had noticed that I was carrying my modern LEKI walking stick. Dick preferred his old-style wooden walking stick. The solid nature of the wood reassured him and he liked the feel of it in his hand. I on the other hand, preferred the spring shock absorbers in my stick and the modelled hand grip of my LEKI. I lifted my stick up to show it off when suddenly and for an unknown reason, it left my hand and tumbled over the wooden bridge parapet, falling down the steep and overgrown sides of the streaming waterfalls. Without saying a word and with the energy and agility of someone you might see in a James Bond film I leapt over the parapet and sprang down the steep slope, brushing aside the vegetation to safely retrieve my stick. Having got my hand firmly on it I took a moment to catch my breath and then looked back up the waterfall to see Dick and Richard way up, back at the parapet looking down on me. Wow I thought. How did I get down here? Did I really hop, skip and jump all the way down here? It was a slow slippery climb back up.

In 1871 the two Naylor brothers from Cheshire walked from John O'Groats to Land's End. In 1916 they published a book by that name. It is a fascinating account and in the first chapter, they too discussed the merits of walking sticks. In the end they armed themselves with stout, oaken staffs or cudgels heavily ferruled by their local blacksmith and especially selected for them by their sword-fencing master. He also gave lessons in how to use the staffs either for defensive or offensive purposes because back then in 1871, coming across robbers and thugs was by no means uncommon. Their staffs could also be used to carry their leather holdalls strung across their shoulders. Luckily for me my stick was used mainly as an aid to walking. I had used it to whack my way through overgrown vegetation and as a defensive stick when approached by aggressive dogs but up until now the people I had met on my walk were all friendly with no thugs or robbers at all - yet.

The walk to the end of the reservoir proved a lot easier and we were soon admiring the massive *'hollow arched dam'* constructed in 1941, the first such dam to be built in the UK. It measures 1,540 feet in length. The lane down to the hamlet of Burn Banks is a leisurely walk dominated by the dam, now behind us. Burn Banks originated as the reservoir builders camp. Today it has many holiday cottages to let. A quiet country lane led us to the small village of Bampton.

We joined a well-signposted river footpath that followed the River Lowther northwards. The river here was wide and slow-flowing through gentle green pastures, the hills being behind us now. We stayed on the river footpath for some time and appeared to be heading towards the village of Askham but at an ornate Victorian suspension bridge we crossed the river to arrive at the unusually-named hamlet of Whale, which has a number of attractive stone-built cottages and at least one working farm. We crossed through the busy farmyard and continued our northward journey through the great, extensive and beautiful Lowther Park. We kept to the high ground with the River Lowther down to our left. Eventually we came through the park woodland to the *'spectacular memorial to past glories'*, (A. Wainwright), Lowther Castle. Sadly today, it is a ruined shell of a building but none the less still a grand and imposing structure, once the home of the famous sporting Earl of Lonsdale.

We gazed in awe at the place and then turning our backs on the castle, walked away through the well-tended grounds and lovely avenues of trees. We could hear the constant roar of the nearby M6 motorway.

Back to the river which we crossed using a graceful, single arch stone bridge, our route followed the river on a wide track through mature woods. Soon we came to a large caravan site with children running and playing all over the place. We walked on and under a massive stone-built viaduct which carries the main London to Glasgow railway line.

The village of Clifton lay across the other side of the river. Clifton claims the distinction of staging the last pitched battle on English soil when, back in 1745, a skirmish took place between the retreating Jacobite force of Bonnie Prince Charlie and the British army under the Duke of Cumberland.

We were making good progress through the woods and our lane soon became metalled. I was enjoying walking in company and the tale-telling kept my mind more than fully occupied. It was 'a stroll in the park'. Our lane joined the A6 which was blessed with a pavement. We headed towards the hamlet of Yanwath and here in a field was the very visible but wrongly named, 'King Arthur's Round Table'. We leant over a stone wall to have a closer look at it. Passing motorists could be forgiven for thinking they had just passed a scene from the TV programme, 'The Last of the Summer Wine'. It was obvious who Dick would be; being tall, lean and military-smart but I'm not sure who I'd have been taken for. Richard, with his full beard could be 'Compo'.

The round table was an obvious earthwork in the form of a circular entrenchment. Sir Walter Scott wrote about it as *'Penrith's table round'*. However, it has been firmly established that this is an ancient henge monument, probably of the Neolithic period. A few yards further on and we had reached the northern boundary of the old County of Westmorland at Eamont Bridge. The River Lowther that we had been faithfully following northwards joined the River Eamont nearby, the latter being crossed by a fabulous 16th-century triple-arched stone bridge.

A hamlet of old and unusual cottages stood on both sides of the river. Many of these buildings had interesting date stones above their doorways, most of them from the 17th-century. A long climb uphill brought us to the massive roundabout on the edge of Penrith which luckily turned out to be easier to cross than I had first thought.

We walked into the town centre along Bridge Lane, the old A6, passing the plague stone, a hollowed-out rock placed here in 1598 when the town was suffering from the Black Death. People from inside the sealed-off town could use the stone, (one of many still existing around the country), to continue to trade with outsiders. Vinegar or some other liquid was used to 'disinfect' the coins placed in the hollow.

When we reached the centre of Penrith, Kay was waiting for us by the town square. We'd had a good days walk and were looking forward to a meal and a drink but first we headed back to Shap, to show Dick the display of orchids (which we had seen the day before) which he later identified as Northern Marsh Orchids. We then drove into Kendal and stopped at the first pub we came to, the 17th-century inn, The Duke of Cumberland.

June Friday 22 — Rest Day *Fine and dry*

A day off from walking.

We moved the motorhome up to Dalston near Carlisle. Driving up the A6 over Shap Fell, we parked in a lay-by to admire the fabulous views and the monument to road-users who as the monument says, *'Struggled for years to keep the social and commercial links between north and south alive by motoring over the old and difficult route over Shap Fell'*.

It was a fantastic place to stop and have a bacon and tomato sandwich.

The drive to Dalston and the caravan site would have been easier if the route instructions to get to it had included the fact that the caravan site was near to the large Nestle factory; a factory that looks more like a chemical plant than a manufacturer of beverages. Having said that the caravan site was quiet, near to the golf course and mature woods, a home to red squirrels.

That evening our daughter Samantha and her fiancé Joe, arrived to stay the weekend with us and we spent it exploring Carlisle.

Samantha and Joe went home today. Because I'd had a couple of days off I was eager to get back out on the stroll. Penrith is a Celtic word. It has many meanings, all disputed. One meaning is 'Red town' which certainly fits as most of the old town is built out of a deep red stone. It has always been an important cattle market town and still is today. By walking in Penrith I joined the long list of noteworthy people who had also passed this way. Richard III stayed here. Mary Queen of Scots, Oliver Cromwell, Bonnie Prince Charlie, John Wesley. Wordsworth was educated here. Anthony Trollope, they all spent time here.

Penrith, like Kendal, was built in a defensive mode with narrow streets and easily-defended yards which today make it an interesting place to wander around. What to me is surprising is the fact that up until 1070 AD, Penrith was the capital of Cambria, a semi-dependent state in the kingdom of Strathclyde, Scotland.

Before leaving the town centre I walked around the churchyard of St Andrew's church, part of which is 14th century. In the graveyard, there is a monument worthy of a closer look; it is said to be the grave of the legendary giant king of Cumbria, Owen Caesarius. It consists of two eleven-foot-high wheel crosses combining Christian and Viking carvings, separated by four 10th-century hog-back tombs, said to be the graves of four wild boars. Penrith in later years gained a reputation as a clock-making town. In the town square, there is a magnificent clock tower which had the correct time and is known as the Musgrave monument. It was erected in 1861 to commemorate Philip Musgrave, (the eldest son of Sir George and Lady Musgrave), who died aged twenty-six years in 1859 in Madrid, Spain.

I walked away from the shops, banks, hotels and pubs, passing the little stream or beck that runs near the square at the back of the buildings. This beck has an unusual name, 'Thacka Beck' and is a man-made water course bringing fresh water diverted from the River Petteril into town. It was the idea of Bishop Strickland back in 1385, to create this water supply, after all the towns' wells became polluted. The townsfolk could draw as much water as they needed if the water flowed freely through the eye of a millstone. The millstone is preserved by the Tourist Information Office. Bishop Strickland later became the Archbishop of Canterbury.

I turned to walk up hill towards the ruined 14th century castle and passed a famous toffee shop. The shop had been visited by Prince Charles and regularly supplies H.M. The Queen with toffee. Unfortunately for me it was shut. A sign in the window declared, *'probably the best fudge in England'.*

I left Penrith by the Gilwilly Industrial Estate, crossing the M6 motorway and London to Glasgow railway line. I walked along a narrow country lane which surprisingly, had a recently-built, well-lit footpath running parallel to it. I made good progress along this path and soon found the reason for its existence. I came to Penrith Sports College; a modern complex with buildings set in a fabulous location overlooking the hills.

The lane leading away was pathless but quiet and level. The only car that passed me was being driven by a vicar; on his way, back from church I presumed.

I arrived at the very quiet village of Newton Reigny which is a place I had been to before. This village, with its neat stone cottages and wide Main Street was the home village of my first wife's Grandfather, who as a railway worker married a Yorkshire woman. In the late 1970's we travelled here with him to view his parents' grave which stood in the well-kept churchyard. I entered it and went to the spot where I had been before. I then went inside St John's church which had been rebuilt in 1876 but still contained some 12th and 13th-century parts. I hadn't noticed when I entered but I actually took a step down into the church.

This apparently, has helped the authorities dedicate the church to John the Baptist, as opposed to John the Evangelist, because no written record exists as to which of these saints the church was originally dedicated to; so, an old church saying was brought into use. Apparently, you walk straight on for John the Evangelist and you step down for John the Baptist, hence the patronal festival is observed on John the Baptist's day. [*A Short History of St. John's church, Newton Reigny*, by Frank Shaw. 2001]

I made a suitable entry in the visitors' book, spent some time in quiet prayer, and then moved on.

As I passed the wood yard at Laithes, huge trunks of trees were stacked up along the lane and my attention was caught by some beautiful ringlet butterflies fluttering along in front of me. The peace and tranquillity of my Sunday stroll was shattered by the noise of motorbikes. The roar of the bikes increased as I climbed the lane which enclosed in mature trees and high hedgerows. At a break in the hedge in the fields below I could see an old-fashioned motorcycling scrambling course like the ones that were very popular back in the 1960's; bikes were roaring around the course throwing mud up everywhere. It was very entertaining and I wondered why you never see it on TV anymore?

I walked on and into the village of Skelton. A sign declared it to be the home of the Skelton Village Show - '*one of the largest village shows in England*'. This is held on the third Saturday in August each year. A crown green bowling competition was taking place. All players were dressed in whites. The game was sedate and relaxing to watch but just as entertaining as the youthful scrambling I'd seen earlier. All this sport spectating was eating into my time but I was in no hurry to get anywhere as I ambled out of the village and followed the lanes that were conveniently marked with the National Cycleway Route 7 marker.

A few cyclists passed me; two lots going in differing directions. Then it happened. One minute I was strolling through the beautiful and peaceful English countryside and the next I was in the middle of a James Bond film set. I'd arrived via a long stretch of road, at the Skelton Transmitting Station. Opened in the middle of World War 2, it allowed the BBC to broadcast to the world. It covers a vast area (750 acres) which is all fenced in. Numerous guards were on duty behind the fences. I had obviously given them something to investigate.

It is an M.O.D. Transmitting base used for sending signals to submarines. To do this it uses a VLF (very low frequency) transmitter and an aerial of the guyed lattice mast-type which at its height is 1,197.6 feet tall (365 metres) - close to a quarter of a mile high. Skelton aerial is the second tallest structure in the UK and it is spectacularly awesome.

I left the 'film set' and headed along an undulating lane through pine woods. I was still following Cycleway No. 7 as I crossed several streams by well-built stone bridges. It seemed to be never-ending as I crossed one stream to immediately walk downhill to cross another. I met no one at all on this lonely stretch. Eventually I arrived at the village of Raughtonhead, more of a hamlet really with its collection of farmhouses and modern, neat bungalows. The village was shut with absolutely no one around. I imagined I saw a curtain or two twitch as I sat on a prominent bench on the village green. I was enjoying my rest when all of a sudden, the heavens opened and a torrential downpour struck me. I quickly threw my raincoat over myself and hopped down the lane to the shelter of All Saints Church. Built in 1761, it has a truly massive square tower which was added in 1881. The church itself was locked and I huddled to its side to get some protection from the rain.

Once the rain stopped I headed for a lane that took me downhill through woodland to the historic stone-built Rose Bridge that spans the River Caldew. The river here was meandering slowly to its end. It starts high up on the back of Skiddaw Mountain and flows into the River Eden near Carlisle. On the hillside opposite stood Rose Castle; a red stone building which, since the 12th century has been the main residence of the Bishop of Carlisle. Amongst its many parts is a visible 13th-century tower, said to have been built on the instructions of Bishop Strickland of Penrith fame. Most of the present building is Victorian. It is in a very beautiful rural setting with walled, terraced gardens leading down to the river. I had to be content with admiring the castle from a distance.

From Rose Bridge, I followed a riverside footpath going with the flow of the River Caldew and heading for Carlisle. The footpath was a good one in an idyllic river and rural setting, what some might describe as 'easy' countryside. The walking was, if not exactly 'easy', then certainly very enjoyable. There is something about walking along a riverbank in the countryside. I found it very peaceful.

I was walking on part of the Cumbrian Way which was well-signposted. It eventually led me into the grounds of a large and imposing public school, Limehouse School. It was founded in 1899 and takes boarders from around the world. I hope they grow up to appreciate the school's setting because it truly is set in a privileged place; one that must rub off on the children. Compare this with being educated in a run-down inner city comprehensive. It's the difference between free-range and battery. I know it comes at a price but we would all prefer free-range.

After taking me through the grounds of the school and giving me tantalising views of the buildings, the footpath took me through cow filled undulating meadows back to the river bank where I spent some time watching the antics of a common sandpiper wading in the muddy embankment.

I then walked through woodland to arrive at a place called Bridge End which had an elegant stone bridge as well as a garage at a cross roads.

The roads were quiet as I climbed up and crossed over to the *'Dalston Sports and Classic Car Garage'*. It was still a petrol station but had specialised in these fantastic cars from a bygone era, several of which were on display in the showroom.

From here it was a short walk along a road lined by large detached houses overlooking pleasant parkland with a stream, into the village of Dalston; pronounced by the locals as DAWSTON which means *'Town of the Crows'*; hence the village motto *'While I live, I crow'*, which is displayed on the millennium monument, a metal arched sculpture topped by a Cockerel set just off the village square in the park.

Dalston won't like me for saying this but it is more of a small town than a village. Being much larger than any of the villages I'd walked through recently. It has a thriving main street with a good variety of traditional shops, pubs, and offices, as well as a large school and two industrial estates.

There are still enough work places to keep some of them in work in the 'village', that is without even mentioning the massive 'Chemical Factory', sorry; Nestlé's Beverage factory.

Here's a thing; the Dalston Secondary School is rated as one of the best Schools in the Country; a good place to be educated but the rich and privileged are not queuing up to send their children here, preferring instead to pay for their children to attend the nearby Limehouse School. My observations were sharpened when I saw two things: The after-school games being played on the school fields, and children making their way home, impeccably behaved and still well turned out.

Dalston wasn't always so 'respectable', in fact back in 1921 the local Vicar complained that the women of the town were competing with the men in Whippet racing. *'Why can't they do something more respectable such as Cockfighting'*, quote from Cumbrian Life magazine June 2008. Apparently, Cockfighting was all the rage in Cumberland; even the Bishop had a cockfighting pit at his house at nearby Rose Castle.

June
Monday
25

Walking Day 48 *Overcast but dry and blustery (rain and floods elsewhere in the UK)*

Dalston to Gretna Green, Scotland - 13 miles - Total Walked 542

Kay and Ripley joined me as I walked down the lane from the camp-site and back to the river bank. The views across to the Lake District fells were stunning with the back of Blencathra being particularly clear. We crossed over the railway line by an unmanned crossing and took the footpath alongside the River Caldew. For some reason the footpath was excessively overgrown and I had to whack away with my stick to clear it. After a few minutes, Kay and Ripley had had enough and decided to turn back. At this rate, it would take me all day to get to Carlisle. Shortly after, the footpath not only became clear but transformed into a well-signposted dual path and cycleway and it became easy walking all the way into Carlisle. I noticed a lot of burdock plants; sticky buds. I'd never seen so many all in one place. I named the path, 'Burdock Way'. The scenery changed from rural river bank to industrial and I was soon walking between the river and factories at Cummersdale. By the time, I got to Denton Holme Weir I was in Carlisle proper. Dog walkers joined me on my route into the city.

Carlisle was known in Roman times as Lugovalum.

When the Naylor brothers visited Carlisle in 1870 (JOG to LE 1916), they looked around the castle, cathedral and town. The main attraction however at that time, was the Carrs Biscuit Manufactory. Thousands were queuing up to take the tour around the world's first biscuit factory. Crowds were, *'excited by the wonder of it all'*. The factory was, in 1815, little more than a bakery. By 1831, Jonathan Dudgeson Carr had taken over and biscuit manufacturing on a massive scale was begun. Carr's Table Water Biscuits are still made at the site today (United Biscuits). However, visitors are restricted to pre-booked groups so I missed getting all excited about it. (Interestingly Elihu Burritt in his 1868 book *'A walk from London to Land's End and back'*, visited the Huntley and Palmer's 1822 biscuit factory at Reading).

I crossed the bridge overlooking the railway station, and I was reminded that from this station I had travelled on some of Britain's most spectacularly beautiful routes including the truly awesome and most spectacular route of Settle to Carlisle.

I left the busy railway station and made my way along through part of the old walls of the city into English Street, the main shopping street which has been pedestrianised. Where English Street meets Scotch Street outside the Visitor Centre, there stands the Carel Cross (in Market Square). It dates from 1682 and it was from the steps of the cross that Bonnie Prince Charlie claimed the throne of England for his father, James Stuart. More recently, at the beginning of the 20th century, the cross was the site of the 'Hiring's', when farm-hands and domestic servants would gather twice a year to offer themselves out as labour.

By the cross is an ornate Victorian post box or pillar box. This box commemorates the fact that the first pillar box in England was erected here in Carlisle, in 1853. I walked through the Streets and Lanes Shopping Centre leaving by a side entrance. Opposite to this entrance was the Market Hall which was built in 1889. It has been restored and made fit for modern purpose but still retains its fabulous cast iron and glass roof. I had a quick walk through. In the meat market section I stopped to admire the columns, each carved on their tops with the animal which was sold at that point. I liked the carved chicken best.

Leaving the market, I crossed over the busy road and entered Bitts Park with its wonderful weeping willow trees. Looking over to my right I could see the red walls of the castle and was reminded that here in the park, the first ever international football match took place between the local team and the French servants of the imprisoned Mary Queen of Scots, who was in the castle and watched the game from her window.

Down by the River Eden I walked through the park on the Hadrian's Wall footpath. I'd been here before, years ago, when I walked the full route of the wall with my young family.

After admiring the RSPB monument of a Cormorant bird, I walked over to the road bridge that crosses the river. A sign declared the high flood level of 8th January 2005 a good few feet above my head. I climbed the stone steps and crossed the river, entering the area of Carlisle known as Stanwix, immediately leaving the busy road by a side road that followed the north bank of the river through pleasant streets of fine houses.

I arrived at the Kingmoor Nature Reserve which, with good foot paths through mixed woodland and heath was a pleasure to stroll through. However, the pleasure was short-lived as most of the reserve covered an area in the opposite direction to that in which I was walking and I was soon back on a country lane that led me past the vast Kingmoor railway goods yard.

In its heyday, it must have been an impressive site with hundreds of freight trains. Even today there were still plenty to see. The yard merged with the Kingmoor wood yard. A huge area was given over to pine wood which was continually being transported into the yard on articulated lorries and freight trains. Once in the yard, huge claw-like machines moved the timbers as if it were matchsticks.

Back in the 16th century this vast area known as Kingmoor was the first venue of the world's oldest surviving horse-racing prize, The Carlisle Bells, which is still run each year in June at Carlisle Racecourse. There are two gold bells, of which the largest is dated 1580 and has engraved upon it, in old-English, something along the lines of, '*To the swiftest horse in Lady Dacre's stake*'.

I walked to the end of the wood yard and along the lane, dodging the never-ending supply of wood-ladened lorries. Right at the very edge of Kingmoor, near to the unusually-named village of Cargo, I came upon a small patch of ground that had a few horses on it; not racing horses; more like children's ponies, but horses nonetheless; a faint reminder of what Kingmoor in the past had been.

A quiet country lane led me to the tranquil village of Rockcliffe where there was a busy pub and a large church with a magnificent spire. The church was locked but in the churchyard, I saw a beautiful war memorial bearing a sculpture of a World War One 'Tommy'.

A wide path led from the church down some rocky cliffs to the beach. I was back at the seaside. I was looking out across the River Eden to the Solway Firth with the mountains of Dumfries and Galloway in the distance. The beach, sheltered by low rocky cliffs, reminded me of the now far distant Cornwall. As I walked along the beach, which I had all to myself, I listened to the gentle and soothing sound of the waves lapping onto the shore.

I picked up a signed footpath, The Cumbrian Coastal Way, which eventually took me back up through the cliffs and away from the beach. A long stretch of country lane bounded on both sides by pine forest, led me back to the A74 at Metal Bridge where the River Esk spills forth into the Solway Firth. I crossed the main London to Glasgow railway line by way of a metal bridge which at both entrance and exit was overgrown with nettles. I had to hack my way through. A train heading for London thundered underneath me whilst I was on top of the bridge.

The Cumbrian coastal path led me through an overgrown nettle field and eventually surfaced at what used to be a pub at Metal Bridge; it was all boarded-up.

The last section of my walk from here to Gretna was not going to be easy; I had studied the maps in detail. No one in their right mind would want to walk this way into Scotland. I do not recommend it at all. All the guide books recommended another way into Scotland via the village of Longtown.

However, this is the way I wanted to go. I wanted to enter Scotland by way of Gretna Green. To do so on foot from Metal Bridge requires both agility of mind and strength of body. Let me explain, A mile or so back from Metal Bridge, the very busy M6 motorway changes to an 'A' road, the A74, which continues north until it crosses the border into Scotland where it reverts to motorway but gains the title of A74 (M); legally therefore, it is possible to walk on the side of the A road. The trouble is that none of the thousands of motorists, including hundreds of drivers of giant articulated lorries, act any differently, believing it to be still a motorway. Anyone who has been unfortunate enough to walk any distance on the side of a busy motorway will know what I mean. At least on a motorway there is usually the hard shoulder between the pedestrian and the speeding traffic. Here on the A74 I had a tiny rough bit of verge between me and certain death! To make matters worse, at the time of my walk the whole of this area was a large building site as the A74 was being widened; whether it becomes a motorway or not I must wait and see. As lorries tried their best to 'suck me' into their wake, I was dodging dumper trucks and JCB's advancing on me from all sides. The stares and glares I received from lorry drivers and builders alike confirmed what I had been thinking: that I must be mad.

I began counting the Eddie Stobart's lorries that were whizzing past me. After I had reached over one hundred I gave up.

The building site was getting busier. My mind was racing. I was finally coming to the end of part one of my adventure; walking the length of my country, England.

The 'Welcome to Scotland' sign appeared in front of me and I took the slip road up away from the traffic which continued northwards. As I walked to Gretna, thankfully a little more peacefully, I walked onto the bridge that crosses the River Sark; the border between England and Scotland. I could see Kay and Ripley waiting for me on the other side. Kay was shouting, "Come on and hurry up. The Gretna Retail Shopping Outlet closes in twenty minutes!"

I was in no hurry. Exactly halfway across the bridge I looked down on the stream-like River Sark with one foot in England and one foot in Scotland. I'd done it!

Back in 1818 when this stone bridge was built, a unique topping-out ceremony took place. The Freemasons from Gretna, Scotland and Longtown, England, walked in full regalia from their respective lodges to this very spot and witnessed the keystone being put in place. I walked across the border into Scotland; a foreign country. As W.B. Dawson wrote in his 1934 LEJOG book;

'I am a native of England and a stranger to Scotland. I have a little knowledge of the latter and not a great deal more of the former'.

June Tuesday 26 — Rest Day *Fine and dry*

Today we moved camp. Leaving England behind us we drove up the M6 and A74 (M), passing the A74 stretch of road that I walked on yesterday, (I must have been mad). We found a quiet camp-site in the small town of Lochmaben a few miles east of Lockerbie. The site, set in mature woodlands, was perfect for our needs, with some good dog walks nearby.

June Wednesday 27 — Walking Day 49 *Dry, cloudy with sunny spells*

Gretna to Ecclefechan - 11 miles - Total Walked 553

Kay dropped me back at the River Sark Bridge at Gretna. From where I walked past the first house in Scotland and the Gretna Retail Outlet. Gretna Green is famous for its history of allowing marriages between runaway couples from England. English and Scottish law, although similar, have some noticeable differences.

The marriages didn't take place in the Kirk (church), but at the blacksmiths on the outskirts of town, on the village green. They were civil registrations; as the blacksmith joins two metals together, so he joined two people together in marriage.

In 1870 when the Naylor brothers passed through here, residents still remembered the marriage heyday and even remembered black couples coming to get married; runaway servants? At that time, Black people were a very minority population in Britain, (Naylor JOG-LE published 1916).

Gretna Green today is still a place where couples come to get married and as I reached the blacksmith's shop, now a visitor centre, I was joined by a coach party of Canadian tourists, none of whom were getting married. I overheard the tour guide announce, "You have fifteen minutes here to see the famous anvil in the blacksmith's shop; fifteen minutes and back on the coach please".

To do the place justice you need at least twenty minutes, and that includes a tea break or toilet stop. One thing that did strike me here at Gretna (setting aside the Canadian accents), the staff all spoke with a Scottish accent, whereas just a few miles south, the accent was English, albeit with a Cumbrian dialect.

What a lot of people may not know is that during the First World War, Gretna and its surrounding area became famous for a different reason; one of the largest munitions factories in Britain was built on the edge of town. Over thirty thousand people, most of them women, were employed on the site, mixing cordite paste by hand.

Leaving Gretna by a long straight, 'B'-road, which at first looked quiet, especially quiet compared to the nearby parallel motorway. I was walking along, listening to chiffchaffs in the hedgerows and examining the unusual 'concrete' milestones indicating Glasgow, 84 miles, when my peace and solitude was shattered by the roar of motorcycles; hundreds of them.

This stretch of road north is as straight as an arrow. Many motorcyclists use it as a kind of speed test track. Today motorcyclists who were wearing distinctive helmets whizzed past me again and again, one way then the other. Luckily for me there was a wide grass verge which I was making effective use of.

Eventually I arrived at the small linear village of Kirkpatrick Fleming. I climbed up onto a bridge parapet to rest whilst looking down on the busy railway line. The motorcyclists were still present in ever-increasing numbers but here in the village they had slowed right down and were gathering in groups.

I studied my map, trying to work out my next bit of route. I discovered that a nearby caravan site had an ancient historic place of interest, King Robert the Bruce's cave. I walked into mature woodland that cleverly housed a pleasant-looking caravan site. The site office was in the old mansion house, built on the foundations of Dunskelly Castle. I discovered that the 'cave' was down a steep, red rock cliff face and to go towards it I had to pay a small entrance fee of one pound.

King Robert the Bruce, born in 1274, died 1329, belonged to an ancient Norman family who came over to England with William the Conqueror. They originated from France in the town of Bruce, or Brix as it is now known. William granted them lands in Yorkshire and somehow, they moved further north to Annandale.

Some histories have him as being born in Lochmaben; others say he was born in Turnberry Castle. He murdered his nearest rival, John Comyn, in a church at Dumfries and later waged a highly successful guerrilla war against the English (whom he had once supported). After the murder, three of his brothers were executed and he went into hiding. Several caves in Scotland lay claim to being 'the cave' where he famously hid. There is also a claim that he hid in a shed on Rathlin Island, off the coast of Antrim in Northern Ireland. However, the cave at Kirkpatrick Fleming has as strong a case as any of being 'the cave'.

Lochmaben is a mere twelve miles away. Relatives of Bruce lived here in Dunskelly Castle. The cave door is now exhibited in the Scottish National Museum in Edinburgh.

Access to this cave is far easier than in Bruce's time. I followed the path downhill and across a wooden platform, crossing the cliff face leading into the cave itself, high up above the River Kirtle (Kirtle Water as it is known locally). Bruce is said to have spent three months hiding in this cave over the winter of 1306. The cave was a secret place; man-made it was carved out of the rock and used as a secure storage place. To gain access to it in those days required being lowered down to it by ropes. I had the cave all to myself. I spent a few minutes in it, which was enough and as

I was leaving I noticed, in the top corner, a spider working away building its web. I took a photograph of it and was reminded of Bruce watching this spider's ancestor, doing exactly the same during his stay resulting in the famous saying, *'If at first you don't succeed, try, try and try again'*, which it is said, inspired Bruce to victory. Bruce eventually left the cave and raised an army that went on to defeat the English at the battle of Bannockburn in 1314.

On my map, I had noticed a footbridge crossed Kirtle Water below me so instead of retracing my steps, I followed a path steeply downhill and came to a volleyball pitch. Nearby I walked along a stretch of sandy beach. The bridge was in the distance beyond a large, high security fence topped with barbed wire, (to keep the caravaners in?). I had three options: one, to climb the fence; two, to wade waist-deep in the water; three, retrace my steps all the way back to the caravan site entrance and then take a country lane around the edge of the site leading to the bridge. The latter option was the easiest of them all and I wearily trudged back up the steep hillside passing the cave once more. When I eventually reached the bridge, it looked for all intent and purposes as if it had been built by a Blue Peter presenter all out of bits of thrown-away junk. It didn't look at all safe as I climbed up a set of rickety steps onto the bridge itself which 'wobbled' as I crossed.

Having got safely to the other side I followed a cart track up the valley side to a few houses in an idyllic location with views over to the water, woods and cave. I walked through the small hamlets of Irvington and Moorend, both with their low stone-built cottages that were becoming a common sight in this part of the world. I followed a very quiet, long, narrow country lane bounded by walls. The sun was beating down on me and the walk was easy and pleasant. The surrounding fields were empty and I wondered where everyone was.

In 1870, when the Naylor brothers passed this way on their JOG-LE (book published in 1916), the fields were full of agricultural workers and the cottages full of hand-loom weavers but not anymore.

I saw some crows on the road in front of me pecking at a small piece of carrion. They flew up as I neared them and I discovered that the carrion was in fact a dead swallow. Its colours were still vibrant and clear even in death.

I next came upon a huge roundabout that looked ridiculous for such a quiet country lane; that is until I realised it took my lane over the M74 which thundered below me in a deep cutting.

The lane now climbed gently uphill through fields full of sheep. My eye was drawn to a grass-covered earth bank. Even to my untrained eye, it looked like a good defensive position, commanding a strong view across the rolling countryside.

On arriving level with the earthwork, I was provided with some answers. I had arrived at Birrens Roman Fort which in 1895 became the first Roman Fort to be excavated in Scotland and has since been described as *'impressive when approached from the south'*. I certainly agree with that and more.

The extensive ditch system and entrance causeway are all visible, covered in a blanket of turf with gorse bushes dotted around. The fort is in the traditional playing card shape and I found it to be a truly peaceful place. It is thought that the Sixth Legion stationed in York originally built the Fort in AD 80. During excavations, some interesting carved stones were found which recorded visits by two Roman legions that were not thought to have been in Britain for any serious period. These were the eighth Augustus legion, thought to have been in Britain for just a few weeks in AD 43 at the time of the very first Roman invasion and the twenty-second legion that were almost completely unknown in Britain.

I reluctantly left the peace of the Fort and continued along the lane to the village of Middlebie and there, in front of a row of cottages, I found a bench to rest on. From here it was downhill all the way to the Welsh-sounding town of Ecclefechan. On the outskirts of town, I came across a gas-powered bird-scaring device which imitates the sound of a shotgun going off. I stood watching it go through its motions. I walked on along the main street of the town which appeared to be closed although it was only four o-clock. At the crossroads, I was met by Kay and Ripley.

June Thursday 28	**Walking Day 50** *Dry, cloudy and overcast, heavy rain later* **Ecclefechan to Lochmaben - 12 miles - Total Walked 565** >

Ecclefechan lies in the valley of the Mein Water, a tributary of the River Annan. The town has a stern look about it. The main street is dominated by a large statue of Thomas Carlyle, b 1795 - 1881, the Victorian polymath who was born here.

Educated at Edinburgh University, he spent most of his adult life living in Chelsea, London. In his time, he was a celebrity, a historical philosopher and a prolific writer. I must admit I have not read any of his works, most of which are now regarded as classics. The History of the French Revolution; the Letters and Speeches of Oliver Cromwell; Heroes and Hero Worship; are some of his better-known writings.

The house where he was born is on the main street. It is a plain, two-storey building of a neat and tidy appearance. Its most distinguishing feature is an open arch leading to a courtyard. The National Trust for Scotland now takes care of it.

Leaving the house behind me I headed west up a side street towards the Gothic red stone-built church with its impressive clock tower, built in 1865. Here in the graveyard, Thomas Carlyle was laid to rest along with Robert Peel, the Great-grandfather of Robert Peel, the Lancastrian and founder of the Metropolitan police force and Archibald Arnott b.1772-1855, the doctor who attended Napoleon whilst he was imprisoned on St Helena. The graveyard is also home to the remains of the ancient church of St Fechan (an Irish saint who also travelled through Scotland and Wales).

Before I left Ecclefechan, I was reminded that I was near to Robbie Burn's country; Scotland's most famous poet. Burns had visited Ecclefechan and one of the last songs he wrote, in 1795, is titled, The Lass of Ecclefechan. I walked out of the town contemplating on the fact that I hadn't seen any lasses, in fact I'd not seen anyone. The town appeared closed and it was only 10am in the morning.

Surrounded by fields full of sheep the long quiet country lane led me eventually to a stone arched bridge over the fast-flowing River Annan, set in mature deciduous woodland. This was Hoddom Bridge and I climbed onto the parapet to have a rest and drink coffee from my flask.

I had not seen a soul all morning. I knew Scotland's population was small, much smaller than Yorkshire but I was beginning to wonder where everyone was. Just then a convoy of cars pulling caravans arrived at the bridge. They were all Dutch; at least the car registration plates indicated so. Everyone gave me a friendly wave as they passed. The caravaners had arrived at their destination, the delightful Hoddom Castle Caravan site which was over the bridge and up the hill in front of me. The mature woods turned out to be a nature reserve with woodland paths going in my direction. I took them. The castle was built in 1560 by Sir John Maxwell, more as a barracks for troops than a home. It was topped with a tower which has an unusual 'beacon' platform.

The woodland path didn't last long and I soon found myself back on a country lane heading north. However, before I moved away from Hoddom I took a footpath on my left and climbed a small hill to have a look at a watchtower which was named Repentance Tower. The tower stands near to a graveyard and has panoramic views south over the Solway Firth to the hills of the Lake District.

The graveyard has some intricately carved head stones, some with the skull and crossbones and is said to include the grave of a black African slave buried there in 1776. I looked for the grave but couldn't find it. I was reminded of Sunderland Point in Lancashire and the burial place of 'Sambo'.

I carried on up the Annan valley, the river always being a few fields away to my right as I walked north along the lane in a rural setting that reminded me of Devon. After a while I came to the village of Dalton. Half of the houses on the main and only street, were up for sale. This Dalton, although sounding very English, (I know of at least four Dalton's in Yorkshire), was yet another 'dour' Scottish village. I wandered down the main street and tried to gain entry into the 18th-century church, (parts of which are said to be 12th-century) but it was locked. It is built of local red stone and has a squat square tower with a spire on top.

I looked in on the pub, The Murray Arms, which served authentic Thai food but at that moment in time it was well and truly closed, in fact the whole village was closed and I didn't see a soul. A sign pointed to Dalton Pottery which has a cafe, one-and-a-half miles in the wrong direction.

The village has an unusual monument that is worth having a look at. At the Millennium, all the children of the village and there were about twenty, made casts of their hands which were then made into blue pottery tiles and placed on the *Welcome to Dalton* sign. Below each hand is the child's name and age. There must be a primary school in the village? However, I didn't see or hear it.

I left the village in a northerly direction; not even a curtain twitched.

I carried on along a very quiet country lane through an undulating rural countryside, dotted now and again with pine woods. In the low dips of the land I saw marshes and bogs. This area on my map was called The Isle of Flosh. As I was walked along it began to rain; gently at first and then very heavily. I covered myself up as best I could and tried to seek shelter in the frequent pine woods. By the time, I reached Lochmaben Castle I was thoroughly soaked. Kay and Ripley were waiting for me and we had a quick look around the ruined 14th-century stone-built castle. Edward 1 had built a wooden castle here in 1298 but it was Edward II who had this stone one built. Historic Scotland now looks after the ruin. It stands on the south side of Castle Loch and well away from the town itself.

I walked into town along a well-made footpath that runs parallel to Castle Loch. This area is a nature reserve. It is a lovely spot. There is dingy-sailing on the loch and a yacht club at the northern end near to the town.

Kay and Ripley had found this spot and had often walked here whilst I was out pushing my way northwards. Disabled access to fishing quays had recently been opened on the sides of the Loch which has for years been a favourite spot for fishing. Bream is one of the main fish caught today. Years ago the very rare Vendace fish was found here as well as at the nearby Kirk and Mill Lochs. The Vendace is a freshwater white fish. It is four to six inches in length and has such a thin membrane on top of its head you can see its brain. It is not found anywhere else in Scotland and is only found in Bassenthwaite Lake and Derwent Water in England's Lake District, where unfortunately, it was declared 'extinct' in the 1990's. It is illegal to fish for them. I'm not sure how one can legally fish for Bream and not for Vendace in the same water?

Kay took me back to the camp where I got out of my wet clothes and had a hot shower. Later we drove to the large Supermarket in Lockerbie and had a stroll up the main street, browsing the local shops. We asked for directions to the memorial to the Lockerbie disaster of 1988 and I was surprised to learn that it was a good few miles out of the town back on the Lochmaben road at a large cemetery and garden of remembrance at Dryfesdale, which sits on a hill overlooking the valley of the River Annan.

It was a neat, tidy and well-kept cemetery with the Pan Am Lockerbie Memorial being particularly well-cared-for. An avenue of cherry trees leads to a quiet spot where a slab of marble bears the names of the victims. There are also smaller memorials to individual victims of the bombing and a separate memorial to the aircraft crew which, along with the names of the victims, bears the airlines famous blue globe *'PAN AM'* logo. Sadly, following bankruptcy of the company in 1991, the logo no longer can be seen on aeroplanes.

It was at 7.03pm on Wednesday, 21st December 1988 that the Pan Am Flight 103, on route from London to New York, exploded above Lockerbie. All two-hundred and forty-three passengers and sixteen crew members were killed, along with eleven residents of Lockerbie. The dead, mainly Americans followed by British, came from twenty-one different countries. Syracuse University in New York lost thirty-five of its students. All murdered by Libyan terrorists. The bombing has had a lasting effect on Lockerbie itself. I gained the impression from these shopkeepers and residents whom

I had asked for directions to the memorial, that they are all weary of having their town forever in the spotlight for such a terrible and horrendous event. If you 'Google' Lockerbie, you get pages upon pages all about the bombing. Try to find some of the town's ancient history or even recent history and you must do advanced searches.

Lockerbie has a wide main street; a relic from the old coaching days. It is the first large town north of the border and the main road and rail lines to Glasgow pass close by. Lockerbie is first mentioned in 1306. The name is Old Norse for Locki's village, evidence of the Vikings having settled here. The town is and has been since the 1700's, Scotland's largest lamb market, the surrounding gentle hills supporting thousands of sheep. The main street has an impressive Town Hall built in 1880 of red-coloured local stone complete with clock tower. Inside, in the council chamber, a stained-glass window, a little-known memorial to the bombing, depicts the flags of the twenty-one countries from where the victims came.

The small provincial police force of Dumfries and Galloway really 'stood up to the mark' on that fatal day. They carried out the successful murder investigation and subsequent policing of the trial which was held in a special Scottish court in The Netherlands. Their website coverage of the event is still one of the best. I have heard nothing but praise for them. Lockerbie will, I am afraid, forever live with this weight of remembrance. We owe it to the two hundred and seventy murdered people never to forget. Lockerbie as a town carries this responsibility extremely well.

That evening my mum and dad, who retired to Dumfries and Galloway from Yorkshire some twenty years ago, came to visit us. We found a hotel and enjoyed a pleasant evening meal in their company.

June
Friday
29 Moved campsite to Abington

We decided to take a day off from walking and move our camp. I'd already discovered that all the sites in Moffat were full so we wouldn't be able to *'stop off at Moffat'*. We did however drive into Moffat. I'd been to Moffat before when I stayed in a lovely B & B near the impressive market square which has a good selection of shops and pubs. I still have the toffee tin, although empty now, which I'd bought there; the famous Moffat toffee. Moffat is surrounded by an impressive range of low hills and I promised myself one day to return to explore them.

Eventually we found a fabulous site at Abington just off the motorway, but far enough away from it to be quiet. The site was clean, friendly and everything that you'd expect and hope for.

June
Saturday
30 Walking Day 51 *Heavy rain*

Lochmaben to Beattock - 13 miles - Total Walked 578

This morning I was in for a treat although I didn't know it as we drove back to Lochmaben in the pouring rain. The town was founded in 1296 and was made a

Royal Burgh in 1440. The wide main street was decked out with bunting and was crowded with excited people.

This was a bit of a shock after days of wandering through countryside devoid of people. Grandparents and parents were out in force with flag-waving children, some perched on top of their dads' shoulders. I strolled through their ranks dodging the umbrellas, wondering what it was all about. Everyone else was walking in the opposite direction to me. The crowds surged into town from its northern end.

The English under Edward 1 had ransacked the town and burnt its ancient charters. So, as I popped into the very busy post office to get my LEJOG certificate stamped, I contemplated disguising my obvious English accent by putting on a Sean Connery-style twang. The post office staff however turned out to be friendly and had obviously forgiven the English for past atrocities so I didn't need the disguise, thank goodness.

"What's going on?" I asked.

"It's the annual children's gala", came the reply.

Back out among the throng, a fully-kilted Scottish pipe and drum band was marching and playing their way up the main street, the traffic having been stopped by the police.

Following the band was a small but impressive convoy of floats representing most local interests as well as tractors and trailers and a big red fire engine bringing up the rear.

I walked across to the tall, standing statue of King Robert the Bruce that dominates the northern end of the main street. Behind the statue stands the town hall built in 1745, complete with two cells; one for debtors and one for criminals. I love the sound of the pipes and drums and tried to find some shelter from the rain by leaning against its solid walls. A plaque above my head declared that William Paterson, 1658 - 1719, co-founder of the Bank of England, (1694), was born here.

I reluctantly left Lochmaben, passing traditional stone-built cottages which now mingled with modern bungalows. These, although practical, lacked the timeless durability of the original stone cottages.

I left the crowds behind and walked along a level and very quiet country lane. I wish I could have left the rain behind; it was still pouring down or as we say in Yorkshire, 'silin it dahn'. The sheep in the fields were all huddled against the hedges and walls for shelter. In one of the fields there was a beautiful Palomino Pony that didn't seem to be bothered by the rain. When it saw me it ran over to the fence to be near me and looked expectantly for some food. I'd nothing to give it other than a friendly word. I walked on in the rain through a rural scene where farms and large houses were set back from the lane at the end of lengthy driveways. One farm had lined its driveway with brightly-coloured milk churns now transformed into flower pots.

Small clumps of trees, some pine, some deciduous, were dotted along the lane and over the undulating fields. At one point the lane was actually higher than the fields.

Suddenly in the distance, a young red deer ran across the lane and jumped, disappearing into the field below me. I walked quickly to get up to the point where it had vanished and I saw a truly special scene. Down below me in the field I saw six red deer, all young and two had the beginnings of antlers. I stood quietly and watched this small herd feeding. I could have reached out and stroked them. I was amazed that none of them had seen or sensed me. I gently moved my arm and managed to get my camera and could take a few photographs. What eventually disturbed them wasn't me, but a huge, red deer which appeared in classic silhouette on top of the opposite hill. It had a full set of antlers. It was as if it had shouted to the herd. "Oi you lot, come on up here". The herd responded by immediately cantering away up the hill and away from me. Even though I was getting soaking wet, I was happy to stand there and watch such a beautiful scene until the last deer disappeared over the hill.

I turned to carry on along my way. Not too much further on I was surprised to see a family of rabbits playing on the grass verge. They were hopping around in the rain seemingly without a care in the world. One rabbit was performing head-over-heels tumbles, repeatedly. I walked on by and again the rabbits, like the deer, didn't seem to notice me.

The rain kept coming down and the lane soon became a stream. A friendly farmer driving a Land Rover, stopped and asked me if I wanted a lift. He looked really offended when I told him, "No thank you". He drove off and I was left sloshing my way along the lane. I'd walked all the way so far and I wasn't going to break my own rule just because of a bit of rain.

I was reminded of 'The Big Walk', a book by A. Walker, which describes the LEJOG walk in 1960, organised by Billy Butlin. Because he had offered prize money to the first few to finish the walk, there was a tremendous amount of cheating. Walkers were getting lifts all over the place. To combat this, Butlin organised an army of his own Red Coats to carry out spot checks on the walkers. Without the aid of any computers, the details of the thousand or so walkers were telephoned back to base; (no mobile phones either). Using the data, he could work out who was miles further on than could possibly be expected. They were then singled out for extra attention and it wasn't long before many were being disqualified, having been caught getting lifts in cars. The Big Butlin Walk started at John O'Groats and finished at Land's End and the winner was a Yorkshire Man, J. Musgrave from Doncaster.

One thing to come out of the Butlin walk was a report by the Institute of Chiropodists who had monitored the walk and the thousand or so walkers, many of whom got blisters and other foot problems. Their report, produced as an appendix to the Butlin book still stands today with general advice on care of feet. My feet were standing up very well and my Brasher boots, liberally dosed in dubbin, were doing an excellent job keeping all the water out.

After an hour of walking along the wet and lonely lane, the friendly farmer in the Land Rover came back, this time driving in the other direction. He stopped and implored me, nay begged me to get in out of the rain. He was sure I would catch my death of cold. I again declined his offer, feeling warm as toast under my wet weather gear which was doing a great job. The farmer drove off in disgust, probably believing he had just met a mad man.

As I approached the village of Beattock the rain eased slightly bringing swarms of midges out. I walked through 'clouds' of them. A flock of swallows appeared from nowhere and began a stunning aerobatic display right in front of my face as they dive-bombed the midges. They seemed to be swallowing more than one or two. I liked to think the swallows were clearing the way so I could walk midge-free into Beattock.

July
Sunday
1

Rest Day *Dry, overcast, and rain in evening*

We found that our Abingdon camp-site was near to Wanlockhead, which is Scotland's highest village at 1,531 feet above sea level. We set off in the car to explore. We had to travel through the Lowther hills passing its near neighbour, Leadhills, the village's name giving away the very reason these two villages exist.

They say the Romans came to these hills looking for lead. Lead mining took off on an industrial scale during the 17th century. The near-treeless hills; looked bleak and desolate. I can understand why this place is known as the 'Auld Grey Glen' as grey scree stones 'litter' the hillsides.

The low stone-built cottages, all painted white at least helped to distinguish them from the grey hills. The centre of the village has a preserved water pump beam engine used for pumping water out of the mines. The last mine closed in 1959; not because the lead had dried up but because it was much cheaper to dig it elsewhere in the world. We went straight into the excellent museum, it being the only museum in Scotland dedicated to lead mining. It also has an historic library; not quite the oldest subscription library in Britain. That title goes to the Miners' Library in nearby Leadhills, which was opened in 1741. Wanlockhead's library opened in 1756.

In 1842 when the Royal Commissioner on *'Employment of children in lead mines'* visited, he commented on how the village children *'are taught writing, arithmetic, book-keeping, Latin, Greek and French'*. He went on to describe, *'the intelligence of the children of this poor and remote village is most remarkable'*.

One of the highlights of the museum is a tour down a mine. The Lochnell Lead Mine is situated a few yards downstream from the visitor centre. The walk to the mine was on a path full of beautiful wild thyme and is part of the Southern Upland Way. As we strolled down to the mine we were passed by a group of long-distance walkers. They all looked wet, hungry, dishevelled and thoroughly miserable but I might have been wrong. They may have been enjoying themselves.

Our guide was very knowledgeable. He told us that the mine was non-productive for the first eleven years owing to the miners having to bore a tunnel through sheer rock to get to the seams of lead and to do this they worked long hours. This perplexed me somewhat. Weren't these the same miners who were strong chapel-goers; who liked to read all sorts of books and in fact had a library in the village? Yet the guide portrayed an image of the miners like the Yorkshire men in the Tim Brooke Taylor/

Monty Python sketch, in that they got up to go to work two hours before they went to bed. In other words, they worked a twenty-six-hour day. "When did they find time to read books and go to chapel?" I asked. "Very rarely", came his serious reply. This was a minor point to what was otherwise an excellent tour.

The Duke of Buccleuch owned this area and the miners had to pay him for the privilege of mining here. We learnt that the present Duke still owns this area. For a while these two villages were the most diverse communities in Scotland. Miners came here seeking work from all over the mining world; Cornish tin miners, Welsh and Yorkshire coal miners, together with hundreds of Italians.

We looked in on the Wanlockhead Inn, Scotland's highest pub, but it was packed so we chose to eat at the Museum Visitor Centre cafe where we had an excellent Scotch broth. Whilst in the cafe we learnt, from the waitress who lives in the village, that back in the 1960's, "the authorities planned to close the village down and move the remaining inhabitants to Dumfries". The villagers dug in and protested and their challenge resulted in their village surviving.

Since the opening of the museum the village has grown in population.

You are never too old to learn new tricks and being recently retired, I was eager to pick up some useful skills that might help me later. I'd therefore booked myself onto the gold panning course which the museum runs. Kay walked Ripley around the village whilst I made my way to the gold panning School.

Surprisingly I found I was the afternoon's only pupil. Having paid my license fee to the Duke of Buccleuch Estate, I learnt that I could keep whatever gold I panned. With a set of instructions from my teacher I was soon in the swing of 'panning'. The stream had been diverted into some large water butts and I could help myself to a pile of recently dug river gravel, quickly separating the heavier gold from the gravel.

I collected my specks of gold in a water-filled test tube. After an hour or so of panning, I had made about fifty pence worth of gold. My license to pan had cost £15, so it wasn't quite economically viable. Having had a full and interesting day out we returned to our camp-site, 'educated' and tired.

 July
Monday
2

Walking Day 52 *Mild and sunny at first, then rain and heavy rain later*

Beattock to Elvanfoot - 15 miles - Total Walked 593

The scenery changed from gently undulating rural fields to steep, pine-forest-clad hills. I walked through Beattock which appeared to be a one street village. It looked drab. It could have been the weather as I am conscious that places look better when they are bathed in sunshine.

I found I was walking on the Southern Upland Way. At 212 miles, it is Scotland's longest long distance footpath. I covered a few yards of it then crossed a stone arched bridge, dominated by a large plaque that declared it had been built in 1819 by John

Macdonald from a design by Thomas Telford. I looked over the parapet down to the Elvan Water below and watched a grey wagtail bobbing about the rocks near the water.

I had studied the maps to find a route north and had reluctantly decided to follow the national cycle trail number 74 which headed north on the B7076. This route ran parallel to the very busy M74 motorway and had previously been the A74 road. Excepting that the motorway was nearby, the route turned out to be very quiet with hardly any traffic and I found it easy walking. In some places, I was joined by the railway; the London to Glasgow line, (known as the West Coast Main Line).

All along the route were truly spectacular displays of white and purple foxgloves, often joined by large clumps of sorrel which were already turning to an autumnal reddy-brown colour. I found a magnetic sign that had obviously been stuck on the side of a vehicle. It read, *'John O'Groats to Land's End – Against breast cancer'*. I pulled it out of the undergrowth and left it in a more prominent position. I figured the charity walkers or cyclists had long since passed by.

At a place marked on the map as Middlegill I stopped to eat my packed lunch. I was in the middle of nowhere with pine tree covered hills all around, but my mobile phone signal was good. I rang Kay who happened to be out in the Nissan and she drove the few miles south to join me for lunch. I was glad to see her and Ripley and to have a sit down on a proper seat; benches in these parts were rare.

After lunch Kay left me and I walked on and up, the route gently climbing uphill. As I got higher I moved into hill country, devoid of trees. I was climbing up Beattock Banks to Beattock Summit which, at 1,033 feet is the highest point on both the nearby Motorway and railway line. For many years' traffic struggled to get up here in winter and it gained a reputation similar to Shap Summit in Cumbria.

In the days of Steam a banker, (an extra engine) was needed here at Beattock to help push the trains up the daunting hill. It was made famous in the poem *'The Night Mail'* by York born poet W.H. Auden... *'This is the Night Mail crossing the border... pulling up Beattock, a steady climb. The gradients against her, but she's on time'*.

At one point I was buzzed by a pair of oyster catchers; those beautiful black and white birds with bright orange beak. I gathered I must be near their nest.

As I came to walk down alongside the motorway I passed the large sign declaring I was entering South Lanarkshire which was *'thriving on safe driving'*, according to the sign. Who dreams up these slogans? I thought this one was particularly 'naff'. I was sure South Lanarkshire had more to thrive on than just 'safe driving'.

It began to rain heavily. For some time, I walked in the valley bottom, squeezed between the motorway, the river, the railway and the cycle-way. At junction 14 on the motorway, I walked into Elvanfoot. A few lonely cottages formed the hamlet at the base of the ever-bigger hills. No one appeared to be at home. I was amazed that these few cottages had been given a motorway junction. Kay and Ripley were waiting for me.

Walking Day 53 *Heavy showers at first followed by a spell of bright sunny weather, then ending in rain*

Elvanfoot to Mainshill - 14 miles - Total Walked 607 ⟩

I set off from the motorway junction in a lay-by full of lorries. It was obviously a favourite stopping-off point. It was raining heavily again as I continued along Cycleway No. 74. Once I was away from the motorway I walked in solitude. As I got into my stride the small village of Crawford came into view.

The village is surrounded by what today looked like the bleak Lowther Hills. In the rain, everything looked very dreary. The sprightly young River Clyde was flowing down on my right and I was fast approaching Abington, the village where we were camped. It is situated on the Edinburgh turn-off at junction 13 on the M74. Most motorists will know it because of its large motorway service station.

Abington is surrounded by mature trees which in these surroundings are a welcome change to the grass-covered hills. I noticed on the map, a faint path running through the wood on the southern approach to the village so I headed for it. I phoned Kay and suggested that she and Ripley could walk into the woods from the village and hopefully we would meet up. As it turned out the wood was small and Kay and Ripley were waiting for me at the southern edge, and we walked the short distance to the village; a surprisingly busy place.

Abington has a Bank, Hotel, Post Office, Shop and a bistro-style Cafe; a much more pleasant place than the nearby Motorway Service Station. Having been camped here for a few days I had grown to like the place; plus, the people were friendly which helps. I left the village, Kay and Ripley behind and walked up to the massive motorway service station which covers an area much larger than the village it shares its name with. The old A74 over the infamous and inhospitable Red Moss was my next goal.

After the motorway was built the old dual carriageway was reduced to a single lane; the other lane was grassed over in parts, leaving bits of tarmac here and there. This was the National Cycleway number 74 and I was going to use it to get over Red Moss. The motorway veered off and away to my right and I eventually lost sight of it as it progressed northwards in a deep cutting. It was a long pull up from Abington. I walked for miles up into the bleak wilderness of Red Moss. As far as the eye could see, all before me was moorland. The old A74 road that I was following was deserted and quiet.

The weather, as it always can and does up in the fells, changed dramatically; dark, dull and depressing clouds rolled over the fell tops and suddenly I was in the middle of a horrendous downpour. There was no shelter to be found anywhere. I covered up and sloshed my way on through streams of flowing water. The weather got worse if that was possible. A swirling mist enveloped the whole moss. It quickly became a total 'white out', except it was a dark grey tinged with purple. My views vanished and I lost my horizon. There was nothing to do but plod on.

In the 1940's and 50's when lorries crossed this route it was known as Suicide Alley. I was not surprised by that name. Here I was in the middle of summer, crossing the moss in what felt more appropriately to be a winter scene. I imagined I was Captain Kirk of the U.S. Starship Enterprise, beamed down to explore the new planet Earth. Landing on this very spot at that moment he would have been speaking into his radio, "Beam me up Scottie. Earth is totally inhospitable and horrible". I sloshed on, peering into the mist as best I could.

I kicked an old, rusty metal sign which declared 'Red Moss Transport Cafe 2 miles'. This lifted my spirits and I walked on and on and on. I watched the shadows in the mist to see if they transformed into something friendly. Most either fluttered away into the mist or turned into gorse bushes. This was a dreary walk.

In 1934, W. B. Dawson, in his 'LEJOG' book, cycled over here. He was delighted by the Red Moss and the Lowther Hills and remarked, '... not remarkable in shape but truly they are beautiful in the summer sun ... All the colours of the rainbow could be seen in the grass bushes: yellows, oranges, reds, shades of greens and blues'. A tinge of purple in the dull grey was the best I could do. These two colours, mixed as they were, can easily cause depression. The Russian-born American painter Mark Rothko, renowned for painting purple blocks on canvas, must have been here or somewhere like here to achieve his inspiration. They say people 'weep' after looking long into his purple pictures. I understand it now. Rothko famously said, "Go forward into nature". Well I was going as fast as I could. I longed for a break in the weather and for a cup of tea. I wasn't going to get either quickly. I sloshed and plodded on.

The rain was now a shower mist that soaked me more thoroughly than the heavy rain itself. The only good thing to say was that at least the cycleway that I was walking along could still be followed but only just. I was thinking that this spot would go down as the worst place on my entire walk but then I remembered those awful shopping malls in Exeter, Bristol, Preston and so on. Yes, without a doubt they were truly awful places and I'd rather be here in the mist on Red Moss than in one of those places. Jesus went into the wilderness for forty days. I'd been in this wilderness for four hours and it was enough for me. I bellowed out a prayer. "Give me a bloody break".

A short time later my prayer was answered. Way out in front of me deep in the mist, I saw a bright light. It was too big a light to be the headlights of a lorry and I thought it might be the lights from the fabled Red Moss Transport Cafe. The light grew larger and larger as I walked towards it; then I hesitated for a moment. Had I not just prayed for this deliverance from the mist? So, I thanked God over and again for bringing this ray of light into my world. I was being sucked towards it like a magnetic pull. Suddenly, as if by some magic and mystic power, all was revealed to me. The mysterious light was the Sun itself in all its glorious, majestic, beautiful and powerful self, shining down on me.

The mist cleared and I was joined by the haunting sound of a curlew flying overhead. It is one of my favourite sounds in nature. Just then a stone chat bobbed up on top of a gorse bush and began singing, "Look at me. Look at me", puffing up its rust coloured breast at the same time. The moss that I'd earlier thought dead and inhospitable was suddenly alive with birds; skylarks flew up above me; insects could be seen flitting from bush to bush and I was back, happily walking in this now cheerful landscape. It was as though I'd walked through a bad dream. What's more I had a good view ahead. There in the distance I could see the famous Red Moss Transport Cafe. I hastened towards it.

Before the coming of the motorway, in the 1950's and 60's, the Red Moss Transport Cafe was the centre of the universe for a lot of travellers struggling north to Glasgow over Red Moss in winter. The Red Moss was the last major hurdle before the relatively easy route down the Clyde valley to Glasgow.

As I approached the cafe I braced myself for disappointment. It looked lifeless. No cars or lorries were parked outside. I was correct in my assumption, for on arrival I discovered it was closed. No one was on site. A sign declared 'Open at 4pm', which I found strange, Why open at 4pm? Until I figured out that the cafe must concentrate its business on the night traffic. There was no chance for a cup of tea here. I walked around the place shaking door handles, hoping that one may be open. It wasn't to be. With still half an hour to go to 4pm, I decided to move on rather than wait. I didn't want to be disappointed again.

It was still an uphill walk but in the distance, I could see the crest of the hill which gave me something to head for. After a while I became aware of a thick black line in the heather up and over to my left. With my eyes, I followed the line away to the left and saw it emerge at a vast area of blackness. I couldn't make out what it was but as I got nearer I saw some movement on the line.

This kept my attention for some time as I tried to think what it could be. As I got nearer I could see that the movement was in fact a huge lorry and the thick black line was a track or lane. I decided it must be some sort of quarry. Eventually, as I reached a point where I was almost parallel to it, I saw that it was the Mid Rig open cast coal mine, a working mine. The huge blackness or black hole was the working end. I stood by the lane that entered the road crossing the cycleway. A car wash contraption was set up here to wash the wheels on the lorries before they entered the road. A coal-laden lorry with wheels as tall as me went through the contraption. The water sprinkled onto the tyres in a pathetic dribble. The lorry moved off and onto the road, taking half the open cast mine with it. A thick black line of coal dust ran on the road for as long as I walked nearby it.

At long last I crested the hill. The featureless horizon now stretched out into the distance. I heard the drone of the motorway. The noise got louder and soon I was again walking parallel to it. I was walking downhill and fast approaching Mainshill at junction 12 of the M74. Kay and Ripley were waiting for me at the bottom of the road. We drove into the nearby town of Douglas.

The town has the remains of a 12th-century castle where in 1307 or 1308, (the exact date is disputed), a massacre of English troops took place. The English, having captured the castle went to pray in the castle chapel. The remnants of the defeated Scots promptly set it on fire killing all those inside. The castle is said to have inspired Sir Walter Scott for one of his many novels, *'Castle Dangerous'*. Most of the castle was demolished as recently as 1938 due to coal mining subsidence.

The town still has its 13th-century church, St Brides, with its heart-shaped effigies on its interior walls. It has a shapely tower which contains what is said to be Scotland's oldest working clock dating back to the 14th-century. It is said to have been a gift from Mary Queen of Scots. In accordance with the Douglas motto the clock chimes Jamais arriere - *'never behind'* and strikes three minutes before the hour. We were soon heading back to the campsite for our evening meal. I hadn't really given Douglas the time it deserved.

July
Wednesday
4

Walking Day 54 *Dry and sunny*

Mainshill (Junction 12, M74) to Lanark - 9 miles - Total Walked 616

After being dropped off I made my way to the Happendon Service Station which once serviced the A74 dual carriageway. Today it is still open but needs a slight diversion from the motorway to get to it. It turned out to be one of the quietest motorway service stations that I'd seen. I crossed what remained of the A74 and on a good footpath, walked through the pleasant mixed woodland of Happendon Wood. After yesterday's moorland yomp this was much more like it but it didn't last long. I reached the end of the wood and before me was a gently undulating rural scene of fields and hedges, dotted with small neat farms and cottages with well-kept flower gardens.

I found a very quiet tree-lined lane to follow and I was soon in my stride passing farm houses with evocative names such as 'Wolf Crooks Farm'. I was walking now parallel to a disused railway line that I had hoped to use but it was so overgrown, my previous experience warned me to leave it well alone. Away over to my right on a hillside I could see the ugly evidence of old mine workings. This was Rigside mine which closed down in the 1960's. Those responsible for the mine; those who made money out of it, hadn't by the look of things kept some money to one side to regenerate and refurbish the area once the mine closed.

On the other side of the lane however, I was surprised to learn that the beautiful green hillside I was looking at had once been a vast opencast coal mine called Broken Cross. Most of it has since been landscaped and it looked pretty good to me; what a contrast.

The village of Douglas Water came into view. This village was a proud mining village which in its heyday, boasted numerous societies, theatres, libraries and even a railway station. Today it looks a sad state and is known as *'The village that once was'*. The last coal mine closed in 1967 and nothing replaced that industry to keep people here. The Louden Pond Nature Reserve which I was skirting around, is the one positive bit of news in the area. There has been talk of opening new mines. The area still has vast untapped coal reserves and nearby, coal-hungry power stations, but cheap Polish coal still floods into the country. The last few villagers cling on to their once active and lively community but for how long?

My route now led me downhill to the village of Kirkfield Bank where I joined the fast maturing River Clyde. I could see over to my right the buildings of New Lanark and above them the woodland that contained the Falls of Clyde, two places of interest that I intend to visit. I walked over an ancient stone arched bridge, now bypassed by a modern road bridge. The stone parapet was low, coming just above my knees, so a metal addition had been constructed raising the parapet above waist height. This metal parapet was clamped into place by many metal clamps all bearing the legend, *'Made in England'*. I thought this a bit ironic as the bridge crossed that mighty Scottish river, the Clyde and led me into the town of Lanark which was the birthplace of William Wallace, Scotland's heroic 13th-century English basher.

As I walked into Lanark it started to rain heavily and I was glad Kay and Ripley were there waiting for me.

 Rest Day *Heavy showers with some dry spells*

July
Thursday
5

Today we were being visited by an old colleague and friend of mine, Phil and his wife Karin. Upon retirement, they moved deep into the Yorkshire Dales. Today they had driven up to see us.

We drove to the World Heritage site of New Lanark where we had a comfortable stroll around the beautifully restored village that surrounds the 18th-century cotton mill on one side and the River Clyde on the other.

Large tenement buildings have been converted, creating modern homes. Some of the other tenement blocks have been preserved as hotels, youth hostels and a visitor centre complete with cafe and museum.

It was good to catch up with Phil and Karin and hear all their news and this place was a great venue.

New Lanark was founded in 1786 by its owner David Dale, as a model village based around its cotton mills. Two thousand, five hundred people were employed here in its heyday; many came from the slums of Glasgow and Edinburgh and some came from as far away as Caithness in the north. New Lanark came to its fore when in 1800, Welsh-born social reformer Robert Owen, b. 1771-1858, came here to manage it. He was already a successful business man and a benevolent employer. However, it was here that he found he could put his ideas into practice; Ideas that are still amazingly relevant and topical today. He believed that the best work could only be expected from happy, prosperous and educated employees. His far-reaching ideas didn't come cheap and Owen eventually gave up his New Lanark commune when financial difficulties forced him out twenty-five years later.

We went for a walk to the nearby Falls of Clyde using a well-kept riverside footpath accessed through a gate in the wall near to the visitor centre. The Bonnington Power station, as it is called, is the only ugly blot in this idyllic scene. Made from concrete and metal, one wonders how they managed to get planning permission for it. One of the generators had the word *'Yorkshire'* built into its facia and had in fact been made in Leeds, Yorkshire. For five days in the year, in April and October, the power station is switched off to allow the waterfalls to be seen to their full effect; these are known as 'waterfall days'.

Passing the power station with its many pipe lines threading up the hillside behind, we entered the world painted by J.M.W. Turner and others and described by Wordsworth and Sir Walter Scott. There are several waterfalls, the top one being Bonnington Linn which has a single cascade and even today (a non-waterfall day) was an impressive sight. We followed the trail back to the Corra Linn waterfall taking advantage of the fenced off viewing point. The fall comprises a series of cascades over benches of near horizontal sandstone. Wordsworth described Corra Linn as *'The Clyde's most majestic daughter'*.

It started to drizzle and the paths quickly became slippery so we slowly made our way back. Kay was in her element because someone had very kindly labelled all the wildflowers that abounded on both sides of the path, the yellow small cow wheat being a special find as it is only found in Scotland. Hedge woundwort, balsam and common comfrey were other riverside plants that helped set the scene.

On arriving back at New Lanark, we headed for the Visitor Centre cafe and a warming, much-needed bowl of soup. A good variety of shops make up Lanark High Street with a fine statue of William Wallace dominating the bottom end. A large modern Tesco supermarket is situated just behind a row of shops which is interrupted by the ginnel, Bulls Close; named because in years gone by bulls were tethered here prior to slaughter.

I noticed a fantastic sweet shop called Sweet Memories. Inside it was decorated in the1950's style and selling sweets from that period.

We drove back to Abington via the top end of town passing Lanark Racecourse which closed in the 1950's, although much of the site remains, including the finishing post. Today much of the course is still associated with horses; the stables are still used as such and a riding school is based in one area.

Our day off with Phil and Karin was over too soon and later that afternoon we waved goodbye to them as they set off to travel back home to Yorkshire.

| July
Friday
6 | **Rest day** *Dry and overcast* |

Today we moved camp, reluctantly saying goodbye to Abington. It had been an excellent well-run site and we had liked everything about it. I found that a site at Strathclyde Country Park, Motherwell, near Glasgow, appeared to be perfectly located for all our needs. It was a big shock driving into an urban area. The huge Muirhouse towers, a set of multi-storey flats, dominate the skyline to the right on the approach to the conurbation that is Greater Glasgow.

Strathclyde Country Park had been the venue for water-based sports for the 1986 Commonwealth Games. The park is beautifully laid out with a large lake separating the park from the motorway. At the northern end of the park near the funfair, we found the council-run campsite. It had been the athlete's village during the Games. The whole park abounded in mint green hazel bushes which were all in nut.

The grass pitches in each pod were muddy and waterlogged. We were advised not to pull onto the grass but to park up on the tarmac where everyone else was. This gave us just enough room between the other vans.

To get to the toilets we had to wade through the waterlogged grass. The toilet block had only one tiny roof light and so appeared dark and dingy. Spiders' webs were everywhere. These toilet blocks were not as clean as the ones at other sites we had visited. On any normal day, we would by now have moved on and found a better site but sites were limited in this area and we resolved to stick it out.

That night, a caravan occupied by a Dutch family pulled in and began setting up opposite us. At the same time a large group of feral-looking kids aged about twelve appeared from the bushes. The kids, boys and girls, began throwing bricks at the caravans and hitting the Dutch family's caravan with a sickening series of thuds. All the caravaners came out and chased the kids away. The Dutch family didn't stay. They packed up and moved on that night. A very Glasgow welcome to Britain. The 'feral' kids were later chased off again after being caught throwing their bricks at a toilet block.

With all the excitement of 'feral', stone-throwing kids, I'd failed to take much notice of a small two-berth caravan that was stuck in the mud in our pod. It was the only caravan parked on the grass. It had seen better times; in fact, it was one of the dirtiest caravans we had seen on the entire journey. The grey slime smearing each of the caravan's windows turned out to be a fusion of net curtains and cigarette smoke. On closer inspection, I could make out a very large television screen. Cartoons were constantly on display. Other than the T.V. I saw no other sign of life emanating from the caravan.

A few days later a flat back lorry appeared and the driver, a large man, went into the smoke-filled caravan. An hour or so later I was amazed to see him emerge with five children aged from about fourteen years down to five or six years, together with an equally large woman who was chain smoking and they all drove off in the van. Kay, who was to spend more time on the site and who had a different view point, wrote home in one of her many letters: *'My vocabulary is being extended by both the parents and the children who spend a lot of their time inside their tiny caravan screaming at one another and using extremely colourful language. At least their neighbours at home are getting a break'.*

Having been slightly depressed by the state of our new home we decided to spend the afternoon in Glasgow. On the way into town we passed a huge, 'out-of-town' shopping centre; The Buchanan Galleries. Kay wanted to have a look. Our daughter Samantha was getting married in August and up until now, Kay's preparations had been limited to telephone planning. She was desperate to look for 'mother-of-the-bride' outfits.

We thus went into the Buchanan Galleries and were swallowed up for a while, in that awful world of shopping. I was pleasantly surprised to see that Pennine Water from Huddersfield, Yorkshire, was on sale from coin-operated machines within the vast underground car park.

The shopping mall was busy, mostly with women. Kay found it difficult to find anything at all suitable. I was in a trance, hoping that soon this torture would be over but at the same time doing my duty. As a man, if I want to buy something I go straight in and buy it. Women have no idea what they want, preferring to browse for ever around similar airless shops, hoping something may jump out and say, 'buy me'. Eventually Kay was beaten and gave me the nod. She had tried her best. Setting off back we wondered if our motorhome would still be safe and sound at the site. Thankfully it was.

July
Saturday
7

Walking Day 55 *Dry and sunny*

Lanark to Motherwell - 14 miles - Total Walked 630

Today I was to follow the Clyde Walkway; a footpath which according to my literature accompanied the River Clyde all the way into Glasgow. I left Lanark and crossed the busy road by the bridge. A footpath sign directed me through some woods to the river bank where I saw another hydroelectric power station, albeit much smaller than the previous one I'd seen. I used the power station's dam wall to cross the river. I then followed the Clyde Walkway through willow trees and fields smothered in meadow sweet, common comfrey and balsam. I nearly missed the Stonebyres Waterfall whose vantage viewpoint was hidden by overgrown vegetation.

I came to a country park of sorts and the path followed a miniature railway line complete with small stations. I gathered it was some kind of children's activity park but no one was around. I arrived at a bridge and the village of Crossford.

I found myself in a sheltered housing complex with neat gardens and seats which I took advantage of. A grey-haired man, his hair in a ponytail, wearing large leather gloves walked past me and crossed over the bridge. I don't think he even noticed me. On his arm, he was carrying a bird of prey, a large falcon.

After my rest, I set off again on a good footpath across level fields at the side of the river. Wooden walkways helped me cross water-filled ditches in lovely surroundings. I was just getting back into my stride when my way was blocked by a gate and large fence. A sign on the gate indicated that the owners of this property had agreed to allow the Clyde Walkway to cross their land providing the walkers and cyclists obeyed the rules. There then followed a list of rules to be observed: *'No camping'; 'no fire lighting'; 'no dropping litter';* etc., etc. The best rule was *'no sauntering'*. I opened the gate and walked along the path. To my left were beautiful manicured lawns leading down to the river; to my right more lawns, gardens, orchards and a beautiful house in spectacular surroundings, the owners of which now had to put up with the likes of me crossing over their lawns. On leaving the 'grounds', I was greeted by yet more signs thanking me for *'not sauntering'*.

I continued along an excellent boardwalk that carried me safely over large patches of wet, boggy land. The boardwalks continued as I climbed rocky knolls and descended deep v-shaped glens. Excellent bridges had been built to help me across the widest ravines. The boardwalk appeared new and went on for some miles, (it must have cost a small fortune). Then just as I was descending a wooded slope, the boardwalk steps finished abruptly. At the bottom of the hill I found a pile of sawn timber and all the builders' paraphernalia to indicate the steps would soon be completed but not today. Not only did the boardwalk stop but also there was no visible sign of a footpath ahead. I still had the River Clyde over to my left. I decided to continue as planned alongside the river bank.

I came to a barbed wire fence that separated woodland from a large meadow. With some difficulty, I climbed the fence and continued along the riverbank through the meadow. At the far end of the meadow my route climbed into another rocky knoll covered by trees. I pushed on through the trees without the aid of a path, always keeping the river, now wide and slow flowing to my left.

The wooded knoll led down a steep slope to yet another barbed wire fence leading to yet another large meadow. As I descended towards the barbed wire fence, I could hear men laughing loudly. I saw the men before they saw me. Directly opposite me on the other side of the fence, was a group of five men sitting around an open fire drinking cans of beer. Their seats were the upturned crates.

Of scruffy appearance, aged between thirty to fifty. They were in possession of two large Rottweiler dogs. As I slithered down the slope towards them, the dogs saw me and began barking ferociously. At the bottom of the slope, I tried to correct myself and stand upright but the bigger of the two dogs made a gigantic leap over the fence and before I could do anything, it was on me. Its sharp teeth snapping at the side of my face. The foul smell of dog breath alone almost knocked me out. The full weight of the dog knocked me backwards and I fell with it on top of me. I was shocked by the sudden attack and for a moment, thought my life was at an end. I struggled to keep hold of my Leki stick and was using it to push the dog off when I felt hot, wet saliva being licked across my face. It took a moment for my brain to engage. This dog wasn't biting my face; it was licking me in true Scooby Doo fashion. It was a big heavy dog and the saliva was truly revolting but infinitely preferable to the painful bloody wounds I had expected.

I pushed the dog off and scrambled to my feet noting that the men at the other side of the fence were a mean-looking bunch. To a man, they had greasy matted hair, their eyes were set in deep, sunken sockets, stubble and beards graced their faces, their teeth were rotten and their fingernails were grubby and black. I'd fallen into the camp of a bunch of real desperado's. Luckily, they were all drunk. As they tried to stand up with their legs crossed, several of them fell back to the ground – fortunately not into the fire. Two of them crawled frantically to the river bank where they tried to hide fishing rods under camouflage netting. They failed miserably, getting tangled up in the net. That left three men and the two dogs. Scooby Doo was now wagging his stump of a tail by my side as if I was a long-lost friend. The other quiet, silent-type-of-a-dog, was circling around to one side and I wasn't at all sure about it. Two men were still laid out on the ground, incapable of standing up. Several empty beer cans were strewn around behind them. That left one man, much smaller than me looking directly at me. He said "Och aye, we thought you were the f...ing water bailiff".

At least I thought that was what he said in his classic, Rab C. Nesbitt, Glaswegian lingo. I replied to him, something along the lines of, "Pardon". He clearly didn't understand and continued in a drunken, slurred speech. "See you Jimmy, you f...ing gave us the shits. We thought you were the water bailiff". He was angry - but not that angry. I decided to confront them head on and climbed over the fence – not very easy to do as I was also trying to keep an eye on the other dog which was now menacingly circling me. On the other side, the lone standing man said something that I took to mean, "Don't be afraid of the dogs, they're harmless". Although he could quite easily have said, "I'd be afraid of the dogs if I were you. That one might be harmless but the other one is a monster". I couldn't understand a word. The other men were now gathering their senses and getting to their feet and I was soon surrounded by an evil-looking group of men, all swaying unsteadily.

They had glazed eyes and foul-smelling breath; they all reeked of stale alcohol, cigarette smoke and foul body odour – truly vile and repugnant. I decided I had been too long in their company, so I told them I was walking along the River Clyde into Glasgow. This caught their attention. I gathered that in all the years they'd been illegally fishing at this spot, they'd never seen anyone come down through the wood from the direction I'd done. I told them about the Clyde Walkway, which I presume will one day be completed to pass this very spot. They had never heard of it. My initial impression of them being evil was, I am glad to say, wrong. They turned out to be very friendly, even offering me a sip of their beer. I was still worried about the silent dog, now right behind me and drooling at the mouth. "Just control that dog, will you?" I asked. One of the men gave the dog an almighty kick on its side and it went scampering away to the river. Whilst I was relieved the dog was away from me, I wasn't too pleased with the way it was achieved.

The soberest man said, "You'll want to see the Roy Memorial". Up to that point, I'd never heard of the Roy Memorial. I had to concentrate hard as he began to giving me directions to it. Apparently, I had to "use the fisherman's' path" which "avoided the big house with walled gardens, the owners being right bastards" and I was warned to "be careful, they'll shoot you if they catch you on their land". I waved goodbye to my new-found friends who quickly resumed drinking, dogs by their sides. I was glad to be breathing fresh air again.

After a while, my way was blocked by a large, stone wall which was too big to look over and obviously belonged to a big house. I crept around the wall on a muddy path that led me back into thick undergrowth with rhododendron bushes. Eventually I emerged onto a private lane that did lead to a big house by the river. I turned away from the house and walked up the lane to a gatehouse, escaping onto a tarmac road. A sign on the fence by the gatehouse declared the drive to be private, with no right of way. Thankfully no "right bastard with a gun" was around.

I'd lost sight of the river and the Clyde Walkway and I was walking up-hill wondering what I was going to do next when I came upon the Roy Memorial; a concrete trig point painted white; once a familiar site on top of many hills and fells across Britain. The memorial was to Major General William Roy, b.1726-1790 who was responsible for the first military ordnance survey of Scotland. He used the then new three-foot theodolite, newly designed by Jesse Ramsden to accurately measure the hills and valleys. His work laid the foundation to what was then called the Trigonometrical survey of Gt. Britain 1791 and later became better known as The Ordnance Survey, a name which survives today.

Using my ordnance survey map I accurately pinpointed my location at Miltonhead, the birthplace of Roy. Studying the map caused me some concern. If I followed the lane I would eventually arrive at Carluke, miles from where I wanted to be. If I set off across the fields and crossed Jock's Burn, a trickle of a stream according to the map, I would eventually arrive back at the riverside footpath heading in the right direction.

I set off across a large field towards a complex of farm buildings but on nearing them I could hear dogs barking. I'd had enough of dogs this morning, so I gave the farm a wide berth and walked the long way around the large field, crossing hedges through narrow gaps. I continued until I reached the top of a deep wooded 'v'-shaped glen. I could see across to the other side, some four hundred yards. Below me was a sheer drop into the valley bottom. I looked for a way down. All around was mud, liberally laced with cow muck where cattle had once been sheltering under the trees at the edge of the field.

The ubiquitous barbed wire fence stood between the field's edge and the wood. This fence was much sturdier and taller than I had been used to. I walked through the knee-deep mud or rather waded through it, looking for an easy way over the fence and a way down into the ravine-like glen. Two buzzards circling and whirling above kept me company as I sloshed my way forward. These fields for as far as my eyes could see were deserted of farm life and people. No one was here except me.

I climbed the fence using one of its posts for support. I took my time resting and balancing, one move at a time as I slowly reached the top. The most difficult bit is swinging a leg over the barbed wire. To give me some protection from the barbs, I placed my rucksack directly on top of them so it was in between my legs as I straddled the fence. There wasn't much room on the other side before the land dropped steeply into the glen. After what seemed like an exhausting eternity I was at last over the fence, in one piece with no rips or tears.

On climbing the fence, I had at least climbed out of the mud. My brain was slow to realise that the fence had been strong, tall and sturdy for a reason. The descent into the glen was a sheer drop and looked dangerous. I can't have been thinking straight as I decided to descend diagonally into the ravine. The ground was loose and shale-like and I began to pick up speed; speed I didn't want or need. Years ago, as a youth, on camping holidays in the Lake District, I'd enjoyed scree running as a means of quickly descending a fell using lots of loose stones and slates to 'ski' down the slope but without the aid of ski's.

My descent into the depths of Jock's Burn was similar but much worse. Before I knew what was happening I was hurtling towards the bottom; ripping up grasses, bushes, shrubs and even young trees as I sped ungraciously towards the stream in the bottom. About ten feet up from the stream I came to a jolting abrupt stop. Looking back, I could see a deep groove or shoot, cleared of all vegetation, marking my descent. It resembled a children's play slide.

A few years ago, I'd spent a happy afternoon with daughters Samantha and Charlotte and the people from Forest of Bradford, planting trees in the grounds of Bingley Grammar School; doing my bit for the environment. My descent into Jock's Burn had just undone all that good work. Most of the vegetation was on me. I stood for a while gathering my senses. No bones felt broken and I was in one piece. On looking down I saw that my feet and legs up to my knees were stuck in a rotten tree stump which resembled an overgrown toilet bowl covered in green mossy slime. I was stuck and try as I might I couldn't get out. I frantically tried to kick my way out but found I couldn't move my feet. I tried reaching for some branches from nearby trees to pull myself out. The branches were either too far away or so slight they came away in my hands. The saying that *'a rolling stone gathers no moss'* is not true. I was completely covered in the stuff and my rucksack, still on my back, resembled a large bush.

I took it off and thought about the situation I had found myself in. The stream below was bubbling away through a primeval setting. I doubt if anyone had been down here in years, or if at all. A jungle lay before me. Looking up I could just make out the blue sky peeping through the canopy of leaves. The buzzards were still to be heard mewling above; my imagination now turning them into vultures, waiting for my demise. I felt in my pocket for my mobile phone but not surprisingly, I couldn't get a signal. I did have a whistle for emergencies and remembered the code; six long blasts, rest, then repeat. I didn't use it. No one was up there and no one would expect anyone to be down here in the first place.

I felt like shouting, screaming and weeping all at once. I dreaded to think what creepy crawlies were stuck in the tree stump, my legs and feet now joining them for company. In the 1960's when cigars, could be advertised on TV, there was an advert for Hamlet cigars. The man, having got himself stuck somewhere, would have a cigar, a hamlet moment which, giving him inspiration quickly enabled him to resolve his problem. I was having a Hamlet moment but without the cigar, I don't smoke anyway. In my rucksack, I found my flask of tea; tea not cigars; this was my Hamlet moment. Pouring the tea into my cup reminded me of another 1960's hero who regularly found himself in similar jams; Popeye the sailor man. Popeye would quickly open a tin of spinach which he always carried and muscles bulging he would be out of this hole in a flash. I didn't have any spinach. I had tea and as I stood there deep in the jungle, stuck fast in a rotten tree stump, I slowly sipped my tea and pondered on my predicament. A new TV advert that was doing the rounds at this time, was *'Visit Scotland - live it'*. I changed it to 'Visit Scotland - stuff it'. My mind was working overtime, not at trying to find a way out but reminiscing on old TV adverts. The chimpanzees moving the piano in the PG Tips advert: *"Dad do you know this piano is stuck on my foot?" "No son. You hum it, I'll play it"*.

Then Bernard Cribbins singing about being stuck in a hole; *"... We was going nowhere so we had a cup of tea"*. This one had my toes tapping... Hang on. I could feel my toes and wriggle them. What if I tried to stand on my tip toes; I hadn't tried to do that. I tried it and my feet moved for the first time in about twenty minutes. I could move my feet. What if I stood on my tip toes and pushed myself up? It was worth giving it a go. With one almighty thrust I pushed upwards on my toes and freed myself from the trap I had been in. My momentum carried me up, up and suddenly down, down, speedily crashing to earth and slithering back down through slimy vegetation to reach the stream.

Exhausted, tired but mightily relieved, I used the stream water to wash some of the slime and mud off me then sat on a rock and rested. I still had the climb up the other side which was as steep as the one I had just slid down. It was a slow climb up; one foot forward and three back. Roots of trees that I grabbed at for support ended up in my hand with the tree falling down over my back, soil, vegetation and slime covered me from head to toe.

Halfway up the cliff face, I had a long rest teetering on the edge and close to sliding all the way back down. I eventually managed to climb out at the top into an overgrown but level wood. I fought my way through the virgin vegetation just pausing for a moment to give a thankful prayer and to thank bridge builders everywhere; they do a great job. The virgin primeval Jock's Burn and this wood at its northern edge reminded me of the poem, *'Nutting'*, by William Wordsworth, in which his hero, whilst walking through a virgin wood *'O'er pathless rocks, through beds of matted fern, and tangled thickets ... I came to one clear nook, unvisited, where not a broken bough drooped with its withered leaves'*.

I was like Wordsworth's hero. Here I was forcing my way through a scene of beauty, leaving behind a scar or blot on the landscape. Wordsworth's hero, *'Rose up and dragged to earth both branch and bough, with a crash and merciless ravage'*; myself, leaving the scene as I did, *'a mutilated bower'*. I eventually emerged onto a quiet lane near to a large garden centre. Most garden centres I have visited have cafes and this one was no exception. As I stood at the counter ordering a pint of tea, I caught sight of myself in a mirror... without any makeup, I would have passed the Army Camouflage course with flying colours. The lady behind the counter declared, "We don't serve tea in pint cups". "Okay", I said. "Give me two mugs of tea please".

As I drank the tea I looked around at the other cafe customers. They were all middle aged to elderly ladies dressed in tartan tweed outfits, sipping tea from dainty cups with their little fingers extended. I'd swear they all had smart blue-rinse hair do's. They were all staring at me in a manner that said, "You are not welcome here". I felt more comfortable and at home with the Glaswegian poachers I'd met earlier than I did with this unfriendly bunch. I drank my tea and refreshed, I was ready for the off.

My crossing of Jock's Burn had taken me one and a half hours. I'd still got miles to walk today. I took a quiet country lane through gentle countryside towards Garrion Bridge, heading down through woodland to meet it. I passed a road sign welcoming me to North Lanarkshire. *'Take the lead, reduce your speed'*. These under sign strap lines just get worse. I also saw a huge sign that told me that Phase six of the Clyde Walkway was yet to be completed. (It would have been nice to have seen a similar sign back up river.) I turned onto a track that led me into the Cambusnethan woods which were once part of the Dalzell Royal Hunting Forest.

I took a fork in the path that led me back to the river bank and onto a concrete road which was newly built and signed along its many miles as the Clyde Cycle Way. I took advantage of it and made progress alongside the river. In the distance, I could hear the roar of the M74 motorway and up to my right, I could see the large, imposing Dalzell House, now converted into flats, prominently sticking out from behind trees.

The woodland was laid out in the 19th century and contains excellent examples of Yews, Cedars of Lebanon, Spanish Chestnuts and Wellingtonia's. Behind the woods and above it were the dominant Muirhouse Towers; a set of five huge tower blocks of flats. I knew I was getting near to camp. The concrete cycleway took me through a vast area of flood plain meadows full of yellow ragwort, balsam and common comfrey. Butterflies were everywhere. The area was also full of birds. I watched a Kestrel hovering above me, suspended in the air as if on a puppeteer's strings.

On a bend in the river I noticed a strange phenomenon. The river, whilst flowing towards Glasgow, appeared to rise, wave like and flow in the opposite direction. It was an unusual occurrence. I watched it for some time. The wave did in fact appear to be moving up river. I learnt later that this was the Clyde tidal bore. The footpath led me pleasantly into the Barons Haugh R.S.P.B. Nature Reserve. I was disappointed to note that Barons Haugh is one of a few R.S.P.B. Reserves that do not have a visitor centre. It didn't appear to have any visitors either. I collapsed into a bird hide and got my binoculars out. Between the river, the footpath and an earth embankment, there was a huge lagoon or small lake full of birds. Behind the lagoon there were some woods and then the ever-present Muirhouse tower blocks. The people who live there must have a fantastic view; so good that they don't need to walk down here. I had the place to myself and I spent a relaxing twenty minutes watching Moorhens, Coots, Mallards, Canada geese and Sand Martins, all very common but enjoyable just the same.

Stretching back into my walk I passed a few other well-built hides, all empty of people. Where was everyone? It was a beautiful afternoon and we were on the edge of a large conurbation; this place ought to be packed. The path led me into a mature wood and soon I had a stone wall to keep me company. It was another high stone wall and I was curious to see what was on the other side. A rare opening in the wall soon provided me with an answer; it was a huge cemetery. The section I was peering at had many war graves, all neat and regimented.

Back on the path I could see ahead of me a railway bridge carrying a busy railway line with trains passing along it regularly. The nearer I got to it the more depressing it became. Graffiti artists had risked life and limb to climb over the parapets to paint their sickening mess all along the wall edges. None of the graffiti was good. It was my 'Welcome to Glasgow' sign.

I climbed up onto a busy road bridge. A road sign declared, 'Welcome to Motherwell'. After being alone on the flood plain for so long it was a bit of a shock to emerge straight back into the busy city. Cars, buses and lorries were whizzing past and I dodged between them to get to the other side. In front of me was the Strathclyde Country Park with the Commonwealth Games Boating Lake.

Over to my left was the River Clyde, the motorway, then Hamilton with its Park Race Course and the Duke of Hamilton's Mausoleum sticking up like a 'big knob', which is what the locals call it. The mausoleum is all that remains of the Hamilton Grand Palace, once described as 'the most regal home in Britain'. H.V. Morton in his 1929 book 'In Search of Scotland' states, 'In its time Hamilton Palace must have looked like a big brother to Buckingham Palace'. The building was demolished in the 1920's when coal mining subsidence rendered it unusable. The mausoleum once housed the tombs of 18 Dukes and their ladies now safely reinterred in a local cemetery. It is reputed that the interior of the vault with its high stone drum like walls, known as the whispering walls or wa's; give the longest lasting echo of any man-made structure in the world; (over six seconds).

Our campsite was at the far end of the country park which I walked through on an excellent path. Here I met lots of other people; dog walkers, joggers and boaters. I passed a well-run toilet block which was staffed and spotlessly clean; it was a shame they didn't sell tea. At the Roman Bath House (whose walls are preserved), I was joined by Kay and Ripley and together we walked back to our camp.

Walking Day 56 *Dry and sunny*

July Sunday 8

Motherwell to Kirkintilloch - 14 miles - Total Walked 644

Kay and Ripley joined me as we walked from the campsite to the Roman fort passing swathes of pink and purple-flowering rosebay willowherbs, mint green-coloured hazel bushes with nuts, damson plants with purple fruit, together with hedge bindweed and crab apple trees. What you may have noticed is that at the beginning of my walk back in Cornwall, I could hardly name or identify any of these wild flowers. Now I knew a good few of them.

This peaceful and tranquil spot I find hard to believe was the scene of a battle. Scots pitched against Scots. The battle of Bothwell Bridge was fought on the 22nd June 1679 between an army of rebellious Covenanters and a government army commanded by James, Duke of Monmouth. The Covenanters were severely beaten. Light blue forget-me-nots 'littered' the scene as if like the poppy, to remind future generations of the futility of war.

We walked across the parkland to Bothwellhaugh and surveyed the remains of the Roman fort that I had arrived at yesterday; discovered in 1973. It had been built between 142 AD and 162 AD. The wonderfully preserved Roman bath house now at my feet, had been carefully rebuilt in 1980, brick by brick and placed here a few hundred feet from its original home which is now submerged under the boating lake. I felt cheated. I said goodbye to Kay and Ripley and made my way uphill through woodland that surrounds the northern part of the country park. I came to a busy golf course. So, this was where everyone was. Soon my path through the wood became fenced-off from the golf course by a massive metal fence, more suitable to an industrial estate. I took it that the golfers had had many problems with thugs and vandals. You wouldn't spend the money on a fence like that otherwise.

I found myself on a road heading into a housing estate; the change of scenery was dramatic and unnerving. One minute I was alone in idyllic woodland, the next in the middle of a huge housing estate. I had arrived in Bellshill or as it is sometimes spelt, Belshill (one L). The 1980's pop star, 'modern girl' Sheena Easton, was brought up here. I walked on along rundown streets of depressing grey pebble dash. It was easy to see why people turn to drink in this kind of place. I began looking at the old cars parked on the road; this one has a bald tyre; that one has an expired tax disc; STOP. What was I doing? I'd retired from the police and this walk was supposed to clear my head. I continued my way looking ahead at the tall run down and depressing blocks of flats.

This place was the pits. High up in one of the blocks a window opened and a modern throw away baby's nappy came flying down to earth, landing a few yards away from me with a sickening splat. I knew what the nappy contained. I'm not sure this is what the manufacturer had in mind when they invented these throw away nappies. I walked through and then around huge piles of litter.

I walked on. I'd spent many years in such estates and didn't want to be here at all. The trouble was the estate went on and on and on. The American, Jessie Barker Gardner, writing in his 1930's book, *'From Lands' End to John O'Groats'*, drove through the Glasgow district when, as he put it, *'... an extensive housing activity ...was taking place with the building of thousands of pretty little houses'*. He at first thought all this building was a sign of prosperity but then learnt it was Britain's solution to the terrible problem of caring for the bodies and souls of destitute citizens. He didn't like what he saw, thinking it very wrong to hand over good houses to the poor when hard-working families lived in more squalid conditions. I'm not saying that I agree with his views except that neither of us liked what we saw.

I passed I suppose, what could have been the town centre, a street of red brick buildings. A church had a sign that read, 'Walk daily - walk with God', which is exactly what I was doing. I crossed over the very busy A8 and some railway lines, which had seen better days. I walked into the town of Whifflet which takes its name from 'wheat fields'. The town didn't look much different to Bellshill. I certainly didn't see any wheat fields. Someone had at least tried to paint the drab grey pebbledash tower blocks a different colour; a mustard-orange colour. This area had once been a significant railway junction servicing the huge coal mining, iron and tin working area. Whifflet merged seamlessly into Coatbridge, once known as 'Iron Burgh' or as someone once described it in 1869, 'There is no worse place out of hell than this neighbourhood'. I was calmly walking through it. It is true, the industry that helped this area grow has gone. No longer do the volcanoes of the blast furnaces and smelting mills spew fire and smoke out into the atmosphere of black, dense smog all day and all night. The great waste heaps or 'bings' as they were known, 'as large as the Great Pyramids of Egypt', have been levelled and the land reclaimed.

Today the area is much cleaner but not quite the natural beautiful woodland with extensive orchards and gardens as it was in 1799. On the main shopping street of Coatbridge I dodged between groups of smoking people, banned from smoking inside the pubs and forced outside onto the pavements. I passed the Quadrant Shopping Centre, (a 1960's monstrosity), past the huge Jackson flats and admired the old traditional solicitor's clock that appeared to be the only thing worth looking at in these parts; hanging like a pub sign on the main street. I began the long walk out of town and couldn't help thinking that all the heavy industry, as hellish as it was once described, would at least have been interesting to view. The views now are nothing but dreary and depressing. I tramped on.

Then in front of me I saw an ice-cream van. Written on the rear of the vehicle was the warning, 'Watch the weans', which in English can be translated, 'Look out, children about'. This ice cream man won my 'Entrepreneur of the year award' unlike many others on this walk. He looked out of his van and on seeing me approaching, waited for me and said, "You look like a man who could do with an ice cream". He was correct and I bought a large one.

At long last and after climbing uphill, the view on my horizon changed. There at a place called Greenhill, I saw in front of me, some green hills; still some distance away were the Campsie Fells. My spirits were lifted by the sight. The Campsie Fells stand guard between the broad farmlands of the Carse of Stirling and the northern fringes of Glasgow. The fells are bypassed by all major roads and are known as 'an oasis of peace, tranquillity and beauty'. It felt like a breath of fresh air just to see and admire the view. However, I still had to walk to them and that involved more urban foot padding amongst dreary housing estates. I tramped on.

At the former mining village of Glenboig I crossed railway lines that could have been part of the historic 1826 Monkland to Kirkintilloch first railway in Scotland. I entered the Glenboig parkland, created in 1999 on land reclaimed from industrial fireclay potteries. The centrepiece of the park was the Garnqueen Loch, a small pool of glacial origin. Both great crested and little grebes were swimming in the loch and a grey heron was fishing at its side. The loch was surrounded by flowering meadow sweet, purple loosestrife, ragged robin, water lilies and thankfully I was transported back to nature.

The locals didn't seem to appreciate this little bit of paradise. I was alone in the park admiring the pool which, according to a sign, contained some brandy bottles. I wouldn't have been surprised to have seen a few empties floating in the loch, be they brandy or whisky but there were none. I learnt from the sign that the brandy bottle was the name for a type of deep water lily. Glenboig Park is small; it deserves to be much bigger and more frequented. I left it by a side gate and headed back into shitsville, keeping my eyes focused on the fells on the horizon as I crossed over the busy M73 motorway.

The housing began to change for the better and by the time I reached Johnston Loch, another small pool of glacial origin, the housing estates had picked up somewhat and looked pleasant. On a bench overlooking the loch I sat down and drank some tea from my flask and ate an orange. I crossed over into the county of East Dunbartonshire; its name I presumed, derives from nearby Dumbarton, albeit one is spelt with an 'n' and the other an 'm'. The urban scenery did get better. The housing was more substantial; Edwardian stone-built terraces and semi-detached houses, all with mature well-tended gardens.

I came to the town of Lenzie which I was told is pronounced locally as Lenyie, the z taking the form of a y. The railway arrived here in 1842 and ever since then the town has been an important commuter town for Glasgow and Edinburgh. It was also the site of an 1875 lunatic asylum; the biggest in Scotland. The 495 patients quadrupled the town's population. Sadly, the patients have now all gone, kicked out into the 'Government's care in the community', or as we all know it, 'lack of care in the community'.

Whatever, I saw no sign of the mentally ill wandering aimlessly on the streets. I did see a group of schoolboys walking into town away from the railway station. I was reminded of my adage that, 'You can tell what an area is really like by the behaviour of their school children when seen walking to or from school'. Lenzie may be pleased to know that on the evidence of these well-dressed, well-behaved schoolboys, I decided this town was up there with Tiverton in Devon and Runcorn in Cheshire. In fact, I found the place to be a really nice area. The sun was shining and I enjoyed my stroll along the suburban streets with their big houses and pleasant gardens which led me agreeably into the town of Kirkintilloch where I met up with Kay and Ripley on the main shopping street. Kay was parked up by a building that had a blue plaque displayed which stated that Archibald Scott Couper had lived here. I had never heard of him and decided to do a bit of research on him as we drove away from town but not before calling in at Sainsbury's supermarket to restock on necessities.

Archibald Scott Couper, b. 1831 – 1892, was a chemist. He was the son of a wealthy Glasgow textile mill owner. He studied in France, publishing his theory on chemical structure and bonding in the scientific language of the day – French. He competed against a German chemist, August Kekule, who worked on similar theories and published his work first. Couper nearly went mad over the subsequent dispute and returned home to his mother. Years later he finally received the recognition he deserved when his work was re-examined. His papers were much better and more resolved than the German's. Couper's formula, style and drawings of molecular structures using elemental symbols for atoms with connecting bonding lines drawn between them, are still used to this day by modern chemists around the world.

Rest day *Hot and sunny*

A day off from walking.

We moved camp, driving up to Loch Lomond via the centre of Glasgow and crossing over to the east side of the loch to find the near idyllic campsite at Milarrochy Bay. It was a beautiful site on the edge of the loch, edged by oak trees with plenty of lawn-like fields. The site was busy with campers and caravaners from around Europe: French, Dutch and Germans were parked up nearby. Boaters were also in good numbers as jetties projected out into the water from the edge of the campsite. A section of the site was also home to good numbers of West Highland Way campers. I was eager to join them but first job that afternoon was a complete launder of clothes and bed sheets using the campsite's excellent laundry facilities.

Walking Day 57 *Dry and sunny*

Kirkintilloch to Dumgoyne - 11 miles - Total Walked 655

I was dropped back at Archibald Scott Couper's former home on the main street of 'Kirkie' as it is known. I made my way straight to the 1960's shopping centre and found the bustling post office where I joined the queue and got my LEJOG papers stamped without any fuss.

Outside I stood and admired the canal with its towpath and preserved canal furniture. This was the Firth and Clyde Canal; a small sea-going-vessel's canal that in 1773 linked the east coast of Scotland (i.e. Edinburgh) to the west coast (i.e. Glasgow).

Kirkintilloch, although many miles inland, became a bustling and busy sea port. It was and still is the 'canal capital' of Scotland. It was also a busy ship building centre. A millennium project of true value reopened the canal and it is back in business.

Sir Giles Gilbert Scott's famous red K2 to K6 telephone kiosks were made here at the Lion Foundry between 1924 and 1984. What a total lack of vision the British Telecom bosses had when they ceased production of them. I know telephone kiosks are hardly ever used these days with everyone on mobile phones but their box like replacements of the 1970's and 1980's are truly vile objects. Thankfully there are many old kiosks still out there, some with listed building status.

I crossed over the busy main street where I was mobbed by a seagull. Why it picked on me I'll never know but it dive-bombed me several times as I dodged between the traffic and pedestrians who all stopped to watch. I decided it must be a Scottish seagull, unhappy with an English stranger in town.

I sought refuge from the mad seagull by a large red polished granite obelisk on the side of the River Luggie. Once the seagull had gone I took time to look at the obelisk and read its inscription. It was put up by public subscription in memory of 17year old Hazelton Robert Robson of Glasgow who lost his life in the flooded River Luggie trying to save the life of a little child on the 5th of September 1876.

Just across from the monument there flows yet another river, the River Kelvin which rises in the Campsie Fells, now nearer than ever.

Prior to leaving 'Kirkie', I walked along beside a Roman fort which forms part of a preserved section of the Antonine wall. The Romans came here in AD142 and just as the canal was built here in 1773 to cross the mainland at its narrowest point, so was the Roman wall.

Kirkintilloch gets its name from the Gaelic, Caerpentaloch, which translates to 'fort at the head of the ridge'. The Antonine wall is 37 miles long and is the largest Roman relic in Scotland. Named after the Emperor Antoninus Pius, it replaced Hadrian's Wall (built 20 years earlier) as the northernmost border of the Roman Empire. Most of it was a ten-foot-high earthen wall with a turf-lined top and a defensive ditch on the northern side. By AD160 the Romans had abandoned the wall and retreated south to Hadrian's Wall. Perhaps they too had been dive-bombed by mad seagulls.

Checking to make sure the seagull was well out of sight, I crossed over into the countryside and into the ' wild territory', as the Romans called it.

I walked along a lane looking at fields of stubble. The yellow dandelion type Catsear plant appeared in vast numbers. I found the area to be tranquil and peaceful with the Campsie Fells looming up in front of me.

I came to a T-junction and found myself at the little village of Milton of Campsie. I had reached the foot of the Campsie Fells, where I was to turn left and follow the lane along the base of the fells. Just before leaving the village I rested on a bench where behind me in the grass, I noticed a memorial which had I not rested, I certainly would have missed. It was a memorial to one Vincent Lunardi, (born 1759 in Naples, died in 1806). He was a famous balloonist who drew crowds of 200,000 people in London to see his spectacle. In 1785, on his fourth out of the five flights he undertook in Scotland, he landed at a spot near here after setting off from Edinburgh.

I took a path that led me onto the disused Strathblane railway, now converted into a footpath. The going was good and I made quick progress along the lonely but easy stretch, passing through fields and woods as I walked along.

At Lennoxtown I was diverted from the path by some building work which on reflection I should have ignored. I should have walked around the back of the diggers and continued along my way. As it was I was 'pushed' into the town and then out along a busy road, not being allowed to re-join the disused railway line for some miles.

I did however, manage to get a pleasant view of the Crow Road, the mountain pass that cuts north through the Campsie Fells. For some reason, it has been associated with death. I couldn't ascertain why; it looked beautiful to me.

Three teenage girls crossed the road in front of me. They were the first people on foot that I had seen since leaving Kirkintilloch. I walked on into the village of Strathblane which had a war memorial with benches where I could rest. A nearby bowling green was flying a Centenary flag, 1907 to 2007. The bowling green was busy with white-suited players.

I crossed into Stirlingshire County and made my way past large houses set in beautiful grounds and then back to the disused railway line. This time the line was bordered with swathes of pinkish-purple flowering ragged robins. Paddocks full of horses lined my route. Judging by the hoof prints, someone had been using my disused railway line as a bridleway. Initially the hoof prints were a small distraction but as the way became muddier, obviously churned up by the horse's hooves, they became an annoyance.

Soon my path had become a total quagmire and was virtually impassable. My disused railway line was joined by a pipeline which I climbed on top of to escape the mud. I later learned that the pipeline carried fresh water from Loch Lomond to Edinburgh.

The route became more and more overgrown with vegetation. The horse hoof prints stopped but the mud didn't and I carried on pushing my way through bramble bushes and gigantic hogweed plants. I pushed on through the undergrowth using my Leki walking stick like a jungle machete, hacking back the foliage.

All this hacking at leaves disturbed the insects and I was soon covered in midge-like flies. Infested would be the correct word to use. They were crawling over my face, into my ears, nostrils and eyes. I probably ate a good number as I pressed on, now crashing and thrashing my way through. I felt as though I was being eaten alive. After what seemed like an eternity I crashed up against a metal gate hidden by giant hogweed plants. Beyond the gate the disused railway line was perfectly clear with no vegetation. At last I had reached the West Highland Way at the point where it crosses Blame Water to join the Strathblane disused railway line. Up until 1951 this line was still in use, taking locals directly into Glasgow. What a fantastic commuter line it would be today if it was still open. The WHW makes effective use of it now.

Milngavie, the official West Highland Way (WHW) starting point was five miles to the south. On reflection, I should have continued following the Clyde into Glasgow, spent some time admiring the city centre with its fantastic Victorian architecture, museums and art galleries and then headed out via pleasant suburbs to Milngavie to pick up the WHW there. Instead I'd gone for days of walking through dull, grey housing estates. I had at last crossed the Glasgow Conurbation. All that lay ahead was beautiful dramatic scenery in spectacular walking country.

The West Highland Way, Scotland's first long distance footpath was opened in 1980. Starting from the edge of Glasgow, the Way soon reaches Loch Lomond's eastern shore before opening out to the broad glen of Strathfillan, crossing wild Rannoch Moor, leading to stunning mountain scenery near Glencoe and ending at Fort William, 95 miles away. I was going to use it to move up northwards. The first thing I had to get used to was a strange style of stile; a metal contraption more like a large mouse trap than a stile. You opened the two metal V-shaped bars and stepped in, holding them open. If you happened to let go they banged shut, trapping your leg in between them. This was my welcome to the WHW, a great big bruise on my thigh. If the mad seagull of Kirkintilloch had appeared, I'd have known for certain all was lost. At least the midge infestation had subsided.

I was supposed to be passing a castle, according to my map, Duntreath Castle, but my view was obscured by trees and bushes and so of it, I saw nothing. It is described as a *'truly magical place'* which it must be because it had vanished.

Ahead of me, hobbling slowly, I saw a teenage couple, both with massive packs on their backs. They were walking so slowly I was bound to catch them up. Having walked alone for so long I didn't fancy bumping into people as I knew I would be doing here on the WHW. It has been described as a walker's motorway, being one of the most popular long-distance walks in the country. Before I caught up with them I glanced over to my left to admire a strange 'blob' of volcanic rock; Dunglass Hill, with wavy rock formations that reminded me of the Giant's Causeway in Northern Ireland. Strangely, it was not marked on my map. On closer inspection, the rocks were hexagonal shapes exactly like those across in Ireland.

Both the young man and woman were limping badly and stopping to rest every few yards. They were slim, young and on the face of it, 'fit'. Something was seriously wrong for them to be so lame after just a few short, easy miles. I caught up with them and found they were from Belgium. They both spoke excellent English. The problem was that both were wearing brand new boots bought for their holiday, and carrying packs that were way too heavy. I suggested that they should ditch at least half of their gear. I wasn't at all surprised to see that the young woman was also carrying a large make-up case and I suggested that that should be the first thing to be thrown away. I handed them a few blister plasters and explained how to use them. They had never seen them before. I wished them well and left them removing their boots.

I strode on along my easy route, lined by fields with good views. Yellow monkey flowers, common valerum and pinkish-purple marsh woundwort were all in flower and stood to attention as I passed them by. At Dumgoyne Road junction, Kay and Ripley were waiting to take me back to base.

Walking Day 58 *Dry and sunny*

July
Wednesday
11

| Dumgoyne to Milarrochy Bay (Loch Lomond) - 13 miles - Total Walked 668 |

Kay and Ripley walked with me for the first mile along the disused railway line, now converted into an excellent footpath. Kay was looking at ALL the wildflowers IN

DETAIL. Photographing this one then that one. That mile was the longest on the entire journey. The trouble for me was that the verges were all alive with many varied and wonderful wild flowers which were all in bloom. It was a lovely sunny day and the surroundings were beautiful. It was like being back on the Scilly Isles or the lanes of Cornwall in spring.

Enough of this; I was itching to get off. I made timely progress on the excellent path which led me to Gartness Bridge. Here, by some pleasant waterfalls on Endrich water, the way leaves the disused railway and takes a quiet lane to reach Drymen, two miles further north.

I passed a large quarry on my way into Drymen, along a sun-drenched lane which was so hot, the tarmacadam was melting in places. The West Highland Way proper doesn't go into Drymen village centre but turns sharp right on the outskirts of town and quickly heads off through the pine forests of Garadhban.

I stuck to the route as I knew we could visit the village any evening during the following week. I marched up hill through the regimented lines of trees on a wide track, coming to some red tape and a sign, 'Tree cutting in progress. Route diversion'. This wasn't what I wanted to see. Neither was the route to which the diversion sign arrow was pointing, back downhill, steeply. I'd experienced tree-felling operations many times before in the Lake District. I know they can be dangerous places and beautiful footpaths can quickly become muddy quagmires. I dutifully followed the diversion arrow, downhill. At a point when I thought I couldn't go any further down the diversion signs took me off to my right, back into the forest along a narrow path which was so narrow in places I was pushing the tree branches aside.

By now I was thinking that I was a victim of some idiotic prank, the kind where someone points the diversion arrow the wrong way, 'Wacky Races' style. Indeed, for a brief moment, I even imagined I was entering Narnia, that fictional land as told by C.S. Lewis in his books, including 'The Lion, the Witch and the Wardrobe'. As if I'd pushed my way through the fur coats at the back of the wardrobe, now transformed into pine tree branches, I was pushing my way through. Then ahead of me in a clearing, I could see someone or something moving. Was it a 'faun'? - half man, half goat. I couldn't see a lamppost but there was something there. I moved closer. Travelling swiftly towards me snapping branches from trees at an alarming rate was... a forestry commission ranger armed with a tree-cutting pruner.

He turned out to be a very friendly chap, certainly not a 'Mr Tumnus'. His Land Rover was parked in the clearing having arrived there via another track. It appeared I'd beaten him to the diversion path. His job was to widen it for the comfort of us WHW walkers.

The ranger reassured me that I was on the correct route and if I carried on, I would soon re-emerge back on the main WHW route. He wasn't wrong; I climbed back up onto the route which, thankfully was level for some way.

Up ahead I could see yet another sun-filled glade. Someone was already there and moving about. I tried to see who or what it was; perhaps the 'faun' was here after all. No, on reaching the clearing I saw my two friendly Belgians. The girl was lying on the ground. Her massive pack which still included her cosmetic case was beside her. The boy was standing but only just. They both looked absolutely shattered, looking at me with eyes that said, 'Help us, we are knackered'.

I discovered they had totally ignored most of my advice and I wasn't surprised to see them here in such a state. They were carrying enough water to supply a small town; someone had told them that our water wasn't good enough to drink. I reassured them that British tap water was the best in the world and that up here in Scotland it was in plentiful quantity. I left them pouring a huge drum of water away into the forest.

The route ahead climbed up onto the tops of Conic Hill which neither of them looked fit enough to tackle. I pointed out an easier option, a cheat which led them to Loch Lomond by the low road.

A bit further on I emerged out of the forest onto wide open moorland where the trees had been felled perhaps a year or two back with just the stumps remaining. I could see my path climbing up over the moor and in the distance the climb up Conic Hill, which at 1175 feet was a modest climb. The route led me down into a deep rocky valley. I crossed the stream at the bottom using stepping stones and climbed up the other side. I'd made it across the Burn of Mar.

I now plodded slowly up the steep side of Conic Hill. In parts the path had been cut into steps. The sun was beating down and I was hot, tired and sweaty. The climb up was made more pleasurable by the huge swathes of flowering wild thyme that lined my route. Further back onto the moor, large patches of fluffy white cotton grass danced in the breeze. I turned and looked back to see if I could spot the couple from Belgium crossing the moor. I couldn't see them and in fact I never saw them again.

I kept going, one step at a time until at last I reached the summit of the hill. Wow. What a spectacular sight. There before me was the full beauty of Loch Lomond stretching north to the mountains. The scenery was breath-taking and well worth the climb. Here I could make out the famous Highland Boundary Fault, a geological feature where two tectonic plates came together millions of years ago, and which today form the easily visible division between the Highlands and the Lowlands.

Even without the loch, the scene before me would still be breathtakingly spectacular. The loch is truly the icing on the cake.

The loch is 24 miles long, five miles wide and 600 feet deep and has the largest surface area of fresh water anywhere in the U.K. Its water today reflected the near blue sky. Its 38 named islands include the enchanting one-mile-long Inchcalloch Island where St. Kentigerna from Ireland brought Christianity to this area in 717 AD.

Loch Lomond has more fish in it than any other loch including the unusual freshwater herring called a powan. With Glasgow, just a few miles south, I thought how lucky

Glaswegians must be to live in a large city yet have all this in their back yard. Where were they? I was up here alone. Their loss not mine. I'd taken the high road and as far as I am concerned, '*I was in Scotland before them*'.

Eventually I dragged myself away and began the long descent on good paths down through rocky terrain towards the woods that lie above the shore edge of the loch. The descent was steep and as I approached the tree line I saw two teenage girls climbing up towards me. One of the girls was carrying a bottle of lemonade and the other a packet of 'fags'. Both were dressed in clothes that looked as if they were about to 'hit the town' on a Friday night. As they drew up alongside me I noticed that both had amazing 'dolled-up' faces, with lipstick and make-up more suited to the women behind cosmetic counters in department stores, than walkers. It turned out the girls were from Poland and were working as chambermaids in the nearby hotels on the edge of Loch Lomond and on their afternoon off they had decided to climb the nearby hill.

The bottle of lemonade would come in handy but I'm not at all sure about the cigarettes. I wished them both well and continued my way down into the cool pine woods.

The path emerged onto the large car park at Balmaha. Crowds of people flocked around the large visitor centre which I had a look around, before beating a retreat to the nearby Oak Tree pub, again crowded with sightseers, most of whom had only walked the short distance from the car park. I was developing into a 'walking snob' in that here I was, having walked from Land's End, desperate for a drink and I was having to queue up with people who'd walked barely five yards. The crowds should have parted and I should have been served first but it didn't happen.

Today the pub was home to coach party visitors. I drank my pint of lemonade with pineapple and made my way back out into the sunshine and down to the loch's edge.

To get down to the water I walked through beautiful park-like flower gardens. Here the loch was awash with boats; big ones, small ones and rowing boats. Even though it was busy with people I found it to be a very peaceful scene. The little steam ferry painted in Royal Mail livery complimented the picture. This little boat takes passengers along with the mail to some of the inhabited islands.

I headed up the shore and left the crowds behind as I gently climbed forward through trees towards the small rocky hilltop called Craigie Fort. For a few minutes, I joined the Balmaha Millennium Forest Path, a mile-long path which explores the different types of woodland, from ancient oaks to modern pine plantations and it has carefully placed information boards.

When I reached the hilltop I again stood alone looking out over the loch. I'd have thought a few of the hordes down below could have managed this little climb. The views were certainly worth it. Just as I was about to move on, an elderly couple came staggering up to join me. They were both clearly delighted to have made it to the top and I was happy for them.

I walked down the other side on good paths through the trees, arriving at our campsite. Nesting swallows were present on the site. Throughout the week, the swallows kept us entertained with their aerobatic displays.

Walking Day 59 *Dry, overcast with gentle breeze*

Milarrochy Bay to Rowardennan - 5 miles - Total Walked 673

Milarrochy Bay, pronounced Milariky, is an idyllic spot and I could see why many of the campers had no intention of leaving this place once they'd arrived here. I on the other hand was, as usual, itching to get off.

Kay and Ripley joined me for their morning walk as I walked away from the site through the woods. I knew before setting off that I was going to have a short day. The motor road finished at Rowardennan a mere five miles further north. Beyond that lay a fourteen-mile rugged stretch through the woods along the east shoreline of Loch Lomond, unsupported by a motor road; a stretch I planned to do in one go but not today. My aim was to get to Rowardennan and then have half a day of rest.

Kay was busy flower spotting as we made our way through Lag an Amair woods. A good patch of beautiful orange-coloured fox and cub flowers lined our way, quickly followed by slender St. John's wort and huge banks of bell heather together with the much rarer lesser cow wheat. The views through the trees to the water's edge with the mountains behind were stunningly beautiful.

I said goodbye to Kay who had to walk back to camp, pick up the car, drive to Rowardennan and wait for me to arrive. I moved on, walking now amongst the ancient oak trees of Ross Wood. I passed some lovely secluded beaches, one of them being a temporary home to some French 'wild campers'. All day along the route, signs indicated that 'wild camping' was not just permitted but actively encouraged, so long as the campers took their rubbish home with them. Sadly quite a few didn't do this as I kept walking past deserted camping spots littered with empty beer bottles and tin cans. I tried not to let it spoil the walk but how anyone can despoil such a lovely place is beyond me.

As I climbed up a hill I came upon an army of small frogs hopping all over the path. The biggest one was about the size of a penny. Kay was parked up and waiting for me by the visitor centre which was busy with walkers about to climb the nearby Ben Lomond, which at 3,951 feet is Scotland's most southerly and most climbed Munro.

We drove the short distance by car to Drymen, pronounced Drumen. At the library, we could check our e-mails and re-acquaint ourselves with family and friends. From there we walked across the village green to The Clachan which is Scotland's oldest licensed pub, dating back to 1734. Ripley joined us as we tucked into an excellent lamb dinner. The barmaid was lovely. Even though she had a busy bar, she managed to sit and chat with us and brought Ripley a biscuit. She told us about Drymen's famous one-time resident, Billy Connolly, who used to be a regular here.

On the way, back to Milarrochy, I tried to get a glimpse of Buchanan Castle, another fabulous ruined castle set in acres of grounds but to no avail as all was hidden behind rows of trees. In 1925 the castle became a hotel and during World War 2 it was used as a military hospital. It was here where Hitler's deputy, Rudolph Hess, was treated after crash landing his plane in Scotland in 1941. In 1950 the roof was removed to avoid paying taxes. It has remained an ivy-covered ruin ever since, although a golf course is sited within the grounds.

Walking Day 60 *Dry and sunny then heavy rain for the last hour*

July Friday 13 | Rowardennan to Inverarnan - 14 miles - Total Walked 687

Kay wrote in one of her many letters home:

'Loch Lomond was really beautiful. Ripley and I did lots of walks along the edge of the loch. It was warm and sunny and the air felt fresher. These were lovely walks with magnificent views of mountains and islands. The ancient, undisturbed woodland around the loch were excellent for testing our growing wild flower knowledge'.

This morning I left Kay and Ripley exploring the flower-filled woods at Rowardennan. I also left a horde of Munro climbers heading up Ben Lomond and I set off along good paths at first, into the lonely woods of the eastern shore. I hadn't gone too far when a slow worm slithered across my path, the first snake, sorry legless lizard, which I'd seen since Devon.

The path climbed gently through the trees affording me good views across the loch to the mountains beyond. One of the many loch cruise boats carrying camera-snapping tourists came close in shore. I doubt if any saw me high up on the path camouflaged by trees but I could see and hear them. The guide was giving them a commentary on the West Highland Way.

The woods went on and on. The good path eventually narrowed into a jungle of gnarled tree roots that I imagine in wet weather could be lethal when slippery.

Bill Bryson in his 1998 book, *'A walk in the woods'*, which tells the story of Bryson and his companion Katz, struggling to hike through the vast, tangled woods of the American Appalachian Trail, describes those woods as, *'Spooky – there is something innately sinister about them – some ineffable thing that makes you sense an atmosphere of pregnant doom with every step and leaves you profoundly aware that you are out of your element and ought to keep your ears pricked. You can't quite shake the feeling that you are being watched'.*

Well today I felt none of this. I was happy and contented to be here and felt totally at one with my surroundings. I walked on. The only creeps and nutters watching me were perhaps the tree creepers and nuthatches that I saw in abundance. On hearing human voices, I realised that I was fast-approaching that tiny spot of civilisation here on the upper eastern shores of Loch Lomond which is the ferry and hotel at Inversnaid. I crashed through the undergrowth to find myself at the back of the hotel and at the top of a flight of steps that led down to both the ferry jetty and hotel grounds. A large group of people were in the process of climbing out of the ferry and beginning the steep climb up to the hotel. None of them saw me at the top as they chattered happily to themselves. I heard some American accents in the crowd. "Gee, look at this". "Yeah, wow", etc. I couldn't proceed until the steps had cleared so I took the opportunity to look across the loch to see the massive power station which, along with its miles of pipes, dominates the western shore hereabouts.

When at last, my path was clear I made my way down to the hotel which was now packed with tourists queuing for the bar. It's a good job I wasn't thirsty. I doubt if I'd have been served. I did feel like shouting, "Make way for Chris Binns, long distance walker, walking Land's End to John O'Groats. Make way. He needs a drink". Unlike Ian Botham who perhaps employed just such a team when he completed his charity walk, I was on my own, so I slunked away to some hotel-owned picnic benches where I sat down and drank some of my own water, ignoring the sign that declared benches and picnic tables for hotel guests only. I knew no one in the hotel would trouble me as they were far too busy making money behind the bar.

Refreshed, I set off again, ready to tackle what all the guide books describe as the hardest, pathless section of the West Highland Way. There actually is a path but it is narrow and full of slippery tree roots and rocks. I hadn't gone far when I came upon a young family; tourists who were clambering amongst the rocks down on the shore edge searching for Rob Roy's cave.

I couldn't help them as my maps were not that exact. A little further on I bumped into two very polite, Dutch teenage boys also searching for the cave. About 100 yards further on, after I had lost sight of the cave searchers, I came across a sign indicating that Rob Roy's cave was down to my left. I climbed down the rocks and came to the place where someone had painted in white paint, large letters indicating 'Cave', for the benefit of the tourists in their cruise boats.

I clambered about searching for a cave; a natural hollow in the rocks but all I could find was a poor shelter formed by two large rocks resting against one another. I couldn't for the life in me remember who Rob Roy was, that is if I ever knew. My education failed me here and I was determined to find out.

The guidebooks state that the way ahead was 'rocky and uneven'- I was soon to find out this was something of an understatement. The path led down to the rocky shore. All along the path, rocks were scattered here and there. Some of my steps had to be gigantic to enable me to stride across. If the rocks were not bad enough, monstrous tree roots erupted from the earth as if determined to break an ankle ... or two. This whole stretch was an assault course. To sprain an ankle here would be especially painful as it is a long way to hobble out. I recommend everyone should carry an elasticated support bandage in their first aid kit just in case.

The surrounding scenery was spectacular with cascading waterfalls flowing down to the loch through the trees and rocks but I am afraid much of it was lost to me as I was concentrating on every step I took, making sure I was safe and sure-footed. I did suffer from one accident here; my gigantic strides through the rocks caused my trousers to split at the seams causing me to be ventilated in parts that at that moment didn't need to be.

Somewhere along here I crossed into another county – Argyll and Bute. Eventually the path became a little easier, although muddier and I made my way through trees to Doune Bothy, a one room stone cottage providing free, basic and dry shelter to any walker who needs it. A pile of uncollected rubbish proclaimed it was still being well used.

Half a mile further on I reached civilisation again in the form of the Ardleish ferry which could be hailed across by use of a hailing ball; a big orange ball that could be pulled up on ropes to tree height. The ferry is for foot passengers only and I could see it at the other side of the loch near Ardlui railway station, pubs and car park. People were swarming about the other side but here on the east I was still quite alone. I began to climb out of the trees and up onto a heather moor at Cnap Mor pass, which is at the northernmost point of the loch.

I looked back to see the length of the loch, its eastern shores softened by the trees. It made a perfect picture. The walk downhill to Beinglas farm and camp-site was spoiled somewhat by heavy rain that came from nowhere; one minute it was hot and sunny, the next a torrential downpour that lasted well over an hour. I slithered across the bridge that carried me over the stream which flowed, further up to my right, from the Grey Mare's Tail waterfall, hidden from view at this point (and missed by many WHW walkers).

The bar at the Beinglas campsite was packed with wet climbers and walkers. I squeezed myself in and slowly worked my way to the front. By the time I got to the bar I was standing in a huge puddle of water. No one seemed to care as everyone in there was in the same drenched state. I detected a wide variety of accents, mostly European, Dutch and German. Even though they were all soaked to the skin they were in good spirits and enjoying their holiday. When I'm tired, cold and wet, I never really fancy a cold drink. What I wanted was a pint of hot tea. The barmaid pointed to a fancy coffee machine and suggested that I have a milky coffee instead, probably because it was easier for her to make. I looked disappointed and said, "I drink coffee in a morning and tea in an afternoon and I really would like a cup of tea".

The message got through and she replied, "I'll see what I can do". A few minutes later I was squeezing away from the bar holding a steaming-hot pint of tea. I took my drink to a quiet area outside the bar but still undercover in a large three-sided, lean-to tent-come-drying room, with picnic benches and washing machines. One or two people sat here quietly reading and watching the rain pour down outside.

From Beinglas it was a short walk to the main road that accompanied the western shore of Loch Lomond. I called Kay - yes, I had a signal - and waited for her. Tony and Di, our friends from home were travelling up to spend the weekend with us and I was pleasantly surprised to find that Di was with Kay when she pulled into the entrance to the camp-site.

Before the long drive back down the western shore of Loch Lomond, I directed Kay to a nearby pub car park just off the A82. From here it is said you get the best view of the Grey Mare's Tail waterfall. With all the rain that had and still was falling, the waterfall looked magnificent.

The drive back to our base became a nightmare as we hit the Open Golf traffic which, spurred on by the rain perhaps, was fast-flowing out of the car parks of the Loch Lomond Golf Course and creating a massive jam. This meant that for us, travelling south on the A82, we were held up for hours; in fact, it took longer for us to return to our camp than it had taken Tony and Di to travel up here from Yorkshire.

Tony and Di had brought our post up to us and all the welcome news from home. That evening, in the motor home we enjoyed a steak meal and afterwards played cards - a game of 'pig'. During the night, we had a heavy storm which shook the motor home.

July Saturday 14 | Rest day *Hot and sunny*

It dawned bright and sunny. We had a lovely walk at Balmaha, through the woods and down by the shore edge. We climbed back up the rocky hill top of Craigie Fort which gave all of us a splendid photo opportunity of the magnificent views over the loch. By the time, we had walked back along the shore to the car, it was lunch-time, so we sat outside the Oak Tree Inn and had soup and a sandwich in the watery sunshine.

After lunch, we drove up to Tyndrum to explore new caravan sites and visit both the Green Welly tourist shop, a huge supermarket-style complex and the National Park Visitor Centre. It was here that Kay and Di bought me a book on that well-known Scottish folk hero, Rob Roy Macgregor, b. 1671-1734. The author, Daniel Defoe of Robinson Crusoe fame, wrote a fictional account of his life in 1723. He described Rob Roy as a Highland rogue, a legend in his own lifetime. He was a glorified cattle thief who fell out with the local authorities and other prominent lairds. In 1817, Sir Walter Scott wrote another biography on him that helped to keep Rob Roy up there in the national mind along with Robin Hood.

Our drive with Tony and Di took us deep into the Trossachs through steep-sided, wooded glens, eventually arriving at the Queen Elizabeth Forest and the David Marshall Visitor Centre, situated on a high promontory overlooking the vast, forested valley. The weather had been improving all day and we now sat in glorious sunshine admiring the views whilst partaking of afternoon tea. Later we made our way back to Balmaha and the Oak Tree Inn where we had our evening meal sitting outside on the terraces overlooking the loch.

July Monday 16 | Rest day *Rain all day, sunny in the evening*

Today we said our goodbyes to Loch Lomond and moved north to Glen Dochart near to Killin to a site a few miles off our route but the best we could find in that area. The campsite was situated on an old disused railway line in beautiful, mountain scenery. The lower slopes here are full of bog myrtle and their lovely scent permeates through the whole area. Waterfalls abound and the sound of fast-flowing water pouring off the hillsides was constant. Kay wrote: *The weather is changeable; one minute lovely and sunny and then in the next instant we have heavy showers; perfect for the midge.* Described by some Scottish travel brochures as *'a small but particularly vicious, biting insect',* with that I would concur.

We had noticed that the owners of the campsite wore full-face midge hats and nets whilst doing odd jobs around the site. By the end of the day we too were wearing them. After setting up camp we drove the few miles into the small village of Killin. Its parade of shops had several outdoor gear specialists. We were advised to buy some 'Avon Skin So Soft', which is an excellent midge repellent. Apparently Royal Marines on exercise in Canada had discovered its qualities.

We bought four bottles of the stuff and can testify that it works for us. For the rest of our journey I carried a bottle and used it liberally. The evocative smell of 'Avon Skin So Soft' stays with me and if I ever catch a whiff of it, I am instantly transported back to Glen Dochart.

After shopping in Killin we went to admire the Falls of Dochart; beautiful cascading waterfalls by the main road. The heavy rain made them look particularly powerful.

Across the road from the waterfalls we found a cosy inn which allowed dogs in. We enjoyed an excellent evening meal served to us by two friendly Canadians who were slowly working their way around Scotland.

Back at the campsite we were busy battening down the hatches to keep the swarms of midges out when my attention was caught by a French family of campers who having arrived late had set up their large family tent. They began to cook and eat a meal sat around on fold-away chairs. Nothing unusual about this you might think, a scene common on many caravan and camping sites at this time of year. Except that the midges here were particularly nasty and were swarming around in huge packs. One finger sticking out unprotected would instantly attract a horde of them. The French campers appeared to be completely unfazed by them. They enjoyed their outdoor evening meal and drinks well into the night.

 Walking Day 61 *Hot and sunny with occasional heavy showers*

July
Tuesday
17 | **Inverarnan to Crianlarich - 7 miles - Total Walked 694**

I was itching to get back walking after my long weekend off. Beinglas Farm had a cafe as well as a bar and we were looking forward to having a bit of breakfast there before setting off. The lady behind the counter looked at me in a puzzled manner when I ordered a well-done bacon and tomato in a tea cake. I realise that tea cake is a Yorkshire term for a bread cake.

She said, "We don't do anything like that".

"What do you do?" I asked.

"I can do you a nice cheese and ham toastie", came her reply.

"What, for breakfast?" I said incredulously.

The eating habits of the nation are so very different. Still, we went outside to the picnic benches and ate our toasties in glorious sunshine and thankfully they still serve coffee for breakfast although some people were drinking Scotland's national drink – no not whisky but Irn Bru.

Kay and Ripley joined me for the first half hour along the old military road which still made a good path alongside the fast-flowing River Falloch. Kay was examining wild flowers as we made our way slowly up a gentle incline. Creeping buttercups, eyebright, northern marsh orchids, foxgloves, slender St. John's wort and tormentil, as well as a good selection of lichens and moss, were all out and on full display.

As we crested the top of the hill, the mountains up ahead seem to close in on us. It started to rain heavily and we sheltered under an information board. As it didn't appear to be going to stop anytime soon, Kay with Ripley decided to turn back.

I pressed on through the trees passing a succession of gorges with rocky rapids and cascades of water, flowing down the hillsides into the already furious River Falloch. The power of the water was mesmerizing. In complete contrast, every now and then the water flowed into a cauldron-like pool; dark and deep; stationary and still.

The path deteriorated into a muddy and rocky, slippery way. On the west side of the River I was joined by a coach party of tourists braving the rain to walk down to the Falls of Falloch. I could hear the roar of these spectacular waterfalls long before I saw them. With the heavy rain the waterfalls looked powerful with water being squeezed through a tight crevice and over rocks. My photographs of the falls don't do them justice. The tourists on the other side waved at me and I at them. They then turned to go back to their coach and I to walk on up into the mountains.

As I climbed up to the top of another ridge I found myself considering a large U-shaped valley, devoid of trees. This was the Glen Falloch. The river here was slow and gentle. A series of electricity pylons caught my attention, ugly and intrusive as they are in such beautiful surroundings. Some workmen were working on the pylons, rewiring them. They were using pulleys and sledges that ran along the wires. It looked dangerous yet fascinating to watch.

I arrived at Derrydaroch Bridge which had been built by a team of engineers from the army. I used it to cross the river and continued for a while on the west side, climbing up and away from the river towards the railway line and road. I passed under the railway line via a small and narrow tunnel which the guide books called a 'sheep creep'. I immediately passed under the A82T road via a modern tube tunnel and climbed steeply up the hillside to re-join the military road which was excellent under foot.

The mountain scenery was breathtakingly spectacular. The rain eased and the sun shone, giving me clear views of Ben More at 3,843 feet across the other side of the valley. In the 18th century, General Wade and his successor Major Caulfield, built a series of military roads in the Highlands to help quell the turbulent Highlanders and prevent further rebellions. I was grateful that the roads, being well constructed, today made excellent walking paths.

I hadn't been going long when I fell upon two young Scots men. One was lying flat on his back; the other was sitting on a boulder. Both were wearing shorts and on their heads, midge nets. I looked around to check and see if there were swarms of midges up here but there weren't any. The young man sprawled along the floor was sobbing and muttering something along the lines of, "Bloody West Highland Way. Next year I'm off to Ibiza". His visible inner thighs were chafed and red raw. When they saw me they both tried to get up but were obviously well and truly knackered.

I got talking to them and discovered that they were both suffering from blisters as big as golf balls. Both men were carrying rucksacks the size of a double bed. It was possible that they had a cosmetic vanity case in their sacks but I couldn't be sure. I gave them some friendly advice on reducing their sack weight, on blister plasters, (neither had heard of them) and on petroleum jelly, (Vaseline), liberally spread between the legs and anywhere else they cared to rub it in. All this advice was given free and what was even better for them was the news that they could have all this soon, at the nearby town of Crianlarich just a few miles away. This appeared to motivate them into action and they began to walk but not at my pace.

I left them behind and made my way along the road until it came to some trees where I descended into the town of Crianlarich (a Gaelic word meaning low pass), which being a major Highland cross road and having two railway stations, a shop, post office, cafe and youth hostel, was a welcome hive of activity.

The post office stamp declared Crianlarich was in Perthshire but all other signs declared we were in Stirlingshire – all very confusing.

July
Wednesday
18

Walking Day 62 *Dry for the first hour then heavy showers for rest of day*

Crianlarich to Bridge of Orchy - 14 miles - Total Walked 708

In glorious sunshine, we climbed through the pine trees, up and out of Crianlarich. After half an hour of climbing we reached a level way and here Kay and Ripley turned back.

It wasn't level for long and the path rollercoastered through the trees passing lively streams. I passed a group of men and women walking in the opposite direction. They turned out to be Germans up early for a morning stroll.

After an hour, I stumbled onto the busy A82 road, crossing it with care. I also crossed under the railway line and over the River Fillan which led me to the small ruined chapel of St Fillan. It began to rain heavily so I found some shelter under the trees that surrounded the chapel. I had a drink of coffee from my flask and read the information board which gave the history of the place.

There were two travelling Irish saints in the 7th century who had the same name. The one remembered here retired to this place from Fife. It was said that he had a mysterious luminous arm that allowed him to read and write at night. Also, that he possessed powers to heal the sick using pebbles and stones to help him do this.

It is said that at the battle of Bannockburn, Robert the Bruce called for his relics to be brought to him; i.e. the bones of one of St Fillan's arms. The Scottish went on to be victors at the battle. To thank St Fillan for helping him, Robert the Bruce had a priory built here to the north of Glen Dochart. The area is now known as the Strath of Fillan.

At Auchtertyre I came to a busy camp-site. As well as a shop, it had wooden heated wigwams (pods) for hire and an internet cafe. This turned out to be a computer situated in a garden shed. I paid my £1 and went in for half an hour. I crossed back over the A82 and walked through immature woodlands on good paths at the side of the fast-flowing River Cononish. The midges were out in force and I was doing all in my power to stop them from eating me alive. I looked up to the mountains above the River Cononish where, until quite recently, gold was mined in a commercial way.

I walked around the edge of a small lake or Lochan surrounded by a good growth of bog myrtle. As I reached the far side (still being pursued by midges), I saw a large memorial stone. It declared that here was the site of the King's Field and the battle of Dalrigh in 1306, where Robert the Bruce suffered a rare defeat at the hands of the MacDougall's of Larne. His men, to aid their escape, threw off their heavy armour and swords into the Lochan.

I climbed gently up, away from the Lochan and the midges and entered a scene of desolation, an ugly scar on the countryside and the remnants of the lead mining industry at Tyndrum. To be fair it did look like someone was trying to clean it all up and regrow grasses and bushes. Information boards had been put up and the dramatic scene-change made a peculiar welcome in an area of otherwise outstanding beauty.

Tyndrum, a Gaelic word meaning 'house on the ridge', is an important crossroads in the Highlands. Overshadowed by Ben Lui, it still has two railway stations and roads lead to either Oban or Fort William. Most people will probably know it because it is home to the Green Welly Service Centre, a cross between a motorway service station, a supermarket, a tourist gift shop and a camping and hiking store.

Yesterday I described Crianlarich as a welcome hive of activity but it was quiet compared to Tyndrum. Hamish Brown, in his 1981 book, *'Hamish's Groats End Walk'*, described a similar situation where, *'the loud, tourist voices jarred and I realised just how attuned I was already to the softer sounds of the wilderness'.*

The Green Welly was packed with people, nearly all of whom had arrived here by coach or motorbike. Into their midst, I plodded along and strangely felt like the odd man out; even as I passed briefly through the hiking store to buy some much-needed dubbin for my boots. People stared at me as they purchased extremely expensive and unnecessary designer fleeces and trousers.

I was glad to get away and climbed out of town on the old road that runs parallel to the new A82 and the Fort William railway line. As I crested the hill the rain came and huge dark clouds enveloped the massive mountain side of Beinn Odhar (2,948').

I walked on in the now increasingly misty and eerie surroundings. My world became blanketed in silence apart from the odd cawing sound of either a raven or hooded crow; I had seen both birds hopping about earlier. I knew by my maps that I was heading towards the mountain of Beinn Doran, (3,524') but I couldn't see it; it was too shrouded in mist or as the Scots call it, 'clag'. 'Dreich' is another word sometimes used for mist with rain and this is what I was now walking through. I walked along on what, until the1930's, had been the old motor road into the Highlands.

The path sloped downwards until I crossed a stream by the farmhouse at Auch. The railway line, now over to my right, had to make a sweeping but level curve to cross the same stream up in Auch Gleann. As I looked a train crossed the bridge.

I came upon three men, one old and two young. The older one reminded me of the prison warder, McKay, in the TV programme Porridge. The two young men were dressed in T-shirts and cut-off trousers. They were soaking wet through. 'McKay' was dressed in mountain waterproof gear and appeared dry and comfortable. As I passed them one of the young men said aloud, "People do this for enjoyment".

I decided that they were in fact prisoners being watched over by their guard on a day release scheme; either that or some sort of social work experiment. I doubt if it was working. The rain became heavier. I briefly took refuge in a railway shelter.

Near the Clach A Bheinn, I came upon an enormous boulder where four young men were all sitting on the soaking wet ground. Their boots were off and I could see that all of them had blisters. On the face of it, here were four young, fit men, debilitated by blisters; blisters that could be prevented by wearing appropriate footwear, including socks. I gave them my by now usual advice on blister plasters. Once again, I was surprised to learn that none of them had heard of them before. I want to claim some sort of reward from these companies who are clearly not advertising their products as well as they might. All the camp-sites and shops along the West Highland Way should stock and advertise them. They could easily boost their sales.

I left the young men who were now rolling on the wet ground and walked on in the rain. I crossed over the railway line at the Bridge of Orchy Railway Station and observed a strange railway contraption. A yellow Bedford lorry was attached to some railway wheels and was on a piece of track. Clearly the road lorry could drive freely on roads and then up onto the railway line and move along as if it was a locomotive.

I descended the steps to the isolated white hotel at the Bridge of Orchy where Kay was waiting for me and I called it a day.

July Thursday 19 — Rest day *Dry and sunny*

Today we moved camp up to Glencoe. Just below the Kingshouse hotel we pulled into a lay-by to take in all the stunning mountain scenery before joining the steady stream of tourist coaches and cars heading down the glen itself.

Many WHW walkers miss this bit as the route climbs up the 'Devil's staircase' and avoids the glen altogether which is a great shame as the views are spectacular. I suppose a few must walk down to the glen to use the camp-site and visitor centre. They're the lucky ones. Why the WHW planners didn't organise the route to allow extra time to explore more of Glencoe is a mystery.

We pulled into the Glencoe camp-site which was not only well-cared-for and clean but a perfect spot, nestled right in between the mountains with awe-inspiring views all around. With the sun beating down, it felt as if I'd arrived in heaven. From the campsite looking back up the Glen, past Meall Mor, The Three sisters (all mountains) and beyond, I saw the glen pretty much as Queen Victoria had seen it from this view point back in 1883 when she wrote, *'Emerging from the village, we entered the Pass of Glencoe, which at the opening is beautifully green, with trees and cottages dotted about – then turning to see the finest, wildest and grandest part of the pass, stern, rugged and precipitous, with beautiful peaks and rocks'.*

We took Ripley for a walk in the pine forests that surrounded the camp-site and found a pool full of tadpoles – in July. That evening we looked up in delight to the enveloping mountain ridges and watched a pair of eagles soaring high into the sky with a large glowing moon appearing to balance delicately upon the highest ridge. We were in heaven.

| July | **Walking Day 63** *Dry and sunny with clouds on mountain tops* |
| Friday **20** | **Bridge of Orchy to Kingshouse Hotel, Glencoe - 13 miles - Total Walked 721** |

As we drove up the Glen we, like hundreds of others, pulled into a newly-built lay-by to view the waterfalls; a spectacular sight. However, I found myself looking at the brilliant piece of engineering that I was standing upon; a viewing platform projecting out above the cascading waters. It looked as though it had been cut into the rock and was so expertly created that it appeared to be part of the scenery. For some reason, I was reminded of that despicable slab of concrete that is the Pomparles Bridge at the entry into Glastonbury. What a contrast. On the way, back over Rannoch Moor we saw a dead red deer; a massive one apparently, a victim of road kill. The many road signs warning us of deer suddenly became relevant.

At the Bridge of Orchy there was a lot of activity with people milling about in the car park and on the hotel steps. We moved away from them and walked down to the actual bridge over the River Orchy. Kay and Ripley joined me for the first mile as we passed through a series of gates in the large deer fence and entered a pine forest on the shoulders of Mam Carraigh. We gently climbed up through the trees, up onto a grassy knoll, to be rewarded with a wonderful view of Loch Tulla.

I said goodbye to Kay and Ripley and walked on across open hill tops surrounded on three sides by mountains and the loch to the north. Now in my stride I caught up with my first walker of the day, a huge man wearing ragged clothing. He was moving fast, feeling the ground before him with a staff. His face was dark, dangerous and secretive. He reminded me instantly of the blind man in Robert Louis Stevenson's

'Kidnapped'; 'We began to go alongside'. This man was not blind but his face was full of character. It turned out that he was French and part of a large party of foreigners walking the WHW who preferred to walk alone yet within sight of one another.

Ahead of me I could see this party spread out across the hills. When he said, "We will all have fun with you tonight at the King's House Hotel", I looked at his face to see if I could register any sinister motive in his words or whether his English was poor. I said my goodbyes and pressed on.

The views across Loch Tulla reminded me of the Lake District with hills and mountains set as a backdrop. I felt at home. I could see many crannogs out in the loch. These are ancient and in the main, man-made islands, fortified against attack. Loch Tulla is one of the best places in Scotland to see them.

At the head of the loch lies the Inveroran Hotel, another splendidly isolated hotel set in tree-covered grounds. The door was open and I walked in. The place was deserted. I called out but no one answered, yet I sensed someone was present in the building. For some reason, they never surfaced. I left the place disappointed and made do with a swig from my water bottle.

A short stroll from the hotel I came to a bridge in an idyllic setting with swards of green fields by a stream. I leant on the bridge and ate some of my snap whilst peering over the parapet. As I bit into my ham sandwich I recoiled in horror, not at what I was eating but at what I saw. Apparently, lots of scummy people had passed this way and finding the place idyllic had camped here, leaving piles of their rubbish behind. Broken tents, umbrellas and garden furniture lay amongst tin cans, bread bags and empty bottles of beer. Someone had tried to sweep this rubbish into a pile but had failed; it was just too big an eyesore, especially in this beautiful setting. I felt physically sick. What kind of people would do such a thing? I knew the answer; the kind of people who walked the WHW; ordinary people.

I moved on and crossed the head of Loch Tulla by Victoria's Bridge, a wonderful stone-built bridge. From there I made my way onto the Thomas Telford-built road across Rannoch Moor. All the way along the West Highland Way, two names put fear into the hearts of the walkers; Rannoch Moor and Devil's Staircase; Rannoch Moor because it can be, in bad weather, very exposed and for a good nine miles offers no shelter or help; Devil's Staircase I will get to later.

Surrounded by mountains, Rannoch Moor is a vast, featureless, boggy moor which, according to Hamish Brown in his 1981 'Hamish's Grout's End Walk', can swallow up the whole of the English Lake District and more. The scale of this area is vast. On the day, I crossed it the weather was fine and route-finding along the excellent Telford road was easy. In addition, I had a party of foreigners to keep me company. I frequently overtook groups of French walkers. "Bonjour", is about as much as my French allows. Then I realised that some were Dutch, some were German and some Scandinavian. They were all friendly.

Over to my left, the large mountain, Black Mount, shadowed my every move. Appropriately, I fell in alongside two German men, 'Goths', dressed from head to foot in black leather with one of them wearing a Dracula t-shirt and the other a large leather cape: For added dramatic effect they both had painted white faces with dark cherry-coloured lips. They were an odd couple. They were heading for the Kingshouse Hotel and said that there they hoped to have some "fun tonight". I thought of the huge Frenchman I'd met earlier and knew they were a match made in heaven. The two blood-sucking 'Goths' were in good company with swarms of midges that filled the air and which I had to fight my way through; just as one swarm abated another larger swarm came upon us and so, it went on - and on.

After a few miles, I was totally fatigued (a nicer word than knackered); not with walking but with fighting the midge. This vast boggy moor is one big, midge-breeding ground and I doubted if Robert Louis Stevenson had ever set foot in it. In his book, 'Kidnapped', his two heroes, David Balfour and Alan Breck, evaded the soldiers by hiding in the heather on Rannoch Moor and, 'bristling' in the sun; scorching on top of two great boulders, listening to the 'drone of the bees'. Not one word was there of the midge that rules supreme hereabouts, the biting little buggers. I quickened my pace, leaving the two Goths enjoying themselves with their blood-sucking midges.

At the bridge over the River Ba, I crossed over into Highland county and had good views across the moor to the Schiehallion Mountain. A group of friendly French walkers were huddled together having a picnic with midges all over them. They waved and I waved back whilst thinking that they must be mad. What is it with the French that the midge doesn't appear to bother them?

I moved on now in a cool breeze that kept the midge away. I was on the lookout for red deer, golden eagle and ring ouzel, all of which are said to frequent the moor. I didn't see any. I did see chaffinches, meadow pipits and lovely eyebright flowers set amongst the rare Rannoch rush grasses. A gentle climb took me up to the cairn that commemorates the death of Peter Fleming who died in 1971 whilst out deer stalking.

I'd nearly done it. On reaching the col, Rannoch Moor lay behind me; ahead was Glencoe and I walked towards it along the old motor road which, up until 1930 was the main road into Glencoe. Today it is traffic-free. This must have been the road that Charles Dickens and others used to enter Glencoe which he described as an area, 'strewn with great boulders'.

I put on a 'gleg' step (a brisk walk), and headed down past the ski centre and down towards Kingshouse. I passed a sign which said 'Welcome - Failte to Glencoe'. The sharp rocky outline of Scotland's most photographed mountain, Buachaille Etive Mor – the Great Herdsman, came into view, as did Kay and Ripley. Kay was in her element in these surroundings and was excitedly looking at the wild flowers. Her latest 'find' being the tiny blue heath milkwort. The Kingshouse Hotel, was another wonderfully isolated place set at the base of the surrounding rugged mountains.

We drove down into the village of Glencoe itself and searched for the memorial to the famous Glencoe Massacre. We found it at the end of the village, set up on a rocky knoll, a tall stone cross atop a stone circular pillar surrounded by iron railings.

The simple monument had been paid for by MacDonald descendants now living in the U.S.A. As a child growing up in the 1960's, if asked, what does the name MacDonald recall, I would almost certainly have said they were the clan of thirty-eight men, women and children who were all massacred at Glencoe on the 13th February 1692 by Government troops.

Today's child would almost certainly, talk about a certain fast-food chain with burger and chips. The National Trust for Scotland, in its excellent booklet on Glencoe (2005), mentions, '*Glencoe's name remains for many synonymous with the brutal slaughter of 1692 and public shock at the massacre ... reverberated throughout the country*'.

Glencoe like Glastonbury, has always been a magical, mysterious and awe-inspiring place in my psyche. Before my LEJOG journey I had not visited either of them but had often heard of them. Glastonbury overall, disappointed me. Glencoe on the other hand, elated me and still does.

Dorothy Wordsworth writing in 1803, said of Glencoe, '*I cannot attempt to describe the mountains*', but then goes on to do so. Many writers have attempted to describe Glencoe or put down on paper their feelings for the place. In my mind, they have all failed. Glencoe beats them every time and retains its magical, mysterious awe.

J.B. Priestley once wrote of the Yorkshire Dales, '*Many places disappoint me on returning to them. The Dales don't. Every return I see them fresh and exciting*'. I agree with him there. I also hope that Glencoe won't disappoint me on returning, as I'm sure I will.

July Saturday 21 | **Walking Day 64** *Dry and clear with grey skies; mountain tops in mist*

Kingshouse Hotel to Kinlochleven - 8 miles - Total Walked 729

By the office at the Glencoe camp-site there was a dry-wipe board with a list of wild flowers that campers had seen growing on the site. Kay could increase that list by a further twenty, bringing the total to thirty-eight. The warden was a bit sceptical at first until Kay dragged her around to the various spots where the species were flowering. Black medic was a new flower to Kay.

Back up the glen to Kingshouse Hotel and I was ready for the off. Today I would be climbing the 'dreaded' Devil's Staircase. Kay was to write: '*As usual, Ripley and I joined Christopher on his walk for the first couple of miles, although I think he was probably glad when we turned back as we were becoming a major distraction - I am now well and truly infected with the desire to hunt for new species of wild flowers and he has instructions to photograph any new examples he encounters. Appropriately, we spotted the blue devils-bit scabious not too far from the Devil's Staircase and the whole area glows yellow with the star-like bog asphodel. Slightly subtler is the yellow tormentil - just as prolific but tiny and just managing to peep through the summer grasses. Yellow rattle was new to us...*'

I said goodbye to Kay and Ripley and set off on a good path that skirted the base of the dark and brooding Beinn a' Chrulaiste 2,805'. At the tiny hamlet of Altnafeadh, the WHW turns away from Glencoe and begins the climb up the Devil's Staircase which is part of the old military road built in 1750. At 1,850' above sea level, it is the highest part of the West Highland Way. There literally are steps cut into the hillside and I found the climb easy and not at all as fearful or as hard-going as some have said.

On the way up I was regaled with fine views across to the eastern flanks of Buachaille Etive Mor, now much more reminiscent of a volcano.

I was passed by a team of young mountain bikers coming down hill and as I neared the top I was approached by two young women, both carrying huge packs. I jokingly said, "You are going the wrong way", to which one of them replied, "We're walking John O'Groats to Land's End".

"Well I...." I said but before I could finish my sentence they were gone, skipping down the staircase at a fast pace.

At the cairn by the top someone had placed a pair of worn-out boots. A party of Russians were having photographs taken by their guide. They looked wealthy, healthy and friendly.

The next section of the WHW is high and exposed and can be *'unpleasant in severe weather'*. Thankfully, the weather was fine and the path good with views over the high moorland towards Ben Nevis in the north.

After a while the huge Blackwater Reservoir came into sight. I walked on, noticing amongst the rocks and bogs, flowering common butterwort and sundew, both insect-eating plants. I took photographs of the tiny trapped flies in both plants. The area also had plenty of delicate Crowberry complete with ripened berries. Meadow pipits kept me company as I walked on across the now desolate moor. Eventually the moorland path began to descend, first to a bubbling stream by a bridge and next to some moorland cottages by the track, which led off one way towards Blackwater Reservoir, the other way towards Kinlochleven.

I headed towards Kinlochleven on a good track that zig-zagged down towards the tree line. On reaching the pine trees I came upon two young boys being shepherded up the hill by their Dad. The boys, aged about eight and six, were moaning constantly, "Can we go back now". "I'm fed up". "I want to go down".

Their Dad was doing his best to motivate them but the little sods were having none of it.

"Oh, come on, let's see what's round the next bend", said their Dad enthusiastically. One boy threw his cap down into the road and had a bad temper tantrum. I knew what this man was going through. As a parent I would try and make these walks an adventure. We would be cowboys riding in a three-wheeled wagon being chased by Cherokees with flaming arrows or soldiers looking up to the hill that suddenly was covered with thousands of Zulu's all banging their spears on their shields. I tried to help by saying, "Just up there, there are some insect-eating plants".

"Great. Come on boys, let's go and see", said Dad.

"Boring", said the oldest boy.

If only the plants ate naughty boys. Luckily, I could walk on, moving away from the moaning brats and their stressed-out Dad.

Six huge ugly pipe lines crashed through the forest, taking a very steep descent down to Kinlochleven. They brought water from the reservoir to a hydro-electric power station. The track continued to zig-zag down through the trees, frequently offering tantalising glimpses of cascading waterfalls and turbulent pools, any one of which, had they been near to a main road, would cause a coach party to stop and admire.

Upon reaching the foot of the hill, I walked out of the trees and into the frontier town of Kinlochleven, heavily scarred by the now demolished aluminium factory. A wooden built hotel, complete with veranda and horse tie-up posts, was full-to-bursting with WHW walkers. An adjacent camp-site was also doing good business. I guessed that most had taken the opportunity to call the Kingshouse to Kinlochleven a half-day walk and were spending the rest of it at leisure prior to their final day tomorrow.

Before the bridge was built over Loch Leven near Glencoe, Kinlochleven had been a busy village, deep inland at the head of the loch. It was nestled at the foot of steep forested mountain slopes and was a necessary place to pass through for traffic heading to Fort William. Today it is by-passed, its industry gone.

The smelter finally closed in 2000, leaving eight hundred people unemployed. Anywhere else, the villagers might have packed up and gone too but some modern-day entrepreneurs were trying to make a go of it. A canoe school was busy down by the loch's edge and a rock climbing school complete with a climber's wall had taken over a rather tall and much out-of-place factory building. Rightly so, the place is now a top destination for outdoor enthusiasts. Kinlochleven has an idyllic mountain setting on the edge of a beautiful sea loch. It deserves to survive. I went into the local shop and bought the local newspaper and some milk. It was a shop that looked like it needed some customers.

July
Sunday
22

Walking Day 65 *Light showers at start and end of day. Dry and grey for rest of day*

Kinlochleven to Fort William - 17 miles - Total Walked 746 >

We had a walk around what was left of Alcan town, as Kinlochleven had been known. Some of the village was very pretty with neat gardens, particularly by the little village school.

It was raining so I donned my WHW poncho, an ideal quick coverall. Kay and Ripley climbed half way up with me through the trees on steep but good paths and then returned to the car.

Eventually I cleared the trees and joined the excellent old military road that led me all the way through the Glen of Lairigmor. The views back to Kinlochleven and the sea loch were stunning. The walk up to the Col of Lairigmor at 1,100' was easy going.

The Mamore Ridge above to the north of me is said to be one of the finest ridge walks in Scotland, boasting eleven Monroe's.

To my south, the large mountain Beinn na Caillich, at 2,502', kept me company for much of the way. (For some reason, it is known as the Old Woman's Mountain). At the ruined croft of Tigh na Sleubhaich, I met a group of German boy scouts, who were the tail-enders of a much larger party, the rest of which I would soon catch up with.

At another ruined croft, Lairigmor, I met the main party resting on the rocks. They looked immaculate in their smart blue uniforms and wouldn't have been out of place on a drill square.

After a chat, I said goodbye to the friendly scouts and marched on into the mountains with ravens for company. I came to a huge cairn marking the end of Lairigmor. Tradition has it, *'a passing MacDonald should add a stone, whilst a Campbell should remove one'*.

At last the mountain path led into forests. A few miles later I wished I was still on the mountain path. The pine forests here are close-planted and offer little to view. They are also, in my opinion, poor for nature as insects, birds and animals all seem to give them a miss.

At Biar a Chaoruinn I could have cheated and walked the four miles into Fort William on the motor road, however I chose to walk six miles through the ever-darkening forest. I came upon a clearing where some forestry workers had begun to fell some of the tight-knit trees. This turned out to be an exception and for miles I walked alone in the dark dense forest.

Somewhere near to the WHW ninety-mile marker, I had a view through the trees to the massive Ben Nevis. Here, shrouded in mist and blocking out the sky, it was dark, brooding and awesome. It rained.

The forest path went up and down like a roller coaster as it led me deeper and deeper into the dark forest, its heavy conifer canopy blocking out the light. Just when I hoped to be descending into Glen Nevis, I began to climb uphill, up and up through the trees in the rain. Untimely, the weather brought on dusk to mid-afternoon. I was fed up and wet. I came to a rare sign indicating a one-mile detour to visit an ancient hill fort. That would be an extra two miles in the rain and gloom. I surprised myself by deciding to take it. A hill fort might afford a view. This one-mile detour was all uphill but eventually at the last bit, the trees gave way to an open hilltop which boasted a large, 'vitrified' fort with easily-seen rampart remains. This was Dun Deardail and I had the place to myself.

After exploring the pear-shaped hill top, I tucked into the remnants of my snap whilst looking out across Glen Nevis to the bulk of The Ben as Ben Nevis is known. The shawl of mist around its shoulders was growing darker and thicker as the day slunk its way into evening.

I could just see the camp-site down the valley; it looked miniature in scale.

I picked myself up and marched on back downhill along the detour path and then onto a wide downhill forest track that led me all the way to that camp-site at Glen

Nevis. Inexplicably, the last mile of the West Highland Way follows the road into Fort William, thankfully on a wide pavement; firstly, in a rural area then ever-increasingly suburban, passing neat gardens and houses on the edge of town.

By Nevis Bridge there is a large thistle sign set in small parkland declaring the end of the West Highland Way. I walked over to touch it. Across to my left on the lawn, soaking and wet, were a group of six women drinking champagne and celebrating. They were nurses from Glasgow who had just completed the walk. They must have always been just ahead of me, as I'd not seen them before. They came over and offered me some champagne, taking my photograph by the sign. They wanted to take me away and celebrate with me. When I told them, my wife would be here any minute they appeared disappointed. I explained that tomorrow I was setting off on the Great Glen Way. They were returning to Glasgow and to work; all of them wished they were going my way.

July **Monday** **23** **Walking Day 66** *Hot and sunny, then light showers with heavy rain at night*

Fort William to Gairlochy - 11 miles - Total Walked 757

Fort William was the biggest town we had visited since Kirkintilloch. It is a seaside resort, industrial centre and pleasant residential area all rolled into one. The town is dominated by Ben Nevis, Britain's biggest mountain, yet unseen by it. From nowhere in the town could I afford a view of The Ben, it being blocked by a wooded shoulder of the Nevis range.

I walked along the promenade looking out across the sea loch that is Loch Linnhe. I crossed the main road, the A82, which unfortunately cuts through the town between the shops and the sea front. I strolled down the busy main street, visiting the post office to buy stamps, send-off postcards and get my LEJOG certificate stamped.

On leaving the post office I noticed a book shop with a huge pile of the new Harry Potter book, a copy of which I promptly went in and bought. It's a massive book and I didn't fancy carrying it all day. Luckily Kay and Ripley were strolling around the parkland that is where the actual Fort William stood. I re-joined them and relieved myself of the weighty tome.

The remains of the fort, originally built in 1654 by Oliver Cromwell, can still be seen in outline in the parkland by the sea wall just opposite from Morrison's supermarket and the bus shelter-like railway station. The great railway journey through the Highlands starts or finishes at Fort William, depending on your view point. Either way its terminus is a shabby bus shelter which, although practical, deserves a much-needed make-over.

The fort is the official starting point of Scotland's newest long-distance footpath, the Great Glen Way.

The Great Glen Way (GGW) has some interesting information posts made of huge slabs of slate, taller than a man and split in the middle by a straight line. This line represents

Scotland's split by the Great Glen (Gleann Mor), a massive depression which follows an easily recognisable geological fault line that effectively cuts Scotland in two; Fort William in the south and Inverness in the north, with Loch Ness in between.

I followed the route out of town, passing signposts for the 'Fort William Mountain Bike Track', Britain's longest downhill track which attracts thousands of mountain bikers each year. I walked along the Shinty ground, home to the Fort William Shinty Club and the Lochy football team. I found myself walking by the side of the River Lochy, in a nature reserve surrounded by young trees and wild flowers, when I came across a group of men. They were stocky, well-built men with fishing rods in their hands. A gamekeeper with two well-controlled dogs was talking to them. The gamekeeper had a well-educated English accent, whilst the four men had that distinctive Glaswegian drawl. It appeared that the gamekeeper had caught them fishing without a licence and was in the process of kicking them off the river bank. Just as I was thinking what a lonely and perhaps dangerous job the gamekeeper had, his radio blurted out and 'backup' was on its way. Surprisingly, the men were very compliant, packing up their fishing rods and moving on. I followed them away, along the river bank to a small car park which led me to a bridge that crossed the river.

The bridge is known as 'Soldiers Bridge' and from it I had some grand views of nearby Inverlochy Castle in its now ruined state. The castle was built in the 12th century by a Norman family, the Cummings or as they were called up here, the Comyns. The castle has been described as 'one of the most important castles in Scottish history'. Built on a natural defensive position against the River Lochy, it witnessed two important battles. The first was a clan battle between the MacDonald's and the Stewarts in 1431. The MacDonald's' won, then during the Civil war, in 1645, (a war I have always thought of as the 'English' Civil War), a Royalist army headed by the Earl of Montrose, defeated a Roundhead force led by the Campbell clan, who were defending the castle. The defenders lost over 1,300 men in the battle. Shortly after this battle, a Cromwellian army led by General Monck, recaptured the castle and built Fort William nearby, thus making Inverlochy Castle forever redundant.

I walked on and soon entered the village of Caol, pronounced Cool or Kool, not only the winner of 'A Village in Bloom' contest but described as 'the largest village in Scotland' with a population of 3,240. It lies on the northern shore of Loch Linnhe. Most of the village resembled a large housing estate more reminiscent of the Glasgow urban scene. I reached what I took to be the centre of the village; a modern square of buildings with an assortment of shops. In the centre of the square, along with some seating I saw an unusual igloo like cairn of local stone.

A plaque declared that this cairn was the centrepiece of the local regeneration of the village. It had been officially opened in April 2007, a month ago, by Princess Anne. Caol beach had, prior to this regeneration, been an ugly blot on the landscape with masses of assorted flotsam and rubbish washed here by the tides. Over fifty years of neglect and rubbish was recently cleared away by a mass litter pick involving the villagers. To their surprise and my delight, they found they had a wonderful and beautiful beach right on their doorstep.

I enjoyed walking along the beach towards Corpach. In World War 2, Corpach was a naval repair base. However, it was in timber, like Caol, where it employed over 900 people. The mill was taking 10,000 trees a day. It closed in 1980.

Corpach is better known for being home to the western end of the Caledonian Canal. When I arrived at the magnificent set of sea locks they were bathed in sunshine. The locks are beautifully maintained. Some boats were waiting to enter them, both from the sea and canal sides, so there was plenty to observe. All the boat crews were smiling and laughing and everyone looked happy. Some were obviously celebrating having successfully navigated the full distance of the canal. I was soaking up this jolly atmosphere when my eye suddenly caught sight of something. There, back the way I had come, I could see Ben Nevis clear of mist, its mountain top visible. I was annoyed. The weather forecast had been good but in all the days that I had been in this area, Ben Nevis had kept its veil hung over its top and I'd reluctantly given the climb a miss. From Corpach I could see both Fort William and Ben Nevis; so very close together yet so far away.

I turned to walk along the tow path of the canal. Hamish Brown in his 1981 book 'Hamish's Groats End Walk', states: 'James Watt surveyed the sixty-mile-long route in 1773 and gave an estimate of £164,000. By 1847 the expenditure had risen to £1,311,270. It was really a sort of 19th-century Concorde, recognised for its incredible engineering feats. The building of the canal enabled sea going vessels to significantly reduce their journey (and costs) between the Baltic and America'.

I had the towpath to myself and enjoyed pushing on, even if I did keep getting tantalising glimpses of the cloud-free, snow-covered, northern slopes of Ben Nevis, which was now over to my right.

At Banavie I arrived at the foot of Neptune's Staircase, a series of eight locks which raise the canal by 64' (20 metres). The locks were mechanised in 1968 but it still takes one hour for a boat to get through them.

A coach park nearby supplied a near-constant stream of visitors. For the clear majority of them, the walk alongside the locks was about as much of the canal towpath walk they would do. They had a lot to see. The locks were busy with pleasure boats either going up or coming down. I gently pushed my way through the throng of ice-cream-licking crowds, peeking in at the gift shop half way up. Within yards of reaching the top, I had left the crowds behind and never saw a walker again for the rest of the day.

I had just got into my stride when I came to the Sheangain Aqueduct. I peered over the wall to look down on it. I couldn't see much as vegetation got in the way. I climbed down a flight of steps and came to a track. The aqueduct was below here. I climbed through some trees and bushes and slithered down a steep path to finally arrive at a fabulous stone-built feature consisting of three tunnels; two carried streams and the third a farm track. They all were beautifully paved with stone flags. The canal was a long way up above me. As I stood back to take a photograph I wondered how many, if any, of the five thousand canal boat users and uncounted walkers, ever got down here to see this engineering delight.

The walk along the canal was a sheer joy; comfortable strolling in good weather. The trees and bushes were all at their summer best. Dorothy Wordsworth described the mountains and hills, as seen from the Caledonian Canal, as being *ethereal or sapphire blue in colour. A beautiful blue which set the scene so perfectly*. (NT for Scotland, Glencoe booklet, 2005)

Birds and butterflies competed for my attention as they flittered around me.

I passed another aqueduct as I crossed the River Loy, which joined the nearby River Lochy that runs parallel to the canal. From here I could see some fishermen down on the river bank.

I strolled on until I came to the Moy Swing Bridge, a beautiful, double Leaf Bridge. Built in 1821, it is the only original cast iron bridge still in use. It is now mechanised and the winch has been preserved.

On the bridge, there was an attendant in a hut. He was a friendly fellow who told me that staff along the canal rotated their duties to various bridges and locks so as not to get bored. He said the Moy Swing Bridge was one of the loneliest positions on the canal. Walking on I passed a weir on the river and arrived at Gairlochy locks; winner of the award for the best length of canal, so a sign declared. Thomas Telford had his base here whilst he oversaw the building of the canal.

The Queen visited the locks in 1958 when she and her then young family toured the canal. Kay and Ripley met me by the isolated telephone kiosk and we went for a walk around the locks and out to the lighthouse on the edge of Loch Lochy. More boats, sometimes huge sea-going motorboats, were here and moored up for the day.

Kay, in a letter home, wrote: *The weather forecast keeps telling us that we are going to have rain. If it does rain, it falls mostly at night. During the day, it is very pleasant. We have heard that it has flooded many areas in the south, even at Loch Lomond and have a feeling that the bad weather seems to be lurking behind us and each time we move up, it moves up. Let's hope it runs out of steam by August*.

July / Tuesday 24 — Rest day *Dry and sunny*

Today we moved camp up to Fort Augustus which is half way between Fort William and Inverness. We found a pleasant site on the edge of the village. The steps on the motor home had broken and we needed to visit a caravan supply shop to buy some temporary ones to use until we could get ours fixed. The nearest caravan suppliers with a shop were in Inverness, a thirty-mile trip up the side of Loch Ness. Reluctantly we set off up the busy A82 road.

At Inverness, we found the caravan supermarket on the edge of town and we purchased quite a few things for the motor home in addition to the set of steps. We finished the day off by having a meal at an Italian restaurant which overlooks the river and castle beyond. The restaurant was a real find with excellent food and atmosphere. Refreshed, we drove back down the still busy road to Fort Augustus and our camp-site.

July
Wednesday
25

Walking Day 67 *Showers at first, then hot and sunny*

Gairlochy to Laggan Lochs - 11 miles - Total Walked 768 >

On the way to Gairlochy, we drove via Spean Bridge. By a dog-leg bend in the road, on the brow of a hill, stands the imposing Commando Memorial. We pulled into the coach park and joined the hundreds of tourists which, even at this early hour of the day were clamouring around the monument, designed in 1949 by Dundee Art College student, Scott Sutherland. The seventeen-foot-high monument, set on a stone plinth, is a bronze statue of three battle-dressed commandos holding a dramatic pose, staring out over the Great Glen, Ben Nevis to the south and the range of hills known as the Grey Corries over to their right.

The monument was unveiled in 1952 by Queen Elizabeth, the Queen Mother and commemorates the thousands of soldiers who passed through Spean Bridge, piped in and out by Scottish pipers on their way to Achnacarry House on the edge of Loch Arkaig. Here, during the height of World War 2, they received their commando basic training which included everything from survival skills to unarmed combat, night-time manoeuvres and boat navigation skills. At the end of the training they were awarded their famous green beret.

Their motto, *'United we conquer'*, is emblazoned across the memorial.

Back at the telephone kiosk at Gairlochy, I was reminded that near this place in 1689, under Viscount Dundee, the gathering of the clans took place at the beginning of the Jacobite Rebellion. After reacquainting ourselves with the beautiful canal lock setting, all three of us took the path uphill into the woods and followed it for a mile as it ran parallel to the road and the loch. We parted company when the path descended then I crossed the road and headed for the loch shoreline.

Before me I could see the full view of Loch Lochy as I headed north. Pine forests dominated the lower slopes of the mountains that formed the picturesque scene. It reminded me of Loch Lomond but without the crowds. The sun was shining and I couldn't wish for a better outlook as I strode on. Up until now on my journey, I hadn't had a deadline to meet. In fact, I'd been *'wandering at fancy's whim with no rules – possibly the best way to see the more civilised and historically interesting places'*, as Hamish Brown put it in his 1981 *'Groats End Walk'* book. He of course, was walking at a ridiculously fast pace; eating and even reading on the move.

However, the deadlines at last caught up with me. For some time, I'd known that in August, one of my daughters was due to get married. I'd skipped going to retirement do's and even funerals but my daughter's wedding? Kay had been spending ever-increasing

194

amounts of time on the telephone – the thought of the bill made me shudder. I consoled myself with the thought that even if we'd been at home, most of her organising would have been carried out by telephone and as it turned out, you can do all that almost anywhere. I'd worked out that Inverness would be a good place to aim for and then take a well-earned break to travel back home and attend the wedding. What's more, I could do it comfortably in my style without missing too much on the way. I had to put my mind to the Father-of-the-Bride's speech. Thankfully, everything else was being taken care of.

I stopped to admire the beautifully isolated houses at Bunarkaig, looking delightful in the sunshine, set up in the trees overlooking the loch. The River Arkaig had been tumbling down a rocky ravine into the loch by a series of cascades and waterfalls. At the mouth of the river a paddle of canoeists were resting, having canoed (or kayaked?) down this fast-flowing river. A Land Rover parked up nearby had a sign declaring, *'Canoe Training School - River Arkaig'*.

At Clunes I joined a forest track that led me along a level way that skirted the loch shoreline, allowing me some breath-taking views of Loch Lochy. I could see virtually all its ten-mile length and its mountain surroundings. The forest track was wide, the pine trees being spread out.

The walk in the sunshine was a joy, joined by my shadow, my only companion on the route today. My path was lined by pink-coloured wood vetch and by its near cousin, bitter vetch which, as an edible plant, was grown here as a subsistence crop. Large black and yellow dragonflies hovered about; speckled wood butterflies flittered here and there and I strode on. I passed the ruined bothy of Glas Dhoire, situated on the loch shore. Someone had recently been wild camping here judging by the remains of a camp fire. Today I had the place to myself.

I moved on. The track crossed numerous fast-flowing streams that tumbled down the steep, pine-covered hillsides, heading for the loch.

The streams contained large numbers of 'humbug'-striped rocks, many looking edible. It looked like someone had spilt a bag of Yorkshire Mixtures into the streams. I resisted the temptations and walked on until finally reaching civilisation at the Kilfinnan Holiday Lodges that dotted the hillside above the loch.

I emerged on the road at Laggan Locks. The locks raise the canal to 106 feet (32 metres) above sea level at its highest point and cuts through some of the hardest rocks in the region, hence here, the canal, which links Loch Lochy to Loch Oich, is at its narrowest. People swarmed over the locks as they always tend to do. I made my way through them and crossed over to a barge that has been converted into a pub. I met up with Kay and Ripley and climbed on board to buy a much-needed drink.

On the short way, back to the car we passed an information board that declared here was the site of the Battle of the Shirts. In 1544, a clan battle between the Frasers and Grants on one side and the MacDonald's, MacDonnell's and Camerons on the other, took place on a really hot day in July; so hot that the men stripped off down to their shirts. It was a bloody, hand to hand skirmish, where over 1,000 men lost their lives. As with a lot of historic battlefields, today it was a beautiful, peaceful spot.

Walking Day 68 *Hot and sunny*

Laggan Locks to Fort Augustus - 11 miles - Total Walked 779

On the way back to Laggan Locks the road passes the unusual monument, 'The Well of Seven Heads', which stands at a spring on the west side of Loch Oich. As the Great Glen Way follows the disused railway line along the south-east side of the loch, I doubt if many walkers of the Way get to see it.

We stopped the car and I got out to examine it. There are seven heads carved in stone, set around the top of a stone obelisk, which is itself topped by a carved hand clasping a dagger. On each of the four sides of the base there was an inscription. I struggled to find the English version, the Gaelic and French being more prominent, followed by the Latin version. The monument was erected in 1812, to commemorate a grisly murder that took place in 1663. The son of the Clan Chieftain, Keppoch, was murdered after a quarrel with his uncle and six sons. The Clan Chieftain demanded that the murderers themselves be killed and their heads brought to him as proof. The perpetrators of this deed washed the severed heads at the spring here before presenting them to their chieftain. The monument is known in Gaelic as, 'Tobar–Nan–ceann'. In the 19th century, an archaeological dig at a nearby mound, uncovered seven headless bodies, adding credence to the story. I climbed down the steps to the stone trough at the bottom of the monument and took a drink of the pleasant spring water that still bubbles up here, fresh and pure.

Laggan Locks were again busy with people. We left them behind as we set off along the path high up on a raised embankment through well-spaced, mature pine trees. We passed a couple of families out dog-walking and obviously up here on holiday.

The path led to the busy A82 road near to the Laggan Swing-bridge which is at the bottom of Loch Oich. Kay and Ripley turned back as I crossed the road and skirted around the Great Glen Water Park, another 'chalet' and lodge holiday centre. A sign declared that 'No dogs' were allowed on this section of the Great Glen Way. There was no explanation as to why this should be so and after walking the 'no dog' section, I am still at a loss as to why dogs were not allowed.

I was now walking on a disused railway line which was thick with mud. The railway had been built from Fort William to Fort Augustus between 1896 and 1903 to link up with the Loch Ness paddle steamer, thereby linking up to Inverness. It was never a profitable line and closed in 1933, briefly reopening during World War 2. I was finding the going tough as I tried to hop, skip and jump through the sloppy mud. The trees were doing their best to overgrow the line and it felt as though I was walking through a tunnel. A group of German Girl Guides marched past me in a long single file. Judging by the lack of smiles, they too were finding the going tough.

After a while, the path left the disused railway line, now completely overgrown and followed along the shoreline of Loch Oich, the highest loch in the Great Glen, being one hundred feet above sea level. Across the loch, through the trees, I got some glimpses of Invergarry Castle, known as the Rock of Raven. Built on a rocky outcrop on the west bank of Loch Oich, it is the ancestral home of the MacDonnell family. General Monck burnt it down in 1654 when fighting for Cromwell's republic. From 1688 until 1715 it was the centre of the Jacobite revolution and was visited twice by Bonnie Prince Charlie. The Duke of Cumberland had the castle destroyed after the Battle of Culloden. Today a hotel has been built amongst its ruins.

I walked along the pebbled beaches of the loch, passing a ruined cottage before climbing up to re-join the disused railway line. I crossed an old railway bridge and emerged from the trees into fields at the head of the loch. The views behind me were wonderful and I had to drag myself away and turn northwards.

I walked up to the modern road bridge at Aberchalder that replaced the original and preserved double cantilevered swing-bridge, built in 1834 by James Drudge. The original bridge was used up until 1932 when traffic levels forced the authorities to build the present, less attractive but more functional bridge. I walked across the beautiful old swing-bridge and then back again. The preserved bridge crosses the River Oich that runs parallel with the canal into the loch. I was again joined by large crowds of holidaying walkers and numerous pleasure boats as I strolled along the wide canal tow-path into Fort Augustus passing first, the beautifully located Kytra Locks surrounded by mature Scots pine trees.

Several memorial benches sited at Kytra bore dedications such as, 'He loved this place'; and 'she was at home here'. I sat on a picnic bench and had a drink of water, soaking in the idyllic atmosphere.

Soon I was again passing dog walkers and ubiquitous holiday chalets on the edge of Fort Augustus. When I got to the six rise locks that led the canal down into Fort Augustus, I was surprised to hear a Yorkshire accent in the team of lock-keepers who were busy with boats moving through the locks. It turned out one of the lock-keepers was from Leeds. Having learnt his skills on the Leeds to Liverpool Canal, he had been head-hunted to work up here. Like Neptune's Staircase, these locks were surrounded by ice-cream-licking crowds and I had to weave my way through them, admiring the boats as I went.

Fort Augustus Locks have more life to them; shops and pubs line the lower lock edges. One pub was packed with people spilling out into a small beer garden and then onto the tow-path itself. A live Scottish folk band was inside, playing music which could be heard for some distance. Beer glasses were being chinked in the sunshine. Everyone I saw was in a happy mood.

I crossed the road, dodging the coaches bringing even more tourists here to have a look at Loch Ness. I had reached its southern tip. I walked on, past the Queen Victoria Jubilee Fountain and through the town back to my camp-site, only pausing to admire a field full of donkeys before finally walking into camp and calling it a day.

Walking Day 69 *Hot and sunny, with showers*

Fort Augustus to Alltsigh - 13 miles - Total Walked 792 >

Our camp-site at Fort Augustus was populated with families from all over Europe with tents in the middle and caravans around the edge. There was a relaxed, friendly atmosphere all the time we were there; it was also 'midge-free'.

I walked into town, passing the original fort that gave the town its name. Built in 1716, when peace finally arrived in the Highlands, the fort was gifted to some Benedictine monks who built the present abbey on the site. I made my way into the town centre. The main grocery store in town doubled up as a newsagent and tourist 'tat', gift shop. It was packed with people and doing a roaring trade. I entered and began searching the displays for some toffee. I had taken to buying a small tablet of toffee to carry with me and nibble at throughout my day. My preferred brand up here in Scotland was 'Highland Cow' toffee. I couldn't see it anywhere. I joined the queue, deciding to ask the girl on the checkout. I asked, "Have you got any Highland Cow toffee"?

The Polish girl on the checkout said, "I'm sorry, I don't understand".

There was I, expecting a Scottish accent to greet me.

"Have you got any Highland Cow toffee", I slowly repeated.

A blank, perplexed look came back from the girl.

In a pathetic Scottish accent, I asked for, "Highland Cooo toffee".

"Ah, yes we do; it's over there", she replied, pointing to some on a display by her side.

Chomping on my newly purchased toffee I walked out of town, passing even more coach-loads of tourists emerging from the very large coach park. I passed too, the large queue at the Loch Ness jetty, where cruise boats were filling with tourists eager to sail across the loch at a leisurely pace – perhaps hoping to catch a glimpse of the monster.

On the edge of town, I entered some woods and began climbing up a steep hillside. On the opposite hillside, I could see a huge shanty town with portable huts and cabins; a blot on the otherwise beautiful landscape. This is where 500 Polish migrant workers were living on a site that resembled a World War 2 prisoner of war camp. They were here to help construct an eight-mile tunnel through the mountains. This is the Glendoe Hydro-Electric Project, the largest of its kind to be built in the U.K. It includes a 1,000-metre dam head and new reservoir situated high up at Glen Tarff and an underground power station inside the mountain. The drop from the reservoir is the highest drop at a power station in the U.K and involves water falling at 200 m.p.h. When completed, the power station will provide electricity for 250,000 homes.

I turned away and concentrated on the climb up through the trees. Within minutes of leaving the town, I had also left behind the thousands of people. I stood in complete solitude on a hillside overlooking Loch Ness and Fort Augustus. I knew none of the 'tourists' would venture this way today. I enjoy solitude. Hamish Brown in his 1981

'Groats End Walk book', remarks: 'Solitude is a singing glory; quite different from the cold pain of loneliness'.

I always carried a small pair of binoculars inside my rucksack. Today I would wear them around my neck, ready to scan the surface of the loch, just in case the monster should appear as I watched.

The views of the loch were disappointing as I walked deeper into the forest. The pine trees grew closer and closer together. I trudged on, mile after mile. Just when I began to feel 'lonely', it began to rain heavily.

The trees appeared totally lifeless with no birds, insects, butterflies or anything else for that matter. Rather than a joyful walk it was soul destroying. I can only hope that in years to come, when this long stretch of trees are felled, the replanting will be carried out with more care and thought, for not only the walker but for nature.

At long last, the track emerged from the dark forest and skirted around a rocky outcrop. Finally, I had some spectacular views of Loch Ness. I also had a spring-like euphoric feeling as I emerged from the dark into the light. From my vantage point, Loch Ness gave the impression of being a large, green-sided bath tub filled with water, with a child's set of toy boats floating on the surface.

Binoculars to my eyes, I scoured that surface, up and down, again and again, searching for an unusual ripple in the water, hoping to catch a view of the monster. It wasn't to be. As I turned away from the edge I noticed I wasn't alone. Behind me and unnoticed up until now was a group of eight or nine... "Rucksack carrying penguins"? Queried my daughter Gemma, in her best Monty Python-style sense of humour.

No, not really. What I saw was a small family of stone people; pebbles and rocks carefully balanced one on top of the other and sculptured into a basic human shape. Some were ten pebbles high; quite an amazing feat. They looked as though they'd been around for a while which was surprising seeing as we were on such an open rocky outcrop. I wondered how these stone people could withstand the weather, even though today was windless. I decided that the group had all been built by the same person, a fellow Great Glen Way walker who, having staggered out of the dark forest in a lonely, delirious and demented state, had 'built' himself or herself, an instant family for company.

I turned back to have another look at Loch Ness, here seen in its full majestic glory; 23 miles long and 1 mile wide. This viewpoint of the loch is not seen by the many motorists who drive along the road by the loch edge. Loch Ness contains more water than in all the lakes and rivers combined in the British Isles; a staggering fact. My attention was drawn to the hillside on the other side of the loch. A great, grey rock-coloured horseshoe-shape carved itself out of the green tree-covered slopes. This is known as the Horseshoe Crags. I scanned the loch a final time before reluctantly re-entering the dark confines of the forest path.

The ground below the trees looked parched; nothing could grow down here where sunlight never penetrates. I was told that the elusive pine martin frequents this forest;

199

I never saw one. I don't believe anything lives in here.

I walked on and on and on. Looking at the map I realised the small village of Invermoriston, my next destination, was frustratingly half a mile away down a steep tree-covered slope. However, there was no way I could get to it; the trees were packed so close together, I couldn't get through them. It was somewhere around here that I first met 'German pork pie hat boy', as I nicknamed the teenager from Germany who was also walking the Great Glen Way (GGW). When I first saw him in the forest gloom, I couldn't quite make out who he was or what he was doing. I hadn't seen a soul in ages when I spotted him crouched down near the ground. I came upon him from behind and startled him. After the initial shock, it was obvious he was in fact making himself a brew of tea using a primus stove. He spoke good English and said he'd offer me a cup except he only carried the one; his own. I left him making tea in the forest gloom.

The GGW liberally marked with wooden, blue-coloured 'thistle' marker posts, took me on a four-mile detour through the forest and down onto the banks of the River Moriston, to eventually arrive at Invermoriston. The busy A82 road passes through the village over a modern road bridge that replaced the beautiful old bridge preserved below. I walked down to it. Designed by Thomas Telford and built in 1805, it took eight years to complete. It's a beautiful, double-arched stone structure that crosses the river at a point where the river is forced through rocks in a series of rapids. It's a lovely scene, spoilt by the ugly, though practical modern bridge higher up.

In 1773, when Johnson and Boswell passed this way, they stayed in a humble turf-built inn. Today we have the white-coloured Glenmoriston Arms Hotel; built in 1740, parts of which are said to be the original Johnson and Boswell inn. It was to this inn also that the famous Scottish author, Gavin Maxwell stayed whilst putting the finishing touches to his best-selling book on wild otters, 'Ring of Bright Water'.

In the Millennium village hall, there was an outdoor clothing sale taking place. I wandered in and had a look around. Carrying on, I came to the junction with the A887, the road that leads to the Kyle of Lochalsh and eventually to the Isle of Skye. I went into the village Post Office which amongst many other things, sold tea; potentially awful stuff from a machine. I bought some and was pleasantly surprised; it wasn't bad. I got talking to the postmaster who it turned out was from Yorkshire; or so he said before correcting himself and saying that he was born in Glasgow and went south as a baby, growing up in Saddleworth near Huddersfield. Saddleworth, a proud Yorkshire village, for over 1,000 years, was placed in turmoil by incompetent politicians when, in 1974 after the local Government changes, it found that it was to be governed by Oldham Council a Lancashire town. This postmaster, brought up in that town, considers himself a Yorkshire man.

Before leaving the village, I walked down some steps to have a look at the ancient St. Columba's well, one of a few that goes by the same name. Legend has it that St. Columba, on his way to visit King Brude and bringing Christianity to the area, blessed this well, defying the local Druids who had cursed it. The well is noted for its remarkable curative properties. I bent down and took a handful of the fresh water to drink. Instantly refreshed I strode on out of the village and immediately began climbing the hillside, covered in trees and back into the forest.

These next few miles of forest paths were at least a little more pleasant than the previous section. The trees were spread out a bit and often opened up allowing views of Loch Ness. I passed a large Dutch family walking the GGW south; they were enjoying the adventure, or so they all said. I also passed a stone cave that would have made a good shelter if it had been raining. A flock of tiny gold crests flying high in the treetops, kept my attention for a while. I was glad to see them as sightings of any birds in these forests had been scarce.

I strode on, the path being easy as it contoured around the base of Creag Nan Eun and Meall Na Srome. Suddenly a large dog fox emerged from the forest, directly in front of me. It was a beautiful fox, in good condition. It looked as surprised as I was, standing still at first, not sure of itself, then quickly shooting off back into the 'dead-looking' forest. Thank God it wasn't a wolf I thought. The rest of the afternoon passed pleasantly as I walked on, photographing the many butterflies that flitted about me. Like some modern-day Colonel Johnson from 'Inja' who, as described by Ray Parkin in his brilliant 1963 book, 'Into the Smother', a journal of the Burma-Siam Railway, danced his way through dreadful conditions as a Japanese P.O.W. in World War 2, collecting and identifying butterflies along the line of the railway construction site.

Here I was on a lonely Scottish forest path, admittedly not in any way like his conditions but 'dancing' from one bush to the next, 'capturing' on film, common blues, speckled woods and Scotch Argus butterflies that fluttered idiosyncratically here, there and everywhere. Time and distance passed by and I soon emerged on that busy road the A82, on the side of Loch Ness. In the car park of Loch Ness Youth Hostel, brilliantly located overlooking the loch at Alltsigh, Kay and Ripley were waiting for me as planned. Another day done.

July Saturday 28	**Walking Day 70** *Heavy showers and rain with the odd dry spell*
	Alltsigh to Drumnadrochit - 11 miles - Total Walked 803

As we all got ready for the off at Alltsigh, Kay's attention was drawn to a large shrubby plant with a red stem and bright golden-yellow flowers, bearing bunches of rich, fleshy red berries. It was a beautiful example of a tutsan; a plant known for its antiseptic qualities, being used before modern medicine to help heal flesh wounds. The French derivative tutsaine means 'all healthy'. I was surprised to see it on the edge of more 'barren' pine forests.

We set off in the rain on a wide track, uphill, through the forest. Kay and Ripley turned back after a mile and I continued, eventually climbing out of the forest and onto a hilly ridge with fine views of Loch Ness. The road 'hair pinned' up the ridge to eventually crest the hill.

This was more like it. I disturbed a deer; a red deer I think, which ran away from me at speed. I then came across a Dutch couple huddled together on some stones on the ground, trying but failing to shelter from the now driving rain. They, like the other Dutch family I'd met earlier, were walking the GGW north to south.

Just as I was beginning to enjoy my walk the path led me back into a thick pine forest, the path being narrow and the trees very close together. The forest path snaked its way slowly along the hillside for miles and miles. I was getting sick of pine forests; sick of the confined state the paths put me in and for the first time on my journey I felt bored, a feeling I'd not experienced for a long, long time.

The forest path was soul-destroying. I plodded on and on in the rain that somehow managed to penetrate the tree cover to find me. Where oh where are those mile-wide fire breaks that bring much-needed light to the forest; not here on this long stretch.

I put my head down and walked on, looking at my feet which had hardly given me any trouble; *'they were seasoned to all roads; hard or soft; and by now hardened up; miles rolling by easily beneath my tread...'*. As Theo Lang put it in his 1948 LEJOG book *'Cross Country'*.

Every morning after my shower I dried my feet and then dusted them with talcum powder, wearing a pair of cotton socks next to my skin, followed by my walking socks, all fitting snugly into my Brasher boots. It all seemed to work as they were performing beautifully.

Just as I was thinking the pine forest would go on forever, I crested a small hill and entered a wonderland. It was a truly euphoric moment, as good as switching on a light in the dark. My whole being was uplifted and I felt on top of the world. I had entered an ancient oak wood, a proper wood, not a manufactured forest. The trees were beautiful. I could see the sky with the sun trying to shine through the rain; birds twittered and insects buzzed. It reminded me of a favourite walk of ours back in Yorkshire and I walked on with more vigour in my stride.

I joined a farm lane that climbed up to meet a motor road and car park at Gortaig. I followed this very quiet road for the next few miles, sometimes on pavements, sometimes on paths that ran parallel to it. The pine forests crept back into view, eventually enveloping me yet again as I descended the steep hill into Drumnadrochit.

The GGW route planners have done a great disservice to walkers by not negotiating a route to Urquhart Castle, whose magnificent remains stand out on Strone Point overlooking Loch Ness. Walkers must face a two-mile uphill detour to visit this famous landmark; many I guess, will miss it completely. I for one would rather have visited it than walked the miles of intolerable pine forest paths. I know that to walk to it involves walking on a good pavement alongside the very busy A82 but after hours of being alone in the forest, a few minutes on the busy road doesn't seem at all bad.

Having Kay with the car made it easy for me and later that day, after we'd met up in Drumnadrochit and were on our way back to camp, we called in at Urquhart Castle (which has featured on many biscuit tin lids over the years). It was one of the largest castles in Scotland; built in 1230 and seized by the English as early as 1296.

Protected by the water on three sides and by a moat on the fourth, it looks an impregnable stronghold. Today its ruins are well-kept and cared for and the car park was big enough to accommodate the hundreds of coaches that call this way. Tourists climbed over every inch of the castle diminishing some of its romantic appeal. I digress... I walked into Drumnadrochit which is set back from Loch Ness, deep at the head of Urquhart Bay.

The Naylor brothers in their 1916 JOG-LE book, quote an unnamed Irish poet who wrote: *'Stop, traveller. With well-packed bag and hasten to unlock it; you'll ne'er regret it, though you lag a day at Drumnadrochit'*. I certainly did 'lag' for some time in the town for the first thing I saw was a Shinty Match. I stood in the rain on the edge of the pitch joining hundreds of other spectators.

It was a fast, physically demanding and skilful game; totally absorbing for me as a spectator. I watched for over an hour as the twelve players per team battled it out with a small leather ball. To my untrained eye, it looked like a cross between hockey, football and boxing. I could see, when struck, the ball whizzed along at fantastic speed, it is claimed, sometimes up to 100 mph.

The Glen Urquhart Shinty Club has played at this Blairbeg Park ground since 1885. Shinty like the Irish hurling, can trace its roots back to warrior training. Glen Urquhart are in the Premier Division which is governed by the Camanachio Association. It's such a good game to watch, I was surprised that it hasn't caught on further south or even been televised. I had to drag myself away from it.

For those Great Glen Way walkers who missed Urquhart Castle there is a perfect model of the castle in the village centre, set amidst the white-harled cottages near to where the River Enrick flows out into the bay. I met up with Kay and Ripley at the bigger of the two Loch Ness monster exhibition sites, our little Nissan car being dwarfed by the huge 'Monster' coaches parked in the car park.

We took Ripley for a walk in the gardens that led downhill to a pond, in the middle of which we saw a model monster – Nessie – the only monster I saw that day. We joined a troop of tourists for a tour of the Monster Visitor Centre which was now housed in what had been the rather grand and imposing Drumnadrochit Hotel.

The exhibition lasted about one hour and presented the facts of the case in an impartial way using film, sounds, photography and up-to-date computer wizardry with laser special effects. It gave details of Loch Ness itself, how it was formed etc. Important, in my view was the fact that the loch has little in the way of food suitable for a monster; the deeper the loch gets, the less food there is.

We passed through rooms that told the story of early sightings right up to the famous sightings and hoaxes then on to the numerous studies and researches; some eccentric but others University-backed and serious. One such study in the 1960's employed students in their summer break stationed at various points along the loch, armed with binoculars, viewing the loch for twenty minutes at a time throughout the day. Another study in the 1980's known as Operation Deepscan drew a sonar curtain along the whole length of the loch using a fleet of local vessels. The exhibition leaves you to make up your own mind; is there a monster or not and with the last words; *'Science is always changing - we don't know everything'.*

Like many such attractions, we left the exhibition via a gift shop which was massive; more like a supermarket. The route out was like a maze. I'd never seen so much tourist 'tat'. Having said that, I did buy myself some miniature whiskies for my collection. Before finally emerging from the building, we entered a cafe. I needed a drink after the mind-blowing explosion of Scottish tourist gifts.

July
Sunday
29

Walking Day 71 *Heavy showers mixed with dry spells*

Drumnadrochit to Abriachan - 7 miles - Total Walked 810

I walked out of Drumnadrochit in the rain on the pavement of the A82; at least I had some good views of Loch Ness and Urquhart Castle. By a prominent tree, I spotted 'German-pork-pie-hat-boy' sheltering under an umbrella. We nodded and smiled at each other but I carried on, protected from the rain in my West Highland Way poncho. A couple of miles later I left the road and began to climb steeply through fields. After a good climb and before entering yet another pine forest, I paused to have a drink of coffee from my flask. From here I had an excellent view of the loch and Urquhart Castle. This spot must be where countless calendar and biscuit-tin-lid photographers climb to capture that popular view; a view not seen at its best by the thousands of motorists who pass by way below on the road.

Wait; what was that just passing in the water in front of the castle? By the time, I got my binoculars to my eyes the 'thing' I'd seen had gone. Was it a boat - or was it the monster?... I'll never know.

Just then the rain stopped and the sun appeared. 'German-pork-pie-hat-boy' also appeared, marching up the hillside. He passed me at speed, smiling but never looking back and not seeing the spectacular view that I was enjoying.

The Naylor brothers in their 1916 JOG-LE book, advise: *'All tourists, on walking expeditions, to look back occasionally, since much of the pleasure and beauty of the tour may otherwise be lost'.* I couldn't agree more. Just before the boy vanished into the forest I quickly searched my brain for the only German word I know. "Halt". I shouted. He stopped immediately and threw his hands up in mock surrender. He turned slowly to look at me. "You are missing this spectacular view", I said.

He returned his arms to his side and smiled. "Thank you", he said.

After admiring the view, he marched off into the tunnel-like opening of the dark pine forest.

A short time later I followed him.

The path went steeply uphill through a long dark patch of forest; the sunlight barely breaking through. I climbed up, all views now lost to the forest. It was another dreary section of 'dead' pine forest. In the distance, I saw some torch lights dancing in the dark. They were heading my way. As they got nearer I realised they were head torches worn on a band around the head. From a distance the torch-wearers had the appearance of miners. There was a long line of them walking in single file. When eventually we met, I saw that they were scouts; boys and girls aged about sixteen to eighteen. Aided by the light from the torches I could see that they were immaculately turned out in smart blue uniforms.

The lead scout was blonde-haired and blue-eyed and even before he opened his mouth I knew he was German. He reminded me of the boy, Rolf, who sang the song, *'I am seventeen going on eighteen'*, from the film *'The Sound of Music'*. They all were friendly and the lead boy explained in perfect English, that they were marching from Inverness to Glasgow via the GGW and the WHW. When he told me where they intended sleeping that night I exclaimed, "Wow, that's some distance".

He replied, "We will do it easily". As I stood to one side to let them pass I believed that yes, they would easily do it. Why hadn't I seen any British teenagers walking on a similar adventure?

One of my most treasured books is a picture book given to me as a boy; *'Kidnapped'* by Robert Louis Stevenson. In it there is a picture of the young David Balfour standing to one side to let a troop of redcoats go marching by. In the book, a murder occurred shortly after this scene and I wondered what my day's walk would next have in store for me; not a murder hopefully.

I wondered if my 'German-pork-pie-hat boy' had met his fellow countrymen; he must have done for the path was narrow. I soon found out as I approached a level sun-lit opening, where I again came upon him, in his by now familiar appearance crouched over his primus stove. "Halt", he said to me. "Just go through the trees here and see the view".

I did as he said and saw another spectacular view of Loch Ness with the pine forest dropping away steeply below me. I asked my German friend if he was enjoying the walk. "No, there are too many trees and not enough mountains to climb", was his reply. I couldn't have put it better myself, albeit the GGW is promoted as a low-level route through the Glen. I left him there sipping his tea, never to see him again.

I climbed on up and eventually reached the top of the forest, walking on a heath-like ridge, the view below obscured by the forest. Rounding a bend, I found myself suddenly confronting a beautiful antlered stag; a roe deer I believe. Why it hadn't detected me I don't know. Even now as I stood within inches of it, it didn't detect me, continuing to graze on the already short grass. "You are a beauty", I said to it as I stood in shocked admiration, then its head jerked. It saw me and with a hop and a leap it was gone, easily making it over the huge, nearby deer fence and without the aid of a Steve McQueen motorcycle. Magnificent. Then I was off again walking on a wide, level forest track where trees were better dispersed.

I continued walking out onto heath-like moorland with the odd white-walled cottage tucked away here and there. Striding towards me was a young woman carrying just a handbag. She looked totally out of place; dressed for a day's shopping. She was Dutch and was walking the GGW alone and utilising the services of a rucksack carrier who move her belongings from bed and breakfast to bed and breakfast thereby allowing her to walk rucksack-free. I hope she has a torch in that handbag I thought. She will need it.

Soon after this meeting I came to a large blue marker post, bigger than all the ones previously seen. It marked, at 1,245', the highest point of the Great Glen Way (although a lot of guides state it as 1,210'). What a disappointment there was no Devil's Staircase or Ben Nevis. Just another nondescript point on a forest track; there wasn't even a clearing. Yet half a mile away across open moorland, there is Carn na Leitire, a modest fell at 1,424'. Why the GGW route planners hadn't made this the highest point was beyond me.

I left the highest point and headed slightly downhill through yet more forest. This time I was in the Abriachan forest. The forestry Commission have laid paths and routes through this forest with green, yellow, red and purple marker posts. Kay and Ripley were waiting for me in the car park which was busy with families.

Kay, in a letter home wrote: *'The car park overlooked a splendid children's adventure playground and whilst I waited for Christopher to arrive - watching families coming and going. I began to feel a bit sad as I realised that that stage in my life was over and I am now getting to a Grandma's age. Charlotte our youngest had already informed me a couple of days previously, "Mum, I am officially an adult now".*

When our children are young, we are busy with life, and them, and we don't really notice that we are getting older - we don't feel older; not in our minds. Then suddenly, parents are our children's' age and we are in the next stage of our life and our children, as children, are just fond memories. This is unavoidable but also very sad - well, it was today'.

The drive back to camp took us back down to the busy A82 alongside Loch Ness which allowed me a glimpse of the two memorials on the side of the loch. The first records the ditching in the loch of a World War 2 Wellington bomber in 1940 after engine failure. The crew swam safely away. The debris of the bomber was located and raised in 1985. The second commemorates John Cobb, who in 1952, as the land speed record holder, lost his life on the loch as he attempted the water speed record, the debris of his jet-powered 'Crusader' not being recovered until 2002.

July
Monday
30

Walking Day 72 *Hot and sunny*

Abriachan to Inverness - 12 miles - Total Walked 822

We all set off together from the Abriachan car park, walking on a good path through bushy moorland. We were joined by an array of butterflies. Kay was again examining the wild flowers that blossomed up here; tiny, purple eyebrights and blue milkwort's were two of the 'new-to-her' species.

A cottage advertised bed and breakfast and morning coffee. We deliberated for a while, thinking that here was an excellent piece of entrepreneurism when suddenly, from out of nowhere, came a large party of chatty and loud foreigners, possibly Dutch, who walked past us and entered the cafe grounds. Knowing that in some places an influx of just two customers can cause massive problems, we knew that immediately following a party of eight or nine people into a cafe is not the sensible thing to do if you want to get on with the rest of your day. Without partaking I said goodbye to Kay and Ripley and walked away from the cottage along a quiet 'B' road which passed isolated farms and green fields, the forest and hills being well back from the road.

Loch Ness was totally out of view as the Great Glen Way left it behind and came into Inverness around the back of the fells of Doire Mhor and the Craig Leach forest. I made good progress along the road, passing fields of cows and horses, a welcome change of scenery from the forests of the last few days. The road climbed up onto heather moorland.

The ling heather was in flower with huge swathes of purple. On closer inspection, dotted amongst the heather, I noticed many bilberry bushes laden with delicious fruit. To make the scene even more idyllic, the GGW route planners had recently built a path running parallel to the road.

Near the farms at Blackfold I came to an information board that declared these heather moors to be an important black grouse breeding area with a few known 'lecks' being nearby. I knew there was no chance of me seeing the rare black grouse breeding ritual, it being carried out earlier in the year and earlier in the day, very early, but possibly, I might just see a black grouse. I took out my binoculars and spent a good half hour scouring the moors for just a sighting. I didn't see any but my time viewing was rewarded by several beautiful stonechats who bobbed up on top of the heather, making their distinctive 'pebble-clapping' sounds.

I walked on in the sunshine until the route left the side of the road and took a wide old drovers' track through some trees and then along the outside of the large forest of Craig Leach. I walked through a picnic area where two or three families were making use of the tables. They were all happily chatting whilst the children of the party scrambled about on mountain bikes.

A moss-covered stone wall separated me from the dark pine forest on my right. Over to my left was a bushy moorland with young trees sprouting up here and there. The track was easy walking and slightly downward-sloping. Eventually I came to a small fenced-off tarn. A sign on the fence declared, 'Private. No fishing'. I saw two teenage boys fishing, their bikes being left by a large hole in the fence. I walked on until I came to a grassy ridge covered by mature trees which were well-dispersed. From this ridge, I had my first view of Inverness, the capital of the Highlands. Directly below and in front of me, I saw a hive of building activity at a large imposing red-bricked building with nine towers of immense charm, which I later discovered to be the old hospital, now being renovated. Beyond that lay immaculate-looking housing estates of white-coloured buildings. Away to my right was the northern tip of Loch Ness and flowing from it, the River Ness that led into town. I descended the hillside dodging the building site and walked along the edge of a busy golf course and parkland before emerging onto the tow-path of the Caledonian Canal.

Instead of following it north a few hundred yards through town to its northern end at the Moray Firth, I followed the route south a hundred yards to the fabulously-named road swing-bridge at Tomnahurich on that busy, A82 road. Both the canal and the road were teeming with traffic and I waited for the swing-bridge to return to its road position before crossing it, along with many pedestrians and cars. Leaving the cars behind me, I stepped into Bught Park which was also very busy with families, passing a bustling Floral Hall and garden centre with a car park that housed temporarily, a mobile cinema, the first I'd seen. The cinema was on the back of a lorry and opened out providing a reasonable amount of seating. I can't recall the name of the film being shown but I remember thinking what a pity, I would have liked to have gone to the mobile cinema but not to watch that film.

I walked on by the well-kept rugby pitches alive with fit, young men at practice and then alongside the River Ness which had a few fly fishermen dressed in waders, standing in the shallow middle, fishing. A sports centre running track was busy with athletes in training. All around, everywhere was clean, which gave me the impression of a well-ordered and lovely place. I walked along the river, overhung by trees and entered Whin Park, crossing the river by beautiful white Victorian suspension foot bridges across two islands that formed much of the park. Lovely well-tended flower-beds adorned the area at every corner. I hadn't seen any litter or graffiti, nor the loud obnoxious young thugs that you might come across anywhere else in a city centre park. I felt like I was walking in wonderland.

I was now on the south bank of the river, passing beautiful stone-built houses with well-cared-for gardens. Some but not all were currently bed and breakfast establishments. I stood in awe at the sheer beauty of the war memorial. It was like a lot of war memorials I'd seen along the way except that here the memorial was set in flower gardens with a working fountain; all immaculate and wonderfully kept.

From here I climbed the busy tourist-filled streets to the red sandstone castle. A Victorian building now utilised as Council offices and courts, surrounded by a car park with a large statue of Flora Macdonald, the Scottish heroine who assisted Bonnie Prince Charles' escape to Skye after the Battle of Culloden. It was here in an earlier castle, in 1039 that, according to Shakespeare, King Duncan was murdered by Macbeth.

By the car parks edge overlooking the river, the park, the cathedral and the town, I came to the sign that signified the end of the Great Glen Way. The sign was like the slab of slate I'd seen in Fort William. A notice read, *'Sign not yet fully completed'*. I asked a grinning Japanese tourist who spoke perfect English, to take my photograph. I'd completed the GGW but had not yet completed my LEJOG walk. Having been walking north-east for the entire GGW I was disappointed to realise that here in Inverness, I was still actually further west than Lancaster. (Look at a map and see.)

I left the castle by the steps which lead down into the town centre where I entered the modern, concrete built Tourist Information Office. Here I joined the queue of yet more Japanese tourists and had my LEJOG verification certificate stamped.

Bill Bryson in his 1995 book 'Notes from a Small Island', writes about this concrete monstrosity of a building; 'I could never live in Inverness because of the sensationally ugly, modern, office buildings that stand by the central bridge and blot the town centre beyond any hope of redemption. Everything about them; scale, materials, design, was madly inappropriate to the surrounding scene. It was awful beyond words'. What's worse is that the even uglier back door service area, 'fronts' onto the otherwise delightful River Ness. The architect who designed this building had obviously never been to Inverness.

I met up with Kay and Ripley and we had a lovely stroll along the otherwise enchanting river bank, our attention being fought over by beautiful buildings on one side and a 'rare to us' bird, a black-throated diver, sleek and streamlined, fishing in front of us in the river. The sun went down and leaving Ripley in the by now cool shade of the car, we went again to the excellent Italian restaurant for a celebratory meal.

July Tuesday 31 — Walking break to Thursday 16th August

I took a few days off. We drove home to Yorkshire to attend our daughter Samantha's wedding; eleven hours driving. It felt strange to be at home but I attended to lots of minor matters that needed attending to whilst Kay busied herself with last minute wedding plans.

Kay was to write: 'The house and garden were a bit of a shock after four months away – all the rain that Yorkshire had been having, and our garden had put on more growth than I had seen over several years – and, I know why dust sheets were popular when families have several residences.' The wedding took place, and in my opinion, went off without a problem, or as Kay wrote: 'It was everything we could have asked for'.

The day after the wedding, we drove back to Scotland, breaking the journey at Abington, where the lady who runs the campsite was given lots of flowers that we had rescued from the tables at the wedding feast.

August Tuesday 14 — We travelled up the A9 via Perth, Stirling, Pitlochry and Aviemore to Inverness and entered the town along the busy A9, passing lots of industrial estates, factories and DIY warehouse shops. What a different approach to that which I had experienced just a few days before when I strolled into town along the GGW through beautiful parkland overlooking the River Ness. We continued over Kessock Bridge and found a campsite at the next town, Dingwall, where we made our base for the next few days.

Fine and dry

Even though I was really itching to be off, another sightseeing day was called for. We drove to the lovely market town of Beauly. Mary Queen of Scots is credited with giving Beauly its name. She stayed here in 1564 and declared; *'C'est un beau lieu'* (It's a beautiful place.)

An eight-hundred-year-old elm tree, said to be the oldest in Europe, stands in the ruined 13th-century priory grounds. The Naylor brothers wrote in their 1916 JOG-LE; *'At Beauly, we saw the biggest key in our entire long journey'*. The key weighed 2lbs 4oz and was used to gain entry to the priory grounds.

W. B. Dawson also visited Beauly and he wrote in his 1934 LEJOG book; *'At Beauly Priory, I got a view through a kind of grill, of a dark, eerie chamber with mouldering tomb, and in striking contrast, a brilliant, all-white, recumbent effigy. Effect quite unearthly and suggestive of Edgar Allan Poe'*.

All of this was lost to me. I saw Beauly as a pleasant, one-shopping-street town with a quaint market square, some quality shops and ample on-street free parking, a place worthy of a revisit. We left the town and drove on to the Strathglass Valley. I'd heard a lot about the valley as friends of ours own a pine cabin hereabouts. We drove along the golf-course-covered valley, admiring the heather-topped hills.

We saw a rare footpath sign and parked up. Joined by beautiful ringlet butterflies, we climbed steeply up the path that led eventually to a spot called Strath View Point. The climb up had been worth it. Here was indeed a lovely rural valley; mild and mellow yet with a wild, untamed look.

My main reason for not walking today was to allow time to visit Culloden, the battle site just south of Inverness. As we drove into the car park a sign declared, *'Dogs are allowed on the battlefield but not in the Visitor Centre'*. So, we all walked the battlefield; first walking between the Government line and then the Jacobite; Highlander line. It was easy to see that the Government troops had the better advantage of height on this windswept moorland, for what turned out to be, in April 1746, the last battle fought on British soil.

We walked across the field of the clans to the drum-like 20-foot 'boulder' cairn memorial to the losers of the battle. Erected in 1881, the inscription commemorates, *'The graves of the gallant Highlanders who fought for Scotland and Prince Charles'*. The fact that many Highlanders fought against fellow Scotsmen is ignored by the memorial.

Back over the line and in the so-called English field, lie the three hundred or so Government troops who died that day, many from the St. Clair Royal Scots Regiment, who lined up on the front rank alongside men from Price's Regiment which later became known as the Prince of Wales Own West Yorkshire Regiment. We found the stone that marked the spot where many Yorkshire men lined up to wait for the famous 'Highland Charge'. They then, with the advantage of height and much better cannon and gun fire, won the day.

A new visitor centre was being rebuilt next door to the 1970's building and half the battlefield looked like a huge construction site. Hundreds of tourist coaches filled the car parks. We made our way inside and had a bowl of soup in the café, watching an excellent short film in the cinema and then finishing off by walking around the exhibition.

Kay was to write: *'I found it hard to believe that the Scottish Highlanders, a race of people reputed to be centred on their own national identity, could be so foolish as to follow an Italian-born prince; who hadn't even lived in Scotland; into a battle so ill-managed on their own soil, that it could almost be described as mass suicide'.*

We drove back into Inverness and parked up by the cathedral. It is built of local deep pink limestone with a roof of green Westmorland slate. The foundation stone was laid in 1866 by Dr. Charles Longley, Archbishop of Canterbury; the first official act in Scotland by an English Archbishop since the establishment of the Presbyterian Church in 1689.

A walk with Ripley in the beautiful park by the river ended a busy day which we finished by having yet another excellent meal at the Italian restaurant; three visits to this one restaurant, all excellent and truly enjoyable.

August / Thursday 16

Walking Day 73 *Dry and clear with heavy showers later*

Inverness to Dingwall - 16 miles - Total Walked 838

I crossed over the bridge to enter Inverness's modern Eastgate shopping area and Victorian market arcade. They blended well together. I weaved my way through the crowded streets of shoppers and then walked down a street that serviced the growing Polish community with cafes, bars and shops.

At a roundabout, I took the road signposted to the B.P. Oil terminals and docks, thinking I could perhaps walk along the harbour wall towards Kessock Bridge. I was of course wrong and my progress was barred by huge metal fencing that secured the B.P. oil terminal from any unwanted visitors. Frustratingly I could see the sea, the Beauly Firth, at the other side of the terminal buildings. The road I was on was called Cromwell Road. By accident I had walked to the citadel or as the locals call it, 'The Sconce'. Obscured by an oil terminal is the site of Cromwell's English fort built from 1653 to 1658.

There is not much of it to see today and it's hard to make out whether the earth embankments around the oil terminal are modern flood defences or ancient ramparts. However, an ancient clock tower still stands, said to have been built in 1693. I found it in good repair surmounted with a slated belfry and a weather vane. A plaque on its wall gives information of Cromwell's fort. Today the tower looks isolated and lonely, surrounded by modern buildings and not a tourist in sight.

I eventually found the right road away from town. Before I left Inverness, I had a text from a friend asking me to take good care of the *'four and twenty'*. Of all the texts and messages, I'd received on my walk, this one puzzled me the most. What on earth did it mean? If I'd been sharp enough or even a rugby fan I could have answered, "They're not here anymore". As most of you will know the text relates to the rugby song, *'four and twenty virgins came down from Inverness and when they went back home again they were four and twenty less'*. I walked on, passing the harbour wall where tourist coaches disgorged their eager passengers into 'Dolphin' sightseeing boats that bobbed up and down on the choppy sea.

At a roundabout I joined the busy A9, on a good pavement and headed towards Kessock Bridge. I passed the Inverness Caledonian Thistle Football Club stadium which, like most football stadiums on non-match days, lay quiet like a sleeping dog waiting to spring into action. I came upon the Kessock Bridge, opened by the Queen Mother in 1982. It shaved twenty road miles off the route north doing away with the long drive round Beauly Firth.

This very striking bridge, of German design, is a copy of a bridge that crosses the Rhine near Dusseldorf. The weight of the road deck is carried by steel cables coming down, harp-like, from four towers. A sign warned of strong side winds. I was separated from the road by fencing.

To my left I could see Beauly Firth, Inverness and the Caledonian Canal sea loch. To my right across the traffic, lay the Moray Firth and the North Sea beyond. The bridge wobbled in the wind and at times I struggled to keep walking in a dignified manner. Traffic thundered by. I was the lone pedestrian today. The Dolphin cruise boats sailed under the bridge and I waved at the tourists. I left the bridge and entered the 'Black Isle'. I had strolled into the old county of Ross and Cromarty, now a district council within the larger Highland council area.

A large visitor centre complete with toilets, *'Winners of loo of the year'*, attracted my immediate attention. As I walked across the car park to the centre, a young woman advanced towards me waving a pair of binoculars. "Come quickly", she shouted at me. Thinking perhaps there might be some emergency I followed her into a hut-like building. Once inside she thrust the expensive-looking binoculars into my hands. We were alone in the well-lit hut, the light coming from large windows looking out onto the Beauly Firth and Kessock Bridge.

"They're here", she said pointing out of the window. I followed her finger pointing out to sea. Peering through the binoculars I had a fabulous view of a pod of 'porpoising' dolphins; about ten in number. They were bottle-nosed dolphins and were the most northerly group of dolphins in the world. It was a spectacular sight. The young woman was an official 'dolphin watcher' and just wanted to share this moment with someone I was the lucky person in the right place at the right time. I wondered if the tourists in the Dolphin cruise boats were getting as good a view as I was. I thanked the woman profusely, only leaving when I was assured I'd seen them all "at their very best".

I walked down some steps that led steeply away from the visitor centre bringing me to the shoreline at North Kessock; once a busy ferry port; now completely bypassed and very much a quiet backwater. The inshore lifeboat station stands under the Kessock Bridge. It's a striking modern building of octagonal shape. A modern building that works. I liked it. It fits in with the surroundings. I walked out of town with its hotel, tearooms and shop, all with fabulous sea views. Making my way along a quiet coast road with rural countryside over to my right and spectacular views of the Beauly Firth over to my left, the whole being surrounded by the hills of Strath Glass in the distance.

At the hamlet of Redcastle and Milton, a bench was strategically placed overlooking the Firth. I made effective use of it and had a drink of tea from my flask. Leaving the Beauly Firth behind me I headed north and inland up good footpaths through fields. I crossed over a disused railway line which headed in the wrong direction. My up-until-then good footpath was now overgrown with hawthorn bushes. There was no way through even though the footpath, an old cart track, could clearly be seen under all the bushes. I climbed into an adjacent field and followed the path line. A deer bolted right in front of me and I watched it dart away across the field. As I turned to carry on a female pheasant nearly got squashed under my boot. She resolutely held her ground; sat on her nest? Until after I'd moved on. This had happened to me before in Shropshire.

The next field I climbed into was full of cows with calves. They were at the far end of the field well away from my path. I plodded on, slightly uphill, keeping an eye on the cows. As I neared the fence which led into the next field I realised it was made of barbed wire that would be difficult to climb. I turned to have one last look at the cows and saw a bull in the middle of them. Worse, they were now all charging towards me at a fast pace. They got to me before I got to the fence. It was as though they hadn't seen a man before. They all pushed each other to get closer to me. They were so packed together I thought some of the calves might get squashed, or worse I might. The bull was truly massive and thankfully a few cows separated me from him. I could feel his breath on my face as he snorted with excitement and trumpeted over the back of his cows. I gently pushed my way to the barbed wire fence and using my rucksack as protection from the barbs I rolled back onto the fence, pushing up with my feet, 'commando-rolling' over the fence and into the safety of a new field.

I continued gently uphill through empty fields. Eventually I came to a hedge of hawthorn which I crashed through and emerged onto a quiet tarmac lane. I followed the lane until at the crest of the hill I came to the Mulbuie Memorial at Rootfield.

Looking like a small lighthouse, it was erected by the local villagers in memory of a local man-made-good; Major General Sir Hector Archibald Macdonald. Being a poor crofter, this Gordon Highlander entered the army as a foot soldier and rose through the ranks distinguishing himself in many battles. The famous bagpipe tune, Hector the Hero, is named after him. His most-noted heroic deed was to save the day and win the 1898 Battle of Omdurman, in Sudan. The monument looked in need of a lick of paint and some tender loving care.

I moved off, this time heading gently downhill, still on my tarmac lane, passing large houses and eventually emerging onto the main road at Bishop Kinkell. This road had been the A9 around Beauly Firth before Kessock Bridge was built. I had a good verge to walk on. I followed it into the Town of Conon Bridge, passing large building sites on its edge. (It seems everyone wants to live up here now the town has been bypassed).

The River Conon had been crossed by a Thomas Telford bridge, still here but now replaced by a practical modern concrete slab of a bridge. An off-licence in the town was busy with friendly people. I walked on and entered the neighbouring town of Maryburgh which merged seamlessly with Conon Bridge. Small cottages now dominated the sides of the road and at one of them, 'Seaforth Cottage', I noticed a blue plaque. A man called Donald Cameron had lived here. He had been a famous Victorian bagpiper. I must admit I'd never heard of him, but as I read the plaque, bagpipe music filled the air; someone in a nearby cottage was practising the bagpipes and doing a pretty good job of it.

I left Maryburgh to the sound of music and joined the main A9 road at a roundabout. The Black Isle, Kessock Bridge and Inverness lay south. To the north and very near, lay Dingwall. I walked along this main road on a pavement, passing the Dingwall Cattle Auction Mart, standing empty, waiting for market day. I entered the county town of Ross-shire and local administration town since Viking times. The name Dingwall derives from the Norse word for parliament, thingvalls. Macbeth was born here in 1005.

I passed the busy railway station, which was packed with commuters and shoppers returning from Inverness and tourists coming back from John O'Groats (Wick). I studied the impressive Seaforth Highlander war memorial in Station Square complete with a statue of a kilted soldier. I crossed the railway line and took the road to the Ross County Football Club stadium at the side of which lay our campsite. On the far side of the campsite lay the most northerly canal in Britain. We later walked along the very short canal that linked the town to the sea. Designed by Thomas Telford, sadly it is now disused.

August
Friday
17

Walking Day 74 *Fine and dry*

Dingwall to Alness - 9 miles - Total Walked 847

I began by walking around Dingwall's town centre, down the high street with its selection of shops including the champion Haggis making butchers, Cockburn's. There is a huge Tesco, built close enough to the town centre to complement rather than detract from it and a museum on the high street with an impressive clock tower, built in 1905. One of the oldest objects of interest at Dingwall is a moss-covered Pictish stone which I found in the church yard. It is said to be Bronze Age and has cup and ring markings on it very like those found in profusion on Ilkley, Rombald's and Baildon moors back home in Yorkshire. Looking at and touching the stone immediately transported me back to those moors in Yorkshire and I had to snap myself out from a wave of homesickness and move on.

It is said by some that Dingwall marks a distinct divide between Scots and Norse. The people living here speak with an almost English accent rather than the by now familiar

Scottish brogue. I was to note this all the way up to John O'Groats. I left Dingwall by climbing a steep hill through a pleasant residential area to arrive at a T-junction. I turned right and passed bungalows which had fantastic views over the town and Cromarty Firth with its bridge.

I walked out of town along a quiet lane following the National Cycleway. Through fields and trees, I could look down and see the busy A9 road that hugs the shoreline of the Firth as it heads north. I carried on, now passing large houses set in grounds. The houses got bigger and their grounds larger until there were just one or two dotted along the hillside looking magnificent.

My view across Cromarty Firth was now directed towards some large oil rigs which had been towed into the deep-water bay for a refit. These were the first oil rigs I had seen on my journey. Looking out to sea, the romantic in me imagined them to be Tall Sailing Ships. They did provide an interesting and different view and have been doing so since the early 1970's when the North Sea Oil and Gas fields were developed.

They have been manufacturing and repairing Oil Rigs from around the World here since that time. Shipbuilding and repair yards already existed during World War 2 a large U.S. Army and Navy camp was based here, carrying out vital repair works. On the outskirts of Evanton I saw, on the hillside above the town, an unusual monument. For some time, I failed to work out what it was. It looked like a small part of Stonehenge with bits falling off. I still couldn't work it out as I walked on and saw it at different angles.

At the next village of Balcanie, I found a pub-cum-cafe which was open and serving tea. I was the only customer and the waitress explained all. The unusual and curious monument on the top of the hill is known as the Fyrish monument. Built in 1785 it is a replica of the gateway to Negapatam, an Indian town sacked by General Sir Hector Munro of Novar as a celebration of his famous victory there against the Dutch in 1783.

The folly-cum-memorial also provided much-needed work for the displaced people during the Highland Clearances. There are a few local walks up through the trees to the monument; an easy climb but one I didn't take and now wish I had. The waitress in the cafe was more interested in telling me all about the Polish invasion with new immigrants everywhere taking local jobs for fewer wages. The local bus driver was now Polish and relied on the locals to direct him around his route, so I was told. I also learnt of violent and drunken knife fights between the Polish themselves, which happened frequently and alarmingly on most Friday nights when lots come into town to get drunk. It all seemed grim and reminded me yet again of work. I drank up and left.

I walked towards Alness on a new cycle-path that had been laid at the side of the road, cutting through trees and bushes. It made easy and excellent walking. I passed an old wartime airfield and the 1839 Dalmore Whisky distillery, said to be the World's most expensive single malt. Alness welcomed me with a sign that declared it to be a winner of both the 'Britain in bloom' and 'Scotland in bloom' competitions. The busy A9 now bypassed the town and I could stroll down the main street which was peaceful and free from traffic. It had a surprisingly substantial number of independent shops.

Above the large High School, I found a Morrison's Supermarket where I met up with Kay and Ripley. A sign above the door declared it was owned and managed by Wm. Morrison plc, Gain Lane, Bradford. I wondered how many people from Alness had ever been to Bradford, let alone to the Morrison's headquarters. We went in to do a bit of shopping. At the checkout, I casually asked the till operator, "Is this the most northerly Morrison's in Britain?"

"Oh, I've no idea", came the reply. "I'll call the supervisor".

My "No, it's okay", came too late as the supervisor had already been called.

"This gentleman wants to know if this is the most northerly Morrison's in Britain", she asked the supervisor.

"Oh, I've no idea", she replied. "I'll ask the manager".

"No, it's really okay", I said.

Too late; the supervisor had already asked for the manager to attend.

"This gentleman wants to know if this is the most northerly Morrison's in Britain?" the supervisor asked the manager.

"Oh, I've no idea", came the manager's reply.

All three women, for they were all women, looked at me with completely puzzled expressions. I tried to help. "Well, above here there are only two big towns that I can see on the map; Wick and Thurso. Do they have a Morrison's?"

All three replied in unison, "We don't know, we've never been so far north".

I thanked them for their help and told them I was heading north and I would seek the answer. The truth is that it was Britain's most northerly Morrison's.

Another thing happened to me whilst I was walking around the store, I developed a small blister on my little toe. To take my mind off it and to clear my head of the Morrison's debate, we headed back into town for a curry at one of the three Indian restaurants.

 August **Saturday** **18**   **Walking Day 75** *Heavy rain*

Alness to Tain - 12 miles - Total Walked 859

I walked out of Morrison's car park with the rain bouncing off the tarmac, passing many large detached bungalows set in immaculate gardens. On the outskirts of town, I walked through a huge building site. The builders were all friendly but most of them were sheltering from the rain in either half-built doorways or little sheds, nearly all of them were smoking. I dodged the muddy parts of the building site and soon found my way onto a very quiet B-road which at first zig-zagged through fields, then headed straight as an arrow to Tain through pine forests dotted with large houses surrounded by fields of horses. The pine trees afforded me little shelter from the incessant rain. I pulled on everything I had to keep the rain off: leggings, cape, rucksack cover and sloshed my way along the road.

At a small hamlet called Scotburn, the trees cleared just enough to allow me to stretch out on a grassy knoll and read a sign that declared *'footpath'*, heading in the wrong direction and leading to Strath Rory, a quiet secluded mountain glen and home to Scottish crossbills and black grouse. It sounded like a nice place, worthy of further exploration but not today.

My route lay north and that's the way I went, hoping that perhaps just one of these big houses had someone inside who on seeing me, felt enough compassion to send out 'their man' with a flask of tea for me. It didn't happen and I just walked on along the road that now resembled a stream. With just a mile or so to go before entering Tain, I came to a roadblock. The signs declared that the bridge had collapsed and a diversion was in place. The diversion would take me four miles, deep into the pine forest of Morangie. Prior to me setting off along the diversion, I did explore the possibility of trying to walk across the stream by the broken-down bridge. The water was flowing at a torrential speed so I decided the long but safe walk was the best option.

Eventually the diversion led me safely back onto the main road into Tain. I walked by big houses, some castle-like, resembling large hotels. I found the main street dominated by its imposing toll house, built in 1630. The street was deserted. A hotel seemed to be packed with people dodging the rain. I walked on, passing a chemist shop which declared itself by a large model of a pestle and mortar above its door.

Tain is the oldest royal burgh in Scotland. Saint Duthus was born here in 1000AD. He is venerated as being The Chief Confessor of Ireland and Scotland. In 1360 they built a collegiate church here in his name and Tain became a pilgrim town. King James IV of Scotland made a pilgrimage here every year for twenty years from 1493. The King's route is a modern long distance walk from Kessock near Inverness to Tain, crossing the Black Isle. Had I known about it I could have explored the possibility of following it.

I saw both the collegiate church and then down by the beach the ruined chapel of St Duthus, said to be near the spot where the saint was born. I met Kay and Ripley in the beautiful rose gardens by the war memorial and called it a day. A thoroughly wet and soggy day. Back at the camp-site at Dingwall the warden was having problems with every pitch being taken and most being waterlogged. He had asked some vans to move onto the site road to ease the situation. We were just alright, but only just; a lake of water took up most of our pitch.

August **Walking Day 76** *Dry and clear*

Sunday 19 | **Tain to Dornoch - 7 miles - Total Walked 866**

I slept in this morning after my wet soggy day yesterday. Today was completely different being dry and clear. Kay and I headed for Tain and found the beautiful though deserted rose garden by the war memorial where we sat and ate our packed lunch. At the side of the rose garden we found a small public convenience. Anywhere else in Britain it would not have been a surprise to find these toilets vandalised and a disgusting mess, but not here; they were immaculate and clean. Fresh flowers in vases welcomed you and so did an attendant. Here on a Sunday afternoon in a very quiet village, the toilets had an attendant. How can they do this when other authorities across the country fail? Well done Tain.

I set off walking along the road; the old A9. I walked past the large and busy Co-op supermarket. So, this is where they all are. Out of town I passed the Glen Morangie field, home to the Tain Highland Gathering (games), which as usual I'd just missed as it took place a few days prior to my arrival. As well as the usual solo piping and highland dancing competitions they have caber tossing, tug o' war and hammer throwing, all set against a magnificent backdrop of the North Sea which today was a brilliant blue colour. They also have a hill race which I found strange, as the field was perfectly flat, so I presume that race must take place away from the main events on one of the now distant hills.

As you may have guessed the next building along the road was the Glen Morangie whisky distillery. I walked down the drive to the beautiful stone structure, looking more like a baronial castle than a whisky distillery.

I'd just missed the guided tour. Another was to take place in an hour which was too long for me to wait. I strolled across to the main building and peered in to see the tallest copper stills in Scotland, being 16' 10¼" tall (5.14 metres). I went back to the visitor centre and shop where I learnt that they have been making whisky here since 1843 using hard water that has been filtered through the nearby limestone. The distillation process is undertaken by a staff of 16 known as The Sixteen Men of Tain, who work year-round. The exact process being a secret held between them. They produce one of the most popular single malts in Scotland. I bought a miniature for my collection.

I then walked back up the drive and out onto the main road, joining the A9 on a pavement that led me down to the beautiful estuary at Dornoch Firth where the Rivers Oykel and Shin meet and head out to sea at the Kyle of Sutherland. The estuary has a beautiful backdrop of mountains and separates the Highland districts of Easter Ross and Sutherland. An old legend has it that fairies could be seen rowing across the firth on cockle shells.

The view I had was stunning if not magical. Some say that the modern bridge, built in 1991 and opened by Queen Elizabeth the Queen Mother spoils this magnificent view. I might agree with them.

The bridge reduces the distance between Tain and Dornoch to a mere seven miles. Prior to 1991, the walk around Dornoch Firth was considerably longer and I would have had to walk to an older bridge at the estuary head at Bonar Bridge. Today, lots of communities once busy with traffic have been bypassed. These new roads and bridges make Scotland 'quicker' but I think they take away some of her mystery and charm. Having said that I took the shortest route and crossed the single carriageway bridge on a pavement. The long low bridge was surprisingly quiet and I could hear the curlews out on the mud flats below.

At the other side of the bridge I immediately entered Sutherland and took a quiet road out onto the Cuthill Links, an area of sand dunes and gorse bushes that led me past detached houses with manicured gardens. Out on the dunes I saw and heard a man hunting with his dog and gun. I never saw what he was shooting at, thankfully not at me; I was very exposed.

I stopped to say hello to a couple of scarecrows, immaculately well-made and standing in a large vegetable plot. On the road, I found an insect that even today I still haven't properly been able to identify. It looked like a small lobster minus its tail and claws, being about six to seven inches in length. It was a deep red to brown colour and its back was protected by armoured plates. It was alive and moving slowly along the road surface. I thought it might be some sort of large cockroach but I know them to be fast-moving. In the end, I decided it was a sea creature dropped here by a seagull who having captured it out at sea, had squabbled with another gull and dropped its prey here onto the road. (We now think it may have been a Dragonfly Larvae). I took a photograph of it then moved on and into the quaint-looking town of Dornoch.

The streets leading to the village centre are built of stone with predominantly low-lying cottages. One of these had been converted into an Italian cafe with seats and tables outside. I plonked myself down and being the only customer outside, or inside for that matter, asked the waitress for a large cup of tea.

"We don't serve tea", came her reply.

"Well a large cup of coffee then", I said.

"We've stopped serving coffee", came her reply.

I looked at my watch; it was barely 4pm. "What do you do?" I asked.

"We're still serving ice-creams", she said.

I didn't want an ice-cream, so got up and left. Welcome to Dornoch I thought.

 Rest day *Dry and clear*

August Monday 20 Today we moved camp from Dingwall calling first at the large Tesco supermarket to stock up and then moving on up north. We called in at Alness to tax our Nissan at the post office and to fill up with fuel at Morrison's. We had the slight fear of the unknown, not knowing how we would manage with supplies and provisions in the picture of the 'empty quarter' that the barren north had become in our minds. We found a superb caravan site on the sandy beach at Brora which was to be our home for the next few days.

 Walking Day 77 *Hot and sunny*

August Tuesday 21 | **Dornoch to Golspie - 11 miles - Total Walked 877** >

Dornoch, with its pleasant stone-built cottages surrounded by flower gardens and hanging baskets certainly looked picture postcard beautiful on a hot sunny day like today. It wasn't always so; the central square, now a car park, had once been a slum-like shanty town, populated by hundreds of displaced Highlanders who had lost their homes in the great glen clearances of the late 18th and early 19th centuries.

They lost their homes, 'Feal houses', again when the powers that be, in an early version of town planning, decided to clear them all away and create a large open square, dominated by the 13th century Cathedral and Bishop's Palace / Castle; the latter is now a hotel.

The Royal Burgh of Dornoch to give it its Sunday name, was busy with people wandering about the square which has an unusual number of varied shops, many of quality designer-clothes-type that wouldn't look out of place in a city centre. The old jail house, Dornoch Jail, has been converted into shops with some retailers occupying the old cells still complete with cell doors. I made my way over to the Cathedral noticing a tailor's standard measure stone placed in the cathedral yard; an early form of trading standards. It apparently dates from the medieval period when it was common for markets to be found in Church yards. This stone goes by the name of The Plainden Ell and is exactly 37 inches long. Later these stone measures were replaced by much more versatile measuring rods which even today, many traditional Kilt makers still use, with their rods measuring exactly 37 inches.

The gargoyles that decorated the outside of the Cathedral were particularly ugly-looking, being noticeable and comical at the same time. Gargoyles are thought to have been used practically as water spouts but also as markers to frighten evil spirits away. These here have friendly smiley faces, not very frightening at all and one even looks slightly drunk. The Cathedral is built like the town, of a beautiful warm-coloured stone and is not much bigger than the parish church in most towns.

Inside the warm feeling continued as coloured light poured in through a large stained glass window which dominates the south side. Three stained glass windows in the north wall of the choir commemorate the American steel magnate and philanthropist, Andrew Carnegie, who visited here many times. I liked the Cathedral and could see why Madonna and Guy Ritchie chose to be married here in December 2000, the day after their son had been christened here.

I said goodbye to Kay and Ripley and began to walk northwards out of town.

Kay, on her way back to camp, witnessed a road accident near the entrance to Dunrobin Castle. She was to write: 'A car, one car in front of me, started to make a right turn across the oncoming carriageway which caused the driver of the oncoming vehicle to panic and swerve at speed into part of the Dunrobin Castle entrance wall, demolishing it. Luckily no one was injured but the car was pretty mangled. I called the police and offered to be a witness but it seems that the driver of the damaged car is now denying being the driver, claiming to have been the passenger because he was a disqualified driver - oh dear'.

There was some excitement on our campsite later that day when two Police Officers called to take Kay's statement. Months and years later we were still receiving letters from insurance companies and Solicitors, the last one being a request to attend court in Edinburgh. Kay ticked the box to say she could attend but we never heard any more about it.

On the outskirts of Dornoch, I came to a cottage with an unusual stone in its garden. An information board informed me that in 1722 (some say 1729), after a short trial, the last Witch in Scotland was burned alive. Janet Hornes was accused of being a Witch after her daughter had been born with a deformed foot. The villagers allowed the baby to live, yet the villagers still accused Janet of turning her daughter into a pony. At her trial, she stumbled over her words whilst reciting the Lord's Prayer; certain proof that here was a Witch indeed. She was tied up and placed in a barrel of tar near to the stone and set on fire.

I left town by the road across the sand dunes that led to the Royal Dornoch Golf Course, reputed to be one of the best 'Ings' golf courses in the world. At the club house, I noticed a sign stating that walkers had right of way across the course to the beach. I marched on. The golfers, all of whom were friendly, did indeed give way to me as I walked close by them, whilst families played on the beautiful, sandy beach which was over to my right.

As I left the golf course behind, walking a sandy lane through the dunes, my path turned into a disused railway line surrounded by gorse bushes. A notice declared the area to be the home of yellow hammers. On a hot day like today I didn't see any. I skirted around a huge caravan site that lay on the outskirts of the small fishing village of Embo and walked through its back streets, picking up a quiet lane that led me pleasantly and easily to the estuary of Loch Fleet, a sea loch which narrows before emerging into the sea.

The tide was out and the estuary was a huge mud bank. A colony of about 50 or 60 common grey seals, were basking in the middle of the estuary. Loch Fleet is a designated National Nature Reserve. Backed by hills in the foreground and mountains in the background it is another stunningly beautiful scene. By the ruined 13th century Skelbo Castle, I sat down on a bench looking out across the Loch. The Castle is now a dangerous ruin. No one appears to be looking after it and pieces of masonry look loose and about to fall. It was built on a natural mound overlooking the Loch to protect the ferry crossing that used to be here.

I ate my snap as I looked through binoculars at the seals. They were not alone; the mud flats were covered with dunlin, oyster catchers, greylag geese, curlews and lots of diving ducks and other wading birds. I could have spent hours here in this natural history wonderland but I was soon joined by a car full of binocular carrying tourists; then another car full followed by yet another. Some even invaded my space and sat on 'My' bench next to me. I was barely able to grunt a "hello" to them. They were all friendly and I was soon in a group of about twenty all looking out onto the mud-flats. A cry went up; someone thought they'd seen an osprey, apparently common here but it wasn't to be.

I had to shake myself out of this and move on. The ever-growing army of tourist twitchers looked on in amazement when I said goodbye and walked off alone into the wilderness.

"Where's his car?" I heard someone say.

The wilderness didn't last that long as I soon arrived at the busy A9. I walked along the wide grass verge and came into the 'Mound' as it is known. An area of rivers and marsh land at the head of Loch Fleet. The bridge was built in 1816 by Thomas Telford. I marched across it and followed the road down into Golspie. On the way into the village I couldn't help but notice the huge statue sitting atop of the purple-coloured mountain, Beinn a Bhragaidh, dominating the scenery.

At the first shop in Golspie, a Spar shop, the girl behind the counter told me that the statue, known locally as 'the wee mannie', was of the Marquis of Stafford who on marrying Elizabeth the Countess of Sutherland, became the 1st Duke of Sutherland. It was he who was responsible for the glen clearances when he realised sheep were more profitable than people. "There are some lovely walks up to the statue", said the shop assistant. "Some other day", I thought and walked across to the car park where some motor homes were parked by the edge of *an award-winning beach*.

I met Kay and Ripley in the car park and we went for a stroll along the beach. We then drove back to Loch Fleet so Kay could see the grey seals. Unfortunately, the tide was now in and the seals had moved further out.

August Wednesday 22 — Walking Day 78 *Dry and sunny with hazy mist in places*

Golspie to Dalchalm (Brora) - 7 miles - Total Walked 884

The A9 road cuts through the heart of Golspie. This low-roofed village has a smattering of shops, pubs and a library along its linear main street. Kay and Ripley joined me on the edge of town at the Bible Garden, created in 2000 as a Millennium project. It was stunning with streams and ponds adorned with little bridges. A very small lump represented the 'green hill far away'. It was beautiful with many of its flowers in full bloom, every one of which gets a mention in the Bible. Plants that are not necessarily identified as flowers are strategically placed around the garden: wheat, apple, vines, willow and brambles for example. Roses, tulips, crocuses, iris and lilies were flowers I recognised. Others such as tamarisk, viburnum and anthemion left me puzzled, as did the unromantically named doves dung.

After enjoying our stroll, we headed out of town, up the hill past the Sutherland Arms Hotel and the busy working stone yard, to the starting point of the Big Burn walk where a modern wooden packhorse or hump-backed bridge gives entrance to a scenic glen of mixed deciduous trees.

We climbed steadily upstream through the woods on a well-signposted path, finding many sunlit glades alive with the colour of yellow pimpernels and primroses. The walk eventually led to a series of deep pools hemmed in by rock walls with an access boardwalk fixed to the walls above the swirling water below. We could hear the thundering noise of the Big Burn Waterfall which kept its full majesty hidden from view till the very end of the boardwalk where we stood on an observation platform.

The noise of falling water terrified Ripley and Kay had to pick her up. Kay was to write: *'The waterfalls, although not as stunning as some we had visited, were still lovely, the sunshine managing to penetrate the deep green foliage and to shine on the cascading water where it created prisms of colourful light'.*

Having admired the waterfall, we retraced our steps. Anywhere else we would have had to squeeze past crowds of people but not here. We had the delightful walk all to ourselves.

Having finished our stroll, we then headed the short distance to Dunrobin Castle. Described as *'a jewel in the Highlands'*, the castle with its fairy-tale towers, spires and turrets is very picturesque and vaguely reminiscent of the Walt Disney castle logo.

It is entered from the back but the best views of it are from the sea as it sits on a knoll above terraced and walled gardens before the shoreline. We headed straight for the kitchen dining rooms where we had an excellent lunch of soup and rolls.

There has been a castle here since the early 13th century and parts of the early castle can still be seen deep in the middle of the building. It is the ancestral home to the Earldom of Sutherland, one of the ancient earldoms of Scotland. The castle and gardens were remodelled in 1845 by Sir Charles Barry who created the fairy-tale appearance that we now see. We joined a crowded tour and walked around some of the majestic rooms resplendent in expensive furniture, curtains and suits of armour, swords and shields.

In the grounds of the castle, in the old stable block, there is a museum dedicated to the ancient carved Pictish Stones, an early form of Celtic art. The gardens were wonderful and we saw several clumps of 'giant rhubarb' or 'Gunnera' with leaves up to 8' across (a native of South Brazil).

The walking community, renowned as they are for making an early start to their walking days, may be shocked by my late starts. Today I was about to set off on my main walk at just before 4 pm. George H Allen in his 1904 record-breaking LEJOG began walking at 4 am each day. Having worked many early turns (6 am to 2 pm), I would often make my way up to the Yorkshire Dales and start a walk at 4 pm, coming down off the fells at 9 pm. I was used to late starts.

I said goodbye to Kay and Ripley at a kissing gate on the bend of the road in Golspie. I walked across fields, dodging the thistles and headed north with the shoreline and mist covered sea over to my right and woods on my left. The woods soon gave way to magnificent views of Dunrobin Castle. I followed a good well-signposted footpath through open fields and alongside the deserted but beautiful beach. The map declared I was passing Sputie Burn Waterfall which turned out to be nothing more than a trickle of water down crumbling sand cliffs. I eventually arrived at the well-preserved Carn Liath Broch, I'd never been to a Broch before but I know Scotland's coastline is dotted with these ancient fortified round houses. I had the place to myself and could climb the steps up and then down into the walled interior.

Hamish Brown in his 1981 'Groat's End Walk' book, quotes a 1726 description:

'A broch is an old building made in the form of a sugar loaf and with a double wall

and winding staircases in the middle of the wall round about. Little places for men to lie in, as is thought. All built of dry stone without any mortar'. I left the Broch in the care of a flock of sheep that were helping to keep the grass short. I walked on passing superb beaches, the footpath remaining on the pebbled edge. On one beach, using my Leki walking stick I drew a rough picture of Britain in the sand and indicated my route from Land's End to John O'Groats.

A sea fret set in and my views out to sea became distorted in the murky light. I noticed what appeared to be some large abstract smiling mouths, like clowns smiling; either that or sausages on sticks, it was like a scene from a Monty Python sketch. For some time, I was perplexed by these images. It turned out that they were grey seals balancing on rocks, bending in the middle with head and tail pointing upwards. In the eerie silence, I could have stayed and watched the surreal shapes for much longer than I did but I had to break myself away and move on. I trudged slowly over wet sand until the sandy beaches gave way to rocky and pebbled beaches. Eventually I climbed some small cliffs to walk an excellent short grass cliff top that led me into Brora.

Blue and white metal sheds surrounded the fishermen's squat stone cottages lining the small harbour. Matching blue and white boats bobbed up and down on the sea. No one was about.

A preserved ice house built of stone like the harbour, with an informative notice board, related facts from the past. Fish, particularly salmon caught in these parts used to be packed into boxes of ice from the ice house and then placed on trains, bound the next day for the big hotels in Edinburgh, Glasgow and London. The railway station with its beautiful, 19th-century buildings is still open but nothing of that Victorian enterprise remains today. I left the harbour area and walked up the banks of the River Brora into the heart of town.

Two things happened on my walk up into the town; first the fog lifted and the sun came out again; second, I left behind a charming coastal resort, a Cornwall like seaside village and entered an industrial town reminiscent of the Lancashire towns I had passed through weeks earlier. Brora town has row after row of terraced housing looking totally out of place. I was shocked by the sight of it. Only when you know some of the local history does it make sense.

Brora was a coal mining town, the most northerly coal mine in Britain and one of the oldest. It remained private with nationalisation after World War 2. The miners were the main shareholders. The mine continued production into the 1970's, finally closing when production costs became too high. It is estimated that over eight million tons of coal remains underground waiting to be excavated.

The town prospered because of the Duke of Sutherland's glen clearances; displaced Highlanders flocked into town where as well as the fishing and coal industries, the Duke opened quarries and brick works. Stone from the Brora quarry was used in rebuilding London Bridge; the one that was sold to the Americans and is now in Arizona. The Duke also operated textile mills in the town, which produced woollen garments much sought after in the fashion industries. Sadly, the brick works closed in the 1980's with the last mill finally closing in 2003.

Brora was also home to a top secret cold war radio listening station but even that closed in 1986. For a town that was once a hive of industry, a town that had electric lights well before Glasgow or Edinburgh, being dubbed 'Electric City', things today looked bleak. With the Beatrice Oilfield, a few miles offshore it's surprising to learn that petrol prices in Sutherland and Caithness are the highest in the U.K and anywhere else in Europe except for Norway, another large oil producer.

The petrol station in town had petrol priced at over £1 a litre whereas everywhere else on our travels it was priced at around 92p a litre. The price display sign couldn't accommodate prices over 99p and black masking tape had to be used to indicate the numeral 1 sign in the pound; i.e. 1:00. Near to the petrol station I saw an old garage at the side of the road with old-fashioned petrol pumps which were rusting away. They should be preserved and the garage turned into a museum I thought.

By a beautiful memorial clock tower, I saw a mish-mash of wooden huts that went by the name of Golden Fry Fish and Chip Shop and Restaurant. A banner sign declared, 'probably the best fish and chips in Scotland'. 'Hmm', I thought, we shall have to see about that.

I walked out of town on a quiet lane passing the only large industry still operating in these parts; The Clynelish Whisky Distillery and then turned onto a country lane that led me to our camp-site by the beach at Dalchalm.

August Thursday 23 — Walking Day 79 *Dry with mist on hills*

Dalchalm to Helmsdale - 19 miles - Total Walked 894

Kay and Ripley joined me as I set off across the sand dunes and out across the golf links of the Brora Course. We soon arrived at a deserted sandy beach.

At a stream the sand dunes returned. After crossing them we came to the railway line, where I said goodbye to Kay and Ripley, leaving them to continue their close study of large thyme and field gentians that were easily spotted in the grass-covered sand dunes.

Crossing the railway line, I marched northwards on the by now very quiet A9 road. Over to my left the purple heather-clad hills of Sutherland were covered in light mist. Between the road, the railway and the sea lay just a narrow strip of farmland. I ploughed on. The road undulated up and down, passing a huge, ugly and out-of-place electric sign more suitable to a motorway than here on this lonely country lane. The sign reminded drivers not to drink and drive. Do they have a big problem with drink-drivers up here? I don't know; I saw very few drivers.

I carried on, arriving at a lay-by at Lothbeg. It was here, half hidden by bushes that I discovered a stone memorial to the killing of the last wolf in Scotland, which it stated was killed by Hunter Polson in 1700. A line from a Ted Hughes poem came into my head:

'The fang of wolf is in the purple heather hills'.

Many motorists heading for John O'Groats miss seeing this memorial as they whiz by. The scenery changed; a mist covered the hills and the low-lying farmland now had ruined crofters' cottages dotted amongst it. Andrew McCloy, in his 2002 LEJOG book wrote; *'It may not have the dramatic bays and towering peaks of the north-west of Scotland but the further along this east coast you travel, the feeling of wildness and emptiness grows'.*

At Loth I walked downhill towards a large church but I found it boarded up and being used as a kind of builder's store room. The graveyard next to it was overgrown except for the entrance path that contained the war memorial and several war graves, all of which were immaculately maintained. Nearby, a road on the left headed up the Strath of Kildonan which heads north into the flow country of Caithness. Here, between 1868 and 1870 a small gold rush took place but it was ultimately foiled when little gold was found and the Duke of Sutherland realised he could make more money from his salmon fishing on the river. I briefly contemplated taking this route north; I could put into practice my newly-learnt gold-panning techniques but decided to head for the town of Helmsdale instead.

Back on the A9 the wide grass verge that I had become accustomed to vanished, just when I needed it. A huge wave of south bound traffic streamed by as I hobbled precariously along the kerb edge. Once the traffic had gone the sun came out and the road, now quiet was again benefitting from a wide grass verge. The views out to sea were magnificent and so were the views inland to the hills. I couldn't decide which way to look; out to sea searching for signs of dolphins, whales, seals and even otters or to the hills, looking for buzzards and eagles, none of which I saw.

Having been in the lonely wilds of Sutherland for most of the day it came as a surprise to walk into the housing estate at Portgower. Some workmen listening to a loud radio were painting the guttering and facia boards on the semi-detached houses covered in the ubiquitous grey pebble-dash. A traditional-style telephone kiosk stood on a road junction. A sign above declared no coins were accepted, just credit cards. I entered it and waving away the cloud of cobwebs I made a call to Kay using my credit card; an easy though expensive thing to do.

I had forgotten about the railway line which reappeared and ran into Helmsdale alongside the road and the sea. I had a good view of the well-laid-out town with its little harbour and turreted war memorial clock tower reminiscent of nearby Brora. Helmsdale had been built by the Duke of Sutherland for the displaced Highlanders from the glen providing them with much-needed jobs in the booming fishing industries.

The reason I had a good view of the town was because I was walking on a modern concrete and steel bridge that now towers over the town. It might be very practical but I found it ugly and totally out of keeping with the rest of the town. I could look down on the original 'in keeping' Thomas Telford bridge of 1811. The new bridge, built in the 1970's used the land previously occupied by Helmsdale's ruined castle which in an act of vandalism for road building purposes was swept away. Today little of the castle remains to be seen. In a field by the side of the road I came to a huge statue of two Highlanders with wind in their hair. The statue titled *'The Emigrants'* by sculptor Gerald Laing, had just been unveiled by Alex Salmond, Scotland's then first minister a few weeks previously in July.

With the railway station now over to my left I walked downhill into town. I meandered up and down the main street looking in at the one or two shops and cafes before heading for The Timespan Heritage Centre down by the harbour. Inside I found a gallery full of information on the herring fishing boom of the 19th century. Helmsdale was once home to over 200 herring boats. The river at Helmsdale is also one of the best salmon rivers in the Highlands.

Kay and Ripley joined me and we went for a stroll 'upriver' to St John's Well which had been renovated as a millennium project. The well head was originally a memorial to Queen Victoria's Diamond Jubilee of 1897. All around the well in the hedgerows were ripe wild raspberries.

We called it a day and headed back to Brora. The smell from the fish and chip cafes in Helmsdale had lingered in my nostrils, so we drove straight back to the fish and chip restaurant in Brora - *'The best fish and chips in Scotland'*. Before entering the restaurant, we read some customer comment cards posted in the vestibule: *'The best food I have ever tasted'*, and *'Wow, what a fantastic restaurant, the food is superb'*. We looked at each other with raised eyebrows and knowing smiles. Kay was to write: *'This evening, we had the best fish and chips I can remember having'*.

August Friday 24 | Walking Day 80 *Dry, hot and sunny*

Helmsdale to Dunbeath - 15 miles - Total Walked 909

I left the neat terraced streets of Helmsdale and almost at once began climbing, passing the Youth Hostel, the last building in town. I had some fantastic views out to sea; up ahead rose the purple heather-covered hill known as the 'Ord of Caithness'. Amongst LEJOG cyclists it has a fearsome reputation; from where I stood it looked huge and mountainous and I knew it would have to be climbed.

The road (the A9) was exceptionally quiet and I walked on a wide grass verge. On a very steep section I came to a sign used in winter to declare the road ahead closed due to snow, which wasn't going to happen today; it was so hot, the tarmac was bubbling up into pools of runny hot liquid. I stopped to watch a shepherd with his Border collie dogs rounding up his sheep; a scene very familiar to me and one I have watched countless times before in the Yorkshire Dales. The commands he shouted to his dogs were almost the same dialect and tone as those heard at home: "Lie down". He shouted. I had to tear myself away and climbed on up the road.

The road continued dramatically upwards snaking its way up and up. I could see the high cliffs of the Ord which now and then are punctured by narrow inlets known as 'geos'. In a large lay-by on the seaside edge I came upon some Japanese tourists all clicking away with their expensive-looking cameras. The views were truly breath taking. I drank some water and watched some ravens floating on the wind above us, their distinctive cawing call being louder than the sea crashing into the cliffs well below us.

I left the Japanese and the bubbling hot tarmac and walked on, soon cresting the hill and entering my last mainland county, Caithness. I had climbed the Ord. Neil Gunn, local lad turned author wrote of his native county; *'It's a good land; wide, high and far, yet it could be encompassed'*. From the top of the Ord the land did indeed look high and far. The hills were behind me and I set off along the side of the road. A sign declared John O' Groats *'47 miles ahead'*. I strode on.

I hadn't been walking long when I came upon a large brown information sign which stated that the Badbea, *'historic clearance village'* was a half a mile away across the moorland towards the cliff tops. I turned off and walked on along a good path across moorland reminiscent of my own Yorkshire moors. The gorse bushes, still in flower, were alive with buzzing insects. I climbed a broken-down stone wall and entered the now ruined village of Badbea, situated on a steep hillside leading to the cliff edge.

Five or six derelict crofts fanned out across the field at the cliff top away from the centre of the village and marked by a tall monolithic monument. In the hot sunshine, backed by the blue Moray Firth it looked spectacular. I could see why the Highlanders, cleared from their glens in 1814 chose to settle here. In winter or on a windy and rainy day the place would be different, even inhospitable but then so are many other places.

Badbea was for the few families who settled here, *'life on the edge'*. They scraped a crofters' living from poor moorland fields, fished in the sea and collected birds' eggs. At that time like many cliff top communities it was a necessary and welcome source of food. Children and animals were tethered down to prevent them from being blown off the cliff's edge.

The 22' high monument was built in 1911 by Donald Sutherland whose father had been born in Badbea but later, as with many others, had emigrated to New Zealand. 1911 was also the year that the last inhabitant left the village, unable to make a living. I left Badbea behind wondering if, with today's modern accoutrements, the villagers might have stayed and given it a go. Back on the quiet A9, the bleak moorland had been broken up by patches of forest; new pine forests with young trees being almost shrub-like.

I pegged on along the moor road; at least the sun was beating down and the sky was a wonderful blue colour. What would this stretch of the walk be like in rain, sleet and hail? I didn't care; it was beautiful and sunny. I was blessed. After a while I came to the top of the steep descent into Berriedale, a much-feared part of the road in winter when it is often impassable due to snow and ice. Motor enthusiasts rave about this section of the A9, it being one of the quietest 'A' roads in the country. It has a dramatic 1-in-9 descent into the steep-sided wooded valley of the Berriedale River, crossing over the same on a Thomas Telford bridge built in 1813 and then climbing out the other side by a series of hairpin bends up a granite and red sandstone cliff face before finally reaching the top alongside a walled burial ground on one side and a lonely church on the other.

The hot sun beat down and each step had me peeling my boots from the bubbling tarmac as I made my way down the steep incline. It reminded me of Devon earlier in my walk when something similar had happened. I walked past an emergency safety lane or gravel trap; the first I had seen on my entire walk. Yorkshire has several of these safety lanes, one being reasonably close to where I live. Surprisingly they are not mentioned at all in the Highway Code. E.W. Fox, writing in his 1911 book '2000 miles on foot - Walks through Great Britain and France', wrote about this very piece of road when he stated: 'Along one of the steepest hills in the U.K., the Duke of Portland - whose deer-hunting estate I was walking through - has made one or two off-shoot roads in case of brake failure'.

So, the gravel trap emergency lanes are not a modern feature, having been around for a century, at least. Near the bottom of the hill an old quarry overlooked the tiny Berriedale harbour with its own ruined and overgrown castle. I walked down to the Telford Bridge and admired the beautiful, wooded glen.

Here the Berriedale River joins the River Langwell before flowing together to reach the sea. I strolled across to a large war memorial; for such a small hamlet of a place it had an unusually large memorial topped with a figure of Saint Andrew. I then noticed that among the names commemorated were all those who served in WW1 as well as those who died. Top of the list of survivors were two very English sounding aristocrats, Lord Henry Bentnick of Derby, and Lord Charles Bentnick the Marquess of Titchfield. The memorial was the first to be built in Caithness after WW1.

The steep hillsides looked delicate being made up in the main of loose sandstone and shale. The hairpin bends appeared to balance delicately on this material. I began the steep climb out of Berriedale utilising the hairpin bends to ease the gradients. Half way up and to my horror, I saw a huge juggernaut-of-a-lorry coming down on the wrong side of the road (enabling the driver to manoeuvre his monster lorry around the hairpins). I guessed this particular lorry driver had done this frequently before. In at least two places the lorry driver was blind to oncoming uphill traffic whilst he was on the other side of the road. I made a mental note of all this as in a day or two, I would be driving my motor home, towing the Nissan up these very same hairpin bends.

I passed the walled burial ground and the locked and lonely-looking church and crested the hill. The road went straight before me, heading over the cliff tops with a beautiful sea view over to my right and on my left, barren moorland dotted with abandoned crofts. As I neared Dunbeath some of these croft buildings, certainly a few near the road, were still inhabited. Large peat stacks stood outside.

Dunbeath has been by-passed by a modern and in my mind ugly flyover bridge. I turned off the main road, walking down into Dunbeath where Kay and Ripley were waiting for me.

Walking Day 81 *Mixed, light showers, then dry and clear with a cold breeze*

Dunbeath to Lybster - 8 miles - Total Walked 917 >

On the drive back up to Dunbeath, (yesterday's finishing point), we passed a slim man with a straggly unkempt beard carrying a huge rucksack. He was walking LEJOG and like me, he was nearing the end of his journey. He looked exhausted as if he had spent the previous night sleeping in a ditch by the side of the road. "The bastard", I exclaimed as we drove away from him. "Drive faster", I said to Kay. "I want to put some distance between him and me". For the first time in my adult life I'd suddenly developed a competitive edge. Kay rebuked me for swearing but that was how I felt. This was my walk and I had become very possessive about it. The thought of passing the finishing line with 'him' on my tail filled me with horror but wait; I wasn't in a race; I could take a day off any time I liked; let him overtake me and get out of my way. I relaxed at the thought. Yet still as we arrived in Dunbeath, I opened the door and jumped out pretending to run down the street shouting "I'm not letting him catch me up".

I walked down and around the small harbour, built in 1800. It was deserted. Boats bobbed up and down on the water and fishing nets and boxes were stacked up along the harbour road as if just dropped there 'Marie Celeste style'. I got the feeling that people were about but hiding from me. It felt like curtains were being twitched in the windows of the low-roofed cottages waiting for the stranger to leave. Before I turned to go I stood and admired the bronze statue of Kenn and the Salmon; a 1991 sculpture by Alex Main which commemorates Neil Gunn (1891 – 1973), author of 'Highland River' (1937), which tells the story of Kenn, a local boy who explores the river, poaches salmon, grows up and goes to war.

Neil Gunn was born in Dunbeath and this book, one of many, is said to be very autobiographical. One of his more famous books was called 'Silver Darlings' and tells about the Herring trade centred here at Dunbeath. The trade has now almost died out. I left Kenn struggling to carry his huge salmon and turned to look back south where over on the opposite side of the harbour, high up above the town, stands the beautiful white-walled 14th-century castle, now a hotel, perched precariously on the cliffs above the village.

I still hadn't seen a soul. As I turned to go I got a full view of the new flyover bridge that takes the few motorists heading north away and out of this now quiet backwater. I could see the concrete bridge had a fine curve in it and was lower in the south, rising considerably at its northern end, it had some beauty to it, that's for sure but I stand by what I said in that to me it was ugly and totally out of place here, completely dominating an otherwise quaint and picturesque fishing village.

The road climbed away from the village and I walked past several boarded-up-hotels and a derelict petrol station. I was back on the tops with views out to sea. I hadn't been going for long when I arrived at the tiny hamlet of Laidhay. Here I saw a white painted stone-built cottage with a heart shaped climbing ivy plant which turns the cottage into a well-known landmark. Just uphill next door to it stands the Laidhay Croft Museum.

The car park of the museum was empty. I walked in and was welcomed by a friendly old lady who was acting curator for the day. Now in her eighties she turned out to be a font of knowledge, having lived the crofting life as a young woman. The curator proper was having a day off and she was standing in. How lucky was I. Almost all of those now living the crofting life, (being self-sufficient with just 30 acres of land), live in modern bungalows built alongside the near-derelict croft buildings. The modern bungalows may be comfortable and practicable but in my opinion they do not 'sit in the land'.

The acting curator showed me around the low-roofed banana-shaped building; it had stables for the ponies at one end and the barn or byre for the cattle at the other end. It was a typical ancient longhouse with rush or heather thatched roof. The Crofter's living space was in the middle and slightly higher than the animal quarters, giving them the benefit from the animal's heat but not their waste. We progressed into the bedroom, a kind of bunk barn with boxed beds where the whole family lived together with very little privacy.

I really enjoyed my private tour of the croft and my chat with the 'curator'. Time whizzed by. Caithness is certainly a place where time stands still. I didn't realise until later that I'd spent nearly two hours talking to her. She spoke with an English accent with a soft Irish lilt. This, she explained was the Caithness accent, related more to Norse than Gaelic, which has never been spoken up in this area of Scotland having reached Golspie and no further. Her accent could easily have been recognised in some of the Yorkshire Dales where the Norsemen dominated. The croft way of life reminded me of the many farms with shippons attached to barns that I'd seen in the Dales.

I thanked the lady for her time and made my way to leave whilst she was still imparting knowledge on planning permission and the term 'De croft', a term used only in this part of Britain and referring to when a family wants to split the croft in half to accommodate a growing family reluctant to move away. It's a fascinating subject.

I was outside now, trying politely to move on. The old lady followed me out still talking away. I dutifully listened. The road was quiet until a group of motorcyclists rode past. They were all dressed as Dalmatian dogs and I guessed there were 101 of them. Banners on their backs declared they were riding LEJOG on a charity fund-raising effort. "They never stop and come in here", said my curator. "It's a great shame; they're missing a real treat", I said.

I realised JOG was getting close and after all this time I hoped that upon my arrival I would have the place to myself for a moment.

As the roar of the motorcycles died away another sound took over. It was the whizzing-sound of pedal cyclists this time, about twenty riders, all with their heads down and pedalling hard. "They never stop to come in here", said my curator. "What a shame", I said. I walked away from the Croft Museum glad to have spent time in there.

In the 1930's a man called J.W. Rossiter from the village of Sennan near Land's End in Cornwall, rode LEJOG in a record 2 days, 13 hours and 22 minutes. The previous record having been held for 20 years by a man called Harry Green. Back in 1773 a celebrated pedestrian, Foster Powell, held the record for walking from York to London.

The Victorians and Edwardians certainly travelled the LEJOG routes in numbers by various methods of transport. Challenge records come and go and today most people travelling LEJOG do so by bicycle; perhaps 9 out of 10. Cyclists take on average 2 to 3 weeks to complete their journey. John Woodburn broke the cycling record in 1982 by completing the route in 1 day, 21 hours, 3 minutes and 16 seconds and probably didn't even notice the ever-changing scenery. He certainly didn't spend a couple of hours in the Laidhay Croft Museum; his loss. I was not trying to break any records. The walker is few and far between but even amongst the walkers, some walk to beat the records; I don't even know what the walking record is and I really don't care.

I walked on along the cliff tops. The sky above was full of birds; kittiwakes, guillemots, fulmar and razorbills. The road turned inland and before descending into a tree-covered valley, I stopped to admire a whale bone arch; a relic of whaling days gone by. It reminded me of the one in Whitby, Yorkshire, except that this one here looked neglected, being a brown-grey colour and standing in an overgrown patch of land.

I descended the hill and for the first time in ages I was amongst native broad-leafed trees; one of the few areas in Caithness where trees such as Birch, Hazel, Rowan and Willow can be found. I crossed the bridge over Reisgill Burn and climbed up the other side, soon leaving the tree cover behind. I came to the village of Lybster where at the crossroads, Kay and Ripley were in the hotel car park waiting for me.

The town, with its striking stone harbour was down to our right. A street planned village, built in the 1830's / 1840's by rich landowner, Sir John Sinclair, it had been the third biggest fishing port in Scotland and provided much-needed jobs for the highlanders displaced by Sinclair, from their glen homelands further northwest during the clearances. Here the traditional fishing boat is called a yawl and is still built in a local workshop. We saw the pitch where the world championship games of Knotty are held every year but today no one was even practising the variant of Shinty.

Just before driving away we stopped to look at a monument to a town called Fort Mackinac in the U.S.A. Lybster is twinned with this place as it was founded by Patrick Sinclair, a member of the Sinclair family who was one of the Black Watch Regiment who fought against the French and local First Nation 'Red Indians' during the years 1759 to 1784. Mackinac was founded by Sinclair between 1779 and 1781. We left Lybster still not having seen a soul and drove up and on into Wick, which we found to be alive with shoppers in its busy town centre with a harbour full of boats.

We parked the car by a park with a lake where we watched birds including greylag geese, greenshanks and common scoter. Ripley had a walk and then we searched out the old Pulteney Whisky Distillery and Visitor Centre among some very grey-looking streets that wouldn't have looked out of place in Preston.

The Lancastrian artist L.S. Lowry, visited Wick in the 1930's and produced a painting of this area entitled 'The Black Steps' and depicting his famous matchstick people ascending and descending the steps that lead from this part of town to the harbour. I was pleased to hear that these famous steps have recently been renovated. This area of town is known as Pulteney Town and was built using money confiscated from Jacobite chiefs after Bonnie Prince Charlie's failed revolution. Sir William Johnstone Pulteney, the 2nd Earl of Bath and an Englishman, gave his name to the town and the whisky; the distillery began in 1826. The Distillery the most northern in mainland Britain was closed to Visitors today but the small shop was open and I bought some whisky as a souvenir of our visit to Wick.

August Monday 27 Rest day

Yet another day off.

Today we moved the van up to Dunnet Bay, Caithness, said to be the windiest caravan site in Britain, having no protection from the fierce winds that regularly roar in from the Atlantic all the way from Canada. We looked at the site and saw that it gently sloped down to the beach; a fabulous white crescent of sand. Some vans were positioned up at the top of the site and looked very exposed and vulnerable. We positioned our van on a pitch located behind a sand dune and toilet block hoping they would form a windbreak and provide some shelter. A light breeze was blowing and I was satisfied that we had picked the best spot on the site.

Safely pitched, we set off in the car on the short journey to Dunnet Head. It is the most northerly point of mainland Britain and is now an SSSI (site of special scenic interest). Here the breeze had picked up and was now a strong cold wind. We were blessed with clear blue skies and beautiful views across the Pentland Firth to The Orkney Islands. We could clearly make out the Old Man of Hoy and other fabulous cliff scenery across a very choppy sea.

A memorial viewpoint indicated all before us. Over to our left we had views of Cape Wrath, the north-westerly tip of mainland Scotland whilst over to our right we saw for the first time, John O'Groats just a few miles away. I was determined that we wouldn't go there until I walked to it. Beyond John O'Groats we could make out Duncansby Head, the most north-easterly point on mainland Scotland. The viewing station also encouraged us to look back where inland, we could see the vast lowland that is Caithness, often described as 'the lowland beyond the Highlands'. The Flow country as it is known, is made up of fifty percent peat bog, the largest expanse of blanket bog anywhere in Europe. Beyond the bogs, we could see the Mountains of Morvern and Maiden Pap far to the south.

Up on the top where the wind was the strongest we explored the now-derelict Royal Navy WW2 observation post. Strange concrete rafts 'floated' on top of the boggy moorland, dotted between red-bricked bunker-type buildings. At least the buildings were open and we explored their insides and sheltered from the wind. Built in 1940, these buildings were the last of six coastal defences; U-boat radar stations, which were set up in Shetland, the Orkney's and here to protect the British fleet harboured in Scapa Flow and Atlantic shipping, from U-boats heading out from the North Sea into the Atlantic.

Before leaving the Trig Point we realised that here at 58° 40› 21" N latitude and 30° 22› 3" W longitude, we were further north than Moscow and parts of Alaska. We quickly dropped down to the lighthouse and surrounding buildings and were joined by a few hardy tourists. The lighthouse, now automated, was built in 1832 by Robert Stevenson, the grandfather of Robert Louis Stevenson, the author. It stands on a tussocky headland some 300 feet above the sea below. The cliff edges are dotted with devil's bit scabious, beautiful blue wild flowers. As we were on top of the cliffs peering down we didn't get the full sense of their magnificence; just an impression of the sheer drop below.

Puffins could be seen flying below us. With their bright-coloured bill and orange feet it is understandable why it is sometimes called the sea parrot. We'd missed seeing those on the Scilly's but there were plenty of them here. For a while these colourful birds brought back that happy feeling. I dug out the pebble that I had carried all the way from the beach at Lizard Point, mainland Britain's most southerly point and ceremonially threw it into the sea, Kay capturing the moment on camera. I imagined that one day some geologist would find the pebble and be puzzled by its appearance up here out of context.

We had journeyed between these two extreme points. Together we had completed a journey. Over the next few days we were to complete some more journeys. Instead of feeling elated I felt a twinge of sadness that our adventure was nearing its end. Back at camp we settled in for a windy night.

August
Tuesday
28

Walking Day 82 *Dull grey day with light showers*

Lybster to Watten - 14 miles - Total Walked 931 >

Amongst the many things that the curator at the Croft Museum had mentioned was the Whaligoe Steps and I was determined to seek them out. Built in a narrow creek the steps lead steeply down a sheer 250-feet cliff face into a tiny unique harbour. No other harbour has been constructed in such an apparently inaccessible place. It is said there are 365 steps, one for each day of the year.

The steps are not signposted as a tourist spot due to health and safety rules. Tourists wanting to venture up and down them do so at their own risk. You really have to want to walk them as finding them isn't at all easy. However, find them we did and, parking round the back of a row of fishermen's cottages we came to the only sign to be seen; a stone, cut in memory of Etta B. Juhle who cared for the steps for many years.

Sticking close to the cliff face we began our descent of the steps which zigzagged down with no safety banister. The steps were dry but in wet weather I could easily see them being slippery and dangerous. I tried to imagine hundreds of women, for it was women laden with heavy fish baskets on their heads, who continually climbed up and down these steps year after year in all weathers.

Whaligoe Haven stands at the foot of the steps; a natural calm sea-green pool surrounded by rocks and caves with a slight crack in the rocks opening out into the busy and noisy sea beyond. It is said that this place earned its name after the local fishermen trapped a whale in here and spent the next few months cutting it up.

At the bottom of the steps we found a rock platform known as the 'Bink'. On here we felt safe at last. It was also on here that the fishermen, using a winch, would hoist their boats up out of the water for repair and to keep them safe in stormy weather. Clumps of Danish scurvy grass kept Kay interested as we hadn't seen the like of it before. We had the place to ourselves and even Ripley, usually frightened by the waves, seemed to be enjoying the adventure. We began the steady climb back out, this time counting the steps as we climbed. At the very top I'd only counted to 330, so what happened to the other 35 I don't know.

A weather-beaten fisherman came out of one of the cottages carrying a mildew-covered photograph of the steps in Victorian times. He told us that his father had been the last herring fisherman to use the haven and steps back in the early 1960's. We admired his photograph and some pencil sketches that he had done. We talked to him for some time as he relished in telling us the history that surrounds the steps. With no Tourist Information boards, we were grateful to listen to his passion for his heritage and his informative way of passing this on. He pointed to the stone remembering Etta B. Juhle. Without her work preserving the steps for over 20 years they wouldn't be here today, he told us.

Eventually we had to tear ourselves away and we drove back down the road to Lybster. I'd sought out a route north to walk across the flow country following a farm track of a road heading for Watten. I said goodbye to Kay and Ripley and set off on a very quiet country lane with grass growing down the middle of it. All around me was the vast empty openness of the flat flow country, now and again dotted with abandoned crofts. The further I walked the more desolate the scenery became. Once, in the distance I spotted a postman's red van but it sped off over the countryside, appearing to float over the bogs and moors. At least the heather of the moors was a beautiful purple colour with here and there, the yellow of marsh ragwort.

Most people who visit this wilderness do so by car. They don't usually walk across it as I was doing. Somewhere out here in this vast open bog where the horizon seems to merge seamlessly with the ground, I came upon the Camster Cairns. The grey cairns of Camster are the best-known Neolithic site in Caithness. They are signposted and have Tourist Information boards, boardwalk footpaths across the bog, car parking, and picnic benches. I had the place to myself.

The chambered cairns, (there are two of them), are built on a fairly flat, terraced piece of land near to the confluence of streams that are the source of the River Wick, one of the main rivers in Caithness. Archaeological excavation has revealed evidence of burning at the centre of the chambers and large amounts of human bone, animal bone and flint have been found but their exact use is still a mystery.

One of the cairns, built of stone like an igloo, has an east-facing entrance and is round in shape, hence it's called Camster Round. The other is about 60 yards long and 2 yards tall and is known by the name Camster Long. Its entrance has a modern iron gate protecting it, although today it was open with no sign of a padlock. I crawled inside and pushed my way into the dark chamber. I had the idea that I could wait here until some hapless tourists came by and then at just the right moment I could begin to make eerie wailing noises that might give them a fright. I gave up on the idea, believing that I might have to wait a heck of a long time.

The cairns deserve to be visited by many more than they obviously are.

I ate my snap at the picnic bench and then walked on alone into the desolate wilderness. Some regimental pine forests now crept in on both sides giving me a much-needed change of scenery but it started to rain which only helped to make the walk depressing and soul destroying.

I had a feeling of being low in the flow and was glad when at last the boggy flat moorland gave way to fields full of sheep and cattle. These eventually gave way to farms, (which actually looked like farms) and eventually the village of Watten, which surprisingly, had tree-lined avenues with neat houses, manicured lawns and well-tended gardens. It all came as a bit of a welcome shock after the wilderness of the mossy moors.

Across the bridge and by the crossroads near to the hotel I stopped by the Alexander Bain memorial. Up to that point I'd never heard of him but according to the memorial, Bain was the inventor of the electric clock. It's remarkable to note that a self-educated crofter's son, (although some would say poorly educated), would go on to be a 'bright light' in the development of the electric industry. He not only developed the electric clock but played a major part in developing telegraphy and the fax machine. He lived from 1811 to 1877 and died in Kirkintilloch where there is a pub named after him. The village of Watten appeared as though time itself had stopped. No one was to be seen. When Kay and Ripley arrived to pick me up the place felt busy.

I'd heard of the Caithness flagstones, which are still cut from the rock at the nearby Spittal Quarry but we travelled in the other direction and didn't catch sight of this famous quarry.

August **Wednesday 29** **Walking Day 83** *Sunny at first then heavy rain later*

Watten to Slickly Hill (Lyth) - 8 miles - Total Walked 939

The hotel at Watten was surprisingly busy with guests and I had to nudge past one or two of them as I set off. There was more to Watten than I had first seen. At the back

236

(or is it the front?) of the hotel there is a loch where you can hire rowing boats, sailing dinghies and fishing rods. The loch is famous for its fly fishing and fishermen travel up here in good numbers to take advantage of it. I walked along the loch edge towards the railway line. Once there had been a railway station here. It closed in 1960 but the line remains. This is the Far North railway line and I crossed over it by the level crossing and carried on. After yesterday's wilderness, it seemed strange to be back in civilisation.

I came upon a small, well-maintained walled cemetery. I opened the gate and had a look around. As with a lot of small cemeteries you often see the same surname repeatedly on different nearby memorials. This cemetery appeared to have three or four common 'local' surnames, one of which I'd heard before; it belonged to a barrister in Leeds. I wondered if he or his family originated from way up here. The man I knew was as Yorkshire as the day is long.

On leaving the cemetery and away from Watten I realised I hadn't seen any sign of its WW2 prisoner of war camp. Here, at the end of the war, between 1945 and 1947, some of Germany's top Nazi's and SS commanders were detained in compound 'O' of Camp 165. It was a secret location picked for its remoteness and the fact that it was surrounded by what was described as *an inhospitable landscape*. The prisoners had been put through a *brain-washing, de-Nazification programme*' before being dispersed around the world. Little remains on the ground of this former activity. Valerie Campbell has written a book on the subject called *'Camp 165 Watten – Scotland's most secretive POW Camp'*; published in 2007. I was now walking along quiet B roads through countryside with walled fields full of sheep and cattle. I hadn't been walking long when my peace was shattered by a convoy of Land Rovers, trailers and tractors. Due to the road being narrow I had to step into the long grass of the verge. The farmers were friendly, waving as they passed me by. They were not alone. Often the cabs of the vehicles were crammed full with family; the trailers were full of sheep. I didn't have to walk far before I discovered what was happening. At Quaybrae farm, or Caithness Livestock Centre (as it was also called), an auction mart was taking place in premises that resembled a large unit on a nondescript industrial estate and looked totally out of place up here. It was packed with even a burger van doing a brisk business. For an area, wild and desolate, I would not have believed it could bring so many people out into the open. The auction mart was obviously a highlight for all the family. Teenage girls gathered in groups and farmers' wives huddled together on seats, drinking tea whilst the farmers and young boys got down to business, leaning over the fences looking at pens full of sheep. I walked away leaving them to get on with their business.

At the top of a slight rise I had a view northwards over yet more moorland, miles and miles of it. There couldn't be much farming taking place up here I thought. At the side of the road someone had built a modern house. It stuck out in this countryside, as alien to the scenery as anything I'd seen. It was a prefabricated wooden kit house more akin to the pine forest areas of middle Scotland.

A man appeared at the gate and saw me 'admiring' his house, "We've not finished it yet", he said in a strong Glaswegian accent; "Come in and have a cup of tea", he went on. I declined his kind offer but listened to him as he told me how he'd escaped the 'rat race' in Glasgow, bought a derelict croft up here and having demolished it, built his home here. For the first time in his life he said he was happy. What his wife and kids thought, he didn't say. Like the lady in the Croft Museum and the fisherman at the Whaligoe steps, he'd certainly got the 'gift of the gab' and I reluctantly dragged myself away from him after a good half-an-hour's talk.

I strode on. It was easy walking on flat terrain. Eventually I crossed the reasonably busy main road between Wick and Thurso and arrived at the hamlet of Hastigrow. The village consists of a few low-roofed cottages that clung ribbon-like along the road to Thurso. Bill Bryson in his 1995 book, 'Notes from a Small Island', visited here and suggested that the name Hastigrow could perhaps be used as a name brand for fertilizer. I walked through the hamlet and discovered on its edge, something 'growing'. This was a builders' compound complete with men in hard hats, dumper trucks and diggers. I discovered it was a project to lay an overhead electric cable with pylons across the surrounding wilderness.

I was glad to leave them all behind and glad that my view of the Caithness flow country was still pure and unsullied by pylons, at least for now. I turned down a narrow lane bounded on both sides by high hedgerows. The lane headed north, long and straight as an arrow. On one side the moss of Wester and on my other, the moss of Killimster, both vast areas of moor-like boggy terrain with wide, open and empty skies, very grey in colour.

It started to rain and I pulled on my poncho rain Mac. As I walked along and slightly uphill I had a feeling, a sensation that I was being followed. I turned around to see a dark car which was stationary in the lane a long way behind me. I thought it strange for a car to be on this lane in the first place; for it to remain stationary was puzzling. I walked on, ever cautious of the car way behind me. As I arrived at the tiny hamlet of Lyth, just a couple of cottages really, I saw that the car was advancing at speed towards me. All soon became clear. My friend Dick who had walked with me at Haweswater in the Lake District, was in the car with his wife Val.

In all the years that I'd known him, this was the first time I'd seen him driving a car; he either cycled everywhere or used the railways. He had travelled north in order to walk into John O'Groats with me. He explained that they had driven around looking for me and after spotting me, they had stopped to take a photograph of me; a lonely long-distance walker out on the flows in the rain. To have a reasonable walk tomorrow (I was now just a few miles from John O'Groats), I decided to finish today's walk at Slickly Hill, a remote and lonely spot out on the flows, identified by a trig point.

Dick joined me and we walked the two miles to Slickly, not a huge hill but just a slight rise in the land. Dick's wife Val and Kay had met up and were waiting for us at the trig point. It was raining so we didn't hang around but arranged to meet back up at their hotel in nearby Castletown.

After a wash and brush up later that evening we drove to Castletown, a small village on the road to Thurso where in their Hotel we enjoyed a lovely meal in Dick and Val's company, or as Kay was to remember it: *'The meal was edible, just, the company excellent and we had a lovely evening'.*

August
Thursday
30
Walking Day 84 *Rain. Rain. Rain*

Slickly Hill to John O'Groats - 7 miles - Total Walked 946

It was a dark grey sky that greeted us as we said our good byes to Kay, Ripley and Val at the trig point at Slickly Hill. It started to rain heavily as Dick and I set off on the final day's walk. A Jack Snipe flew up and away from us as we walked on the springy grass turf at the side of the narrow tarmac strip of road. There are no footpaths up here across the bogs, only the tarmac lane we were walking on. We were joined by a small flock of lapwings which helped raise our spirits as we watched them 'floating' in the sky. They didn't seem to mind the rain as they performed their 'acrobatics'.

A communication tower came into view and for the next hour it was our walking goal. We strode along in unison. For someone who had walked alone for much of the way, I soon adapted to walking in company and we strode on, battling against the rain.

We began to get a patchy view of the sea and Scotland's north coast. It wasn't at all clear but we could make out the Orkney's. We passed deserted crofts, the land once farmed, now slowly being swallowed up by the boggy moorland; accumulated farm junk was also slowly rusting and rotting away, huge piles of the stuff. It was a dreary walk in dreary and wet surroundings on tarmac! I felt sorry for Dick who'd travelled all the way up here to walk with me on the last day. Eventually we arrived at the coast road. Turning right we headed for John O'Groats passing through the hamlet of Canisbay. The road was long with hardly any traffic. The crofts turned into habited crofts, still with piles of rotting junk stored outside and with cultivated strips of farmland running down to the sea.

We walked into the hamlet of Huna which had some neat bungalows with well-maintained gardens. We also saw the John O'Groats Youth Hostel which was a bit odd being that John O'Groats was still a few miles away. It was now lunchtime and we looked around for somewhere to sit and eat our snap. We couldn't see anywhere suitable and eventually decided that a large garden hedge provided some cover from the pouring rain. We found that if we leant back into the hedge, although still standing, we could eat and drink without rain washing our faces.

On the whole of my walk, this had to be the worst lunch break I'd experienced. Dick's company, with his many humorous tales, helped raise my spirits as we finally trudged the last mile into a very wet John O'Groats.

239

A sign read, '*A welcome at the end of the road*'. The rain and the wind welcomed us here.

John O'Groats is another hamlet really with its few buildings scattered along the road, ribbon-like. We walked down towards the harbour passing a large coach and car park which looked dreary in the drizzle. Over to our left the large white-coloured hotel with distinctive turret-shaped tower dominates the scene but looked sad and neglected with many of its windows boarded up, although the hotel bar remained open. It all painted a bleak scene.

Kay, Ripley and Val were waiting in the rain for us by the Last House in Scotland, a folk museum which turned out to be closed. There were no brass bands, no flag-waving crowds. No one else knew or cared that I'd just walked from Land's End. Kay later wrote: '*We arrived at John O'Groats just in time to see the bedraggled duo trudging the last hundred yards, already pretty soggy*'.

Dick produced a hip flask of whisky and Kay, a bottle of champagne from a parcel our friends Tony and Di had given her with instructions that it had to be opened only on our arrival at John O'Groats. It contained the bottle of champagne, cakes, chocolate and other goodies to aid our celebrations. We huddled together in the pouring rain, smiling.

I'd done it. I'd walked from Land's End to John O'Groats in 84 walking days, having 60 rest days along the way. A total of 946 miles averaging 11.3 miles a day which it must be said is a very relaxed rate; a comfortable stroll if ever there was one. We'd stayed at 28 caravan sites. This was safe and simple adventuring.

Hamish Brown, in his 1981 '*Groat's End*' book wrote, wishing that he had had more time to walk the route in the fashion of what he called, '*a slacker wanderer*', ensuring he would see far more. '*If only we could buy the hours in which others are bored*'. I was that 'slack wanderer'. We couldn't get wetter than we already were when after a while, we moved towards the famous sign post pointing to, amongst other places, Land's End.

The photographer was ensconced in his little hut and at first refused to come out in the rain to take our photograph. "Come back later when the rain has stopped", he said. My pleasant relaxed warm feeling of satisfied accomplishment nearly left me as I explained to the 'prat' that I'd just walked from Land's End to John O'Groats and that a bit of rain wouldn't spoil the photograph; it would probably add to its character. He eventually agreed to take the shot and quickly put the pieces into place, spelling the sentence, 'Land's End, 946 miles in 84 days' and 'Bingley' as our home town.

As we were standing being photographed, a coach party made their way from the gift shop to the coach park bringing a bit of life to the otherwise dull place. A voice shouted, "Chris, Chris". I assumed this was someone from the coach party shouting to a friend and ignored it. The shouting grew louder. "Chris, Chris", and then I saw a friend of mine, John, with his wife Kath. They were walking towards us. "We are your brass band and flag-waving crowd", he declared as he gave me a wet sloppy handshake and hug in the rain. "Come over to the bar and I'll buy you a drink".

Photographs completed we sloshed across the rain-sodden car park to the bar. Wet coats pulled off and drinks all round, John explained that he and Kath were celebrating their wedding anniversary and were staying at John O'Groat's other hotel, 'The Sea View', situated a mile inland up the road and they had been following our progress via text messages with me and others waiting for me to arrive. It was a lovely pleasant surprise. We sat around the bay window chatting and drinking.

Outside there was a white line painted on the tarmac by the bar entrance. (I'd crossed it to get into the bar) This was the official start or end line and before long a group of cyclists arrived to start their journey to Land's End. Photographs were taken and people waved as the four or five cyclists set off at speed in the rain.

The excitement over, we resumed our chat in the warm dry surroundings. I sent a text message to all the people who'd been following me by text up the country and immediately received back messages of congratulations including one that asked me to check with the barman for a letter addressed to me. I duly did so and the barman produced a letter addressed to Mr Christopher Binns, Land's End to John O'Groats walker, John O'Groats Hotel.

The barman said that he'd had the letter for weeks and was beginning to give up hope for me. He was used to cyclists completing the journey in three or four weeks, not months. The letter turned out to be a congratulations card from Bob and Joan, friends of mine from Bradford. Bob had walked LEJOG a few years ago, and had given me a lot of help and advice at the beginning of the year. We closed our afternoon celebrations and agreed to meet back up at the Sea View Hotel later that night for a celebratory meal.

Before leaving John O'Groats we did three things:

Signed the book behind the bar and I had my LEJOG certificate stamped, before reading pages after pages of entries from LEJOG cyclists and motorcyclists with just one or two from walkers.

Visited the gift shop and bought postcards to write to those people not on our circle of 'texter's' and purchased a miniature bottle of 'One for the Road Whisky'.

Visited the harbour office of the Orkney Ferry Company and bought day tickets to visit there tomorrow.

That evening we arrived at The Sea View Hotel where we again celebrated the achievement with our friends. Having completed my walk virtually alone, it could be taken as a contradiction to be here celebrating the achievement in a group. Other walkers write about the loneliness and wander off to celebrate their achievement with a packet of crisps and bottle of beer in a quiet corner of the pub. Not I. As the 'slacker wanderer', this was as fitting an end celebration as could be mustered and I really appreciated Dick, Val, John and Kath being there with us to celebrate in style.

I can't say enough about Kay and Ripley. I wouldn't have been able to do it without them; the best back-up team ever.

Celebrations over we huddled in the hotel porch to say our goodbyes. The wind had 'got-up', so we made our separate ways quickly. John and Kath were staying at the Sea View; Dick and Val made their way back to Castletown and we made our way back to Dunnet Bay Caravan Site. The wind nearly blew our little car away as we drove back along the quiet lanes. The famous Caithness wind was blowing its strongest tonight, continuous gusts of up to 90 mph and more. We scrambled for safety into the motor home, holding onto the door for fear of it being ripped out of its sockets. The caravans pitched higher up the site looked extremely vulnerable.

Our motor home rippled, rocked and groaned in the wind; a wind that was trying to bully its way inside our shelter as they say.

Visiting Orkney tomorrow seemed a bad idea as we tried to settle down for the night; sleep was impossible. The windy night we'd previously experienced at Aust on the Severn estuary appeared calm compared to tonight's buffeting battle. We expected to be either blown over and away or the roof ripped off at any minute. After about an hour a loud knocking noise could be heard on the side of the van. At first I thought we were being struck by a tree branch before realising it couldn't be a branch as trees cannot survive up here in these winds and none were nearby in any case.

The knocking continued for some time, appearing to become more desperate; if a knock could sound desperate these were desperate knocks. I eventually decided enough was enough and I would investigate. I climbed out of the warmth and comfort of my bed and peered out of the window into the pitch blackness of the night. I couldn't see anything yet the knocking continued. I switched the outside light on but still nothing was obvious. Holding on for grim death I opened the motor home door. Bizarrely Dick and Val, both dressed as Nanuk of the North, blew inside. I fought to close the door behind them. "Why, look what the wind has blown in", I said, thinking at the same time, 'it's a bit late for visiting'. They both looked as if hypothermia was beginning to set in and between gasps for air, Dick explained, "We are locked out of our hotel. When we got back all was in darkness and locked up. We can't raise them".

"Tough". I said, jokingly.

Kay swung into action making the spare double bed up, putting on the kettle and other assorted tasks. It felt like the middle of the night but turned out to be only 10.30pm. "You're welcome to stay here; we need the ballast", I wasn't joking about the ballast. "Don't forget we are up early to go to Orkney".

Dick and Val appeared to fall asleep as soon as their heads hit the pillow. I on the other hand, lay awake worrying that at any minute we'd all end up tipped out into the field. Morning came and Dick and Val were up, dressed and ready for the off well before us. They left without even so much as a cup of coffee and headed back to their hotel where we learnt later that on walking into the breakfast room they were greeted with a friendly, "Good morning. Did you sleep well" as though none of what they'd experienced had taken place.

We set off back to John O'Groats in miserable rain and wind. Finally reaching it yesterday, my initial impression was of a bleak scene. On my return, there this morning the feeling remained with me even more so. The car parks were empty and the souvenir shops were closed.

We made our way to the ferry ticket office where we were greeted by a friendly man who checked our tickets and directed us down to the harbour to the waiting ferry which was to take us to the Orkney Islands. The walk down a stone jetty lashed by rain and wind felt like 'walking the plank'. Safe on board the 'Pentland Venture' we made our way to the passenger seats deep in the bowels of the boat where we found thirty or forty other passengers already there waiting for the off.

The passenger lounge was clean and tidy but lacked any comforts. We were on hard plastic seats. Our fellow passengers looked foreign to me and I was surprised to find that most of them were Spanish tourists. An announcement over the ship's Tannoy told us that due to the weather, the crossing would be rough and we were advised to remain inside the passenger lounge during the crossing. The engines started and immediately the lounge filled with the smell and wispy smoke of engine oil. Kay had Ripley tucked inside her coat with just her head peeping out, attracted a lot of attention and both she and Ripley became instant celebrities with the dog-loving Spaniards who began taking photographs.

I left Kay and Ripley at the centre of attention and moved through the crowd to the doors onto the deck. At least here I could get a bit of fresh air. Looking out I saw groups of Spanish tourists taking photographs and getting wet by spray from the waves. Hadn't these people heard the warning announcement?

Although the crossing was rough, no one appeared in danger of being swept overboard and certainly none of the ferry crew seemed concerned that groups of passengers were ignoring their safety advice. I opened the door and went out on deck to join them but not venturing out as far as some of them, who were now having Titanic-style photographs taken at the bow of the boat. My attention was 'grabbed' by the rocks at the Old Man of Hoy that I could see over to my left. To my right I could see the two small islands of Stroma and Swona situated roughly in the middle of the Pentland Firth, a stretch of water that links the Atlantic Ocean with the North Sea.

Our boat bobbed about in the waves as it battled its way across to Orkney. Here the Pentland Firth is subject to several strong tidal currents known locally as 'roosts'. They are renowned for being amongst the fastest tides anywhere in the world, reaching speeds of up to 16 knots. These 'roosts' have individual names depending on their exact location; names such as the Merry Men of Mey and the Boars of Duncansby. The Swelkie which is a famously strong whirlpool is a Norse Viking name meaning 'the swallower'.

We were being buffeted by the wind, waves and rain but at least I felt better up on deck than inside the hold with those engine fumes. I reassured myself with the fact that our captain had probably made this journey thousands of times and was aware

243

of the tidal races and whirlpools; aware enough to avoid them. Suddenly on deck, the crowds grew excited and rushed to the barriers. I cautiously moved across with them and was rewarded with a view of some dolphins 'porpoising' out to my right. They'd gone before I'd got chance to get a photograph.

I went back inside to inform Kay of what she had just missed, again. I found her still surrounded by the dog-loving photographing Spaniards. Eventually, after what was described as a 'choppy crossing' we arrived at Orkney; at Burwick on the Island of South Ronaldsay to be exact, which is exactly 10 miles north of John O'Groats. Burwick appeared to be little more than a concrete jetty with a hut or two and surrounded by barren moorland.

A coach was parked on the jetty and everyone filed off the boat and climbed aboard where we were welcomed to Orkney by our driver and guide for the day, a Londoner who had long ago relocated up here. In his welcome our driver-cum-guide told us we were 'ferry loupers'; what the Orkneyan's call 'off aimdens' and what we Yorkshire folk call 'off cumdens' or non-natives.

The Orkney Islands comprise over 70 islands of which 17 are inhabited by a population of around 21,000. The Greek Pytheas wrote about the Islands as early as 325 BC. We set off across the moor-like landscape and skirted around the natural landlocked harbour.

Scapa Flow has deep entrances where, one month into World War 2 the Germans, using a U-boat sank HMS Royal Oak with a loss of 833 crew; a massive blow to the British. During World War 2 the natural harbour was still being used as the main Royal Navy base for the British Home Fleet. To add protection to it Churchill 'negotiated' with Italian prisoners of war to build U-boat barriers across one of the entrances. The Prisoners of war agreed to this work, (which on the face of it went against the Geneva Convention) because, it was argued that the barriers would be beneficial to the islanders long after the war was over. Indeed, they are; we were using them as they linked lots of tiny islands together in a causeway.

We drove on looking out across the large, calm and now quiet harbour with just a few small boats bobbing about. It was here at the end of World War 1 that the German High Sea Fleet surrendered after sailing into the harbour with 74 ships. However, before the British could get their hands on the ships the German sailors opened the sea-cocks and sank them, scuppering the entire fleet onto the sea bed. Most of the wrecks were later salvaged but a sizable number, including 3 battleships, remain and have become a favoured haunt for scuba divers.

I wasn't at all surprised when our coach pulled up at a hamlet of cottages and picked up a passenger; a lady off shopping for the day. Further on we picked up more passengers and dropped off two young campers who were going to spend a fortnight here camping near a beach.

Our coach trundled along the quiet road, eventually arriving in the sunny picturesque seaside town of Stromness. Here we were allowed some free time. We walked around the excellent harbour with its many fishing boats. We were informed that the Canadian Hudson Bay Company, founded in the 17th century, had their British base here and that the company had recruited many of its early employees from here on Orkney, the sailing skills of the local islanders being much sought after.

Later we walked down the town's narrow pedestrian precinct; a winding flagstone paved street lined by neat, clean but grey buildings (every other one a shop, the others being residences, many being shore-side houses with their own piers). We found a pleasant cafe with tables and seating outside.

As we sat in the sun and watched the world go by, a lady with a Yorkshire terrier dog arrived and stopped to talk to Ripley. Amazingly, it turned out she was from Ripon in Yorkshire and had moved up here on retirement. Londoners may now get everywhere but they are closely followed by Yorkshire folk. I remembered the Yorkshire men I met on the Scilly Isles at the beginning of our Journey.

Having been independent travellers for so long I was impressed with how quickly we fell back easily into the tourist herd. We meekly followed when called back to the coach; our allotted time in Stromness was over and we were off to see some further delight of Orkney.

We drove to the cliff tops at Yesnaby where the wind nearly blew us away. The cliff tops were awash with flowers, sea thrift and birds foot trefoil being prominent. We had some excellent views of The Old Man of Hoy to our south and up the coast to the cliffs at Marwick Head where there is a memorial to Lord (Horatio) Herbert Kitchener, he of 'Your country needs you' WW1-poster-fame. Kitchener, together with all the crew of HMS Hampshire, died off the coast of Orkney in 1916 after their ship exploded upon hitting a German mine.

Kay, in her last letter home wrote: '*Yesnaby is the site of a fantastic coastal viewpoint; a battleground of earth, sea and sky where wind and waves have attacked the coastline since the end of the last Ice Age; 10,000 years ago; slowly scouring away sandstone, formed 400 million years ago, producing dramatic cliffs. The day was sparkling with white clouds racing across a pale blue sky but the wind was ferocious as we stood on the cliff top at Yesnaby Head. The sea was a beautiful Air Force blue and it was being whipped to a foaming frenzy below us. As usual Christopher nonchalantly strolled to the cliff edge to get spectacular views of the coastal drama ... I hate it when he does that. I am frightened of heights and just the thought of the vertical drop has my stomach somersaulting*'.

With fresh sea spray in our hair and faces, we gladly climbed back onto the coach and were off again, soon arriving at a sheltered bay, the home of the World Heritage site, Skara Brae, a perfectly preserved stone village dating from around 3,100 BC. It is Europe's best preserved Neolithic settlement, predating the pyramids of Egypt.

Judging by the number of coaches and cars in the car park we were not to have the place to ourselves. We joined the queue to get in. As we moved along we were taken back in time by a series of date stones showing important dates in history. All the big dates were there: WW2, WW1, Queen Victoria's Golden Jubilee, the American War of Independence and so on, heading back in time. We followed them back as the queue grew smaller. I know 1066, the date the Norman French invaded England doesn't mean much to the Scots let alone the Orkneyan's, but I'd have thought that date would have been set in stone but it was not and we jumped back to an obscure date of 967 AD when something unremarkable happened.

We eventually found ourselves in a large reconstruction of a stone house complete with roof which allowed us to feel what a house here would have been like. It felt like a large wigwam or tepee except in stone. In my opinion the reconstructed house was the best bit of Skara Brae, of which we were now given a guided tour along a series of paths and gantries. We looked down on the stone village which had been preserved under sand dunes and midden rubbish until a violent storm in 1850 had revealed them to modern man. The 'village' consists of at least six stone houses joined by a 'street'. They were well-constructed with drains, cupboards, worktops and beds, all of stone. The Fred Flintstone-type people who lived here were farmers and fishermen, evidenced by tools and equipment found on the site together with food remnants found in their rubbish piles.

Later the tour guide rounded us up with skill, showing he'd done this lots of times before, walking us across a short windy moor to a rather Spartan-looking mansion house that stood nearby. It turned out that Skaill House, a 17th-century mansion with its walled gardens, was a little oasis in its otherwise bleak surroundings.

Ripley, who had been allowed in Skara Brae wasn't welcome at the house so Kay went for a walk with her around the gardens whilst I toured inside. The house was said to be typical of many in Scotland, set out in the style of a 17th-century laird. It had been the home of Sir Joseph Banks, the famous naturalist and companion of Captain Cook. The house contains the complete dinner service of Captain Cook's ship, HMS Resolution. I was a little surprised to find a piece of Yorkshireman Captain Cook history up here. That wasn't thanks to Sir Joseph Banks but to Captain King who, after Captain Cook was murdered near Hawaii, successfully brought his little fleet of ships home, watering in the harbour at Stromness.

Our coach driver-cum-guide appeared and was soon back at it, rounding us up like a shepherd herd's sheep. As we drove to our next destination he expertly told us that evidence of our early ancestors had been found nearby in the form of a charred hazelnut, showing evidence of cooking by our Mesolithic nomadic tribes from 6820 -6660 BC. He also told us that we were still within the World Heritage Site as we pulled into the coach park at the massive stone circle known as The Ring of Brodgar. We joined the crowds of others who were scurrying about the windy hillside like ants. The Neolithic stone circle, dating from about the same time as Skara Brae, was huge, covering at least three football pitches in size and surrounded in glorious purple heather. It forms a perfect circle surrounded by a rock cut ditch. Of the original 60 stone monoliths, 27 remain. Many have sharp angular faces and are up to 12 feet tall, looking like huge broken teeth. We stood in awe at the construction of it, as impressive at least, as its more famous similar structure, Stone Henge, though a lot less well-known.

It frustrates me that 'we', 'modern man', can only conjecture as to why and for what purpose these circles were built. My favourite theory is linked to the annual cycle of seasons and night skies, it being something our ancient ancestors, without our modern-day distractions, probably spent a lot of time studying.

As we approached Kirkwall, the capital of the Orkney's, we passed the Highland Park Distillery, the most northerly distillery in Scotland hence in the United Kingdom. It was founded in 1798 and is advertised as *'the best spirit in the world'*, and *'Orkney Gold'*. This triggered our coach driver into action and we soon learnt about the Orkney Wine Company the United Kingdom's most northerly winery, the Orkney Brewery and Orkney Farmhouse Cheese, all local products that have a large following. I was hoping that we weren't going to have an exam about all these things as we disembarked from the coach in Kirkwall by its massive, St. Magnus Cathedral. "Don't forget to visit the St. Magnus Centre, with its free film show before you do anything else", barked the coach driver.

Too late. Most people were walking downhill into the large square in front of the cathedral. We were the only ones to follow his advice and went into the centre, a cross between a church hall and a community centre with a small cafe and cinema. We were the only visitors at that time but the two ladies behind the reception (that doubled as cafe), positively shuddered when they saw Ripley. "Dogs are not allowed in", they both said in unison. So, we left without seeing the free film that was to explain who St. Magnus was and why he had a cathedral built in his name.

We crossed the road and had a look around the ruins of the Bishop's Palace.

With a population of just 7,000, the city and Royal Burgh of Kirkwall is little more than a village; anywhere else wouldn't warrant a cathedral church of such magnificent size. The cathedral, which dominates the town, is built in the Norman, early Gothic style with alternating bands of red and yellow sandstone. It was founded in 1137 by Earl Rognvald-Kali, nephew to the martyred Earl Magnus. When opened, it was part of the Norwegian arch-diocese of Trondheim, (Orkney remained part of Norway until 1468). When sold to Scotland, the cathedral was given to the care of the people. The last bishop left in 1688 and whilst now it retains the name 'cathedral', it technically isn't one.

Kay waited outside in the sunshine whilst I went to explore the cathedral. Even though I followed crowds of people around the church, it managed to retain a peaceful ambience. Its high windows and red stonework left me with a disappointing impression of a building with a dark interior and this on a sunny day. It must be hard for such a small population to maintain such a big church. I went back outside into the sunshine and fresh air and looked after Ripley whilst Kay went inside.

When Kay re-joined us, we went for a walk down some of the narrow streets of the town. Here at New Year, an ancient traditional, football game is played called the 'Ba', which is a cross between rugby and football and involves trying to get the 'ba' into one of two goals at the opposite ends of the street. Health and safety rules have set in and now they have a boys' game in the morning and a men's game in the afternoon. The crowds join in. The streets were predominantly residential with the odd shop, sometimes a large one, dotted amongst the houses. The narrow streets led to the harbour which today was very quiet.

Back at the cathedral square we found it bedecked with the Orkney flag, a blue and yellow cross on a red background. It is a beautiful flag, very like the Norwegian flag and is a constant reminder that the Orkney's were once part of Norway. After looking around some more shops we decided to find a cafe; the few we saw all declared 'No Dogs allowed'. Then we spotted a cafe which was packed full of diners but more importantly, allowed dogs in so we squeezed in on a small table and enjoyed a light lunch served by friendly staff.

Back in the sunny square we congregated with our fellow coach travellers; our allotted two hours in Kirkwall were nearly up. On the coach as we headed away from Kirkwall, our driver-guide was asking whether we'd managed to see the famous Kirkwall scroll which is a carpet tapestry and tells the story of how Norsemen from the Orkney's back in 1066, discovered America long before Christopher Columbus. Apparently, it shows the route they took from here to Iceland then on to Greenland and on to what we now know to be Canada.

Most of us on the coach said, "No, we haven't seen it".

It wasn't on display in the cathedral but was tucked away in the Masonic Hall which we hadn't found either. "Did you also know", our coachman went on, "that those same Orkney Norsemen joined the Viking Army and, with their Orkney princes, Paul and Erland, fought against Harold at the Battle of Stamford Bridge in Yorkshire in 1066". 'Ah', I thought. 'The Norsemen lost that battle so perhaps that's why it is not mentioned on the date stones at Skara Brae'.

The coach rumbled on until we arrived back at Scapa Flow and the Churchill Barriers. Here we stopped at what was to be our last stop of the day on the tiny island of Lambholm. The Italian chapel here, left behind by the Italian prisoners of war who'd built the Churchill Barriers, has been described as 'the miracle of camp 60'.

The rest of their POW camp had been cleared away after the war but the two Nissen huts that formed the camp's chapel were left behind as a kind of war memorial. Outside the chapel, we saw a large sculpture of St George and the Dragon which had been made using left over barbed wire and cement. Amongst the numbers of Italian prisoners, were a group of skilled craftsmen; painters, artists, sculptors, blacksmiths and builders who were led by the skilled Domenico Chiocchetti, who had earlier sculpted the statue of St George and the Dragon.

The prisoners set about building themselves a chapel from two Nissen huts placed end to end. The result is a beautifully decorated chapel with a large painting of the Madonna and Child behind the altar and a superb vaulted ceiling which looked like a perfect carved marble ceiling instead of being a mural. Metal candelabra, rood-screen and gates and a belfry on top, finish off the beautiful chapel. It remains a reminder of what once was here. The Orkneyan's are rightly proud of their little Italian chapel and have since made numerous contacts with the original prisoners; Chiocchetti, himself, returned in 1960, to complete renovation work.

Since then others have returned and now their relatives carry on this tradition to keep alive this symbol of peace and hope. It was a fitting end to our day on the Orkney's.

We'd barely scratched the surface of these islands. The tour literature reminded us that no visit to Orkney is complete without discovering and exploring the northern smaller islands. Well we didn't get there. We hadn't seen Papa Sound where the shortest scheduled flight in the world takes place, taking just two minutes to cross between Westray and Papa Westray.

We'd only been here for one day, yet I collected more information pamphlets and leaflets than anywhere else on our journey. Like the Scilly Isles at the beginning of our journey, we could say that we'd been there, seen them and we'd like to come back and see some more of them.

Sunny and fair

Sept Saturday 1

Today we would pack up at Dunnet Bay and make our way south for Dingwall. As we set about breaking camp I broke a key, the main key in the motor home door. I consulted the camp warden who informed me that a locksmith could be found in Thurso. I ended up taking the whole lock out of the door with the broken key still in it and headed for Thurso whilst Kay was left behind with Ripley 'guarding camp'. The warden gave us his permission to leave the site later than the 12-noon time that was expected.

I followed the warden's instructions and drove through Thurso, mainland Britain's most northerly town, where I found the locksmith at the far end of the town. The premise was a small hut and like most locksmiths, he doubled as a cobbler and was busy with shoe repairs. "Leave it with me. I'll have a fiddle with it and see what I can do. Will next Wednesday be all right?" he said.

"No", I replied, "we are leaving today and please, I need it doing straight away". The old man looked at me and said, "Okay, you will have to wait. I'll see what I can do".

Two hours later he had removed the broken key from the lock and made me a replacement key with a couple of spares just in case. I thanked him profusely and made my way back to Dunnet Bay where Kay and Ripley were all ready for the off. They had spent the morning walking on the beach, a beach that Kay reported as being one of the best she had seen. In her letter home, she wrote: *'Dunnet Bay was glorious; the weather was beautiful; blue skies and even bluer seas with foaming white waves*

249

that crashed onto the miles of beautiful, pale golden sands, all of which are framed in a half-moon bay with towering headlands at their furthest points . . . Ripley, who doesn't usually like beaches, took to this beach with absolute delight, tail up and her body almost quivering with excitement. Ripley loves the smell of fish... especially rotting fish! If she can find a spot where a fisherman has laid his catch she will roll on the spot in absolute ecstasy. This beach seemed to be the point where all the flotsam and jetsam of the Pentland Firth is washed up, including the biggest prize of all – a dead seal! Instead of dragging Ripley onto the beach, I had to drag her off'.

Heading back along the road to John O'Groats, we hadn't been travelling long when we came to the late Queen Mother's residence, Castle Mey. I turned into the grounds following the road around until by the garden walls I found a large enough parking space. The wall was also providing excellent shade and we were comfortable leaving Ripley in the car whilst we went inside to explore the most northerly castle on the UK mainland, built in the 16th century by George Sinclair, the 4th Earl of Caithness. The castle remained in the Sinclair family until the line died out. In a state of disrepair, it was bought in 1952 by the then recently widowed Queen Mother, as a Scottish summer home.

Once renovated she visited it every summer for the rest of her life. Since her death in 2002, Prince Charles has continued the tradition by spending a week here in August. It is said to be, *'a royal residence which never feels in any way grand or intimidating'*. I'd agree with that description. The main rooms, living rooms, dining rooms and bedrooms, all gave the impression of a little old lady's home, which I suppose it was.

We had what I would describe as a pleasant look around, including the 1950's 'state of the art' kitchen, still preserved as such, it even had a fridge! We went outside to look at the walled garden where, on the other side, we hoped Ripley and our motor home were waiting for us. The garden was laid out in a traditional Scottish kitchen garden design with a greenhouse containing a magnificent floral display. Roses, shrubs and climbers complimented the scene which all in all, considering the bleak, rugged emptiness of Caithness just the other side of the wall, was a testament to hard work and vision. The garden was breathtakingly beautiful. No wonder it was said to be one of the Queen Mother's favourite places.

We tore ourselves away and reunited with Ripley we were soon off again, heading for John O'Groats. I'd barely got out of second gear when I stopped again, this time to have a look around Canisbay Kirk, a bleak white-washed building, the most northerly place of worship on the Scottish mainland which just a few days earlier I'd walked past without looking in. The Queen Mother made this her place of regular worship during her summers up here. As well as her royal pew, the church contains the huge engraved tombstone just inside the vestibule, of Dutchman John de Groot.

In the 16th century he had been granted a licence to operate a ferry between the mainland and the Orkney Islands. He died on the 13th April 1568. A mound and a flagpole at John O'Groats are all that remain of his famous octagonal house, built between 1488 and 1513. The Groat family continued to run the ferry service for over 200 years and it is believed descendants of theirs are still involved in the ferry service today. There was something else I had to do before leaving the area. John O'Groats is not the most north-easterly point on mainland Britain; Duncansby Stacks lay claim to this; they lie just a mile or so away from John O'Groats.

There are two routes to Duncansby; one follows the coastline and is indicated by Caithness flagstones. This route touches one or two beaches where the famous 'Groatie buckies', small cowrie shells (once used as currency) can be found. The other, more direct route is over land on a roller coaster tarmac lane. We parked our motor home and car in a large lay-by and set off overland for Duncansby, soon arriving at the coastguard station and fog horn situated on the actual north-eastern tip. It was all fenced off with barbed wire so even if I'd wanted to touch the actual north-eastern tip I wouldn't have been allowed to do so.

We turned away from the station and walked south on a short grass path towards the Duncansby Stacks. Ripley was enjoying this walk. The sea was well below us, hidden from view. In the bracing sea air we walked on, not knowing what to look at first. Our goal was the sea stacks but all around us we were presented with fabulous views of sea birds and their antics. Out to sea we saw gannets diving into the water; shags, fulmars and kittiwakes were everywhere along with beautiful puffins.

To reach the stacks we walked around the edges of two spectacular narrow inlets with sheer perpendicular sides, just being able to see the water crashing into the rocks below. And then we arrived at the sea stacks, just offshore from the high red sandstone cliffs. All around were caves, natural arches and bridges, complementing the tall pyramid shaped, sharp pointed sea stacks. Andrew McCloy, in his 2002 LEJOG book, described them as, *'rising like sharks' teeth from the sea'.*

We had the place to ourselves, surrounded by natural beauty and the power of the sea. We took in as much as we could before walking back to the motor home. Kay's attention now being firmly fixed on the wild flowers that grew here in abundance; thrift, primroses, red campion and devil's bit scabious; some now perhaps past their best but they were here in masses.

We drove south back through Caithness, down through the hairpin bends of Berriedale, down the steep Ord of Caithness, through Sutherland and Ross and back to the camp-site at Dingwall where we again set up camp. We then drove to Beauly to enjoy another celebratory meal with our friends David and Isabel who own a pine lodge cabin here in Strath Glass.

David was waiting for us on Beauly Main Street. We followed him up and along narrow country lanes until we eventually arrived at the lodge which was situated half way up a wooded hillside. It was dark by the time we got there so we missed out on the stunning views across the valley and hills of the beautiful Strath Glass. We did see a fantastic night sky ablaze with stars, made even more dramatic due to lack of light pollution. I could have just stayed outside looking at the stars but that would have been bad manners and the midges were biting! Inside the lodge, we discovered a warm, deceptively large and very comfortable home where we spent the next few hours relaxing in good company enjoying a lovely meal with our friends.

As expected the drive home was to be a big anti-climax. Before setting off I'd telephoned our travel agent and planned for us to fly up to Shetland and stay for a week, I was determined to travel the full length of the country. I appreciated that we could travel by ferry with our motor home and stay on the one or two caravan sites that they have in Shetland but decided against it, favouring a week in a Bed & Breakfast instead. In the meantime, we had to get the motor home and Ripley (she wasn't coming to Shetland with us), home.

Sept
Saturday
22
We'd had a few days at home where we spent time reclaiming our small garden from the jungle it had become. Today we set off on the last leg of our journey to the Shetland Isles and to the most northerly point of the British Isles, our end goal, Muckle Flugga. We were both disappointed that Ripley wouldn't be coming with us but in the time we'd given ourselves it just wasn't practical so she went to stay with Kay's parents, Kevin and Margaret and their dog Jesse.

We flew from a packed and manic Leeds Bradford Airport into an almost deserted, calm and serene Aberdeen Airport. Unfortunately, there was no immediate connecting flight to the Shetland's until early the following morning so we had to settle for a night at one of the airport hotels which can be best described as a 1970's motel for oil rig workers. At least it was fairly clean and friendly.

Having settled into our room we left for a walk into the town of Dyce. This was not quite as easy as it sounds. The roads around the airport were built for cars not pedestrians. However, after crossing a few busy roundabouts we arrived at what we took to be Dyce Main Street where we found a Chinese Restaurant. It was busy with a buffet-style service and we joined the queues of happy eaters for what turned out to be a reasonable Chinese meal.

Sept
Sunday
23
Dry and sunny

We were up very early, skipping the hotel breakfast and heading straight for the airport where we had an excellent breakfast. Kay, in her last letter home, captured what happened succinctly: *'There were only eleven passengers for our flight and we were all herded into a dim and narrow corridor where we sat making small talk as we looked at a windowless wall waiting to board. We were saved from desultory conversations and awkward silences when our attention was dragged from the wall by cheerful whistling which was travelling towards us from some distant point along the corridor. A door opened and the Captain of our flight strolled through smiling, his flight cap pushed to the back of his head and swinging his briefcase. He winked and greeted us cheerfully. With upper class enunciation, he said, "Not long now chaps. I'll just go wind the elastic band. Toodle pip"'.* His good humour seemed to light up the corridor leaving us all smiling.

The aeroplane, a British Airways 35-seater Saab was very intimate and our happy and eccentric pilot kept us entertained through the pre-flight introductions. When he introduced his co-pilot, he said his name sounded like a complicated stomach ache and that was because he was Swedish.

We made good time to mainland Shetland with an 85-mph tail wind, arriving 30 minutes before the airport had opened. Our pilot cheerfully announced that rather than circling the airport, we would go off on a jaunt to explore the nearby island of Foula. The weather was clear and sunny with beautiful blue skies dotted with fluffy white clouds. We descended through the clouds into bone-jarring turbulence and flew low over the island to reach the far side. Foula means 'Bird Island' in Old Norse.

We followed the line of the Sneug which is a steep hill rising to 1,371 feet before it drops into the sea at the Kame; a spectacular, wind-buffeted sea cliff with a sheer drop 1,200 feet into the foaming water of the Atlantic. The plane banked around the end of the island giving us all fantastic views of these majestic cliffs ----WOW! Even the captain was impressed. He stated that in twenty years of flying this route it was the first time he had managed to see the cliffs; and said that we had all now joined a very small select group of people who had actually seen them.

At the airport at Sumburgh in the very south of the main island, we saw the modern, award-winning terminal building, built in 1979, which resembled a white cardboard shoe box and did nothing for me. It certainly stood out in its surroundings. Here we collected our hire car and set off to explore.

First stop was nearby Sumburgh Head Lighthouse run by the Northern Lighthouse Board. It was built in 1821 by Robert Stevenson, the grandfather of author R. L. Stevenson. Its 56-foot tower stands with a few lighthouse buildings atop some magnificent cliffs. We were at the southernmost tip of the Shetlands which shares the space with an RSPB nature reserve. We were the only ones there apart from the 10,000 sea birds that were all around us; guillemots, razorbills, kittiwakes and shags. My favourite sea bird is the gannet; its spectacular plunge dive into the water is always a delight to see. Blue seas, huge waves crashing against the rocks below, fabulous cliffs and green hills really completed a beautiful, if a little windy scene.

The cliff tops around Sumburgh Head were protected by a solid stone wall that gave us good protection and allowed us to admire the views in a degree of comfort. This is also one of the best places in the British Isles for seeing humpback, minke and killer whales and common harbour porpoises; but not today. We didn't even see any seals! We were later informed that July and August are the best whale-watching months.

The sight of Shetland ponies grazing in nearby fields was icing on the cake as we stopped to admire them. They have short legs, a short back, small ears, a thick neck and a large head. They thrive on a poor diet and can cope with severe weather. They have been used as pack animals all over the world and trading in ponies boomed after the 1847 Mines Act banned children from working in mines.

We left Sumburgh Head and drove north on the road that skirts around the airport runway. As our road nearly completed the journey around the airport we came to Old Scatness Broch with its visitor centre. The Broch and Iron Age village were rediscovered in 1975 when the new airport was being constructed. Since 1995, a team of archaeologists from Bradford University have been painstakingly revealing the wonderfully preserved site. From the highest point in the village it all looked rather complicated and confused.

As well as the Broch, the site contained stone houses, both square and circle paths, staircases and such. As the site had been inhabited continuously for over 2000 years from the Picts to the Vikings right up to recently modern times, the jumbled and confusing site was explained by 'actors' from the Living History group who were in attendance. A stone slab with a carved picture of a bear was my favourite 'find'. We entered a replica stone wheel house and sat around the peat fire in the middle of the room. There we were entertained by Elizabeth who passionately told us stories and 'relived' the lifestyle of the hut dwellers. She certainly knew her stuff. It was windy outside but we were warm and comfortable inside, if not a little too smoky.

As we moved on, I thought that had this site been anywhere else in Britain we'd have had to queue to get in. Here we were the only visitors. The archaeologists use a converted croft as their residence when they are here during the summer. This croft was once the home of Betty Mouat who became famous in 1886. She left home in the fishing smack, The Columbine to sell her knitwear at Lerwick. Enroute in bad weather, the skipper fell overboard. The two-remaining crew launched a boat to save him leaving Betty alone in the fishing smack which caught the wind and sailed away. Nine days later she was rescued on the Norwegian coast.

We headed north driving through South Mainland, (or as known by the old name Zetland), on a well-maintained road through miles of productive agricultural land, before driving into Lerwick, pronounced 'Lerrick'.

Big 'ships' in the harbour dominated the town and took some of our attention as we searched for our 'bed & breakfast' which we found in the centre of town. The owners were out and we found a note on the unlocked door 'welcoming' us to our base for the week. We let ourselves in and were soon settled in a basic but clean attic room. After a quick wash and brush-up, we were off to explore the town. Lerwick, Nordic for Muddy Bay, started life as an unofficial market place for the 17th-century Dutch herring fleets. Now it is a thriving and busy port with yachts and cruise liners crowding the waterfront alongside the more traditional working fishing boats. Lerwick describes itself as 'Britain's top port'. At the heart of the town is its traditional shopping street and market cross which is incongruously overlooked by huge yachts and cruise liners appearing to be parked in the town itself.

23,000 people live on the Shetland's; a group of one hundred islands, ninety miles long, thirteen of which are inhabited, 8,000 people live in Lerwick. The streets are stone-flagged and flanked by tall granite buildings. We found them quite charming as we wandered through narrow and intimate closes. It seemed very Victorian until, as Kay was to write: *'Suddenly and quite unexpectedly, we stumbled upon a huge, horrible, concrete block which sprang up from the middle of a lovely stone square, towering high above the beautiful traditional buildings. We were staggered as to who could have got planning permission for such an ugly monstrosity in such a lovely street. A large sign on the building told us, unsurprisingly, it was the local council'*.

In many ways, it reminded me of that other 1970's ugly concrete mess on the banks of the river in Inverness. Writing in the 1870's the Naylor Brothers wrote about Lerwick in their book, *'From John O'Groats to Land's End'*, having travelled by ship to Lerwick, (making what was then the normal route to John O'Groats), *'...the houses in Lerwick had been built in all sorts of positions without any attempt at uniformity and the rough flagged passage which did duty for the 'main street' was to our mind the greatest curiosity of all and almost worth going all the way to Shetland to see. It was curved and angled in such an abrupt and zigzag manner that it gave us the impression that the houses had been built first and the street, where practicable, filled in afterwards'*.

Today these 'Lons and Klosses' as they are known, would appear to make good affordable housing accommodation. Yet Lerwick, like most towns in Scotland, is dominated by the ever-present grey pebble-dashed housing estates that the masses seem to prefer. In my mind these estates are a blot on the town, indeed a blot on Scotland.

Just before we left the market square I noticed a public clock and barometer which appeared to be positioned on top of the old market cross. Neither clock nor barometer appeared to be working. The clock maker was declared as Potts of Leeds, a firm I know is still going strong, maintaining and repairing church clocks in Yorkshire. I hope one day they'll be called back to fix this clock up here. By the clock, we found a *'Welcome to the Shetland Isles'* sign, presumably for the cruise ship tourists and we dutifully had our photograph taken by it.

Lerwick is also known for its lodberries, houses with a place where boats could be brought alongside to load or unload. All this sightseeing was making us hungry and we adjourned to the Grand Hotel where we ate a meal in the bar. We were served by an Australian barman who had found his way here whilst seeking hotel work in Britain during his 'walk about'. We were his only customers and the Grand dining room lay empty, ready for some other occasion. The Australian paid us respectful attention in between watching a rugby match on a small TV set he had with him behind the bar.

Sept

Monday

24

Rain but brighter later with blue skies

At breakfast, we met our hosts for the first time. They were a young couple with small children. The landlady served us before explaining that she was "off on the school run and would be back soon".

We walked back into the town centre, ducking into the now-open shops to dodge the heavy rain. In the bookshop, I bought the local newspaper, *'The Shetland Times'*. We visited the small Tourist Information office and then moved on, passing Britain's most northerly barber shop.

We climbed up a steep cobbled street to reach the well-maintained walls of Fort Charlotte. We found a five-sided artillery fort with bastions on each corner with cannons pointing out to sea and a large, lawned area with a flag on a pole at its centre. We had seen the distinctive Shetland flag which is a white cross on a blue background, flying everywhere we had been on Shetland. The fort saw action in all three Anglo-Dutch Wars between 1652 and 1673. It was the French who caused most damage to the Dutch herring fleet when they attacked it at Lerwick during the Napoleonic Wars. Today the fort is well-kept, some of its buildings still having a military use as the base for the local Territorial Army Unit.

Our walk led us to the northern part of town to the old Hay's harbour and to the modern well-designed Shetland Archive and Museum. From the outside, parts of this building resemble the sails of a yacht. It is a striking modern building that blends in as it stands out at the same time and should be award-winning. I believe the architects and designers have 'got it together' since those awful buildings of the 1960's and 1970's.

The museum has a three-storey Boat Hall, a theatre and a cafe/restaurant that looks out across the harbour. The museum houses thousands of objects and archives. We spent a leisurely morning mooching around the museum. Amongst many things, the famous Shetland knitwear story was told. All around, loudspeakers allowed you to listen to the recorded stories of and by local people. Outside, along the harbour which housed more historical crafts, serpentine rocks polished into 'receivers' were playing a selection of the recordings from the stories and music told and performed by Shetlanders. These speakers were on all the time and later, when we visited at night they were still playing creating an 'other time' atmosphere in the otherwise quiet harbour. The serpentine rocks created a link with the beginning of my journey down at Lizard Point in Cornwall being the only other area in the British Isles where these rocks can be found.

After a good look around, we made our way to the museum cafe and picked a window seat. We ate lunch watching the antics of a rare bird, a grey phalarope, a scarce migrant that only appears in small numbers in the extremities of the British Isles. We were enthralled by it whilst it swam and dived in the crystal-clear waters of the harbour. Our meal was delicious and the waitress assured us that the restaurant opened on an evening with a more extensive menu.

The Shetland Museum and Archive is an excellent local museum, one of the best we'd seen and we thoroughly enjoyed it. After lunch, we drove six miles to the west of Lerwick to visit the pretty village of Scalloway, once Shetland's ancient capital, when Earl Patrick Stewart built Scalloway castle and moved the court here from Tingwall. Now a ruined castle, it still dominates the harbour.

We parked up by the quayside and looked across a very busy harbour. It was raining heavily. My attention was drawn to a memorial and I walked over to get a closer look. The memorial was built of metal and was of a fishing boat rising in a wave-tossed sea. It was set on top of a stone-built drum. It was a beautiful monument designed by a Mr D. Cooper and completed in 2003. A plaque declared that it remembered those (mainly Norwegian and Shetlanders) who, during WW2, used this harbour as a base for the 'Shetland Bus', the supply chain that kept the Norwegian Resistance Movement in supplies. Several 'Shetland Bus' stories deserve retelling.

In 1942, in the Norwegian fishing village of Telavag, a German Gestapo officer was killed by two 'Shetland Bus' agents; Norwegian resistance officers, trained in Scotland with the commando's. The Germans retaliated by killing all thirty-one male villagers, placing all the others in a concentration camp, before finally raising the village to the ground. Leif Larsen, or 'Shetland Larsen' as he was known, made over fifty trips across to his native Norway as skipper of a fishing boat. In March 1943, his boat was shot at by German planes. Six of the eight-man crew died; Larsen was saved and continued his hazardous trips, gaining the Distinguished Service Order and becoming the most highly decorated naval officer of WW2 and at the time, no other man, British or foreign, had ever received more military honours than he had gained. The little monument at Scalloway is a poignant memorial.

As we drove out of Scalloway we saw a huge warehouse-type building; the North Atlantic Fisheries College where the young men of Shetland learn all they need to know about fishing the high seas. Years ago, they learnt these skills from their fathers but today knowledge is both passed down from father to son and from academics at the college. Attached to the college is a seafood restaurant, The Da Haaf which specialises in Shetland's seafood including halibut, lemon sole, turbot, plaice, salmon and trout. Not being a lover of Seafood I was thankful it appeared to be closed; some other day perhaps.

We moved on and drove up the narrow inland loch valley to Tingwall and saw the little island field which is joined to the mainland by a causeway where Shetland's old parliament used to be held. Today the site is nothing more than a field; the buildings were demolished in the 18th century.

A small flock of whooper swans glided easily across the lonely water. It was here that the Norse-derived legal system known as Udal Law was practised. It is totally different from Scottish law which abolished feudal law and thought it had abolished Udal law but it hadn't; it is still preserved here today, land being passed down to the eldest son with no written record necessary other than perhaps proof of the father/son relationship.

Around the 60° latitude line which is marked on the road, were Alaska and Canada that way and Siberia and Northern Scandinavia the other. It was cold and windy; it's nearly always ten degrees cooler up here than on mainland Britain. We drove down to Sandwick and looked out to the small island of Mousa with its famous broch dominating the scene. The broch which is well preserved was already 1,000 years old in Viking times; it is now home to thousands of storm petrels. It is described as 'a hard place to get to' and today we couldn't find a boat going out there so had to rely on just our long-distance sighting.

We then moved down the coast to Hoswick, a small village of half traditional stone crofts and half portakabin-style huts. One of these ugly huts, which were shabby, smelt of damp and turned out to be a shop selling Shetland jumpers and knitwear. It was open and signs and photographs indicated that the Queen had shopped here on one of her visits to the Shetland's. What was good enough for the Queen must surely be good enough for us and I bought some jumpers of excellent quality with Kay buying some gloves with matching scarf.

Crossing the island to St Ninian's bay and Isle, we saw a beautiful sandy bay with the Isle joined to the mainland by an 'ayre'; a crescent-shaped ribbon of golden sand forming a narrow causeway which separated St Ninian's bay on one side and Bigton bay on the other; it was spectacular, with a glorious sky of blue with white clouds, reminiscent to us of our time in the Scilly Isles. We parked up and walked across the 'ayre' following someone else's footprints in the sand. I felt a bit like Robinson Crusoe as no one else was to be seen and we had the place to ourselves. Kay wrapped herself up in her new scarf and gloves as the wind chased us across the exposed 'ayre'.

On the Bigton bay side of the barrier, energetic waves crashed against the sandy beach whilst on the Ninian bay side, the deep blue sea was 'lake calm' and still. Strong gusts of wind made the walk across exhilarating and we arrived on the island having had any cobwebs blown away. On the green windswept island, not far from the beach, we came to the ancient ruined chapel of St Ninian, now a protected ancient building. Here in 1958, a young boy found the remains of a larch box containing twenty-eight pieces of Pictish silver, probably a family collection hidden in the church in time of danger. The treasure is now held at the Royal Museum in Edinburgh, much to the chagrin of some locals who feel that the treasure should be rehoused in their beautiful new museum - I agree.

Heading back across the 'ayre' we saw the wind at work, sculpting the sand into valleys and peaks with pebbles perched on little towers with the wind winnowing away their support. We enjoyed this walk. We'd parked the car near to a hamlet that goes by the name of Ireland; 'hmm, that's part of the British Isles I haven't walked across yet'.

A further exploration of the main island led us to drive down the west-coast road. I'd hoped to visit the most photographed village in the Shetland's which shares its name with a similar much-photographed village on the Orkney's. The two villages go by the unpleasant name of Twat and people queue up to be photographed alongside the village sign.

In the Yorkshire Dales people do the same at the village of Crackpot. Indeed, I have a prophetic photograph of my younger brother standing under the Crackpot sign when he was about 8 years old. The Shetland and Orkney word, twat, is related to the English village name Thwaite. Unfortunately, we seemed to get lost down a long lane with Twat still some distance away on a lonely side road so we gave it a miss and continued south-west down the main road. As we drove along a straight piece of bleak moorland road a very strange thing occurred. Ahead of me I could see a set of traffic lights which were at red. I blinked to make sure I wasn't imaging them. I wasn't. There wasn't a crossroads and there wasn't any traffic. Yet here we were being held up by a set of traffic lights at red. These were definitely the most unusually placed traffic lights I have ever seen. Soon all became clear as a private jet flew in low over the road to land on the nearby Sullom Voe Oil Plant airfield.

The old RAF Scatsta airfield, now fully modernised for oil executives to fly in and visit Sullom Voe, was built in the 1970's. The oil terminal operated by BP is vast and handles all the oil from the Brest and Ninian pipeline systems. Oil production peaked in 1984 but even today the flow of oil is measured in millions of tons. Oil has brought a lot of money to the Shetland's. The sprawling white buildings and associated tanks and drums were a sign of human life in an otherwise bleak scene.

Sullom Voe saw action in WW2 when so it is said, the very first German bomb to land on British soil exploded here on the 13th November 1939 killing a rabbit! The wartime song 'Run Rabbit Run' became popular as a result. We drove on soon passing through the large village of Brae which had hotels and shops. One was called the Northern Lights Bar; the Shetland's are the best place in Britain to see this phenomenon but it wasn't to be for us.

Brae had a shanty-town-feel. It expanded rapidly after the oil finds – like a modern 'gold town' of the west. A lot of the buildings are of wood; built temporarily in the 1970's they have a shack-like appearance. The lights of Lerwick soon appeared on the horizon. We made our way to 'Osla's' in Lerwick, Shetland's only Italian restaurant where we enjoyed a very delicious meal.

Sept — *Rain*

Tuesday 25

It was raining heavily as we drove north across bleak, even harsh-looking peat moorland. I love moorland but these looked desolate and unloved. I know everywhere looks glum in the rain and shadowed by grey skies. At home, we joke that 'even Bradford looks good in the sun'. A closer look at the moors revealed them to be a riot of colour from gold, yellow and brown to pale greens, brown, red and rust.

Summer was over and autumn was here. Today it felt more like winter. We drove on and on across the moors, the odd flock of sheep being the only points of interest. As the rain eased the wind became stronger. The lochs were sheets of slate grey. Mists swirled on the tops of the hills. I was glad I was in the car and not walking. Perhaps if we had visited in spring we would have seen the romantic soft benign Shetland's which the brochures wax lyrical about.

At a large sea loch, we saw the first signs that day of human activity; salmon fishing. The waters were covered with nets and cages and a small fishing boat was patrolling the perimeter. We passed the Shetland Golf Course, the second most northerly golf Course in the British Isles, a very lonely and isolated golf course which was wrapped in the gloom of mist and lashed by rain. We didn't see the most northerly Golf course in Britain which is nearby on Whalsey Island a few miles out to the north-east. Soon we arrived at the small hamlet of Toft where a huge modern car ferry was waiting for us. We drove on, joining the few other passengers and then the ferry set off. These ferries were built in Gdansk, Poland and were very clean and comfortable. They were also excellent value at only £10 on the first ferry with the others free for the rest of the day.

The Island of Yell is the gateway to the North Isles and is the second largest of the Shetland Isles. It is allegedly the best place in Europe to see otters or Dratsies as they are known here. The brochures also state that, 'if lucky', you will see killer and pilot whales gambling alongside the ferry. We were not lucky. Yell was even bleaker and more inhospitable than the mainland; the moors were more yellow than green and the wind just ripped across the whole island. It is not surprising that trunks of trees and other debris from northern Canada are washed ashore here.

We drove up through Yell from Ulsta on a new two carriageway road. We were told that oil money has helped pay for the roads and ferries. At Whale Firth, the island is nearly split in two by sea lochs. Here in WWI, it being so remote German u-boats sheltered and took on board water, food and sheep, all under the noses of the locals. As well as new roads, oil money has helped provide Shetland with more swimming baths per head of population than anywhere else in Britain and we saw quite a few of them tucked away in the smallest of hamlets.

We pulled into a parking spot on the very quiet eastern side of Yell at Otterswick, for a walk along the coastline to a promontory. Here we were told we might see some otters. The path was waterlogged and muddy but eventually led us to The White Wife, a striking figure of a woman dressed in white apparently staring out to sea with a bible clasped to her bosom. The White Wife was the figurehead from a German barque, a great iron ship, The Bothus, which grounded on Yell and was dashed to pieces on the rocks in 1924. The figurehead came ashore and was erected within sight of where the ship foundered. Three of the thirty-nine people on board were killed. Most of the survivors owed their lives to the quick action of the people of East Yell.

Today we couldn't see where any locals lived; not around this cove which was isolated and quiet. We soon arrived at Gutcher, another small hamlet where we caught the next big ferry to Belmont on the island of Unst which is the most northerly populated island in the British Isles. It looked very like Yell. A modern road cuts across bleak featureless moorland. We drove up and on across this dreary landscape. The rain eased a little when eventually we arrived at Balta Sound; not a village you'd recognise as such but a collection of crofts scattered across a hillside. In one of the crofts we found Britain's most northerly post office. I braved the biting wind to go inside and send off some postcards.

The lady in the post office behaved as if she oversaw any post office anywhere else in Britain. She wasn't; she was in the most northerly post office in Britain! However, in her actions and words there was not one hint of the wonderful and unique location in which she was situated. It was as if I had just walked in to buy some stamps. I left feeling slightly uneasy. Here I was, at the top of Britain and nearing the end of my journey whilst all around me people were acting 'normal'; that's the way it is.

Back in the warm car we drove further north and soon arrived at an isolated yellow-coloured bus shelter. Inside were everyday items; a fridge, TV, computer, microwave, chairs, and curtains, all yellow in colour. We had arrived at Britain's most northerly bus shelter. I couldn't understand who used the shelter as it was surrounded by the ever-present bleak moorland.

Further on we arrived at Haroldswich Methodist Church, Britain's most northerly church, it was open and we went inside. It is a beautiful modern building which sits neatly amongst crofters' cottages. We said our prayers and signed the visitors' book and donated by putting some money in the collection safe.

The church, like most, was fund-raising to help defray the cost of the brand-new roof; the old one had been blown off by strong gusts of wind! With the winds, we were experiencing today this was very understandable. We drove on arriving at the hamlet of Skaw, Britain's most northerly inhabited house which has an upturned boat shed and is set in a little cove. We saw lots of these 'boat sheds' in the Shetland's. Skaw, sheltered from the wind, has a fabulous beach which we strolled across.

On driving further north we came upon the old RAF Saxavord Accommodation Estate where lo and behold, we saw not one but two other bus shelters, surely more northerly than the previously proclaimed one? At this stage, we didn't stop to look at the Accommodation Village which, since the actual base has been mothballed, has been turned into a hotel, (Britain's most northerly).

As the weather prohibited the use of a boat I had been told by a villager in Balta Sound that the best way to see Muckle Flugga at this time of year was to drive up the MOD road to the RAF base; no one was there as it is now disused (or to be correct, operated electronically from afar). "Don't worry about the 'No Trespassing' notice boards", he declared. The two servicemen who turn up from time to time to service things were not currently there; he should know, as when they do they stay with him.

We soon arrived at the gates and the 'No Trespassing' signs. Luckily, we opened the gates easily and drove up the rough cinder track road. As we crested the brow of the hill the wind hit us and we felt the car buffeted by it. We continued and the views opened in front of us. Looking down we could see the large bay or sea loch that is Burra Firth. Across the other side, we saw the huge moorland that is the Hermaness Nature Reserve which in summer is home to 100,000 birds. Up to our right, perched on top of rocks was a 'James Bond'-bunker-style complex of buildings, obviously military. Keeping going we expected at any minute, a helicopter to buzz overhead and to lower commando troops dressed in black, on ropes to halt our progress; if not that then at least the local bobby in his panda car. We were not interrupted. We drove on, our goal now in sight.

Out in front of us lashed by waves, we could see Muckle Flugga, the lighthouse at the top of Britain and out, even beyond that, the rock, Out Stack, the most northerly island and known as the 'full stop' of the British Isles. We moved as close as we could before the road veered inland and back on itself to head up to the bunker military buildings. Here we stopped and got out of the car. Roaring gusts of wind nearly blew me away. Kay initially refused to get out of the car but I wanted a photograph of Muckle Flugga. Clinging to the car she timidly got out, quickly and heroically took some photographs then climbed back in. The lighthouse, like most others, long since unmanned and remotely controlled, was built by Thomas Stevenson, the father of Robert Louis Stevenson who came here to see his father at work.

It is said that the map depicted in 'Treasure Island' closely resembles the outline of the island of Unst. I walked on a bit and looked over the edge down to the sea below. Then using my binoculars, I looked out to sea and searched for any signs of a boat or ship; nothing. I turned my attention upwards and looked at the sky for any signs of a plane or jet; nothing. I scoured the Hermaness mass for signs of human activity; nothing. I scoured Muckle Flugga for signs of human activity; nothing.

I scoured the rock of Out Stack; no sign of human activity. There wasn't a brass band although I believe there should have been! I stood up tall and braced myself against the wind. With a homemade fanfare of sounds I then declared myself as Britain's 'Top Man' or to be even more precise 'The Top Man in the British Isles!', Kay as Britain's 'Top Woman' and we as 'Britain's 'Top Couple'. We already knew that Ripley was Britain's 'Top Dog' but we were sad that she wasn't here to join us in our windy celebrations. I took a moment to reflect and savour our achievement; ambition accomplished. We had journeyed North across Britain from Bishop Rock to Muckle Flugga. We'd done it.

I walked back to the car, or rather crawled whilst clinging to the cinder rocks.

We headed back to the old RAF Saxavord accommodation village. Ian Marchant, in his 2006 book, 'The Longest Crawl', says that when he visited here he needed an invite to get into Britain's most northerly bar; then the Sergeants' Mess. Today it's a public bar and part of the hotel. We entered the bar as a large group of Dutch motorcyclists were leaving. We celebrated by having a cup of tea. The barmaid, who served us was a local girl of about 18 or 19 years; a true Shetlander. She told us that she had been south a few times; to Lerwick she said, "She didn't like it much".

As we drank our tea I pondered on the thought that here was a Scot who had hardly seen any of her native country. I'd seen much more but then I realised that few Shetlander's seemed to call or think of themselves as Scottish.

We left the bar and drove south. Our ferry crossing back to the mainland Zetland was smooth and uneventful.

Sept
Wednesday
26 Back in Lerwick we had decided to return to the museum and try the evening menu at its 'Hay Dock' restaurant, our last meal out before travelling home. This proved to be one of the best steak meals we'd eaten on our entire trip from Bishop Rock to Muckle Flugga. It's a shame it's so far away as we'd go again and again if nearer to home. We walked slowly back from the